Penguin Education

Penguin Critical Anthologies
General Editor: Christopher

Alexander Pope

Edited by F. W. Bateson and N. A. Joukovsky

Alexander Pope
A Critical Anthology

Edited by

F.W.Bateson and N.A.Joukovsky

Penguin Books

Penguin Books Ltd, Harmondsworth,
Middlesex, England
Penguin Books Inc, 7110 Ambassador Road,
Baltimore, Md 21207, USA.
Penguin Books Australia Ltd,
Ringwood, Victoria, Australia

First published 1971
This selection copyright © F. W. Bateson and N. A. Joukovsky, 1971
Introduction and notes copyright © F. W. Bateson and N. A. Joukovsky, 1971

Made and printed in Great Britain by
Hazell Watson & Viney Ltd,
Aylesbury, Bucks
Set in Monotype Bembo

Contents

Preface 19

Table of Dates 23

Part One **Contemporaneous Criticism and the Eighteenth Century**

Introduction 25

Alexander Pope 39
from a letter allegedly to William Walsh (1706)

Alexander Pope 41
from a letter to Henry Cromwell (1710)

Alexander Pope 42
from *An Essay on Criticism* (1711)

Joseph Addison (anonymously) 44
from the *Spectator* (1711)

John Dennis 47
from *Reflections Critical and Satirical upon a Late Rhapsody Called 'An Essay upon Criticism'* (1711)

Alexander Pope (anonymously) 49
from the *Guardian* (1713)

Alexander Pope 56
Advertisement in the *Postman* and the *Evening Post* (1716)

Sir Richard Blackmore 56
from 'An Essay upon Writing' (1716)

John Dennis 57
from *Remarks upon Mr Pope's Translation of Homer* (1717)

Francis Atterbury 58
reported in *Gray and his Friends* (c. 1725)

Daniel Defoe 59
from *Applebee's Journal* (1725)

6 Contents

Joseph Spence 59
from 'Evening the First', *An Essay on Pope's 'Odyssey'* (1726)

Alexander Pope 71
in conversation with Joseph Spence (*c.* 1728)

Alexander Pope 71
in conversation with Joseph Spence (1728)

Anonymous 72
from *Sawney, An Heroic Poem Occasioned by 'The Dunciad'. Together with a Critique of that Poem* (1728)

Ambrose Philips 72
from *Codrus: or, 'The Dunciad' Dissected, Being the Finishing-Stroke. To which is added Farmer Pope and his Son, A Tale* (1728)

John Dennis 73
from *Remarks on Mr Pope's 'Rape of the Lock', in Several Letters to a Friend* (1728)

Thomas Hearne 74
from *Remarks and Collections* (1729)

Alexander Pope 74
in conversation with Joseph Spence (1730)

Edward Young 75
reported in Spence's *Anecdotes, Observations, and Characters of Books and Men* (in conversation *c.* 1730)

Alexander Pope 76
from *A Master Key to Popery; or, A True and Perfect Key to Pope's 'Epistle to the Earl of Burlington'* (1731)

Alexander Pope 79
from a public letter to John Gay in the *Daily Journal* (1731)

Jonathan Swift 79
from *Verses on the Death of Dr Swift* (1731)

Henry Fielding 79
from Prolegomena to *The Covent-Garden Tragedy* (1732)

Alexander Pope 80
from a letter to Jonathan Swift (1733)

Alexander Pope (anonymously) 80
from *Sober Advice from Horace to the Young Gentlemen about Town* (1734)

7 · Contents

John Hervey, Baron Hervey 81
from a letter to Count Francesco Algarotti (c. 1735)

Alexander Pope 81
in conversation with Joseph Spence (1735)

Alexander Pope 82
in conversation with Joseph Spence (1735)

Alexander Pope 82
Advertisement inserted in the second volume of his *Works* (1735)

Lady Mary Wortley Montagu 83
from a letter to John Arbuthnot (1735)

T. B. 83
from the *Prompter* (1735)

Alexander Pope 84
in conversation with Joseph Spence (1736)

Isaac Hawkins Browne 85
from *A Pipe of Tobacco* (1736)

Alexander Pope 85
Advertisement prefixed to *Imitations of Horace*, II vi, by Swift and Pope
(1738)

Alexander Pope 86
in conversation with Joseph Spence (1739)

Joseph Warton 86
from *The Enthusiast; or, The Lover of Nature* (1740)

Alexander Pope 86
in conversation with Joseph Spence (1742)

Colley Cibber 87
from *A Letter from Mr Cibber to Mr Pope* (1742)

Anonymous 88
from *A Letter to Mr C--b-r On his Letter to Mr P---* (1742)

Alexander Pope 89
in conversation with Joseph Spence (1743)

Alexander Pope 89
in conversation with Joseph Spence (1743)

8 Contents

Alexander Pope 90
in conversation with Joseph Spence (1743)

Alexander Pope 91
in conversation with Joseph Spence (1744)

Alexander Pope 91
in conversation with Joseph Spence (1744)

Alexander Pope 91
in conversation with Joseph Spence (1744)

Thomas Gray 92
from a letter to Horace Walpole (1746)

Philip Dormer Stanhope, Earl of Chesterfield 92
from a letter to his son (1747)

Anonymous 92
from 'Of Some Hyperboles in Pope's Homer' (1748)

Samuel Johnson (anonymously) 93
from the *Rambler* (1751)

Henry Fielding (anonymously) 94
from the *Covent Garden Journal* (1752)

Philip Dormer Stanhope, Earl of Chesterfield 94
from a letter to his son (1752)

Henry Fielding (anonymously) 94
from the *Covent Garden Journal* (1752)

Samuel Johnson (anonymously) 95
from 'A Dissertation on the Epitaphs Written by Pope' (1756)

Joseph Warton 101
from *An Essay on the Genius and Writings of Pope* (1756, 1782)

Oliver Goldsmith 118
from *The Life of Richard Nash* (1762)

Adam Smith 119
from lectures (1762–3)

Oliver Goldsmith 119
from *A History of England in a Series of Letters from a
Nobleman to his Son* (1764)

William Shenstone 120
from 'Essays' (1764)

Philip Dormer Stanhope, Earl of Chesterfield 120
from a letter to his son (1770)

Oliver Goldsmith 120
from The Life of Dr Parnell (1770)

Percival Stockdale 121
from An Enquiry into the Nature and Genuine Laws of Poetry,
including a particular Defence of the Writings and Genius of Mr Pope (1778)

William Cowper 121
from Table Talk (1781)

Samuel Johnson 122
from 'The Life of Pope' (1781)

William Cowper 149
from a letter to William Unwin (1782)

Vicesimus Knox 150
from Essays, Moral and Literary (1782)

Hugh Blair 150
from Lectures on Rhetoric and Belles Lettres (1783)

Thomas Warton 152
from the Preface to his edition of Milton's Minor Poems (1785)

John Hookham Frere 153
from the Microcosm (1787)

Henry Headley 153
from Select Beauties of Ancient English Poetry (1787)

Joseph Weston 154
from An Essay on the Superiority of Dryden's Versification over
that of Pope and of the Moderns (1788)

James Boswell 155
from The Life of Samuel Johnson, LL.D. (1791)

Alexander Tytler, Lord Woodhouselee 161
from Essay on the Principles of Translation (1791)

Part Two The Continuing Debate

Introduction   163

Robert Southey   169
from the Preface to *Joan of Arc* (1795)

William Wordsworth   169
from the Appendix to *Lyrical Ballads* (1802)

William Lisle Bowles   169
from 'Memoirs of the Life and Writings of Pope' (1806)

William Lisle Bowles   170
from 'Concluding Observations on the Poetic Character of Pope' (1806)

William Wordsworth   173
from a letter to Walter Scott (1808)

Charles Lamb   173
reported in Hazlitt's essay 'Of Persons One Would Wish
to have Seen' (*c.* 1808)

William Blake   174
from his Notebook (*c.* 1808–11)

William Blake   174
from 'Public Address' (*c.* 1810)

Henry Fuseli   174
reported in *The Life and Writings of Henry Fuseli* (1831)

William Wordsworth   175
from 'Upon Epitaphs' (1810)

Francis Jeffrey, Lord Jeffrey (anonymously)   178
from an article on *The Dramatic Works of John Ford* (1811)

Samuel Taylor Coleridge   179
from a lecture (1813)

Isaac D'Israeli   179
from 'Pope and His Miscellaneous Quarrels', *Quarrels of Authors* (1814)

James Henry Leigh Hunt   180
from Notes on *The Feast of the Poets* (1814)

Sir Walter Scott   183
from 'Memoirs of Jonathan Swift' (1814)

Robert Southey (anonymously)   184
from an article on Alexander Chalmers's *English Poets* (1814)

William Wordsworth   186
from 'Essay Supplementary to the Preface', *Poems* (1815)

James Henry Leigh Hunt   187
from the Preface to *The Story of Rimini* (1816)

Samuel Taylor Coleridge   188
from *Biographia Literaria* (1817)

Samuel Taylor Coleridge   189
from *Biographia Literaria* (1817)

John Keats   190
from 'Sleep and Poetry' (1817)

John Keats   191
from a letter to B. R. Haydon (1817)

James Henry Leigh Hunt (anonymously)   191
from a review of Keats's *Poems* (1817)

James Henry Leigh Hunt   191
from the Preface to *Foliage* (1818)

William Hazlitt   192
from 'On Dryden and Pope', *Lectures on the English Poets* (1818)

Samuel Taylor Coleridge   198
from a lecture (1818)

Samuel Taylor Coleridge   198
from a lecture (1818)

Thomas Campbell   199
from 'Essay on English Poetry' (1819)

William Lisle Bowles   201
from *The Invariable Principles of Poetry, in a Letter Addressed to Thomas Campbell, Esq.* (1819)

George Gordon Byron, Baron Byron   201
from 'Some Observations upon an Article in *Blackwood's Magazine*' (1820)

Isaac D'Israeli (anonymously)   202
from a review of Spence's *Anecdotes* and Bowles's *Invariable Principles of Poetry* (1820)

12 Contents

George Gordon Byron, Baron Byron 203
from a letter to John Murray (1820)

George Gordon Byron, Baron Byron 203
from *Letter to **** ****** [John Murray], Esq. on the Rev. W. L. Bowles's Strictures on the Life and Writings of Pope* (1821)

George Gordon Byron, Baron Byron 207
from a letter to John Murray (1821)

George Gordon Byron, Baron Byron 208
from 'Observations upon "Observations": A Second Letter to John Murray, Esq. on the Rev. W. L. Bowles's Strictures on the Life and Writings of Pope' (1821)

William Hazlitt (anonymously) 209
from 'Pope, Lord Byron, and Mr Bowles' (1821)

John Clare 211
from his Journal (1824)

John Henry Newman (anonymously) 211
from an article on *The Theatre of the Greeks* (1829)

William Wordsworth 211
from a letter to Alexander Dyce (1829)

William Wordsworth 212
from a letter to Alexander Dyce (1830)

Thomas Babington Macaulay, Baron Macaulay (anonymously) 212
from 'Moore's Life of Lord Byron' (1831)

Edward FitzGerald 213
from a letter to W. M. Thackeray (1831)

James Henry Leigh Hunt 214
from the Preface to *Poetical Works* (1832)

Samuel Taylor Coleridge 214
from *Table Talk* (1832)

Samuel Taylor Coleridge 214
from *Table Talk* (1833)

Samuel Taylor Coleridge 214
from marginal notes on Donne

Samuel Taylor Coleridge 215
from Notebook 17

Robert Southey 215
from 'Life of Cowper' (1835–7)

Thomas De Quincey 216
from 'Pope', *Encyclopaedia Britannica* (1842)

Thomas Babington Macaulay, Baron Macaulay
(anonymously) 217
from the *Edinburgh Review*, reprinted as 'The Life and Writings of Addison'
(1843)

Thomas Babington Macaulay, Baron Macaulay 218
marginal note on Pope's *Imitations of Horace*

James Henry Leigh Hunt 219
from 'An Answer to the Question, What is Poetry?' (1844)

James Henry Leigh Hunt 219
from *Wit and Humour, Selected from the English Poets* (1846)

Thomas De Quincey 220
from 'Schlosser's Literary History of the Eighteenth Century' (1847)

Thomas De Quincey (anonymously) 220
from an article on Roscoe's edition of Pope (1848)

James Henry Leigh Hunt 228
from *Autobiography* (1850)

Charles Augustin Sainte-Beuve 229
from 'Qu'est-ce qu'un classique?' (1850)

Thomas De Quincey 230
from 'Lord Carlisle on Pope' (1851)

John Ruskin 230
from a letter to his father (1851)

William Makepeace Thackeray 231
from 'Prior, Gay, and Pope', *The English Humourists of the Eighteenth
Century* (1853)

Thomas De Quincey 234
from 'Pope's Retort upon Addison' (1855)

Walter Bagehot (anonymously) 234
from 'William Cowper' (1855)

John Ruskin 236
from 'Of the Pathetic Fallacy', *Modern Painters* (1856)

George Gilfillan (anonymously) 238
from 'Satire and Satirists' (1856)

George Eliot (anonymously) 239
from 'Worldliness and Other-Worldliness: The Poet Young' (1857)

John Ruskin 239
from 'Claude and Poussin', *Modern Painters* (1860)

Matthew Arnold 240
from *On Translating Homer* (1861)

Hippolyte Adolphe Taine 242
from *Histoire de la littérature anglaise* (1863)

Gerard Manley Hopkins 245
from letter to A. W. M. Baillie (1864)

John Ruskin 245
from 'The Relation of Art to Morals', *Lectures on Art* (1870)

Whitwell Elwin 247
from his introduction to *An Essay on Criticism* (1871)

James Russell Lowell 247
from 'Pope' (1871)

Mark Pattison (anonymously) 248
from 'Pope and His Editors' (1872)

Matthew Arnold 249
from his Introduction to *The English Poets* (1880)

Matthew Arnold 252
from 'Thomas Gray' (1880)

Mark Pattison 253
from 'Alexander Pope' (1880)

Leslie Stephen 255
from 'Epistles and Satires', *Alexander Pope* (1880)

Algernon Charles Swinburne 259
from 'A Century of English Poetry' (1880)

Alfred Tennyson, Baron Tennyson 261
in conversation (c. 1880–83)

George Saintsbury 262
from 'Pope and the Later Couplet', *A History of English Prosody* (1908)

Francis Thompson 269
from 'Pope' (1910)

J. C. Squire 271
from 'How They Would Have Done It', *Tricks of the Trade* (1917)

T. S. Eliot (anonymously) 272
from 'John Dryden' (1921)

Lytton Strachey 272
from *Pope* (1925)

Virginia Woolf 274
from *Orlando: A Biography* (1928)

Allen Tate 275
'Mr Pope' (1928)

Edith Sitwell 276
from 'Some Notes on Pope's Poetry', *Alexander Pope* (1930)

A. E. Housman 281
from *The Name and Nature of Poetry* (1933)

Part Three Modern Views

Introduction 283

William Empson 297
from *Seven Types of Ambiguity* (1930)

Aldous Huxley 306
from *Texts and Pretexts* (1932)

Ezra Pound 307
from *ABC of Reading* (1934)

Geoffrey Tillotson (anonymously) 308
from 'Alexander Pope' (1934)

F. R. Leavis 315
from 'Pope', *Revaluation: Tradition and Development in English Poetry* (1936)

Arthur O. Lovejoy   326
from *The Great Chain of Being: A Study of the History of an Idea* (1936)

W. H. Auden   328
'Alexander Pope' (1937)

Cyril Connolly   343
from 'Imitations of Horace' (1939)

W. K. Wimsatt   345
from 'One Relation of Rhyme to Reason' (1944)

T. S. Eliot   355
from *What Is a Classic?* (1945)

George Sherburn   356
from 'Pope at Work' (1945)

Cleanth Brooks   360
from 'The Case of Miss Arabella Fermor', *The Well-Wrought Urn* (1947)

W. K. Wimsatt   377
'Rhetoric and Poems: Alexander Pope' (1948)

Maynard Mack   393
from 'Wit and Poetry and Pope: Some Observations on
His Imagery' (1949)

F. W. Bateson   409
from his Introduction to the Twickenham edition of Pope's
Epistles to Several Persons (*Moral Essays*) (1951)

W. K. Wimsatt   419
from 'The Augustan Mode in English Poetry' (1953)

Donald Davie   424
from *Articulate Energy: An Enquiry into the Syntax of English Poetry* (1955)

Hugh Kenner   426
from 'In the Wake of the Anarch' (1958)

J. S. Cunningham   433
from *Pope: The Rape of the Lock* (1961)

Marshall McLuhan   433
from *The Gutenberg Galaxy* (1962)

Winifred Nowottny   443
from *The Language Poets Use* (1962)

Donald Davie   447
from *The Language of Science and the Language of
Literature, 1700–1740* (1963)

J. B. Broadbent   449
'The Rape of the Lock', *Poetic Love* (1964)

Allan Rodway   455
from 'By Algebra to Augustanism' (1966)

Maynard Mack   460
from his Introduction to the Twickenham edition of Pope's
Iliad and *Odyssey* (1967)

Yvor Winters   482
from *Forms of Discovery* (1967)

Peter Dixon   483
from 'Alexander Pope of Twickenham' (1968)

Appendix: Notes   487

Select Bibliography   493

Acknowledgements   495

Index   497

Preface

The criticism of Pope reflects the qualities and limitations of the poetry that it criticizes. What we admire in his poems – and remember most vividly from them – is not a vertebrate aesthetic structure, such as Milton, for example, always provides, so much as an almost haphazard shimmer of epigrams, characters, aphorisms and innuendoes. If the parts hold together – as, miraculously, they almost always do – it is the tone of voice and the metrical virtuosity that are the principal adhesive agents. The critical consequence or complement is that it is almost impossible to find coherent essays on Pope's poetry, as distinct from his personal life, which can be compared with those of Matthew Arnold or A. C. Bradley on Wordsworth, or T. S. Eliot on Dryden, or C. S. Lewis on Spenser. Instead one has generally to be content with a single stimulating paragraph, or the odd sentence imbedded all too often in boring or irrelevant circumambient prose.

The best anthology I know of Pope criticism is the section on him in *The Poets and their Critics* by Hugh Sykes Davies, which was originally published as a Penguin sixpenny in 1943. In its revised form (1960) Pope is allotted thirty-five pages, into which Mr Davies managed to squeeze eighteen critics. Dr Joukovsky and I have followed Mr Davies's excellent example in also preferring excerpts of special interest to whole treatises, essays, lectures or letters. If even so some of the items included will not seem very exciting today, they do at least fill out the history of the changing fortunes of Pope's reputation in far greater detail than is available, to the best of our knowledge, anywhere else. And, since the reaction to his poetry has been a sort of litmus test to more general changes in English literary taste over the last two and a half centuries, the wide range of our selection will, we hope, justify itself.

Dr Joukovsky has been responsible for the choice of criticism between 1800 and 1930, including the introduction to this section;

I must accept responsibility for the rest of the collection as well as for some general supervision. The introduction to the post-1930 section is longer than I had originally intended; but as I assembled the more reputable modern specimens some counterpoise clearly became necessary to the chorus of eulogy from specialists and scholar-critics. I have therefore inserted parts of an unpublished paper of my own that I read to the Modern Language Association of America with the deliberately provocative title 'Isn't Pope Overrated Now?' Grammatically, of course, my question 'expected' the answer, 'Yes, he is'. Critically, however, I expected – and in general obtained – a more tentative and less depreciatory answer. Overrated? Well, yes, perhaps a little – especially, for reasons I don't fully understand, in the United States. If this collection succeeds at least in reopening some of the old controversies and problems it will have more than justified itself. A great poet can only benefit by the critical discussion of *all* his qualities – his limitations as well as his positive achievements.

The reactions to Pope's extremisms – personal, political, aesthetic – resulted in an exceptionally large body of comment and counter-comment, attack and counter-attack. To assist the reader in the complexities of this earlier criticism a short Appendix of Notes has been compiled.

Since they are not strictly critical no excerpts have been included either from W. K. Wimsatt's *The Portraits of Alexander Pope* (1965) or from Maynard Mack's *The Garden and the City* (1969). Nevertheless these are probably the two most important books recently devoted to Pope. No serious student can afford to ignore either of them. And this is perhaps even more true of the Twickenham edition of the poems, now complete in eleven volumes (1939–67). Quotations from Pope's poems throughout our selection have been brought into conformity with the Twickenham text, which has however been modernized (as Pope 'modernized' the spelling, punctuation, capitals and italics in his own quotations from Shakespeare, Milton, Dryden, etc.). Line references are also to the Twickenham edition.

Table of Dates

1667   Birth of Swift.

1672   Birth of Addison.

1688   *21 May* Alexander Pope born in London of elderly
        middle-class Roman Catholic parents.

1700   *April* Death of Dryden.
        The Pope family move to Binfield in Windsor Forest,
        perhaps to comply with anti-Catholic regulations.

1705   Pope begins to move in the literary society of London.

1709   After much revision *Pastorals* published by Tonson in his
        Miscellanies (part VI), a series initiated by Dryden.

1711   *An Essay on Criticism* published – attacked by Dennis but
        praised by Addison in the *Spectator*.

1712   *The Rape of the Lock* (first version) published in Lintot's
        Miscellany. Pope joins Swift, Gay, Arbuthnot and others
        in forming Scriblerus Club.

1713   *Windsor Forest* published.

1714   Revised and enlarged version of *The Rape of the Lock*.
        Death of Queen Anne. St John (Viscount Bolingbroke)
        impeached and escapes to France.

1715   Books I–IV of *Iliad* translation published. Quarrels with
        Addison; becomes acquainted with Lady Mary Wortley
        Montagu.

1717   *Works* published (including *Elegy to Memory of an
        Unfortunate Lady* and *Eloisa to Abelard*).

1718   Settles at Twickenham with his mother. Advises his
        aristocratic friends on landscape gardening.

1720   *Iliad* completed.

1723   Bolingbroke pardoned and returns to England.

1725   Edition of Shakespeare published, also *Odyssey*, vols 1–3.

1726   Swift's first visit. *Gulliver's Travels* published.

1727   *The Dunciad* (in three books, Theobald as hero). Martha Blount becomes Pope's mistress about this period.

1729   *The Dunciad Variorum* (with elaborate facetious notes, etc.).

1731   *Epistle to Burlington* (*Moral Essay IV*). Other *Moral Essays* 1733–5.

1733   First *Imitation of Horace*. Others 1734–8. Death of Pope's mother.

1733–4 *An Essay on Man* (published anonymously).

1735   *An Epistle to Dr Arbuthnot*. Death of Arbuthnot. Vol. 2 of *Works* published. Curll's edition of Pope's letters (Pope connived in this piracy).

1738   Warburton defends Pope against charges of deism in the *Essay on Man* made by Crousaz.

1742   *The New Dunciad*; added in 1743 to *The Dunciad* as Book IV (Cibber hero instead of Theobald).

1744   *30 May* Pope dies.

Part One Contemporaneous Criticism and the Eighteenth Century

Introduction

The author of *An Essay on Criticism* might be expected to be the best critic of his own poetry. And so, in one sense, Pope was. But this criticism is not often to be found in the preliminary notes or dedications with which he prefaced many of the poems. Such things as the early 'Discourse on Pastoral Poetry' (written, Pope later alleged, when he was only 'sixteen years of age') and the Preface to the first collection of his *Works* (1717) have a certain elegance. (The 1717 Preface has the striking and memorable phrase 'The life of a wit is a warfare upon earth'.) It was after all the golden age of English prose, and Pope's was certainly no worse, considered simply as prose, than the next man's. The critical content, however, of these performances – even of the spirited Preface to his translation of the *Iliad*, of which he was particularly proud – is inconsiderable. The footnotes to the *Iliad* and the Postscript to the *Odyssey* (a translation in which at least two and perhaps three poetic hacks collaborated with him) do retain some critical interest. Pope's maternal uncle had been Samuel Cooper, perhaps the greatest of English miniaturists, and his precocious nephew inherited all his paint-brushes and pigments. He was therefore a natural exponent of the new fashion for 'picturesque' poetry, and its later cousin 'landscape' gardening, which began to appear at the beginning of the eighteenth century. Pope's *Windsor Forest* is a very 'picturesque' poem indeed, much more so than Denham's *Cooper's Hill* (1642) on which it is modelled, and the word itself in its modern sense, an adaptation of the French *pittoresque*, seems to have been Pope's actual coinage. It is, significantly, the 'descriptions' to which he calls particular attention in the Advertisement preceding *The Temple of Fame*, a neo-classic version of Chaucer's *House of Fame*. Similarly, just as he had made Chaucer more picturesque, in his version of the *Iliad* he tried to make Homer more picturesque. In case the reader should not have noticed, the pictorial possibilities of the various epic episodes are explained to him in elaborate footnotes. A typical one is that to line 194 of Book XVI (which begins, as translated by Pope, 'Grim as voracious wolves . . .'):

There is scarce any picture in Homer so much in the savage and terrible way as this comparison of the Myrmidons to wolves. It puts one in mind of the pieces of Spagnolett [José Ribera, nick-named Lo Spagnoletto, a painter in the manner of Caravaggio] or Salvator Rosa. Each circumstance is made up of images very strongly coloured and horridly lively.

It is hardly the way a modern commentator on Homer would go about it, but Pope's pictorial interpretation is no doubt a kind of criticism.

Such passages, however, scarcely ever show us Pope in any obvious sense criticizing Pope. The glimpses we get of Pope satisfied or dissatisfied with himself at a textual or technical level are more interesting because more natural, more spontaneous. He could never leave his poems alone, and this process of continuous revision – a series of desperate efforts in edition after edition to give the words and the word-order just that much more point and pungency – must be allowed to be in a sense critical.

T. S. Eliot complained with some justice, in 'The Function of Criticism', that Matthew Arnold – in *his* 'The Function of Criticism at the Present Time' – tended to overlook the element of criticism in literary creation. No doubt what Eliot calls 'the labour of sifting, combining, constructing, expunging, correcting, testing' varies between one writer and another. But in Pope's case, as indeed in Eliot's too, creation almost always included much successful conscious criticism. Unlike the typical Romantic or seventeenth-century poet Pope was rightly hardly every satisfied with every detail in the first version of any one of his poems. The changes may be limited to single words or phrases, as for instance in lines 17–19 of 'Spring':

Soon as the flocks shook off the nightly dews,
Two swains whom love kept wakeful (and the Muse)
Poured o'er the whitening vale their fleecy care.

When originally published in 1709 the lines had been:

Daphnis and Strephon to the shades retired,
Both warmed by love and by the Muse inspired;
Fresh as the morn and as the season fair,
In flowery vales they fed their fleecy care.

It is not one of Pope's most brilliant passages, but 'the whitening vale' is an effective and memorable phrase. As Gilbert Wakefield, an almost forgotten eighteenth-century scholar and critic, put it, 'The epithet *whitening* most happily describes a *progressive* effect'. But the happy epithet was not introduced into the text of *Spring* until 1736. It had taken nearly thirty years to rouse Pope's critical sense into a creative dissatisfaction with the conventional 'flowery vales'; but the quality of the revision is a guarantee of its final effective presence. The line has been greatly improved. In other words, critical dissatisfaction has here stimulated momentarily an expression of the creative process.

Almost every page of Pope's poetry exhibits some such combination of criticism and creation. Dr Johnson's comment on Pope's 'parental attention' to his works was that 'It will seldom be found that he altered without adding clearness, elegance, or vigour'; and George Sherburn, the greatest of recent Pope scholars, has agreed that 'Pope seldom altered without improvement'. And this critical awareness that improvement was necessary or at any rate desirable was not, of course, confined to minor changes in the phrasing. *The Rape of the Lock* and *The Dunciad* both underwent structural rehabilitations of a major order, and other lesser examples are to be found throughout Pope's work. The *Epistle to Burlington* (*Moral Essay IV*) is a good example of such minor structural revision. To the casual eye there may seem to have been no great change from the first edition, but the *shape* of the poem is in fact different, with the separate points of emphasis achieving a new and better balance.

The recognition that a particular passage or poem could be improved might be called implicit criticism. A critical process is clearly the point of departure in such cases, though the reader can only infer the precise nature of the aesthetic dissatisfaction from the change that Pope's text has undergone. But there is also some *explicit* criticism of Pope by Pope, the most familiar examples occurring in the *Epistle to Dr Arbuthnot* (1734), a sort of *apologia pro vita sua* – even if attack is more obvious in it than defence. In lines 147–50 Pope's earliest poems are described and dismissed as follows:

Soft were my numbers. Who could take offence
While pure description held the place of sense?
Like gentle Fanny's was my flowery theme:
A painted mistress or a purling stream.

If, as seems probable, 'soft numbers' are those that exploit assonance and alliteration ('vowel-music'), Pope may be taken to be criticizing his *Pastorals* here, which carry these devices to an insipid extreme and are without any of the 'sense' or intellectual force that is to be found in the best English poetry of the Augustan school. But 'Spring', 'Summer', 'Autumn' and 'Winter' are also at the opposite extreme from Thomson's *Seasons*, written only twenty years later, in the kind and quantity that they provide of 'pure description'. In this phrase Pope is probably apologizing for *Windsor Forest* (published in 1713), *The Temple of Fame* (published in 1715), and even possibly *The Rape of the Lock* (enlarged version 1714). This had been Pope's 'picturesque' period when he was taking lessons from a professional painter (Charles Jervas) and actually painting, or copying paintings, with some success himself. The 'painted mistress' presumably refers to Belinda and the other ladies of fashion in *The Rape of the Lock*, even if the main point of the line is to parody Addison's

A painted meadow or a purling stream.

(Addison had used 'painted' metaphorically for brightly coloured, that is, 'flowery', as in Pope's previous line.)

The consciousness that Pope's early poems had lacked 'sense' is repeated in the claim made in lines 340–41 of the *Epistle to Dr Arbuthnot*. At least, he asserts, with the *juvenilia* long behind him, it can *now* be said,

That not in fancy's maze he wandered long,
But stooped to truth and moralized his song.

Stooping to truth was a hawking term that Pope had picked up from a poem by Sir John Denham, the originator with Edmund Waller of Augustan poetry in England, and the image means something like 'grappling' with truth. To escape from fancy's maze was an ascent, not a descent. And in moralizing his song Pope was declaring himself a man with a serious concern for human values like Spenser, whose *Faerie Queene* begins (line 9 of the Proem),

Fierce warres and faithfull loves shall moralize my song.

In his own special terms, then, Pope was disowning in these passages the ivory-tower elegance of his early work and issuing a kind of critical manifesto on behalf of his later and more socially conscious poetic mode. Fancy (a word synonymous at the time with imagination) is deplored, and sense, truth and morality are the more substantial criteria by which he wishes his poetry – all poetry, indeed – to be judged. With the hindsight of history we can see today that the conversion from a rococo or neo-classic elegance to the poetry of the social conscience – seen at its best, I suppose, in the *Imitations of Horace*, but with the so-called *Moral Essays* and

Book IV of *The Dunciad* confirming the nature of Pope's
maturity – was primarily due to the personal and literary influence
of Swift. But Pope himself, while always honouring and often
imitating Swift, seems to have attributed the change in the nature
of his poetry in the 1730s to the influence of Henry St John,
Viscount Bolingbroke, who had now recanted his Jacobitism and
was allowed to return from exile. The *Essay on Man*, a more
disastrous failure essentially even than the original *Dunciad*, was
the reflection of Bolingbroke's interest in philosophy, and its fourth
book ends with a similar confession of literary faith to those in the
Epistle to Dr Arbuthnot. Thanks to the help of his ambiguous
'guide, philosopher and friend' (whose abuse of him after Pope's
death seems to us today an unforgivable treachery),

> I turned the tuneful art
> From sounds to things, from fancy to the heart;
> For wit's false mirror held up nature's light . . . .

It was at least Pope's honest critical ambition at the time to
do something like that. Similar avowals occur elsewhere in
his later verse. What does not occur in any of these ventures
into self-criticism is any theory of satire – such as Swift
provided in the prefaces to both *The Battle of the Books* and
A Tale of a Tub – or even any apparent awareness that the
best of his poetry is satiric. Such terms as *truth*, *things* and
nature seem totally inadequate as the definition of a poetry
capable of so many variations in so many genres – pastoral,
didactic, picturesque, complimentary and 'Pre-Romantic'
(*Eloisa to Abelard*, for example) – but whose special triumph
was in personal satire. It is possible that the satiric impulse
in Pope was essentially instinctive, almost sub-rational
indeed, outside the area of any self-criticism. The brilliant
passage on Appius in *An Essay on Criticism* (lines 584–7) can
only be excused on some such premise:

'Twere well might critics still this freedom take;
But Appius reddens at each word you speak,
And stares, tremendous, with a threatening eye,
Like some fierce tyrant in old tapestry.

As personal satire it is splendidly memorable. But personal satire usually implies a personal grievance, and John Dennis, who was much the most distinguished critic of the period, though also the author of a tragedy that had flopped called *Appius and Virginia*, had supplied Pope with no obvious motive whatever for so offensive a comment. It is as if a clever modern undergraduate had written a review in the *New Statesman* in which he incidentally cocked a snook at F. R. Leavis. And Pope was to go on with this sort of thing, not exactly picking quarrels but *needing* quarrels, thriving on quarrels. As he put it in one of the *Imitations of Horace* (*Satires*, II, i, 14),

Fools rush into my head, and so I write.

James Sutherland has summed up the habit more moderately in his excellent introduction to the Twickenham edition of *The Dunciad*:

The dunces complained loudly of what they called an unprovoked attack; and it is true that Pope was sometimes – though again not so often as has generally been assumed – the aggressor. But what the dunces could not see – how should they? – was that they annoyed by merely being themselves. 'Gentlemen should consider [as Pope put it] that to some people dullness is provoking; and that in such case, to call gentlemen dull is no abuse, though it may be a rudeness.' At the same time there was about Pope – and, for that matter, about Swift – an assumption of critical infallibility which was extremely annoying to their contemporaries, who frequently

complained that Pope and Swift seemed to think that they and
their friends had a monopoly of wit and good sense.

The assumption of such a monopoly was in fact what
'inspiration' was for a Romantic poet, a *sine qua non* for the Pope
of his best poetry. 'Fools, in my opinion,' Swift wrote in a letter
to Pope of 3 August 1716 that speaks for both of them, 'are as
necessary for a good writer as pen, ink and paper.'

The creative basis, then, of Pope's best poems was satire,
personal satire. But this necessity entailed as a consequence that
Pope's immediate critics were its victims; they are in fact almost all
included in *The Dunciad*. It is not surprising therefore to find little
or no objective criticism of his work during his life-time. Dennis
replied to Pope's personal satire by equally personal though less
witty abuse. And what is true of Dennis is true of all the writers
of the period outside Pope's circle of intimates. One or two young
men, who had not hitherto committed themselves publicly,
prudently began their critical careers by eulogizing Pope, no doubt
in order to secure his favour. Joseph Spence, a Fellow of New
College, who wrote a not uninteresting critique of Pope's
Odyssey, is one such case. But Spence, who was acidly described
by Horace Walpole as 'more of a silver penny than a man', has
his niche in literary history only because of the records he kept of
Pope's conversation (now known as *Spence's Anecdotes*) rather than
for anything he wrote himself. William Warburton, who
defended the *Essay on Man* against the charges of deism made by
Crousaz, a Swiss theologian, is a similar case. Warburton's
forthcoming edition was proclaimed in Pope's will the official
edition of the poems, and its tedious, verbose notes apparently
helped the editor up the ladder of ecclesiastical preferment.
Addison's *Spectator* essay on *An Essay on Criticism*, if not exactly an
acute piece of criticism, is the most interesting of the contemporary
comments because of the latent distrust it exhibits underneath the

compliments. Although the battle that developed over the rival translations of Homer had not yet been joined, Pope's literary credo as well as his temperament were the opposite of Addison's. The key-term in Addison's critical system was Simplicity. To write 'simply' – for Addison and his literary protégés like Ambrose Philips. Thomas Tickell and Henry Carey (the author of 'Sally in Our Alley') – was to write sincerely and sentimentally. Traditional ballads and folk-songs like *Chevy-Chase* and *The Babes in the Wood* had also been the subject of *Spectator* essays by Addison, and he was happier praising them than any contemporary satire, however brilliant its phrasing. Pope got his revenge for Addison's neglect in the satirical portrait of 'Atticus', which was composed in Addison's life-time although it was not officially published until it appeared in the *Epistle to Arbuthnot*. No doubt Addison's advice to his 'little Senate' in Button's Coffee-House was, 'Ignore the fellow'. A blatant example of such criticism by omission is the series of essays on pastoral poetry written by Tickell in the *Guardian*, Addison and Steele's sequel to the *Spectator*. Tickell sprinkles these essays with quotations from the feeble pastorals of Ambrose Philips – which had originally been published in 1709 in the same miscellany as Pope's own – but he is almost ostentatiously careful not to quote any of Pope's pastorals. Pope was not the man to stand this sort of thing, and Tickell was put in his place by the devastating irony of the *Guardian* no. 40, which Steele, a man always in a hurry, had apparently accepted at its face value as a eulogy of Ambrose Philips. It will be found below (pp. 49–55), and the way Pope selects Philips's silliest moments to advertise his own pastorals is now immediately apparent. The Button's Coffee-House school of criticism had been routed, and the rest was silence at its tables on the subject of Mr Pope. But we can regret the incident today because the one group of contemporary critics capable of intelligent criticism of Pope were in fact the Buttonians, especially Addison himself. Pope's poems,

several of them at any rate, would have been much better, less
rhetorically complacent, if he had had critics to whom he was
prepared to listen. In their absence some of the poems – or at any
rate some parts of some of the poems (it is important not to
overstate the point) – must be written off as affected and/or
pretentious.

Pope was already a classic when he died. The Dunces had
belonged for the most part to an older generation and by 1744
Grub Street knew them no more. Of their aristocratic allies such
as Hervey (the 'Sporus' of the *Epistle to Arbuthnot*), only Lady
Mary Wortley Montagu survived and she had already deserted
England in 1739. If she had not forgotten the disagreeable
alternatives presented in the first *Imitation of Horace*,

From furious Sappho scarce a milder fate,
Poxed by her love or libelled by her hate,

most of Pope's readers of the 1740s will not have realized that
'Sappho' was Lady Mary – and for those who did, like Horace
Walpole, the insult was only a relic of spicy gossip from an
earlier age.

A glimpse of what Pope meant for the younger generation is
provided by a passing allusion in a letter to the poet Gray from
Richard West (of Gray's famous sonnet) as early as 1737:

I have been very ill and am still hardly recovered. Do you
remember Elegy 5th, Book the 3rd, of Tibullus ... and do
you remember a letter of Mr Pope's in sickness to Mr Steele?

For clever undergraduates, as West and Gray were at the time,
Tibullus and 'Mr Pope' were both already part of the timeless past
of literature – who could be mentioned in the same breath although
the Roman elegist had been dead some seventeen hundred years
whereas Pope's letter to Steele, originally written on 15 July
1712, had only been printed in 1735.

The Age of Pope and Swift ended with their deaths in the
early 1740s. And it left literary England (of which Dublin was then
the second capital) without a Great Cham until Johnson stepped
into the role some thirty years later. In a review reprinted in his
Mixed Essays Matthew Arnold rebukes a certain Stopford Brooke,
who had written a short history of English literature, for failing
to recognize 'a second period in the eighteenth century,
sufficiently distinguishable from the period to Addison and Pope,
and lasting down to a period of far more decisive change, the
period of the French Revolution'. More recently Northrop Frye
has gone even further. In his seminal study of Blake called *Fearful
Symmetry* Frye has suggested that Romanticism, far from beginning
with *Lyrical Ballads* in 1798, really begins in the 1740s with poets
like Gray, Collins and Akenside and their lesser contemporaries
such as Joseph and Thomas Warton, Shenstone and Smart. And
it has long been agreed that these poets if not Romantic are at
least Pre-Romantic.

In the 1740s the novel, with Richardson and Fielding, first
established itself as a major literary genre. The Restoration comedy
of manners, of which Pope's satires and Swift's 'ironies' may be
considered by-products or sequels, had pre-deceased them. (It
should not be forgotten that Wycherley was one of Pope's
earliest literary friends, or that he chose Congreve, whom he
knew less well, to dedicate the *Iliad* translation to.) In brief, the
Age of Satire was succeeded by the Age of Sensibility. The
ultimate criterion was no longer Common Sense (Pope's 'sense'),
at least as the term was defined by Nicholas Amhurst, a Whig-
turned-Tory pamphleteer and the editor of Bolingbroke's
Craftsman, in his *Terrae Filius* (1726):

By common sense we usually and justly understand the
faculty to discern one thing from another, and the ordinary
ability to keep ourselves from being imposed upon by gross

contradictions, palpable inconsistencies and unmasked imposture. By a man of common sense we mean one who knows, as we say, chalk from cheese.

Ne pas être dupe. Sensibility on the other hand was a very different faculty from Voltaire's scepticism. Its earliest definition so far recorded is in *The Prompter* (1735), a periodical run by Aaron Hill, and William Popple, two of the Dunces, where it is described as the ability to feel 'the misery of others with inward pain'. Hill was a friend of Richardson's, both of them fairly hard-headed sentimentalists, but as the century progressed the ability to discriminate between literary chalk, such as the forgeries of Ossian and Chatterton, and the cheese of literature declined disastrously – and with it the awareness of what is genuine and what is factitious in Pope's poetry. Even Johnson, the defender of the old Augustan order, could occasionally make serious mistakes.

Pope had congratulated Dodsley, the author-bookseller, on publishing Johnson's first poem, *London*, an imitation of Juvenal's third satire similar to Pope's *Imitations of Horace*. And Johnson contributed a detailed and generally laudatory criticism of Pope's epitaphs to the *Visitor* in 1741. But the two never met. Perhaps it would have been embarrassing to both of them if they had. Johnson, the *ursa major* (as Gray once called him), resented patronage and Pope would certainly have been condescending. As it was, Johnson proved himself the doughtiest champion of Pope's reputation against the new Pre-Romantic generation. Indeed, the long account of Pope's life and writings in *The Lives of the Poets* is still the best criticism that we have of Pope's poems, though the biographical sections have been superseded by George Sherburn's masterly *Early Career of Alexander Pope* (1934) – which, however, stops at 1727. But the modern reader may not realize that Johnson's comments are primarily intended as a refutation of the new posthumous image of Pope created above all by Joseph

Warton's *Essay on the Genius and Writings of Pope* (1756; a second and tamer volume followed in 1782). The polemical background adds zest to Johnson's criticism. It is true Warton's name is not mentioned when Johnson reaches his familiar critical conclusion:

After all this, it is, surely, superfluous to answer the question that has once been asked, whether Pope was a poet? otherwise than by asking, in return, if Pope be not a poet, where is poetry to be found?

But the allusion cannot be mistaken. The one public sceptic at the time was Warton, who had not denied *some* merit to Pope's verse but had raised the question of his genres. Could satire, however brilliant, ever be *great* poetry? The question was repeated by critic after critic until it received its most memorable answer from Matthew Arnold. If Pope's status has been restored in the twentieth century it has been by evading or denying the whole hierarchy of genres to which Warton appealed. In the last analysis, we can see that both Johnson and Warton were applying irrelevant criteria. A simple proof of their error is that they both overestimate what Blake's friend Fuseli called the 'hot ice' of *Eloisa to Abelard*. Wherever Pope's best poetry may lie it is not in *Eloisa to Abelard*, clever though the poem certainly is.

Alexander Pope

from a letter allegedly to William Walsh   22 October 1706
(see Note A in Appendix, p. 487)

After the thoughts I have already sent you on the subject of English versification, you desire my opinion as to some farther particulars. There are indeed certain niceties which, though not much observed even by correct versifiers, I cannot but think deserve to be better regarded.

1. It is not enough that nothing offends the ear, but a good poet will adapt the very sounds, as well as words, to the things he treats of. So that there is (if one may express it so) a style of sound. As in describing a gliding stream, the numbers should run easy and flowing; in describing a rough torrent or deluge, sonorous and swelling, and so of the rest. This is evident everywhere in Homer and Virgil, and nowhere else, that I know of, to any observable degree . . . .

This, I think, is what very few observe in practice, and is undoubtedly of wonderful force in imprinting the image on the reader. We have one excellent example of it in our language, Mr Dryden's Ode on St Cecilia's Day entitled *Alexander's Feast*.

2. Every nice ear must, I believe, have observed that in any smooth English verse of ten syllables, there is naturally a *pause* at the fourth, fifth, or sixth syllable. It is upon these the ear rests, and upon the judicious change and management of which depends the variety of versification. For example:

At the fifth:
Where'er thy navy | spreads her canvas wings.

At the fourth:
Homage to thee | and peace to all she brings.

At the sixth:
Like tracks of leverets | in morning snow.

Now I fancy that, to preserve an exact harmony and variety, the pause at the fourth or sixth should not be continued above three lines together without the interposition of another; else it will be apt to weary the ear with one continued tone; at least it does mine. That at the fifth runs quicker, and carries not quite so dead a weight, so tires not so much, though it be continued longer.

3. Another nicety is in relation to expletives, whether words or syllables, which are made use of purely to supply a vacancy. *Do* before verbs plural is absolutely such; and it is not improbable but future refiners may explode *did* and *does* in the same manner, which are almost always used for the sake of rhyme. The same cause has occasioned the promiscuous use of *you* and *thou* to the same person, which can never sound so graceful as either one or the other.

4. I would also object to the irruption of alexandrine verses of twelve syllables, which, I think, should never be allowed but when some remarkable beauty or propriety in them atones for the liberty. Mr Dryden has been too free of these, especially in his latter works. I am of the same opinion as to triple rhymes.

5. I would equally object to the repetition of the same rhymes within four or six lines of each other, as tiresome to the ear through their monotony.

6. Monosyllable lines, unless very artfully managed, are stiff, or languishing; but may be beautiful to express melancholy, slowness, or labour.

7. To come to the hiatus, or gap between two words, which is caused by two vowels opening on each other (upon which you desire me to be particular): I think the rule in this case is either to use the caesura or admit the hiatus just as the ear is least shocked by either: for the caesura sometimes offends the ear more than the hiatus itself, and our language is naturally overcharged with consonants. As for example, if in this verse,

The old have interest ever in their eye

we should say, to avoid the hiatus,

But th' old have interest.

The hiatus which has the worst effect is when one word ends with the same vowel that begins the following; and next to this those vowels whose sounds come nearest to each other are most to be avoided. O, A, or U will bear a more full and graceful sound than

E, I, or Y. I know some people will think these observations trivial, and therefore I am glad to corroborate them by some great authorities, which I have met with in Tully and Quintilian. . . .

If I am not mistaken, Malherbe of all the moderns has been the most scrupulous in this point; and I think Ménage in his observations upon him says he has not one in his poems. To conclude, I believe the hiatus should be avoided with more care in poetry than in oratory, and I would constantly try to prevent it, unless where the cutting it off is more prejudicial to the sound than the hiatus itself.

Alexander Pope

from a letter to Henry Cromwell   25 November 1710

Your mention in this and your last letter of the defect in numbers of several of our poets puts me upon communicating a few thoughts – or rather doubts – of mine on that head, some of which 'tis likely I may have hinted to you formerly in conversation. But I will here put together all the little niceties I can recollect in the compass of my observation.

1. As to the hiatus, it is certainly to be avoided as often as possible; but on the other hand, since the reason of it is only for the sake of the numbers, so if to avoid it we incur another fault against their smoothness, methinks the very end of that nicety is destroyed. As when we say, for instance,
But th' old have interest ever in their view
To avoid the hiatus (in 'The old have interest'), does not the ear, in this place, tell us that the hiatus is smoother, less constrained, and so preferable to the caesura?

2. I would except against all expletives in verse (as *do* before verbs plural, or even too frequent use of *did* and *does*) to change the termination of the rhyme – all these being against the usual manner of speech and mere fillers-up of unnecessary syllables.

3. Monosyllable lines, unless very artfully managed, are stiff, languishing and hard.

4. The repeating the same rhymes within four or six lines of each other – which tire the ear with too much of the like sound.

5. The too frequent use of alexandrines, which are never graceful but when there is some majesty added to the verse by 'em, or when there cannot be found a word in 'em but what is absolutely needful.

6. Every nice ear must, I believe, have observed that in any smooth English verse of ten syllables there is naturally a pause either at the fourth, fifth or sixth syllable – as, for example, Waller:

at the fifth Where'er thy navy | spreads her canvas wings

at the fourth Homage to thee | and peace to all she brings

at the sixth Like tracks of leverets | in morning snow

Now I fancy that, to preserve an exact harmony and variety, none of these pauses should be continued above three lines together without the interposition of another. Else it will be apt to weary the ear with one continued tone; at least it does mine.

7. It is not enough that nothing offends the ear, that the verse be, as the French call it, *coulante*, but a good poet will adapt the very sounds as well as words to the things he treats of, so that there is, if one may express it so, a style of sound. As, in describing a gliding stream, the numbers should run easy and flowing; in describing a rough torrent or deluge, sonorous and swelling. And so of the rest. This is evident everywhere in Homer and Virgil – and nowhere else that I know of to any observable degree. . . . This, I think, is what very few observe in practice and is undoubtedly of wonderful force in imprinting the image on the reader. We have one excellent example of this in our language – Mr Dryden's ode on St Cecily's Day entitled *Alexander's Feast, or the Power of Music.*

Alexander Pope

from *An Essay on Criticism*   1711

But most by numbers judge a poet's song,
And smooth or rough, with them, is right or wrong;
In the bright Muse, though thousand charms conspire,
Her voice is all these tuneful fools admire,
Who haunt Parnassus but to please their ear,

Not mend their minds; as some to church repair,
Not for the doctrine but the music there.
These equal syllables alone require,
Though oft the ear the open vowels tire;
While expletives their feeble aid do join,
And ten low words oft creep in one dull line;
While they ring round the same unvaried chimes,
With sure returns of still expected rhymes.
Where'er you find 'the cooling western breeze,'
In the next line, it 'whispers through the trees';
If 'crystal streams with pleasing murmurs creep',
The reader's threatened (not in vain) with 'sleep'.
Then, at the last and only couplet fraught
With some unmeaning thing they call a thought,
A needless alexandrine ends the song,
That like a wounded snake drags its slow length along.
Leave such to tune their own dull rhymes, and know
What's roundly smooth, or languishingly slow;
And praise the easy vigour of a line,
Where Denham's strength, and Waller's sweetness join.
True ease in writing comes from art, not chance,
As those move easiest who have learned to dance.
'Tis not enough no harshness gives offence,
The sound must seem an echo to the sense.
Soft is the strain when Zephyr gently blows,
And the smooth stream in smoother numbers flows;
But when loud surges lash the sounding shore,
The hoarse, rough verse should like the torrent roar.
When Ajax strives some rock's vast weight to throw,
The line too labours, and the words move slow;
Not so, when swift Camilla scours the plain,
Flies o'er th' unbending corn, and skims along the main.
Hear how Timotheus' varied lays surprise,
And bid alternate passions fall and rise!
While at each change the son of Libyan Jove,
Now burns with glory, and then melts with love;
Now his fierce eyes with sparkling fury glow;
Now sighs steal out and tears begin to flow.

Persians and Greeks like turns of nature found,
And the world's victor stood subdued by sound!
The powers of music all our hearts allow;
And what Timotheus was is Dryden now.
(337–83)

Joseph Addison (anonymously)

from the *Spectator*, no. 253   20 December 1711 (see Note A in
Appendix, p. 487)

There is nothing which more denotes a great mind than the abhor-
rence of envy and detraction. This passion reigns more among bad
poets than any other set of men.

As there are none more ambitious of fame than those who are
conversant in poetry, it is very natural for such as have not succeeded
in it to depreciate the works of those who have. For since they cannot
raise themselves to the reputation of their fellow-writers, they must
endeavour to sink it to their own pitch, if they would still keep
themselves upon a level with them.

The greatest wits that ever were produced in one age lived together
in so good an understanding, and celebrated one another with so
much generosity, that each of them receives an additional lustre from
his contemporaries, and is more famous for having lived with men
of so extraordinary a genius than if he had himself been the sole
wonder of the age. I need not tell my reader that I here point at the
reign of Augustus; and I believe he will be of my opinion that neither
Virgil nor Horace would have gained so great a reputation in the
world, had they not been the friends and admirers of each other.
Indeed all the great writers of that age, for whom singly we have so
great an esteem, stand up together as vouchers for one another's
reputation. But at the same time that Virgil was celebrated by Gallus,
Propertius, Horace, Varius, Tucca and Ovid, we know that Bavius
and Maevius were his declared foes and calumniators.

In our own country a man seldom sets up for a poet without
attacking the reputation of all his brothers in the art. The ignorance
of the moderns, the scribblers of the age, the decay of poetry, are the

topics of detraction with which he makes his entrance into the world; but how much more noble is the fame that is built on candour and ingenuity, according to those beautiful lines of Sir John Denham, in his poem on Fletcher's works:

But whither am I strayed? I need not raise
Trophies to thee from other men's dispraise;
Nor is thy fame on lesser ruins built,
Nor needs thy juster title the foul guilt
Of Eastern kings, who, to secure their reign,
Must have their brothers, sons and kindred slain.

I am sorry to find that an author who is very justly esteemed among the best judges has admitted some strokes of this nature into a very fine poem; I mean the *Art of Criticism* [really *Essay on Criticism*], which was published some months since, and is a masterpiece in its kind. The observations follow one another like those in Horace's *Art of Poetry* without that methodical regularity which would have been requisite in a prose author. They are some of them uncommon, but such as the reader must assent to, when he sees them explained with that elegance and perspicuity in which they are delivered. As for those which are the most known, and the most received, they are placed in so beautiful a light, and illustrated with such apt allusions, that they have in them all the graces of novelty, and make the reader who was before acquainted with them still more convinced of their truth and solidity. And here give me leave to mention what Monsieur Boileau has so very well enlarged upon in the preface to his works, that wit and fine writing doth not consist so much in advancing things that are new as in giving things that are known an agreeable turn. It is impossible for us, who live in the later ages of the world, to make observations in criticism, morality, or in any art or science which have not been touched upon by others. We have little else left us but to represent the common sense of mankind in more strong, more beautiful, or more uncommon lights. If a reader examines Horace's *Art of Poetry*, he will find but very few precepts in it which he may not meet with in Aristotle, and which were not commonly known by all the poets of the Augustan age. His way of expressing and applying them, not his invention of them, is what we are chiefly to admire.

For this reason I think there is nothing in the world so tiresome as the works of those critics who write in a positive dogmatic way, without either language, genius, or imagination. If the reader would see how the best of the Latin critics writ, he may find their manner very beautifully described in the characters of Horace, Petronius, Quintilian and Longinus, as they are drawn in the essay of which I am now speaking.

Since I have mentioned Longinus, who in his reflections has given us the same kind of sublime which he observes in the several passages that occasioned them, I cannot but take notice that our English author has after the same manner exemplified several of his precepts in the very precepts themselves. I shall produce two or three instances of this kind. Speaking of the insipid smoothness which some readers are so much in love with, he has the following verses:

These equal syllables alone require,
Though oft the ear the open vowels tire;
While expletives their feeble aid do join,
And ten low words oft creep in one dull line.
(344–7)

The gaping of the vowels in the second line, the expletive 'do' in the third, and the ten monosyllables in the fourth, give such a beauty to this passage as would have been very much admired in an ancient poet. The reader may observe the following lines in the same view:

A needless alexandrine ends the song,
That like a wounded snake drags its slow length along.
(356–7)

And afterwards,

'Tis not enough no harshness gives offence,
The sound must seem an echo to the sense.
Soft is the strain when Zephyr gently blows,
And the smooth stream in smoother numbers flows;
But when loud surges lash the sounding shore,
The hoarse, rough verse should like the torrent roar.
When Ajax strives some rock's vast weight to throw,
The line too labours, and the words move slow;

Not so, when swift Camilla scours the plain,
Flies o'er th' unbending corn, and skims along the main.
(364–72)

The beautiful distich upon Ajax in the foregoing lines puts me in mind of a description in Homer's *Odyssey*, which none of the critics have taken notice of. It is where Sisyphus is represented lifting his stone up the hill, which is no sooner carried to the top of it, but it immediately tumbles to the bottom. This double motion of the stone is admirably described in the number of these verses; as in the four first it is heaved up by several spondees intermixed with proper breathing places, and at last trundles down in a continued line of dactyls [quotes *Odyssey*, XI 593–8].

It would be endless to quote verses out of Virgil which have this particular kind of beauty in the numbers; but I may take an occasion in a future paper to show several of them which have escaped the observation of others.

I cannot conclude this paper without taking notice that we have three poems in our tongue, which are of the same nature, and each of them a masterpiece in its kind: the *Essay on Translated Verse* [by the Earl of Roscommon], the *Essay on the Art of Poetry* [by the Duke of Buckingham], and the *Essay upon Criticism*.

John Dennis

from *Reflections Critical and Satirical upon a Late Rhapsody Called 'An Essay upon Criticism'* 1711

Wherever this gentleman talks of wit, he is sure to say something that is very foolish . . .

What is this wit that does our cares employ,
The owner's wife that other men enjoy?
The more his trouble as the more admired,
Where wanted scorned, and envied where acquired.[1]

1 Pope acknowledged the justice of some of Dennis's remarks by subsequently altering a number of passages in *An Essay on Criticism*, including the lines quoted here, 500–503, and 566 and 567, below. [Ed.]

Here again I desire leave to ask two or three questions. First, how can wit be scorned where it is not? Is not this a figure frequently employed in Hibernian land? The person who wants this wit may indeed be scorned; but such a contempt declares the honour that the contemner has for wit. But secondly, what does he mean by acquired wit? Does he mean genius by the word 'wit', or conceit and point? If he means genius, that is certainly never to be acquired; and the person who should pretend to acquire it would be always secure from envy. But if by wit he means conceit and point, those are things that ought never to be in poetry, unless by chance sometimes in the epigram, or in comedy, where it is proper to the character and the occasion; and even in comedy it ought always to give place to humour. . . .

In the beginning of the thirty-third page there is a couplet of advice, the first line of which is very impertinent, and the second very wrong.

Be silent always when you doubt your sense.

Now who are the persons to whom he is giving advice here? Why, to poets or critics, or both; but the persons to whom he ought to be speaking are critics, that is, people who pretend to instruct others. But can any man of common sense want to be told that he ought not to pretend to instruct others as long as he doubts of the truth of his own precepts?

But what can be more wrong or more absurd than the latter verse of the couplet?

Speak when you're sure, yet speak with diffidence.

Now I should think that when a man is sure, 'tis his duty to speak with a modest assurance; since in doing otherwise he betrays the truth, especially when he speaks to those who are guided more by imagination than they are by judgement, which is the case of three parts of the world, and three parts of the other part. . . .

Thus are his assertions and his precepts frequently false or trivial, or both, his thoughts very often crude and abortive, his expressions absurd, his numbers often harsh and unmusical, without cadence and without variety, his rhymes trivial and common. He dictates perpetually, and pretends to give law without anything of the simplicity or majesty of a legislator, and pronounces sentence without anything of the plainness or clearness or gravity of a judge. Instead of simplicity we have little conceit and epigram, and affectation. Instead of majesty we have something that is very mean, and instead of gravity we have something that is very boyish. And instead of perspicuity and lucid order, we have but too often obscurity and confusion.

Alexander Pope (anonymously)

from the *Guardian*, no. 40   27 April 1713 (see Note B in Appendix, pp. 487–8)

I designed to have troubled the reader with no farther discourses of pastorals; but, being informed that I am taxed of partiality in not mentioning an author, whose eclogues are published in the same volumes with Mr Philips's, I shall employ this paper in observations upon him, written in the free spirit of criticism, and without apprehension of offending that gentleman, whose character it is that he takes the greatest care of his works before they are published and has the least concern for them afterward.

I have laid it down as the first rule of pastoral that its idea should be taken from the manners of the golden age, and the moral formed upon the representation of innocence; it is therefore plain that any deviations from that design degrade a poem from being true pastoral. In this view it will appear that Virgil can only have two of his eclogues allowed to be such. His first and ninth must be rejected, because they describe the ravages of armies, and oppressions of the innocent; Corydon's criminal passion for Alexis throws out the second; the calumny and railing in the third are not proper to that state of concord; the eighth represents unlawful ways of procuring love by enchantments and introduces a shepherd whom an inviting precipice tempts to self-murder. As to the fourth, sixth, and tenth, they are given up by Heinsius, Salmasius, Rapin, and the critics in general. They likewise observe that but eleven of all the Idyllia of Theocritus are to be admitted as pastorals; and even out of that number the greater part will be excluded for one or other of the reasons above-mentioned. So that when I remarked in a former paper that Virgil's eclogues, taken altogether, are rather select poems than pastorals, I might have said the same thing, with no less truth, of Theocritus. The reason of this I take to be yet unobserved by the critics, viz. 'They never meant them all for pastorals.' Which it is plain Philips hath done, and in that particular excelled both Theocritus and Virgil.

As simplicity is the distinguishing characteristic of pastoral, Virgil has been thought guilty of too courtly a style; his language is perfectly pure, and he often forgets he is among peasants. I have frequently wondered that since he was so conversant in the writings of Ennius he had not imitated the rusticity of the Doric as well by the help of the old obsolete Roman language, as Philips hath the antiquated English. For example, might he not have said 'quoi' instead of 'cui'; 'quijum' for 'cujum'; 'volt' for 'vult', etc., as well as our modern hath 'welladay' for 'alas', 'whilome' for 'of old', 'make mock' for 'deride', and 'witless younglings' for 'simple lambs', etc., by which means he had attained as much of the air of Theocritus as Philips hath of Spenser?

Mr Pope hath fallen into the same error with Virgil. His clowns do not converse in all the simplicity proper to the country. His names are borrowed from Theocritus and Virgil, which are improper to the scene of his patorals. He introduces Daphnis, Alexis, and Thyrsis on British plains, as Virgil had done before him on the Mantuan; whereas Philips, who hath the strictest regard to propriety, makes choice of names peculiar to the country, and more agreeable to a reader of delicacy, such as Hobbinol, Lobbin, Cuddy, and Colin Clout.

So easy as pastoral writing may seem (in the simplicity we have described it), yet it requires great reading, both of the ancients and moderns to be a master of it. Philips hath given us manifest proofs of his knowledge of books; it must be confessed his competitor hath imitated some single thoughts of the ancients well enough, if we consider he had not the happiness of a university education; but he hath dispersed them here and there, without that order and method which Mr Philips observes, whose whole third pastoral is an instance how well he hath studied the fifth of Virgil, and how judiciously reduced Virgil's thoughts to the standard of pastoral; as his contention of Colin Clout and the Nightingale shows with what exactness he hath imitated Strada.

When I remarked it as a principal fault to introduce fruits and flowers of a foreign growth in descriptions where the scene lies in our country,

I did not design that observation should extend also to animals, or the sensitive life; for Philips hath with great judgement described wolves in England in his first pastoral. Nor would I have a poet slavishly confine himself (as Mr Pope hath done) to one particular season of the year, one certain time of the day, and one unbroken scene in each eclogue. It is plain Spenser neglected this pedantry, who in his pastoral of November mentions this mournful song of the nightingale.

Sad Philomel her song in tears doth steep.

And Mr Philips, by a poetical creation, hath raised up finer beds of flowers than the most industrious gardener; his roses, lilies and daffodils blow in the same season.

But the better to discover the merits of our two contemporary pastoral writers, I shall endeavour to draw a parallel of them by setting several of their particular thoughts in the same light, whereby it will be obvious how much Philips hath the advantage. With what simplicity he introduces two shepherds singing alternately:

HOBBINOL
Come Rosalind, O come, for without thee
What pleasure can the country have for me?
Come, Rosalind, O come; my brinded kine,
My snowy sheep, my farm, and all is thine.

LANQUET
Come, Rosalind, O come; here shady bowers,
Here are cool fountains, and here springing flowers.
Come, Rosalind; here ever let us stay,
And sweetly waste our live-long time away.

Our other pastoral writer, in expressing the same thought, deviates into downright poetry:

STREPHON
In spring the fields, in autumn hills I love,
At morn the plains, at noon the shady grove —
But Delia always; forced from Delia's sight,
Nor plains at morn nor groves at noon delight.

DAPHNIS
Sylvia's like autumn ripe, yet mild as May,
More bright than noon, yet fresh as early day;

Ev'n spring displeases when she shines not here,
But, blest with her, 'tis spring throughout the year.
(Spring, 77–84)

In the first of these authors, two shepherds thus innocently describe the behaviour of their mistresses:

HOBBINOL
As Marian bathed, by chance I passed by;
She blushed, and at me cast a side-long eye;
Then swift beneath the crystal wave she tried
Her beauteous form, but all in vain, to hide.

LANQUET
As I to cool me bathed one sultry day,
Fond Lydia lurking in the sedges lay;
The wanton laughed and seemed in haste to fly,
Yet often stopped, and often turned her eye.

The other modern (who it must be confessed hath a knack of versifying) hath it as follows:

STREPHON
Me gentle Delia beckons from the plain,
Then, hid in shades, eludes her eager swain;
But feigns a laugh, to see me search around,
And by that laugh the willing fair is found.

DAPHNIS
The sprightly Sylvia trips along the green;
She runs, but hopes she does not run unseen;
While a kind glance at her pursuer flies,
How much at variance are her feet and eyes!
(Spring, 53–60)

There is nothing the writers of this kind of poetry are fonder of than descriptions of pastoral presents. Philips says thus of a sheep-hook:

Of seasoned elm, where studs of brass appear,
To speak the giver's name, the month and year,
The hook of polished steel, the handle turned,
And richly by the graver's skill adorned.

The other of a bowl embossed with figures:

> ... where wanton ivy twines,
> And swelling clusters bend the curling vines;
> Four figures rising from the work appear,
> The various seasons of the rolling year.
> And what is that which binds the radiant sky,
> Where twelve bright signs in beauteous order lie?
> (Spring, 35–40)

The simplicity of the swain in this place, who forgets the name of the Zodiac, is no ill imitation of Virgil; but how much more plainly and unaffectedly would Philips have dressed this thought in his Doric?

> And what that height, which girds the welkin sheen,
> Where twelve gay signs in meet array are seen?

If the reader would indulge his curiosity any farther in the comparison of particulars, he may read the first pastoral of Philips with the second of his contemporary, and the fourth and sixth of the former with the fourth and first of the latter, where several parallel places will occur to everyone.

Having now shown some parts in which these two writers may be compared, it is a justice I owe to Mr Philips to discover those in which no man can compare with him. First, that beautiful rusticity, of which I shall only produce two instances out of a hundred not yet quoted:

> O woeful day! O day of woe, quoth he,
> And woeful I, who live the day to see!

That simplicity of diction, the melancholy flowing of the numbers, the solemnity of the sound, and the easy turn of the words, in this dirge (to make use of our author's expression), are extremely elegant.

In another of his pastorals a shepherd utters a dirge not much inferior to the former, in the following lines:

> Ah me, the while! ah me, the luckless day!
> Ah luckless lad, the rather might I say;
> Ah silly I! more silly than my sheep,
> Which on the flowery plains I once did keep.

How he still charms the ear with these artful repetitions of the epithets; and how significant is the last verse! I defy the most common reader to repeat them without feeling some motions of compassion.

In the next place I shall rank his proverbs, in which I formerly observed he excels. For example,

A rolling stone is ever bare of moss;
And, to their cost, green years old proverbs cross.
... He that late lies down, as late will rise,
And, sluggard-like, till noon-day snoring lies,
Against ill luck all cunning foresight fails;
Whether we sleep or wake it naught avails.
... Nor fear from upright sentence wrong.

Lastly, his elegant dialect, which alone might prove him the eldest-born of Spenser, and our only true Arcadian; I should think it proper for the several writers of pastoral to confine themselves to their several countries. Spenser seems to have been of this opinion; for he hath laid the scene of one of his pastorals in Wales, where, with all the simplicity natural to that part of our island, one shepherd bids the other good morrow in an unusual and elegant manner.

Diggon Davey, I bid hur good day;
Or Diggon hur is, or I mis-say.

Diggon answers

Hur was hur while it was daylight:
But now hur is a most wretched wight, *etc.*

But the most beautiful example of this kind that I ever met with is in a very valuable piece which I chanced to find among some old manuscripts, entitled *A Pastoral Ballad*; which I think, for its nature and simplicity, may (notwithstanding the modesty of the title) be allowed a perfect pastoral. It is composed in the Somersetshire dialect, and the names such as are proper to the country people. It may be observed, as a farther beauty of this pastoral, the words, Nymph Dryad, Naiad, Faun, Cupid, or Satyr are not once mentioned through the whole. I shall make no apology for inserting some few lines of this excellent piece. Cicily breaks thus into the subject, as she is going a-milking:

CICILY:
Rager go vetch tha kee,[1] or else tha zun
Will quite be go, bevore c'have half a don.

[1] That is, the kine or cows.

ROGER:
Thou shouldst not ax ma tweece, but I've a be
To dreave our bull to bull tha parson's kee.

It is to be observed that this whole dialogue is formed upon the
passion of jealousy; and his mentioning the parson's kine naturally
revives the jealousy of the shepherdess Cicily, which she expresses
as follows:

CICILY:
Ah Rager, Rager, chez was zore avraid
When in yond vield you kissed the parson's maid:
Is this the love that once to me you zed
When from tha wake thou broughtst me gingerbread?
ROGER:
Cicily thou charg'st me false. I'll zwear to thee,
The parson's maid is still a maid for me.

In which answer of his are expressed at once that 'spirit of religion',
and that 'innocence of the golden age', so necessary to be observed
by all writers of pastoral.

At the conclusion of this piece, the author reconciles the lovers,
and ends the eclogue the most simply in the world:

So Rager parted vor to vetch tha kee,
And vor her bucket in went Cicily.

I am loath to show my fondness for antiquity so far as to prefer this
ancient British author to out present English writers of pastoral; but
I cannot avoid making this obvious remark – that both Spenser and
Philips have hit into the same road with this old west-country bard
of ours.

After all that hath been said, I hope none can think it any injustice
to Mr Pope that I forebore to mention him as a pastoral writer; since,
upon the whole, he is of the same class with Moschus and Bion,
whom we have excluded that rank, and of whose eclogues, as well
as some of Virgil's, it may be said that, according to the description
we have given of this sort of poetry, they are by no means pastorals,
but 'something better'.

Alexander Pope

Advertisement in the *Postman* (31 July) and the *Evening Post*
(2 August) 1716 (see Note C in Appendix, p. 488)

Whereas there have been published in my name certain scandalous
libels, which I hope no person of candour would have thought me
capable of, I am sorry to find myself obliged to declare that no
genuine pieces of mine have been printed by any but Mr Tonson
and Mr Lintot. And in particular as to that which is entitled 'A
Version of the First Psalm', I hereby promise a reward of three guineas
to anyone who shall discover the person or persons concerned in the
publication of the said libel, of which I am wholly ignorant.

A. Pope

Sir Richard Blackmore

from 'An Essay upon Writing', *Essays upon Several Subjects*,
vol. 2 1716

... a petulant set of writers, who have no way to popularity and
fame but by making their court to the vices and follies of the ages,
from a rooted and inflexible enmity to piety and virtue, and immortal
hatred to good men. ... Pity it is that these intrepid conspirators
against Heaven and religion, animated with deliberate malice, should
go on by their impious turns of wit and raillery to expose all modest
and prudent behaviour, and give the last blow, if they are able, to
sobriety and manners; and thus, by recovering and confirming the
vitiated relish of the nation, unto all that the other writers by their
excellent labours have, to their great honour, done in the service of
virtue and their country.

I cannot but here take notice that one of these champions of vice
is the reputed author of a detestable paper that has latterly been handed
out in manuscript and now appears in print, in which the godless
author has burlesqued the First Psalm of David in so obscene and
profane a manner that perhaps no age ever saw such an insolent

affront offered to the established religion of their country, and this, good Heaven!, with impunity. A sad demonstration this of the low ebb to which the British virtue is reduced in these degenerate times.

John Dennis

from *Remarks upon Mr Pope's Translation of Homer* 1717

Indeed it is impossible for any translator, and much less for this, to express in a translation the poetical language of Homer. By the advantage of the language in which he wrote, he had several ways of rendering his language poetical which a translator can never have: as the frequent use of compounded and decompounded words; the use of words which were as it were at one and the same time both Grecian and foreign, as being confined in their vulgar use to some particular part of Greece; as likewise the use of words which were purely poetic, and which were seldom or never used in prose; the contracting or lengthening the words which he used, and the frequent transposing of syllables; and, lastly, the altering the terminations of words, by means of the different dialects. But a translator of Homer has but one way of rendering his diction poetical; and that is the frequent use of figures, and above all figures of metaphors. And therefore, wherever in the late translation of Homer there is no use of figures, there we may justly conclude that the diction is prosaic; though at the same time the diction of the original, in that very place, even without figures, may be truly poetical, for reasons mentioned above. Now, in the late translation of Homer, there are, modestly speaking, twenty lines where there is no figure, for one that is figurative; and, consequently, there are twenty prosaic lines for one that is poetical. Indeed, the late translator of Homer, by his want of genius, and by his writing figuratively where the Grecian has writ plainly, has often made his diction the very reverse of that of the original – where the original is pure, the translation is often barbarous; often obscure where the original is clear and bright; often flat and vile where the other is great and lofty; and often, too often, affected and unnatural where the original is simple and unaffected, as it is frequently stiff and awkward where the original is easy, graceful, and numerous. In short, the Homer which Lintott prints does not talk like Homer but like Pope, and is so far from expressing the beauty of Homer's language that he makes him speak English as awkwardly as other foreigners do; and sometimes makes him talk as merrily as a Monsieur who comes to live among us in his old age, and, with a great deal of pains, acquires English enough to be laughed at. So that the little gentleman who translated him, with a most comical and unparalleled assurance, has undertaken to translate Homer from Greek, of which he does not know one word, into English, which he understands almost as little. And from hence it proceeds that instead of making him English, he sometimes makes him Irish, and one would swear that he had a hill in Tipperary for his Parnassus, and a puddle in some bog for his Hippocrene. . . .

I am, for the present, weary of raking in the dirt of this translation, where, in so little space, there are so many faults to be found. . . . The reader may easily see that, through all the verses I have cited, and 'tis true of all that I have not cited, instead of a pleasing variety of numbers, there is nothing but a perpetual identity of sound, an eternal monotony. The trumpet of Homer, with its loud and its various notes, is dwindled in Pope's lips to a Jew's-trump. The Pegasus of this little gentleman is not the steed that Homer rode, but a blind, stumbling Kentish post-horse, which neither walks, nor trots, nor paces, nor runs, but is upon an eternal Canterbury, and often stumbles, and often falls. The Pegasus which Homer rode would carry fifty Popes upon his back at a time, and throw every one of his riders.

Francis Atterbury

in conversation *c.* 1725 reported in D. C. Tovey (ed.),
Gray and his Friends (1890)

Bishop Atterbury, while in France, lost much of the friendship he had once had for Pope, and has been heard to say of him that he was as crooked in mind as in body.[1]

1 More familiar in the Latin of *Mens curva in corpore curvo*. [Ed.]

Daniel Defoe

from *Applebee's Journal*   31 July 1725

. . . a merry fellow of my acquaintance assures me that our cousin Homer himself was guilty of . . . plagiarism. Cousin Homer you must note was an old blind ballad singer at Athens, singing his ballads from door to door; only with this difference, that the ballads he sung were generally of his own making. . . . But, says my friend, this Homer, in process of time, when he had gotten some fame – and perhaps more money than poets ought to be trusted with – grew lazy and knavish, and got one Andronicus, a Spartan, and one Dr S[ewel]l, a philosopher of Athens, both pretty good poets, but less eminent than himself, to make his songs for him; which they, being poor and starving, did for him for a small matter. And so the poet never did much himself, only published and sold his ballads still, in his own name, as if they had been his own; and by that got great subscriptions, and a high price for them.

Joseph Spence

from 'Evening the First', *An Essay on Pope's 'Odyssey'*
1726 (see Note D in Appendix, pp. 488–9)

Antiphaus managed his affairs so as to get this winter sooner than usual to the country-seat of his friend Philypsus. It is there that he passes his time, whenever he can clear himself from the hurry of business, in a retirement every way agreeable, and in a full enjoyment of those pleasures which attend on a particular friendship, in an open and improving conversation. The conversation there does not run in the present polite way of saying and saying nothing; when alone, they usually fall into some points of learning, and as both of them are particularly fond of poetry, their disputes turn more frequently on that subject than any other. Indeed their differing in sentiment can scarce be called disputes, for whenever their thoughts do not meet, each of them shows a diffidence in his own opinion and a willingness to submit to the judgement of his friend.

It is by this means that they fall into each other's sentiments more than could well be expected from men of so different a turn. The enlarged genius of Philypsus always led him to dwell upon the most beautified parts of a poem with the greatest pleasure, while Antiphaus, who has a very clear head and has given much into a strict way of thinking, is taken most with just descriptions and plain, natural ideas. The one was so possessed with the pleasure which he felt from fine thoughts and warm expressions that he did not take a full satisfaction in low beauty and simple representations of nature; the other, on the contrary, had such an aversion to glitterings and elevation that he was distasted at any the least appearance of either. If the latter was too much prejudiced for the ancients, from the purity and justness which we find in most of their works, Philypsus has his foible too, and was sometimes caught by the flourish and colouring of the moderns. In a word, if Philypsus would sometimes contemn a point as low and mean, though in reality proper enough and naturally expressed, Antiphaus, in his turn, might happen now and then to blame a passage which required a good degree of ornament as being too glaring and artificial.

Among several other topics one evening they happened to fall into a discourse on Mr Pope's new translation of the *Odyssey*. As they both found beauties in that piece agreeable to their particular tastes, they had read it over with a great deal of pleasure; however, Philypsus was the person who admired it the most. 'There are some lines,' says he to Antiphaus (pointing to the *Odyssey* which lay before them), 'there are some favourites of mine in that poem which you must not look upon with your usual severity. Prithee, Antiphaus, be more sensible to the flame and spirit of a writer who is evidently our present laureate in genius and the most enlivened translator of the age.'

'I will very readily allow what you say of that great man,' returned Antiphaus, 'and shall always pay a deference to your more lively taste of the fine and sublime in poetry, but you must give me leave to dissent from you in some particulars. If I do not agree with your sentiments in relation to several lines and passages of that translation, 'tis perhaps because I fall so much short of you in your inward sense of the high and elevated beauties of language.' 'As I cannot imagine that to be the reason,' says Philypsus, 'I beg to hear those particulars you talked of; I am persuaded several of the passages which I have observed you to be less taken with in reading the translation will upon a closer view appear to be really beauties; to tell you the truth, I long to make a convert of you, and beg you would be full and large in communicating whatever remarks you have made on this performance. The evenings are long; we have sufficient time upon our hands; and I know not how we can pass it away more agreeably.'

Antiphaus paused for some time and seemed to be taken up in recollecting his thoughts on this point. At last, taking a tablet out of his pocket, 'Since you desire it,' says he, 'I will show you what observations I made as I went over the work; they are the thoughts which struck me *en passant*, and many of them will perhaps appear little and trifling.

'You will allow me, I believe, in the first place, that lines very good in themselves may be bad when considered as a translation. The aim of a translator is to give us the spirit of the original; and where the original is just, the very *manner* is to be observed. By the manner I would not intend the express words, or the mere turn of a period, but that the imitation ought to be easy, simple, and unadorned wherever the first writer uses either of those styles with judgement. You are well acquainted with that plain, humble manner of Homer, which is more particularly kept up by him in the *Odyssey*; and as much as I admire several parts in this translation, I cannot but think there are places in it which differ from the manner of Homer without sufficient reason for a change. The poet in several parts of that work seems to me to have let fall some lines that are forced, some of too much flourish and ornament, and a few even swelling and unnatural, where the original is with good reason plain, and natural, and unadorned.

'Where we admire the simplicity of Homer with justice, we cannot avoid blaming the want of it in his translator. Mr Pope intimates in one of the notes that no reproach has ever fallen upon Homer in relation to his sinking too low or being too familiar, that as to these particulars he preserves a universal justness, and that there is not any one place in his poem which can be justly censured upon this account. If so, a translator of Homer has no occasion for raising anything beyond what it is in the original. If he follows his master it is sufficient; all additional flourish and glitterings where we should meet with the plain and the familiar are at best so many beautiful excrescencies.

'There is one case which seems more particularly to lead Mr Pope into a glaring style: 'tis almost ever to be found in the descriptions of day, of light, and of the morning. 'Tis true, these are subjects which in themselves may require some brightness in the language, but there is a great difference between giving one light and dazzling one's eyes. Beside the conformity to the original, there is another certain and easy way of judging whether the brightening in these or any other points be proper or not: that light, we may be sure, falls in a wrong manner or an undue proportion, which does not make the thing more visible.

'There are of these descriptions, Philypsus, which seem both to refine too much upon the original and according to this rule. Did you ever observe those lines on one of the most agreeable images in the world, the break of day? They are in the beginning of the third book; if you will give me leave, I will read them to you.

The *sacred* sun, above the waters raised,
Through heaven's *eternal brazen portals blazed*;
And wide o'er earth diffused his *cheering* ray,
To gods and men to *give the golden day*. [III 1–4; Pope]

Several of these expressions seemed to me at first sight to take from the nature and simplicity of the description, and when I turned to the Greek, I found those very expressions to have no foundation there. 'Tis the same case in the following lines:

Soon as the morn, *in orient purple dressed,*
Unbarred the portal of the roseate east. [IV 411–12; Fenton]

But when the morning star with early ray
Flamed in the front of heaven. [XIII 112–13; Pope]

You will find these short sketches in Homer to be much more simple and natural; I leave it to your judgement whether they appear better with these colourings, or not. To add one instance more of the same thing: Is it more proper for Circe to tell Ulysses that he should stay that night with her, and 'set sail the next morning', or to hear her giving him leave to

Spread [his] broad sails, and *plough the liquid way,*
[Soon as] the morn *unveils her saffron ray.* [XII 36 35; Broome]

'I must own,' says Philypsus, 'this would have been more fit for the description of a voyage than for a speech – in a place, too, where we only find orders given for setting sail at such a time.'

'To me,' proceeded Antiphaus, 'Mr Pope seems to beautify too much in several other points beside those topics we have been talking of – as where he calls the nobles of Phaeacia "a radiant band of noblemen" [VI 306; Pope] and where he introduces Helen with "a gale of rich perfume breathing before her" [IV 158; Fenton]. If Homer mentions cups of solid gold, in the translation

The gold gives *lustre* to the *purple* draught. [I 188; Fenton]
And in the *dazzling* goblet *laughs* the wine. [III 608; Pope]

'You cannot but observe, by the way, that the original here is designed to signify the real intrinsic value, while only the outside and more glittering circumstances are what the English dwells upon entirely. But to go on. The horns of a bullock are in this new language "budding honours" [III 493; Pope]; and those of a ram (if I am not much mistaken) "translucent crescents" [IV 107; Fenton]. Pallas is well known to have had blue eyes given her by the ancients; now it is

Celestial azure brightening in her eyes. [I 408; Fenton]

'This heightening of things by a severe critic might be thought blamable, and indeed whenever it interferes where the passions ought to be touched, it certainly is so in a higher degree. The reader is delighted when, after a melancholy scene, he sees Penelope revived by a message from the gods and secretly enjoying the satisfaction of her soul; but what passion, what idea, has he when instead of this he is told of her heart's "dilating", and glowing "With florid joy" [IV 1096; Fenton]? Paint to him that unhappy princess in her distress, retiring silently and crying herself to sleep; only show the circumstances, and the reader must be moved. Does her behaviour and her sufferings strike him so forcibly when he finds it embellished into "echoing grief," and "silver-streaming eyes" [I 462,464; Fenton]?

'But however these passages may seem to be weakened by the finery and luxuriance of the language, this certainly is not so much the fault of Mr Pope as of the age: we give much into an airy way. If a verse runs off smooth, 'tis no matter for depth and clearness; and as the ancients valued thoughts more than sound, we seem to be taken with sounds more than thought. To speak out, we are got into an idle manner of versifying, and if Mr Pope sometimes falls into it, we are not so much to blame him for those particulars as to wonder that he does not do it more frequently in so general a debauch of taste among us.'

'Hold!' interrupted Philypsus. 'If you go on at this rate, you will seem only to be got into the old cant of running down our own times. I do not believe but that I could name some poet among us to answer any of those who flourished in the Augustan age. As to the present point, we rarely hear of any such thing as translation among them. In satire, we have the great names of Rochester, Dryden, and Oldham (not to mention the new kind of satire introduced among us by Butler). In critical poems, there are, you know, two or three very good ones beside that incomparable piece by Mr Pope, all to weigh against poor Horace. As for miscellaneous subjects, think of Cowley, Pope, Waller, and Prior, to mention no more of them. In the epic, Milton may dispute the laurel with either Virgil or Homer; and in dramatic pieces of either kind, we have writers that indisputably exceed any of the ancients.'

Antiphaus was not inclined to enter into a dispute of this nature. 'I was only speaking,' says he, 'of our present taste in poetry and the prevailing manner of those writers who are now upon the stage. As to this, Philypsus, give me leave to say that the language of our writers, and the practice of the world, is much infected with the *finesse*. I think 'tis Mr Locke observes that "the humours of a people may be learnt from their usage of words". This symptom of the disease is very strong in the present case: thus, to say that a verse is *bien tourné* is the highest commendation among the French critics; as a *fine* scholar, *polite* literature, and the *belles lettres* are the leading expressions when we would speak of learning in the best sense. And I appeal to you, who are so well acquainted with all our poets, whether their practice in particular does not fall more and more into the *finesses* we have been complaining of. We may partly judge of this from some lines in the best of them, the writer whose works lie before us. I was just going to give you a few more instances of it from the *Odyssey*.

'Is there any figure so much abused by the moderns as what they call the antithesis? They run it into a downright playing upon words. Cowley's poetry could not live without it; Dryden uses it almost perpetually in his translation of Virgil, and was ridiculed, you know, on that head by the late Duke of Buckingham. I have observed with pleasure that Mr Pope in his translation very much avoids this little beauty, which the other affected so excessively; yet I have a place before me where one of this kind has slipped from his pen; it runs thus (he is speaking of a stranger's arrival at the court of Penelope, disordered so much by the riot of the suitors):

Or when, to taste her hospitable board,
Some guest arrives, with rumours of her lord;
And these *indulge their want*, and *those their woe*;
And *here the tears, and there the goblets flow*.' [XIV 413–16; Pope]

'Pardon me,' says Philypsus, 'there you do not seem to do the translator justice; the figure is countenanced by Homer himself. You see, here is an antithesis in the original.' 'That,' answered Antiphaus, 'seems rather to be a contrast, to set the riot of the suitors in a stronger light. But call it what you please, it is only single there, whereas you see it multiplied and worn to rags in the translation. This overdoing a point is observable in many other cases as much as in the former, and in some is carried on to a degree which borders upon the forced and unnatural.

'Telemachus, bursting into tears at the name of his father, endeavours to hide his sorrow from Menelaus, who was then talking with him. Homer says only that Menelaus observed him, which words Mr Pope draws out into this couplet:

The conscious monarch pierced the coy disguise,
And viewed his filial love with vast surprise. [IV 153–4; Fenton]

'For a humble natural description of a tripod (or cauldron) set upon the fire, I would recommend you to the following lines:

The flames *climb* round it with a *fierce embrace*;
The fuming waters *bubble o'er the blaze*. [VIII 473–4; Broome]

'But above all, in my opinion, are these on a person tired and quite spent:

… *Lost in lassitude lay all the man,*
Deprived of voice, of motion, and of breath;
The soul scarce waking, in the arms of death. [v 585–7; Pope]

'Or these:

Ye Gods! since this *worn frame refection knew,*
What scenes have I surveyed of dreadful view! [vi 261–2; Pope]

'Would you imagine that all which countenances this in the original is a passage in Ulysses' speech after his shipwreck in which he intimates that he had not bathed for a considerable time?'

'I find it so,' says Philypsus, 'and own the lines to be somewhat forced and unnatural; indeed, those you have repeated seem generally to draw too near to that character. But I cannot conceive by what means they sound so harsh to me at present. When I read the piece, there was scarce a line of them which gave me any offence. Yes, it must be by your tearing them from the body of the work that they now seem not so agreeable. Really, Antiphaus, this is not fair usage of an author; you rob them of their order and connexion, and 'tis thence that they perfectly lose the beauty which they had in the whole.'
'Very true,' replied Antiphaus; 'the warmth of reading, the thread of the story and a general tunableness in the verse will carry a man on strangely, and may sometimes cheat him into a false pleasure. But then it is for this very reason that I should think the justest method of forming a judgement on particulars is to consider them apart. However, let us try it for once in a more entire passage than any of the former. Let me see: the place I have dipped upon is where Minerva tells Ulysses that she will transform him into the figure of an old man that he may view the posture of his affairs unsuspected and unknown. The lines in Homer may be thus read into English.

I will make you (says that goddess to the hero) entirely unknown to all men; the beauty and smoothness of your skin shall be taken away, your limbs bent, and the hair of your head turned grey. I will then fling a garb over you that shall make you frightful and odious to those that see you. All that flame and life in your eyes shall be lost; I will so far deform them that you shall look contemptible to all the suitors, to your own Penelope, and to your son, whom you left yet an infant in your palace. (XIII 397ff.]

'You know that Mr Pope, in comparing some passages in the prophesies of Isaiah with the famous *Eclogue* of Virgil, turns the latter into prose; if we follow that example in the present case, his translation of these lines runs thus:

It fits thee at present to wear a dark disguise, and walk secret, unknown to the eyes of mortals. For this my hand shall wither every beauty and every elegance of form and face, spread a bark of wrinkles over thy smooth skin, turn the auburn honours of thy head hoar, disfigure with coarse attire every limb, and extinguish all the fire in thy eyes; add all the decays of life, and all the wants of it, estrange thee from thy own, thy son and thy wife; every sight shall turn from the loathed object, and the blind suitors scorn their destruction. [XIII 453–64; Pope]

'Give me leave to go out of my way a little to try the same experiment on a single passage from the *Iliad* which is flourished and set off in an extraordinary manner. It is in the nineteenth book, where we have a poetical account of a fine breed of horses. The original runs thus:

Three thousand mares grazed these meads, with their young foals running by them. Boreas was enamoured of them as they fed there, and, turning himself into the shape of a fine black horse, accomplished his desires. Of this breed were twelve of the colts.

'Mr Pope's translation (only allowing equivalent expressions to blind the rhymes) runs thus:

His *spacious pastures bred three thousand mares, and* three thousand *foals fed beside* their mothers. *Boreas, enamoured of the* sprightly train, *concealed his* godhead in the locks of hair *that flowed over his shoulders; he* neighed *to his* loves with dissembled voice, *and* coursed the dapple beauties *o'er the meadow. Twelve others of* unrivalled sort *sprung hence*, swift as their mother *mares* and father *wind*. [*Iliad*, XX 262–9]

'This, if overwrought, is the more blamable because the matter is carried very far even in the original and so is the less capable of being stretched any farther. Mr Pope, in his note upon the place, observes that "Homer has the happiness of making the least circumstance considerable"; and that "the plainest matter shines in his dress of poetry". It is true, it shines sufficiently in that. Some brightening is necessary in poetry, but an excess of it, Philypsus, may dazzle, or may blind our eyes; it can never assist or delight them.

'By comparing these passages, you will see that which I intend: the difference of manner in the ancient and modern poetry. In the latter we find expressions added which seem to be added for beauties, and which in reality perhaps only turn the plainness and strength of the original into the fine and the artificial.'

Upon Philypsus' acknowledging that he thought the point too much laboured, and the translation unequal: 'Yes,' says Antiphaus, 'the translator himself seems to be sensible of it in the present case, for soon after, when the former passage is repeated in the original, he gives an entirely new turn to it, and I believe upon hearing the lines you will be of opinion that (excepting a word or two) it is rendered with a better grace and with more justice than we find in the former.

She spake, then touched him with her powerful wand:
The skin shrunk up, and withered at her hand:
A swift old age o'er all his members spread;
A sudden frost was sprinkled on his head.
Nor longer in the heavy eye-ball shined
The glance divine, forth-beaming from the mind.
His robe, which spots indelible besmear,
In rags dishonest flutters with the air. [*Odyssey*, XIII 496–503; Pope]

'Mr Pope without question is happy in a great share of judgement, as well as vivacity and spirit in writing, but it is next to impossible in so long a translation, especially as it is in rhyme, not to give sometimes into sound and ornament, when, to crown all, the vogue of the world goes so strong for both. Do not ask whether I should desire to see both of them banished out of poetry; far from it. Expressive sounds are of use in the most natural, and a variety in the management of them is necessary to keep up attention in the reader. That, and ornament, is what sets poetry above prose. All I would say is this, that sound is not sufficient where we might expect sense, and that in humble passages, in natural descriptions, or in moving most of the passions, additional ornaments are so many blemishes. Dressing up the expressiveness of Homer in such fineries is much the same as if one should throw a very gay modern dress over the Hercules Farnese, or any of the most nervous statues of the ancients.'

'But you will allow ornament where the subject will bear it, and where the original leads the way?' – 'In a translation,' answered Antiphaus, 'it is proper, perhaps, only in the latter case; but allowing it in both, it should never be overwrought in either. Too much finery is always affectation, and I wish our writers at present were not so generally given to "elevate and surprise, and all that," as Mr Bayes calls it.

'The running into this excess so much is what has unsinewed our poetry. It is in poetry as it is in building : the being vastly studious of ornament does not only take away from the strength of the work, but is a sure token of a vitiated taste in the designer.'

'You are always blaming the modern refinements,' says Philypsus; 'but will you not allow that this taste of the age is a sufficient justification at least of Mr Pope, in those cases where he complies with it? – We must *write* so as to please the world, and *speak* so as to be most easily understood. Custom will often wear away the propriety of things of this nature, and as for the propriety of language, that depends upon it entirely. I allow, to use your own thought, that a profusion of lace and embroidery would be a disguise upon an old hero, but they are so far from being improper that they are becoming on the heroes of our age.'

'They may become the heroes of our age,' replied Antiphaus smiling, 'perhaps on a far different account: there is another character now wove into and blended with that of a soldier to which these things are very agreeable. How many are there of these heroes, as you call them, whose courage reaches no farther than their sword-knot, and whose conduct is taken up wholly in their dress? But consider a man barely as a soldier, think of him in the midst of some warm action, and these little ideas of him will disappear. Then it is that posture, that pressing on the foe, that grasping of his sword, that fierceness in his eyes, that serenity, and that eagerness on his countenance which strike us wholly and take up all our attention. Yes,

Philypsus, if you view a real modern hero in a true light, those fineries do not sit well upon him; and I think I never saw anything more truly ridiculous than the piece we were laughing at the other day in your picture gallery. – Good heaven! The Duke of Marlborough in the heat of an engagement, with a full-bottomed wig very carefully spread over his shoulders!

'But to return to the present taste in poetry. If this corruption of the age could excuse a writer for what he composes now, must it be carried down as far as Homer's days? Must his heroes love, and talk, and fight à la mode? Must his strong, sententious lines be set to the new polite airs of Handel and Buononcini? Yet were what you would allege of any force, it would carry the matter thus far, and the whole *Iliad* and *Odyssey* ought to be enervated down to the present taste. No, whatever may be allowed to any of the proper genuine productions of this age, it ought not to make an inroad upon all others. Let Homer's energy and pathos be violated as little as is possible; nature ought to rule in his works and those of the ancients, as ornament and surprise and elevation have, in their turn, the empire of the modern world.

'You see I begin to show the old heat that this subject (I think) always betrays me into. I beg pardon, Philypsus, and will attend more to what I am about for the future. I should have given you some instances of this elevation from the translation before us. Apropos, what a glaring description of a sword have we in the eighth *Odyssey*:

> whose blade of brass *displays*
> *A ruddy gleam;* whose hilt, *a silver blaze;*
> Whose ivory sheath *inwrought* with *curious pride,*
> Adds *graceful terror to the wearer's side.* [VIII 437–40; Broome]

'Homer says that Hermione was as beautiful as Venus; this is low and humble in comparison of Mr Pope's Hermione:

> On whom *a radiant pomp of graces* wait,
> Resembling Venus in *attractive state.* [IV 19–20; Fenton]

'Where a prodigy is sent to the Ithacensians in council, Homer says that "they were struck at the sight of it, and revolved in their minds what it might presage to them". This Mr Pope renders after the following manner:

The wondering rivals gaze with cares oppressed,
And chilling horrors freeze in every breast. [II 183-4; Broome]

'How mean is it, and how much like prose, to tell us, that "Penelope heard the mirth of the suitors!" To elevate this sufficiently, you must say:

The shrilling airs the vaulted roof rebounds,
Reflecting to the queen the silver sounds. [I 425-6; Fenton]

'This false way of animating poetry, as no doubt many will be pleased to call it, grows particularly prejudicial and absurd in any case where the passions are to be raised in the reader or described in the persons of the poem. Where we would move pity, in particular, nothing is "more odious than a show of eloquence" [Quintilian]. Nature has provided a sympathy in our souls, she has put a bias into our temper that inclines us forcibly to compassion; and we should leave her to her own work in such points, without any of the impertinent assistances of art.'
(387-98)

Alexander Pope

in conversation with Joseph Spence *c.* 1728 (see Note E in Appendix, p. 489)

Mr Pope said that he was seven years unlearning what he had got (from about twenty to twenty-seven).

Alexander Pope

in conversation with Joseph Spence just after speaking of his *Dunciad* 1728

A poem on a slight subject requires the greater care to make it considerable enough to be read.

Anonymous

from *Sawney, An Heroic Poem Occasioned by 'The Dunciad'.
Together with a Critique of that Poem* 1728

[*The Dunciad* is] a strange, wild, linsey-wolsey composition ... an idle, empty, trifling piece of nonsense. . . . The whole piece is so notoriously full of pride, insolence, beastliness, malice, profaneness, conceits, absurdities, and extravagance that 'tis almost impossible to form a regular notion of it. I would venture to give you some proofs of each, were I not afraid of making you sick, on the one hand, at their abominable nastiness and ashamed, at the other, that any persons who bear some likeness to the human shape should give a loose to those sordid passions that are entirely unworthy of it.

Ambrose Philips

from *Codrus: or, 'The Dunciad' Dissected, Being the
Finishing-Stroke. To which is added Farmer Pope and his Son,
A Tale* 1728

Satire was certainly of admirable use among the ancients, and is of no less among the moderns; but then they always chose for their theme some reigning vice, or growing folly. But where can you find a Persius, a Juvenal, or Horace lashing of personal defect, or turns of providence? These pious heathens well knew that calamities were not crimes, and always exempted such from being the subject of satire. They knew it was not in the power of a man to make his own fortune, any more than he could his own person, and therefore paid a modest deference to the decrees of an over-ruling power, though this enlightened age thinks scorn to own one. *The Dunciad* is a recent instance of this, wherein Dullness, which in plain English is want of capacity, deformity, a want of comeliness, and Poverty, a want of substance, are the only subjects he can find to work up – which how well they become his pen has been said already. . . .

The large profit Mr Pope has made by a nominal translation of Homer, and the little pains he took to deserve it, need no repetition;

he has acquired fame, purchased an estate, dubbed himself a 'squire, and, one would have thought, might have raised an altar to fortune, and sat down contented; but instead of that, weary of a tranquil life and wanting some particular object to fix on, he lampoons both church and state, all that he knows, and all that he knows not, and bids an open defiance to human kind in terms so coarse and filthy that few readers can forbear puking at his bare ideas. Much good may they do him. He has opened Pandora's box, which perhaps he may never be able to shut again.

John Dennis

from *Remarks on Mr Pope's 'Rape of the Lock', in Several Letters to a Friend* 1728

The author of *The Rape* has run counter to this practice both of the ancients and moderns. He has not taken his machines from the religion of his country, nor from any religion, nor from morality. His machines contradict the doctrines of the Christian religion, contradict all sound morality; there is no allegorical nor sensible meaning in them; and for these reasons they give no instruction, make no impression at all upon the mind of a sensible reader. Instead of making the action wonderful and delightful, they render it extravagant, absurd, and incredible. They do not in the least influence that action; they neither prevent the danger of Belinda, nor promote it, nor retard it, unless, perhaps, it may be said, for one moment, which is ridiculous. And if here it be objected that the author designed only to entertain and amuse, to that I answer for that very reason he ought to have taken the utmost care to make his poem probable, according to the important precept of Horace:

Ficta voluptatis causa sint proxima veris.

And that we may be satisfied that this rule is founded in reason and nature, we find by constant experience that anything that shocks probability is most insufferable in comedy....

The machines that appear in this poem are infinitely less considerable than the human persons, which is without precedent. Nothing

can be so contemptible as the persons, or so foolish as the understandings of these hobgoblins. Ariel's speech, for the first thirty lines,
is one continued impertinence: for, if what he says is true, he tells
them nothing but what they knew as well as himself before. And
when he comes at length to the point, he is full as impertinent as he
was in his ramble before; for after he has talked to them of black
omens and dire disasters that threaten his heroine, these bugbears
dwindle to the breaking a piece of china, the staining a petticoat, the
losing a necklace, a fan, or a bottle of sal volatile. . . .

Discord is described by Homer with her feet upon the earth and
head in the skies – upon which Longinus cries out that this is not so
much the measure of Discord as of Homer's capacity and elevation
of genius. Even so these diminutive beings of the intellectual world
may be said to be the measure of Mr Pope's capacity and elevation of
genius. They are, indeed, beings so diminutive that they bear the
same proportion to the rest of the intellectual that eels in vinegar do
to the rest of the material world. The latter are only to be seen
through microscopes, and the former only through the false optics of
a Rosicrucian understanding.

Thomas Hearne

from *Remarks and Collections*, vol. 10   18 July 1729

This Alexander Pope, though he be an English poet, yet he is but an
indifferent scholar, mean at Latin, and can hardly read Greek. He is a
very ill-natured man, and covetous and excessively proud.
(158)

Alexander Pope

in conversation with Joseph Spence   1–7 May 1730

There are three distinct tours in poetry: the design, the language, and
the versification (to which he afterwards seemed to add a fourth, the
expression, or manner of painting the humours, characters, and things
that fall in with your design).

The first epistle [of the *Essay on Man*] is to be to the whole work what a scale is to a book of maps, and in this, I reckon, lies my greatest difficulty – not only in settling and ranging the parts of it aright, but in making them agreeable enough to be read with pleasure. [Spence adds: 'He at that time intended to have included in one epistle what he afterwards addressed to Lord Bolingbroke in four.']

After writing a poem one should correct it all over with one single view at a time. Thus for language, if an elegy: 'these lines are very good, but are not they of too heroical a strain?', and so vice versa. It appears very plainly from comparing parallel passages touched both in the *Iliad* and *Odyssey* that Homer did this, and 'tis yet plainer that Virgil did so, from the distinct styles he uses in his three sorts of poems.

In versification there's a sensible difference between softness and sweetness that I could distinguish from a boy. Thus, on the same points, Dryden will be found to be softer and Waller sweeter.[1]
I wrote things I'm ashamed to say how soon. Part of an epic poem when about twelve. . . . That couplet on the circulation of the blood in *The Dunciad* [III, 47–8] was originally in this poem word for word, as it is now.

Edward Young

in conversation *c.* 1730 reported in Spence's *Anecdotes, Observations, and Characters of Books and Men* (1820)

Pope was so superior to all the poets his contemporaries in versification that if he met with a good line (even in a much inferior poet) he would take it (like a lord of the manor) for his own. Thus even from Ambrose Philips [*Epistle to Lord Halifax* (1714), l. 36], 'nor shall his promise to his people fail' to his *Iliad* [v 77].

1 Spence comments that Thomas Blacklock (1721–91) identified *sweetness* with management of the pauses (= iambic regularity) and *softness* with assonance and alliteration. Pope uses the same terms in the *Essay on Criticism*. [Ed.]

Alexander Pope

from *A Master Key to Popery, or, A True and Perfect Key to Pope's Epistle to the Earl of Burlington*   probably February 1731 (see Note F in Appendix, pp. 489–90)

I have undertaken, at the request of several persons of quality, the explanation of a piece very loudly and justly complained of; or more properly a dissection of the bad heart of the author. It cannot be displeasing to any man of honour to see the same fair opinions and good reasons in print which he has vented and propagated in all conversations; it must be pleasing to see here the proofs of many charges against him, which have hitherto been advanced without full demonstration; and it must be an additional satisfaction to find him guilty of many others, which I shall prove upon the same principles.

The poet's design is twofold, to affront all the nobility and gentry, and to starve all the artisans and workmen of this kingdom. Under pretence of destroying the vanity of the former, he aims to ruin the support of the latter; and, by rendering the patrons discontented with all such works, put a stop to the arts, and obstruct the circulation of money, in this nation, to send a-begging the industrious mechanics we have at home, and introduce Italians, Frenchmen, Papists and foreigners in their stead.

I appeal to all my superiors, if anything can be more insolent than thus to break (as I may say) into their houses and gardens, not, as the noble owners might expect, to admire, but to laugh at them? Or if anything can be more grating and vexatious, to a great peer or an opulent citizen, than to see a work, of the expense of twenty or thirty thousand pounds, which he thought an ornament to the nation, appear only a monument of his own folly? Insolent scribbler! that, being unable to tax men of their rank and worth with any vice or fault beside, is reduced to fall upon their taste in those polite expenses and elegant structures which are the envy of all other nations, and the delight of our own! God forbid it should hinder any of those magnificent persons from enjoying their noble fancies, and delighting in their own works! May every man *Sit peaceably under his own vine*, in his own garden; may every *man's house be his castle*, not only against thieves, but against ill eyes and envious observers;

and may those who have succeeded the worst meet with a better fate than to be at once ill-lodged and ridiculed.

To avoid the imputation of any envy against this poet, I shall first confess that I think he has some genius, and that it is only his morals that I attack.

But what seems very unaccountable is that a man of any genius (which one would think has its foundation in common sense) should be the greatest fool in his age, and constantly choose for the objects of his satire the best friends he has? All the noblemen whom we shall prove him to abuse in this Epistle are such whose esteem and distinction he seemed most to court, and to possess; or whose power and influence could best protect or credit him; nay, all the critics who have been most provoked at it are such as either had been his friends or called themselves so, or had made some pretence to his acquaintance or correspondence.

It is to some of these that I am beholden for many inlets into his meaning and thoughts; for a man's meanings and thoughts lie too remote from any such as could make the discovery [but] from private conversation, or some degree of confidence, or familiarity. The honour and veracity of such I will not doubt; especially of so honourable persons as Lord Fanny, Mr Dorimant, the Lady De-la-Wit, the Countess of Methusalem, and others.

I confess further that I am, in many instances, but the collector of the dispersed remarks of his majesty's Poet Laureate, his illustrious associate Sir William Sweet-Lips, the Lady Knaves-acre and Mrs Haywood (those ornaments of their sex), and Captain Breval, and James Moore Esquire – and Mr Concanen, and Mr Welsted, and Henry K—y Esquire, of the two last of whom I ought in justice to say we owe to the one the most considerable writings and to the others the longest discourses on this subject.

My first position is that this poet is a man of so bad a heart as to stand an exception to the rule of Machiavel, who says 'No man, in any nation, was ever absolutely wicked for nothing.' Now this poet being so, it is fair to suppose that of two or more persons whom he may be thought to abuse, we are always to understand it of the man he is most obliged to; but in such cases where his obligations seem equal, we impartially suppose the reflection on both. Secondly, when so malevolent a man draws any character consisting of many circumstances, it must be applied, not to the person with whom most but with whom fewest of those circumstances agree – and this for a plain reason, because it is a stronger mark of that artifice and cowardice on the one hand, and of that injustice and malice on the other, with which such a writer abounds.

I am nevertheless so reasonable as not to insist, as some critics on this occasion have done, that when a circumstance will not suit with a father, it should be applied to a son or grandson, but I must insist on my two former positions, upon which depends all which others have said, and which I shall say on this subject.

To begin with his title. It was first 'Of Taste,' now 'tis 'Of False Taste, to the Earl of Burlington.' Is this alteration made to impute false taste to that Earl, or out of unwillingness to allow that there is any true taste in the kingdom?

Nothing is more certain than that the person first and principally abused is the said Earl of Burlington. He could not well abuse him for want of taste, since the allowing it to him was the only channel to convey his malignity to others; but he abuses him for a worse want, the want of charity (one from which his lordship is as free as any man alive). This he tells him directly, without disguise, and in the second person,

– What thy hard heart denies,
Thy charitable vanity supplies.

So much for malice; now for ill-nature,

Another age shall see the golden ear
Embrown thy slope and nod on thy parterre,
Deep harvest bury all thy pride has planned,
And laughing Ceres re-assume the land.
[cf. lines 171–6]

That is, 'My lord, your gardens shall soon be ploughed up, and turned into cornfields.'

Alexander Pope

from a public letter to John Gay, *Daily Journal*   23 December 1731

I am astonished at the complaints occasioned by a late epistle to the
Earl of Burlington.... Some fancy that to say a thing is *personal* is the
same as to say it is *unjust*, not considering that nothing can be *just* that
is not *personal*. I am afraid that all such writings and discourses as
touch no man will *mend no man*.... But I find myself obliged to touch
a point on which I must be more serious; it well deserves I should:
I mean the malicious application of the character of Timon, which I
will boldly say they would impute to the person the most different in
the world from a *man-hater* and the person whose taste and encouragement of wit has often been shown in the rightest place. The author
of that epistle must certainly think so, if he has the same opinion of
his own merit as authors generally have; for he has been favoured by
this very person.

   Why, in God's name, must a portrait apparently [obviously]
collected from twenty different men be applied to one only?

Jonathan Swift

from *Verses on the Death of Dr Swift*   1731

In Pope I cannot read a line,
But with a sigh I wish it mine;
When he can in one couplet fix
More sense than I can do in six,
It gives me such a jealous fit
I cry, 'Pox take him and his wit.'

Henry Fielding

from Prolegomena to *The Covent-Garden Tragedy*   1732

I have been long sensible that the days of poetry are no more, and
that there is but one of the moderns (who shall be nameless) that can
write either sense or English or grammar.

Alexander Pope

from a letter to Jonathan Swift   20 April 1733

That I am an author whose characters are thought of some weight appears from the great noise and bustle that the Court and town make about any I give, and I will not render them less important or interesting by sparing vice and folly, or by betraying the cause of truth and virtue. I will take care they will be such as no man can be angry at but the persons I would have angry. You are sensible with what decency and justice I paid homage to the Royal Family at the same time that I satirized false courtiers and spies, etc., about 'em. I have not the courage, however, to be such a satirist as you, but I would be as much or more a philosopher. You call your satires libels; I would rather call my satires epistles. They will consist more of morality than wit and grow graver – which you will call duller. . . . I have met with some complaints – and heard at a distance of some threats – occasioned by my satires. I sent fair messages to acquaint them where I was to be found in town and to offer to call at their houses to satisfy them. And so it dropped. It is very poor in anyone to rail and threaten at a distance and have nothing to say to you when they see you.

Alexander Pope (anonymously)

from *Sober Advice from Horace to the Young Gentlemen about Town*   1734 (see Note C in Appendix, p. 488)

To Alexander Pope, Esq.

Sir, I have so great a trust in your indulgence toward me as to believe you cannot but patronize this imitation, so much in your own manner, and whose birth I may truly say is owing to you. In that confidence I would not suppress the criticisms made upon it by the reverend Doctor [spoof footnotes supposed to be by Richard Bentley, the editor of the Cambridge Horace], the rather since he has promised to mend the faults in the next edition with the same goodness he has practised to Milton [Bentley's notorious edition of *Paradise Lost*, 1732]. I hope you will believe that, while I express my regard for

you, it is only out of modesty I conceal my name – since, though perhaps I may not profess myself your admirer, I cannot but be with as much inward respect, good will and zeal as any man,
Dear Sir,
Your most affectionate and faithful servant.

John Hervey, Baron Hervey

from a letter to Count Francesco Algarotti   *c.* 1735

I forgot, in speaking of the English poets, to mention Pope – but you know my opinion of him is that when other people think for him nobody writes better, and few people worse when he thinks for himself.

Alexander Pope

in conversation with Joseph Spence   February or March 1735

The things that I have written fastest have always pleased most. I wrote the *Essay on Criticism* fast, for I had digested all the matter in prose before I began upon it in verse. *The Rape of the Lock* was written fast. All the machinery, you know, was added afterwards, and the making that and what was published before hit so well together is (I think) one of the greatest proofs of judgement of anything I ever did.

I wrote most of the *Iliad* fast – a great deal of it on journeys, from the little pocket Homer on that shelf there, and often forty or fifty verses on a morning in bed.

The Dunciad cost me as much pains as anything I ever wrote.

After my reading the *Persian Tales* [*Arabian Nights*] (and I had been reading Dryden's *Fables* just before them), I had some thoughts of writing a Persian Fable in which I should have given a full loose to description and imagination. It would have been a very wild thing if I had executed it, but might not have been unentertaining.

If I am a good poet (for in truth I don't know whether I am or not, but if I should be a good poet), there is one thing I value myself upon and which can scarce be said of any of our good poets – and that is that I have never flattered any man, nor ever received anything of any man for my verses.

'Tis a great fault in descriptive poetry to describe everything (that is one fault in Thomson's *Seasons*). The good ancients (but when I named them I meant Virgil) have no long descriptions, commonly not above ten lines, and scarce ever thirty. One of the longest in Virgil is when Aeneas is with Evander, and that is frequently broken by what Evander says [*Aeneid* VIII 314–61].

Alexander Pope

in conversation with Joseph Spence   1735

There is nothing more foolish than to pretend to be sure of knowing a great writer by his style.[1]

Alexander Pope

Advertisement inserted in the second volume of his *Works*   1735

The occasion of publishing these *Imitations* was the clamour raised on some of my 'Epistles' [especially *Moral Essay IV*]. An answer from Horace was both more full and of more dignity than any I could have made in my own person. And the example of much greater freedom in so eminent a divine as Dr Donne [whose second and fourth satires Pope imitated] seemed a proof with what indignation and contempt a Christian may treat vice or folly in ever so low or ever so high a station. . . . The satires of Dr Donne I versified at the desire of the Earl of Oxford, while he was Lord Treasurer, and of the

1 Spence comments that Pope "had the greatest compass in imitating styles that I ever knew. . . partly from his method of instructing himself after he was out of the hands of his bad masters, which was at first wholly by imitation". [Ed.]

Duke of Shrewsbury, who had been Secretary of State, neither of whom looked upon a satire on vicious courts as any reflection on those they served in. And indeed there is not in the world a greater error than that which fools are so apt to fall into – and knaves with good reason to encourage – the mistaking a satirist for a libeller; for the same reason as to a man truly virtuous nothing is so hateful as a hypocrite.

Lady Mary Wortley Montagu

from a letter to John Arbuthnot   3 January 1735

I wish you would advise poor Pope to turn to some more honest livelihood than libelling. I know he will allege in his excuse that he must write to eat, and he is now grown sensible that nobody will buy his verses except their curiosity is piqued to see what is said of their acquaintance, but I think this method of gain so exceeding vile that it admits of no excuse at all .... I am seriously concerned at the worse scandal he has heaped on Mr Congreve, who was my friend and whom I am obliged to justify because I can do it on my own knowledge, and which is yet farther being witness of it from those who were there often with me that he was far from loving Pope's rhyme. Both that and his conversation were perpetual jokes to him, exceedingly despicable in his opinion, and he has often made us laugh in talking of them.

T. B.

from the *Prompter*, no. 108   21 November 1735

Mr Pope, in an advertisement before *Satires of Horace Imitated*, says there is not in the world a greater error than that which fools are so apt to fall into, and knaves, with good reason, to encourage, the mistaking ... a satirist for a libeller .... One might easily dilate upon the opposition, and it has been often done. As 'tis criminal to abuse the innocent, so is it also in a high degree to fall foul upon whole nations or bodies of men. It cannot possibly be true, let the vice or vanity censured be what it will, that whole countries, or whole numbers, are guilty of it, as one man.

'Tis the province of a satirist to attack covetousness and prodigality, lust and idleness, and intemperance, vanity and folly, and low pursuits in all shapes. But then to say that all men are vicious, and vain, and wicked is a libel upon human kind, quite intolerable, and worthy only of a Gulliver. . . .

Upon this foot, I have a mind to try whether Mr Pope himself may not be proved, what he says deserves the odium of all mankind, a libeller. . . .

Proceed, great days! till learning fly the shore,
Till birth shall blush with noble blood no more,
Till Thames see Eton's sons for ever play,
Till Westminster's whole year be holiday,
Till Isis' elders reel, their pupils sport,
And *alma mater* lie dissolved in port!
(*The Dunciad* IV 333–8)

These verses being to live much longer than any of us, as Mr Pope prophetically tells us himself, what will posterity say when they read them? Why, that about the year 1735 there was a total neglect of all study in the greatest schools of the kingdom, and that drunkenness prevailed in both the universities to such a degree that the Masters and Fellows of colleges lay dead drunk in heaps, like people in the plague of Marseilles. . . .

Upon the whole, I take this also to be a *libel*, and so glaring that I believe the fondest admirer Mr Pope has will only smile and say nothing.

Alexander Pope

in conversation with Joseph Spence 1736

'Tis idle to say that letters should be written in an easy familiar style; that, like most other general rules, will not hold. The style in letters, as in all other things, should be adapted to the subject.

Isaac Hawkins Browne

from *A Pipe of Tobacco* (written in the style of Pope)   1736
(see Note G in Appendix, p. 490)

Blest leaf! whose aromatic gales dispense
To Templars modesty, to parsons sense;
So raptured priests, at famed Dodona's shrine
Drank inspiration from the steam divine.
Poison that cures, a vapour that affords
Content more solid than the smile of lords,
Rest to the weary, to the hungry food,
The last kind refuge of the wise and good.
Inspired by thee, dull cits adjust the scale
Of Europe's peace, when other statesmen fail.
By thee protected, and thy sister, beer,
Poets rejoice, nor think the bailiff near.
Nor less, the critic owns thy genial aid,
While supperless he plies the piddling trade.
What though to love and soft delights a foe,
By ladies hated, hated by the beau,
Yet social freedom, long to courts unknown,
Fair health, fair truth, and virtue are thy own.
Come to thy poet, come with healing wings,
And let me taste thee unexcised by kings.

Alexander Pope

Advertisement prefixed to *Imitations of Horace*, II vi, by
Swift and Pope   1738

The world may be assured this publication is no way meant to interfere with the *Imitations of Horace* by Mr Pope. His manner and that
of Dr Swift are so entirely different that they can admit of no invidious
comparison, the design of the one being to sharpen the satire and
open the sense of the poet, of the other to render his native ease and
familiarity yet more easy and familiar.

Alexander Pope

in conversation with Joseph Spence   June 1739

I have nothing to say for rhyme, but I doubt whether a poem can support itself without it in our language, unless it be stiffened with such strange words as are like to destroy our language itself.

The high style that is affected so much in blank verse would not have been borne even in Milton, had not his subject turned on such strange out-of-the-world things as it does.

They are quite destroying our language (speaking of [Henry] Brooke's *Universal Beauty* buskin style [described in Pope's *Peri Bathous* as raising 'what is base and low to a ridiculous visiblity']).

Joseph Warton

from *The Enthusiast; or, The Lover of Nature*   1740

What are the lays of artful Addison,[1]
Coldly correct, to Shakespeare's warblings wild?

Alexander Pope

in conversation with Joseph Spence   6–10 April 1742

When I [Spence] was looking on his foul copy of the *Iliad* and observing how very much it was corrected and interlined, he [Pope] said, 'I believe you would find upon inquiry that those parts which have been the most corrected read the easiest.' The only copy of the

1 When Warton published this poem in 1744, he claimed that it had been written in 1740; and it would presumably have been overbold to write 'artful Pope' instead of 'Addison' when Pope was still alive. But Warton *meant* Pope; of this there can be little or no doubt in view of his *Essay on the Genius and Writings of Pope* (see pp. 101–18 below). [Ed.]

Odyssey is not near so much blotted. 'That shows that I was got to a greater knack of translating him.'

If I may judge myself, I think the travelling Governor's speech one of the best things in my new addition to *The Dunciad* [IV, 282-334].

Those two lines on Alsop and Friend [*The Dunciad*, IV, 223-4] have more of satire than of compliment in them, though I find they are generally mistaken for the latter only. . . . I scarce meet with anybody that understands delicacy.

Colley Cibber

from *A Letter from Mr Cibber to Mr Pope*   1742 (see Note H in Appendix, p. 490)

I wrote more to be fed than be famous, and since my writings still give me a dinner, do you rhyme me out of my stomach if you can. And I own myself so contented a dunce that I would not have even your merited fame in poetry if it were to be attended with half the fretful solicitude you seem to have lain under to maintain it – of which the laborious rout you make about it, in those loads of prose rubbish wherewith you have almost smothered your *Dunciad*, is so sore a proof. And though I grant it a better poem of its kind than ever was writ, yet when I read it, with those vainglorious encumbrances of notes and remarks upon almost every line of it, I find myself in the uneasy condition I was once in at an opera, where sitting with a silent desire to hear a favourite air by a famous performer, a coxcombly connoisseur at my elbow was so fond of showing his own taste that by his continual remarks and prating in praise of every grace and cadence my attention and pleasure in the song was quite lost and confounded. . . .

For what you gained by it? A mighty matter! A victory over a parcel of poor wretches that were not able to hurt or resist you, so weak it was almost cowardice to conquer them. . . . If your revenge upon them was necessary, we must own you have amply enjoyed it. But to make that revenge the chief motive of writing your *Dunciad* seems to me a weakness that an author of your abilities should rather have chosen to conceal. A man might as well triumph for his having killed so many silly flies that offended him. Could you have let them alone, by this time, poor souls, they had been all peaceably buried in oblivion! But the very lines you have so sharply pointed to destroy them will now remain but so many of their epitaphs, to transmit their names to posterity – which probably too they may think a more eligible fate than that of being totally forgotten. . . . In a word, you seem, in your *Dunciad*, to have been angry at the rain for wetting you. Why then would you go into it?

Anonymous

from *A Letter to Mr C--b-r On his Letter to Mr P---*   1742

To all his 'strokes of satire', as he impudently and proudly calls them, and you civilly and ignorantly allow his squab abuse to be, I have just the same sort of objection that I have to what he may style 'invention' – because I can no more look upon coarse language to be true satire than I can rank gross lies under the head of poetic fiction. And as all his manner of satirizing consists in scurrility, and calling names, I can no more admit that Mr Pope has any merit in this sort of writing, or deserves the title of a satirist, than, if I heard a drunken scold of an apple-woman quarrelling with a foul-mouthed hackney-coachman, I should think in my next visit of describing what had passed by saying I had seen at the corner of the street, coming thither, two of the keenest satirists I had ever met with in my life. . . .

Another proof of Mr Pope's want of judgement as well as invention, and that he understands the best of his late writings no more than his readers can understand the worst, is his *Essay upon Man*; in which resolving to turn philosopher, he has, in order to fit himself for the execution of that task, read every speculative book upon the subject he treats, and whenever a passage happened to strike him in any of these different authors, writing upon different principles, though on the same subject, and consequently maintaining different sentiments, he has put them in most harmonious verse, I confess, but such discordant sense that he has jumbled together my Lord Shaftesbury, Montaigne, Lord Herbert [of Cherbury], Mandeville, and fifty *et ceteras*, till, from these fine uniform originals drawing only some incongruous scraps, his whole work is nothing but a heap of poetical contradictions, and a jarring series of doctrines, principles, opinions and sentiments, diametrically opposite to each other, making together just such an olio, hodge-podge mess of philosophy as one of Cloe's best dinners would make of food.

Alexander Pope

in conversation with Joseph Spence   January 1743

Considering how very little I had when I came from school, I think I may be said to have taught myself Latin as well as French or Greek, and in all three my chief way of getting them was by translations.

I did not follow the grammar, but rather hunted in the authors for a syntax of my own, and then began translating any parts that pleased me, particularly in the best Greek and Latin poets. By that means I formed my taste, which I think verily at about sixteen was very near as good as it is now.

Alexander Pope

in conversation with Joseph Spence   March 1743

[When] about fifteen, I got acquainted with Mr Walsh. He encouraged me much and used to tell me that there was one way left of excelling, for though we had had several great poets, we never had any one great poet that was *correct* – and he desired me to make that my study and aim. [Spence comments: 'This I suppose first led Mr Pope to turn his lines over and over again so often, which he continued to the last, and did it with a surprising facility.']

I learned versification wholly from Dryden's works, who had improved it much beyond any of our former poets and would probably have brought it to its perfection, had not he been unhappily obliged to write so often in haste.

Dryden always uses proper language: lively, natural and fitted to the subject. 'Tis scarce ever too high or too low, never perhaps except in his plays.

The idea that I have had for an epic poem of late turns wholly on civil and ecclesiastical government; the hero is a prince who establishes an empire. That prince is our Brutus from Troy, and the scene of the establishment England.

I endeavoured (says he, smiling) in this poem [his epic on Deucalion] to collect all the beauties of the great epic writers into one piece. There was Milton's style in one part and Cowley's in another, here the style of Spenser imitated and there of Statius, here Homer and Virgil, and there Ovid and Claudian. 'It was an imitative poem, then, as your other exercises were imitations of this or that story?' [asked Spence]. Just that.

Mr Pope thought himself better in some respects for not having had a regular education. He (as he observed in particular) read originally for the sense, whereas we are taught for so many years to read only for words.

In the scattered lessons I used to set myself about that time, I translated above a quarter of the *Metamorphoses* [by Ovid], and that part of Statius (*Thebais*, I) which was afterwards printed with corrections of Walsh.

Alexander Pope

in conversation with Joseph Spence   December 1743

In most doubts whether a word is English or not, or whether such a particular use of it is proper, one has nothing but authority for it. Is it in Sir William Temple, or Locke, or Tillotson? If it be you may conclude that it is right, or at least won't be looked upon as wrong.

The great matter to write well is 'to know thoroughly what one writes about', and 'not to be affected' (or as he expressed the same thing afterwards in other words, 'to write naturally and from one's knowledge').

Alexander Pope

in conversation with Joseph Spence   10–14 January 1744

I must make a perfect edition of my works, and then I shall have nothing to do but to die.[1]

Alexander Pope

in conversation with Joseph Spence   5–7 April 1744

There is scarce any work of mine in which the versification was more laboured than in my *Pastorals*.[2]

Though Virgil in his pastorals has sometimes six or eight lines together that are epic, I have been so scrupulous as scarce ever to to admit above two together even in the *Messiah*.

Alexander Pope

in conversation with Joseph Spence   1–4 May 1744

I have followed that (the significance of the numbers and the adapting them to the sense) much more even than Dryden, and much oftener than anyone minds it – particularly in the translations of Homer, where 'twas most necessary to do so, and in *The Dunciad* often, and indeed in all my poems.

1 Unfortunately Pope left the preparation of the 'perfect edition' almost entirely to the verbose and uninformative Warburton, who published it in 9 volumes in 1751. Pope had died on 30 May 1744. [Ed.]
2 Spence adds: "The last (the *Messiah*) his own favourite of them all". [Ed.]

Thomas Gray

from a letter to Horace Walpole   3 February 1746

I can say no more for Mr Pope – for what you keep in reserve may be worse than all the rest. It is natural to wish the finest writer, one of them, we ever had should be an honest man. It is not from what he told me about himself that I thought well of him.

Philip Dormer Stanhope, Earl of Chesterfield

from a letter to his son   9 October 1747

I used to think myself in company as much above me, when I was with Mr Addison and Mr Pope, as if I had been with all the princes in Europe.

Anonymous

from 'Of Some Hyperboles in Pope's Homer', *London Magazine* June 1748

An hyperbole, used with discretion, is a noble and majestic figure in rhetoric; it pleases and surprises at the same time; but if it be not used with caution, it becomes monstrous, or ridiculous. I have a great esteem for Mr Pope's writings, not only as a poet, but also as a master of the English tongue; yet, as diamonds have their flaws, and there are spots in the most glorious of all visible bodies, the sun, so I cannot think that celebrated author's works without their faults. I am going to give an instance or two in the hyperbole, which I think cannot be defended by any rules in criticism.

The first is this, taken from the fifth book of the *Iliad* [lines 687–8]. Aeneas kills the two brothers, Crethon and Orsilochus.

Prostrate on earth their beauteous bodies lay,
Like mountain firs, as tall and straight as they.

The words *as tall and straight as they* have the air of a false sublime, and are contrary to Longinus's direction, in the use of this figure, who says that *those hyperboles are the best which carry in them the least appearance of an hyperbole*. ...

A second instance I shall quote from the eighth book of the *Odyssey* [lines 303–4; translated by Broome], where, describing a dance of the Phaeacians, he says:

Light-bounding from the earth, at once they rise,
Their feet half viewless quiver in the skies.

This is really monstrous. The hyperbole, as Longinus again observes, is entirely destroyed, and loses all its force, as the string of a bow, by being strained too far. If any, in defence of such hyperboles, should urge some examples from Holy Writ, as that passage in Deuteronomy i, 28, where it is said 'The cities are great, and walled up to heaven': here the genius of the Eastern languages is to be considered, which are full of pomp, and amplification, and are no standard for the purity of ours. Were we to copy after their sublime, our style would become, in many cases, ridiculous and bombastic. Besides, the Greek of Homer, ... 'the vibrating splendours of their feet,' does not in the least countenance that extravagance of expression that our English Homer falls into.

Samuel Johnson (anonymously)

from the *Rambler*, no. 92   5 February 1751

[Onomatopoeia in *An Essay on Criticism*, lines 337–84.] From these lines, laboured with great attention and celebrated by a rival wit [Addison], may be judged what can be expected from the most diligent endeavours after the imagery of sound. The verse intended to represent the whisper of the vernal breeze must be confessed not much to excel in softness of volubility, and the smooth stream runs with a perpetual clash of jarring consonants. The noise and turbulence of the torrent is indeed distinctly imaged, for it requires very little skill to make our language rough; but in those lines which mention the effort of Ajax there is no particular heaviness, obstruction or delay. The swiftness of Camilla is rather contrasted than exemplified; why the verse should be lengthened to express speed will not easily be discovered . . . the alexandrine, by its pause, is a tardy and stately measure, and the word *unbending*, one of the most sluggish and slow which our language affords, cannot much accelerate its motion.

Henry Fielding (anonymously)

from the *Covent Garden Journal*, 18 January 1752

I heard drop from the late Mr Pope that nature never produced a more venomous animal than a bad author.

Philip Dormer Stanhope, Earl of Chesterfield

from a letter to his son   2 March 1752

A gentleman should know those which I call classical works in every language – such as Boileau, Corneille, Racine, Molière, etc., in French, Milton, Dryden, Pope, Swift, etc., in English.

Henry Fielding (anonymously)

from the *Covent Garden Journal,* no 23   21 March 1752

He [Dryden] died nevertheless in a good old age, possessed of the kingdom of wit, and was succeeded by King Alexander, surnamed Pope.

The Prince enjoyed the crown many years, and is thought to have stretched the prerogative much farther than his predecessor; he is said to have been extremely jealous of the affections of his subjects, and to have employed various spies, by whom he was informed of the least suggestion against his title. He never failed of branding the accused person with the word DUNCE on his forehead in broad letters; after which the unhappy culprit was obliged to lay by his pen for ever; for no bookseller would venture to print a word that he wrote. . . . But without diving any deeper into his character, we must allow that King Alexander had great merit as a writer, and his title to the kingdom of wit was better founded at least than his enemies have pretended.

Samuel Johnson (anonymously)

from 'A Dissertation on the Epitaphs Written by Pope',
Universal Visitor and Monthly Memorialist May 1756
(reprinted with the *Life of Pope*, 1781)

I

On Charles Earl of Dorset, in the church of Withyham in Sussex

Dorset, the grace of courts, the Muses' pride,
Patron of arts, and judge of nature, died!
The scourge of pride, though sanctified or great,
Of fops in learning and of knaves in state;
Yet soft his nature, though severe his lay,
His anger moral and his wisdom gay.
Blest satirist! who touched the mean so true,
As showed vice had his hate and pity too.
Blest courtier! who could king and country please,
Yet sacred keep his friendships and his ease.
Blest peer! his great forefathers' every grace
Reflecting, and reflected in his race;
Where other Buckhursts, other Dorsets shine,
And patriots still, or poets, deck the line.

The first distich of this epitaph contains a kind of information which few would want, that the man for whom the tomb was erected *died*. There are indeed some qualities worthy of praise ascribed to the dead, but none that were likely to exempt him from the lot of man, or incline us much to wonder that he should die. What is meant by *judge of nature* is not easy to say. Nature is not the object of human judgement; for it is in vain to judge where we cannot alter. If by nature is meant what is commonly called *nature* by the critics, a just representation of things really existing and actions really performed, nature cannot be properly opposed to *art*; nature being, in this sense, only the best effect of *art*.

The scourge of pride

Of this couplet, the second line is not, what is intended, an illustration of the former. *Pride* in the *great* is indeed well enough connected with knaves in state, though *knaves* is a word rather too ludicrous and light; but the mention of *sanctified* pride will not lead the thoughts to *fops in learning*, but rather to some species of tyranny or oppression, something more gloomy and more formidable than foppery.

Yet soft his nature

This is a high compliment, but was not first bestowed on Dorset by Pope. The next verse is extremely beautiful.

Blest satirist!

In this distich is another line of which Pope was not the author. I do not mean to blame these imitations with much harshness; in long performances they are scarcely to be avoided, and in shorter they may be indulged, because the train of the composition may naturally involve them, or the scantiness of the subject allow little choice. However, what is borrowed is not to be enjoyed as our own, and it is the business of critical justice to give every bird of the Muses his proper feather.

Blest courtier!

Whether a courtier can properly be commended for keeping his *ease sacred* may perhaps be disputable. To please king and country, without sacrificing friendship to any change of times, was a very uncommon instance of prudence or felicity and deserved to be kept separate from so poor a commendation as care of his ease. I wish our poets would attend a little more accurately to the use of the word *sacred*, which surely should never be applied in a serious composition, but where some reference may be made to a higher Being, or where some duty is exacted or implied. A man may keep his friendship *sacred*, because promises of friendship are very awful ties; but methinks he cannot, but in a burlesque sense, be said to keep his ease *sacred*.

Blest peer!

The blessing ascribed to the *peer* has no connection with his peerage; they might happen to any other man whose ancestors were remembered, or whose posterity were likely to be regarded.

I know not whether this epitaph be worthy either of the writer or the man entombed.

II

On Sir William Trumbull

One of the principal Secretaries of State to King William III, who, having resigned his place, died in his retirement at Easthamsted in Berkshire, 1716.

A pleasing form, a firm yet cautious mind,
Sincere, though prudent, constant, yet resigned;
Honour unchanged, a principle professed,
Fixed to one side, but moderate to the rest;
An honest courtier, yet a patriot too,
Just to his prince, yet to his country true;
Filled with the sense of age, the fire of youth,
A scorn of wrangling, yet a zeal for truth;
A generous faith, from superstition free,
A love to peace, and hate of tyranny.
Such this man was, who now, from earth removed,
At length enjoys that liberty he loved.

In this epitaph, as in many others, there appears, at the first view, a fault which I think scarcely any beauty can compensate. The name is omitted. The end of an epitaph is to convey some account of the dead; and to what purpose is anything told of him whose name is concealed? An epitaph, and a history of a nameless hero, are equally absurd, since the virtues and qualities so recounted in either are scattered at the mercy of fortune to be appropriated by guess. The name, it is true, may be read upon the stone; but what obligation has it to the poet, whose verses wander over the earth and leave their subject behind them, and who is forced, like an unskilful painter, to make his purpose known by adventitious help?

This epitaph is wholly without elevation and contains nothing striking or particular; but the poet is not to be blamed for the defects of his subject. He said perhaps the best that could be said. There are, however, some defects which were not made necessary by the character in which he was employed. There is no opposition between an *honest courtier* and a *patriot*; for an *honest courtier* cannot but be a *patriot*.

It was unsuitable to the nicety required in short compositions to close his verse with the word *too*; every rhyme should be a word of emphasis, nor can this rule be safely neglected except where the length of the poem makes slight inaccuracies excusable, or allows room for beauties sufficient to overpower the effects of petty faults.

At the beginning of the seventh line the word *filled* is weak and prosaic, having no particular adaptation to any of the words that follow it.

The thought in the last line is impertinent, having no connection with the foregoing character nor with the condition of the man described. Had the epitaph been written on the poor conspirator who died lately in prison, after a confinement of more than forty years without any crime proved against him, the sentiment had been just and pathetical; but why should Trumbull be congratulated upon his liberty, who had never known restraint?

VI

On Mrs Corbet, who died of a Cancer in her Breast

Here rests a woman, good without pretence,
Blest with plain reason and with sober sense;
No conquests she, but o'er herself desired,
No arts essayed, but not to be admired.
Passion and pride were to her soul unknown,
Convinced that virtue only is our own.

So unaffected, so composed a mind,
So firm yet soft, so strong yet so refined,
Heaven, as its purest gold, by tortures tried;
The saint sustained it, but the woman died.

I have always considered this as the most valuable of all Pope's epitaphs. The subject of it is a character not discriminated by any shining or eminent peculiarities; yet that which really makes, though not the splendour, the felicity of life, and that which every wise man will choose for his final and lasting companion in the languor of age, in the quiet of privacy, when he departs weary and disgusted from the ostentatious, the volatile, and the vain. Of such a character, which the dull overlook and the gay despise, it was fit that the value should be made known and the dignity established. Domestic virtue, as it is exerted without great occasions, or conspicuous consequences, in an even unnoted tenor, required the genius of Pope to display it in such a manner as might attract regard and enforce reverence. Who can forbear to lament that this amiable woman has no name in the verses?

If the particular lines of this inscription be examined, it will appear less faulty than the rest. There is scarce one line taken from commonplaces, unless it be that in which *virtue only* is said to be *our own*. I once heard a lady of great beauty and excellence object to the fourth line that it contained an unnatural and incredible panegyric. Of this let the ladies judge.

XI

On Mr Gay. In Westminster-Abbey, 1732

Of manners gentle, of affections mild –
In wit, a man, simplicity, a child;
With native humour tempering virtuous rage,
Formed to delight at once and lash the age;
Above temptation in a low estate,
And uncorrupted, ev'n among the great;
A safe companion and an easy friend,
Unblamed through life, lamented in thy end.

These are thy honours! not that here thy bust
Is mixed with heroes, or with kings thy dust;
But that the worthy and the good shall say,
Striking their pensive bosoms – *Here* lies Gay.

As Gay was the favourite of our author, this epitaph was probably written with an uncommon degree of attention; yet it is not more successfully executed than the rest, for it will not always happen that the success of a poet is proportionate to his labour. The same observation may be extended to all works of imagination, which are often influenced by causes wholly out of the performer's power, by hints of which he perceives not the origin, by sudden elevations of mind which he cannot produce in himself and which sometimes rise when he expects them least.

The two parts of the first line are only echoes of each other; *gentle manners* and *mild affections*, if they mean anything, must mean the same.

That Gay was a *man in wit* is a very frigid commendation; to have the wit of a man is not much for a poet. The *wit* of *man* and the *simplicity* of a *child* make a poor and vulgar contrast and raise no ideas of excellence either intellectual or moral.

In the next couplet *rage* is less properly introduced after the mention of *mildness* and *gentleness*, which are made the constituents of his character; for a man so *mild* and *gentle* to *temper* his *rage* was not difficult.

The next line is unharmonious in its sound, and mean in its conception; the opposition is obvious, and the word *lash* used absolutely and without any modification is gross and improper.

To be *above temptation* in poverty and free from corruption *among the great* is indeed such a peculiarity as deserved notice. But to be a *safe companion* is praise merely negative, arising not from the possession of virtue but the absence of vice, and that one of the most odious.

As little can be added to his character by asserting that he was *lamented in* his *end*. Every man that dies is, at least by the writer of his epitaph, supposed to be lamented, and therefore this general lamentation does no honour to Gay.

The first eight lines have no grammar; the adjectives are without any substantive and the epithets without a subject.

The thought in the last line, that Gay is buried in the bosoms of the *worthy* and the *good*, who are distinguished only to lengthen the line, is so dark that few understand it, and so harsh, when it is explained, that still fewer approve.

Joseph Warton

from *An Essay on the Genius and Writings of Pope*   1756, 1782

To the Reverend Dr Young, Rector of Welwyn, in Hertfordshire

Dear Sir,

Permit me to break into your retirement, the residence of virtue and literature, and to trouble you with a few reflections on the merits and real character of an admired author and on other collateral subjects of criticism that will naturally arise in the course of such an inquiry. No love of singularity, no affectation of paradoxical opinions, gave rise to the following work. I revere the memory of Pope, I respect and honour his abilities, but I do not think him at the head of his profession. In other words, in that species of poetry wherein Pope excelled he is superior to all mankind; and I only say that this species of poetry is not the most excellent one of the art.

We do not, it should seem, sufficiently attend to the difference there is betwixt a man of wit, a man of sense, and a true poet. Donne and Swift were undoubtedly men of wit and men of sense, but what traces have they left of pure poetry? It is remarkable that Dryden says of Donne, 'He was the greatest wit, though not the greatest poet, of this nation.' Fontenelle and La Motte are entited to the former character, but what can they urge to gain the latter? Which of these characters is the most valuable and useful is entirely out of the question. All I plead for is to have their several provinces kept distinct from each other and to impress on the reader that a clear head and acute understanding are not sufficient alone to make a poet; that the most solid observations on human life expressed with the utmost elegance and brevity are morality, and not poetry; that the *Epistles* of Boileau in rhyme are no more poetical than the *Characters* of La Bruyère in prose; and that it is a creative and glowing imagination, *acer spiritùs ac vis*, and that alone, that can stamp a writer with this exalted and very uncommon character which so few possess and of which so few can properly judge.

For one person who can adequately relish and enjoy a work of imagination, twenty are to be found who can taste and judge of observations on familiar life and the manners of the age. The satires of Ariosto are more read than the *Orlando Furioso*, or even Dante. Are there so many cordial admirers of Spenser and Milton as of *Hudibras*, if we strike out of the number of these supposed admirers those who appear such out of fashion and not of feeling? Swift's 'Rhapsody on Poetry' is far more popular than Akenside's noble 'Ode to Lord Huntingdon.' The epistles on the characters of men and women and your sprightly satires, my good friend, are more frequently perused and quoted than *L'Allegro* and *Il Penseroso* of Milton. Had you written only these satires, you would, indeed, have gained the title of a man of wit and a man of sense, but, I am confident, would not insist on being denominated a poet merely on their account.

Non satis est puris versum perscribere verbis.

It is amazing this matter should ever have been mistaken, when Horace has taken particular and repeated pains to settle and adjust the opinion in question. He has more than once disclaimed all right and title to the name of poet on the score of his ethic and satiric pieces.

Neque enim concludere versum
Dixeris esse satis.

are lines often repeated, but whose meaning is not extended and weighed as it ought to be. Nothing can be more judicious than the method he prescribes of trying whether any composition be essentially poetical or not, which is to drop entirely the measures and numbers and transpose and invert the order of the words, and in this unadorned manner to peruse the passage. If there be really in it a true poetical spirit, all your inversions and transposition will not disguise and extinguish it, but it will retain its lustre like a diamond unset and thrown back into the rubbish of the mine. Let us make a little experiment on the following well-known lines [Pope's *Moral Essay I*, 1–10]:

Yes, you despise the man that is confined to books, who rails
at human kind from his study, though what he learns he
speaks, and may perhaps advance some general maxims or
may be right by chance. The coxcomb bird, so grave and so
talkative, that cries whore, knave, and cuckold from his cage,
though he rightly call many a passanger, you hold him no
philosopher. And yet, such is the fate of all extremes, men
may be read too much, as well as books. We grow more
partial, for the sake of the observer, to observations which we
ourselves make; less so to written wisdom, because another's.
Maxims are drawn from the notions, and those from guess.

What shall we say of this passage? Why, that it is most excellent
sense, but just as poetical as the 'Qui fit Maecenas' of the author who
recommends this method of trial. Take ten lines of the *Iliad*, *Paradise
Lost*, or even of the *Georgics* of Virgil, and see whether, by any
process of critical chemistry, you can lower and reduce them to the
tameness of prose. You will find that they will appear like Ulysses
in his disguise of rags, still a hero, though lodged in the cottage of
the herdsman Eumaeus.

The sublime and the pathetic are the two chief nerves of all
genuine poesy. What is there transcendently sublime or pathetic in
Pope? In his works there is, indeed, *nihil inane, nihil arcessitum; puro
tamen fonti quam magno flumini proprior*, as the excellent Quintilian
remarks of Lysias. And because I am, perhaps, unwilling to speak out
in plain English, I will adopt the following passage of Voltaire, which
in my opinion as exactly characterizes Pope as it does his model
Boileau, for whom it was originally designed:

Incapable peut-être du sublime qui élève l'âme, et du
sentiment qui l'attendrit, mais fait pour éclairer ceux à qui la
nature accorda l'un et l'autre, laborieux, sévère, précis, pur,
harmonieux, il devint, enfin, le poète de la raison.

Our English poets may, I think, be disposed in four different
classes and degrees. In the first class I would place our only three
sublime and pathetic poets: Spenser, Shakespeare, Milton. In the
second class should be ranked such as possessed the true poetical
genius in a more moderate degree, but who had noble talents for

moral, ethical, and panegyrical poesy. At the head of these are Dryden, Prior, Addison, Cowley, Waller, Garth, Fenton, Gay, Denham, Parnell. In the third class may be placed men of wit, of elegant taste, and lively fancy in describing familiar life, though not the higher scenes of poetry. Here may be numbered Butler, Swift, Rochester, Donne, Dorset, Oldham. In the fourth class the mere versifiers, however smooth and mellifluous some of them may be thought, should be disposed. Such as Pitt, Sandys, Fairfax, Broome, Buckingham, Lansdowne. This enumeration is not intended as a complete catalogue of writers, and in their proper order, but only to mark out briefly the different species of our celebrated authors. In which of these classes Pope deserves to be placed the following work is intended to determine.

I am, Dear Sir,
Your affectionate and faithful servant

From Section I, 'Of the *Pastorals* and the *Messiah*, an Eclogue'

Princes and authors are seldom spoken of during their lives with justice and impartiality. Admiration and envy, their constant attendants, like two unskilful artists, are apt to overcharge their pieces with too great a quantity of light or of shade, and are disqualified happily to hit upon that middle colour, that mixture of error and excellence which alone renders every representation of man just and natural. This, perhaps, may be one reason, among others, why we have never yet seen a fair and candid criticism on the character and merits of our last great poet, Mr Pope. I have therefore thought that it would be no unpleasing amusement or uninstructive employment to examine at large, without blind panegyric or petulant invective, the writings of this English classic in the order in which they are arranged in the nine volumes of the elegant edition of Dr Warburton. As I shall neither censure nor commend without alleging the reason on which my opinion is founded, I shall be entirely unmoved at the imputation of malignity or the clamours of popular prejudice.

It is somewhat strange that in the pastorals of a young poet there should not be found a single rural image that is new, but this, I am afraid, is the case in the pastorals before us. The ideas of Theocritus,

Virgil, and Spenser are, indeed, here exhibited in language equally mellifluous and pure, but the descriptions and sentiments are trite and common. . . .

A mixture of British and Grecian ideas may justly be deemed a blemish in the Pastorals of Pope, and propriety is certainly violated when he couples Pactolus with Thames, and Windsor with Hybla. Complaints of 'immoderate heat' and wishes to be conveyed to cooling caverns, when uttered by the inhabitants of Greece, have a decorum and consistency which they totally lose in the character of a British shepherd; and Theocritus, during the ardours of Sirius, must have heard the murmurings of a brook and the whispers of a pine with more home-felt pleasure than Pope could possibly experience upon the same occasion. We can never completely relish or adequately understand any author, especially any ancient, except we constantly keep in our eye his climate, his country, and his age. Pope himself informs us in a note that he judiciously omitted the following verse,

And listening wolves grow milder as they hear,

on account of the absurdity, which Spenser overlooked, of introducing wolves into England. But on this principle, which is certianly a a just one, may it not be asked why he should speak, the scene lying in Windsor Forest, of the 'sultry Sirius', of the 'grateful clusters' of grapes, of a pipe of reeds, the antique fistula, of thanking Ceres for a plentiful harvest, of the sacrifice of lambs, with many other instances that might be adduced to this purpose. That Pope, however, was sensible of the importance of adapting images to the scene of action is obvious from the following example of his judgement, for in translating

Audiit *Eurotus*, jussitque ediscere *lauros*,

he has dexterously dropped the *laurels* appropriated to Eurotas, as he is speaking of the river Thames, and has rendered it,

Thames heard the numbers as he flowed along,
And bade his *willows* learn the moving song.
(IV 13–14)

In the passages which Pope has imitated from Theocritus and from his Latin translator, Virgil, he has merited but little applause. . . .

I cannot forbear adding that the riddle of the Royal Oak in the first *Pastoral* [85-6], invented in imitation of the Virgilian enigmas in the third *Eclogue*, savours of pun and puerile conceit.

Say, Daphnis, say, in what glad soil appears
A wondrous tree that sacred monarchs bears?

With what propriety could the tree whose shade protected the king be said to be prolific of princes? . . .

Upon the whole, the principal merit of the *Pastorals* of Pope consists in their correct and musical versification, musical to a degree of which rhyme could hardly be thought capable, and in giving the first specimen of that harmony in English verse which is now become indispensably necessary, and which has so forcibly and universally influenced the public ear as to have rendered every moderate rhymer melodious. Pope lengthened the abruptness of Waller and at the same time contracted the exuberance of Dryden.

From Section II, 'Of *Windsor Forest* and Lyric Pieces'

Descriptive talent was by no means the shining talent of Pope. This assertion may be manifested by the few images introduced in the poem before us [*Windsor Forest*] which are not equally applicable to any place whatsoever. Rural beauty in general and not the peculiar beauties of the Forest of Windsor are here described. Nor are the sports of setting, shooting and fishing included between the ninety-third and one-hundred-and-forty-sixth verses, to which the reader is referred, at all more appropriated. The stag-chase that immediately follows, although some of the lines are incomparably good, particularly verse 151 ['Th' impatient courser pants in every vein], is not so full, so animated and so circumstantial as that of [William] Somerville [*The Chase*, 1735]. . . .

It is one of the greatest and most pleasing arts of descriptive poetry to introduce moral sentences and instructions in an oblique and indirect manner in places where one naturally expects only painting and amusement. We have virtue, as Pope remarks, put upon us by surprise and are pleased to find a thing where we should never have looked to meet with it. I must do a pleasing English poet [Denham] the justice to observe that it is this particular art that is the very distinguishing excellence of *Cooper's Hill*, throughout which the descriptions of places and images raised by the poet are still tending to some hint or leading into some reflection upon moral life or political institution, much in the same manner as the real sight of such scenes and prospects is apt to give the mind a composed turn and incline it to thoughts and contemplations that have a relation to the object. This is the great charm of the incomparable *Elegy Written in a Country Churchyard*. Having mentioned the rustic monuments and simple epitaphs of the swains, the amiable poet falls into a very natural reflection:

For who, to dumb forgetfulness a prey,
This pleasing anxious being e'er resigned,
Left the warm precincts of the cheerful day,
Nor cast one longing, lingering look behind?

Of this art Pope has exhibited some specimens in the poem we are examining, but not so many as might be expected from a mind so strongly inclined to a moral way of writing. After speaking of hunting the hare, he immediately subjoins much in the spirit of Denham,

Beasts, urged by us, their fellow-beasts pursue,
And learn of man each other to undo.
(123-4)

Where he is describing the tyrannies formerly exercised in this kingdom,

Cities laid waste, they stormed the dens and caves,
(49)

he instantly adds, with an indignation becoming a true lover of liberty,

For wiser brutes were backward to be slaves.
(50)

But I am afraid our author, in the following passage, has fallen into a fault rather uncommon in his writings, a reflection that is very far-fetched and forced,

Here waving groves a chequered scene display,
And part admit and part exclude the day;
As some coy nymph her lover's warm address
Nor quite indulges nor can quite repress.
(17-20)

Bouhours would rank this comparison among false thoughts and
Italian conceits, such particularly as abound in the works of Marino.
The fallacy consists in giving design and artifice to the wood as well
as to the coquette, and in putting the light of the sun and the warmth
of a lover on a level.

From Section III, 'Of the *Essay on Criticism*'

Such late was Walsh – the Muse's judge and friend.
(729)

If Pope has here too magnificent an eulogy to Walsh, it must be
attributed to friendship rather than to judgement. Walsh was in
general a flimsy and frigid writer. The Rambler [Johnson] calls his
works pages of inanity. His three letters to Pope, however, are well
written. His remarks on the nature of pastoral poetry, on borrowing
from the ancients, and against florid conceits, are worthy of perusal.
Pope owed much to Walsh. It was he who gave him a very important
piece of advice in his early youth, for he used to tell our author that
there was one way still left open for him by which he might excel any
of his predecessors, which was by correctness, that though, indeed, we
had several great poets, we as yet could boast of none that were
perfectly correct, and that therefore he advised him to make this
quality his particular study.

Correctness is a vague term, frequently used without meaning and
precision. It is perpetually the nauseous cant of the French critics, and
of their advocates and pupils, that the English writers are generally
incorrect. If correctness implies an absence of petty faults, this perhaps
may be granted. If it means that because their tragedians have avoided
the irregularities of Shakespeare and have observed a juster economy
in their fables, therefore the *Athalia*, for instance, is preferable to
Lear, the notion is groundless and absurd.

From Section IV, 'Of the *Rape of the Lock*'

Our poet still rises in the delicacy of his satire when he employs, with the utmost judgement and elegance, all the implements and furniture of the toilette as instruments of punishment to those spirits who shall be careless of their charge. ... If Virgil has merited such perpetual commendation for exalting his bees by the majesty and magnificence of his diction, does not Pope deserve equal praises for the pomp and lustre of his language on so trivial a subject?

From Section V, 'Of the *Elegy to the Memory of an Unfortunate Lady,* the Prologue to *Cato,* and the Epilogue to *Jane Shore*'

If this elegy be so excellent, it may be ascribed to this cause, that the occasion of it was real, for it is certainly an indisputable maxim that Nature is more powerful than fancy, that we can always feel more than we can imagine, and that the most artful fiction can give way to truth. ... Events that have actually happened are, after all, the properest subjects for poetry.

From Section VI, 'Of the Epistle of *Sappho to Phaon* and of *Eloisa to Abelard*'

No part of this poem [*Eloisa to Abelard*], or indeed of any of Pope's productions, is so truly poetical and contains such strong painting as the passage to which we are now arrived – the description of the convent – where Pope's religion certainly aided his fancy. It is impossible to read it without being struck with a pensive pleasure and a sacred awe at the solemnity of the scene, so picturesque are the epithets.

In these *lone* walls (their days' eternal bound),
These *moss-grown* domes with *spiry* turrets crowned,
Where *awful* arches make a noon-day night,
And the *dim* windows shed a *solemn* light,
Thy eyes diffused a reconciling ray. . . .
(141–5)

All the circumstances that can amuse and soothe the mind of a solitary are next enumerated in this expressive manner, and the reader that shall be disgusted at the length of the quotation, one might pronounce, has no taste either for painting or poetry:

The darksome pines that o'er yon rocks reclined
Wave high, and murmur to the hollow wind;
The wandering streams that shine between the hills,
The grots that echo to the tinkling rills,
The dying gales that pant upon the trees,
The lakes that quiver to the curling breeze –
No more these scenes my meditation aid,
Or lull to rest the visionary maid.
(155–62)

The effect and influence of melancholy, who is beautifully personified, on every object that occurs and on ever part of the convent, cannot be too much applauded or too often read, as it is founded on nature and experience. That temper of mind casts a gloom on all things.

But o'er the twilight groves and dusky caves,
Long-sounding aisles, and intermingled graves,
Black melancholy sits, and round her throws
A death-like silence, and a dread repose;
Her gloomy presence saddens all the scene,
Shades every flower, and darkens every green,
Deepens the murmur of the falling floods,
And breathes a browner horror on the woods.
(163–70)

The figurative expressions 'throws' and 'breathes' and 'browner horror' are, I verily believe, some of the strongest and boldest in the English language. The image of the goddess melancholy sitting over the convent and, as it were, expanding her dreadful wings over its whole circuit and diffusing her gloom all around it is truly sublime and strongly conceived.

From Section IX, 'Of the *Essay on Man*'

The *Essay on Man* is as close a piece of argument, admitting its principles, as perhaps can be found in verse. Pope informs us in his first preface 'that he chose his epistolary way of writing, notwithstanding his subject was high and of dignity, because of its being mixed with argument which of its nature approacheth to prose.' He has not wandered into any useless digressions, has employed no fictions, no tale or story, and has relied chiefly on the poetry of his style for the purpose of interesting his readers. His style is concise and figurative, forcible and elegant. He has many metaphors and images artfully interspersed in the driest passages, which stood most in need of such ornaments. Nevertheless, there are too many lines in this performance plain and prosaic. The meaner the subject is of a preceptive poem, the more striking appears the art of the poet. It is even of use, perhaps, to choose a low subject. In this respect Virgil had the advantage over Lucretius. The latter, with all his vigour and sublimity of genius, could hardly satisfy and come up to the grandeur of his theme. Pope labours under the same difficulty. If any beauty in this essay be uncommonly transcendent and peculiar, it is brevity of diction, which, in a few instances, and those pardonable, has occasioned obscurity. It is hardly to be imagined how much sense, how much thinking, how much observation on human life is condensed together in a small compass. He was so accustomed to confine his thoughts in rhyme that he tells us he could express them more shortly this way than in prose itself. . . .

The subject of this essay is a vindication of providence in which the poet proposes to prove that of all possible systems, infinite wisdom has formed the best; that in such a system, coherence, union, subordination are necessary; and if so, that appearances of evil, both moral and natural, are also necessary and unavoidable; that the seeming defects and blemishes in the universe conspire to its general beauty; that as all parts in an animal are not eyes, and as in a city, comedy, or picture, all ranks, characters, and colours are not equal or alike, even so, excesses and contrary qualities contribute to the proportion and harmony of the universal system; that it is not strange that we should not be able to discover perfection and order in every instance, because in an infinity of things mutually relative a mind which sees not infinitely can see nothing fully. This doctrine was inculcated by Plato and the Stoics, but more amply and particularly by the later Platonists, and by Antoninus and Simplicius. In illustrating his subject Pope has been much more deeply indebted to the *Théodicée* of Leibnitz, to Archbishop King's *Origin of Evil*, and to the *Moralists* of Lord Shaftesbury, than to the philosophers above mentioned. The late Lord Bathurst repeatedly assured me that he had read the whole scheme of the *Essay on Man* in the handwriting of Bolingbroke and drawn up in a series of propositions which Pope was to versify and illustrate, in doing which, our poet, it must be confessed, left several passages so expressed as to be favourable to fatalism and necessity, notwithstanding all the pains that can be taken and the turns that can be given to those passages to place them on the side of religion and make them coincide with the fundamental doctrines of revelation.

Awake, my St John! leave all meaner things
To low ambition and the pride of kings.
Let us (since life can little more supply
Than just to look about us and to die)
Expatiate free o'er all this scene of man;
A mighty maze! but not without a plan.
(1 1–6)

This opening is awful and commands the attention of the reader. The word *awake* has peculiar force and obliquely alludes to his noble friend's leaving his political for philosophical pursuits. May I venture to observe that the metaphors in the succeeding lines, drawn from the field sports of setting and shooting, seem below the dignity of the subject, especially,

Eye nature's walks, shoot folly as it flies,
And catch the manners living as they rise. . . .
(1 13–14)

But vindicate the ways of God to man.

This line is taken from Milton:
(1 16)

And justify the ways of God to man [sic].

Pope seems to have hinted by this allusion to the *Paradise Lost* that he intended his poem for a defence of providence as well as Milton, but he took a very different method in pursuing that end, and imagined that the goodness and justice of the Deity might be defended *without* having recourse to the doctrine of a future state and of the depraved state of man. ....

The lamb thy riot dooms to bleed today,
Had he thy reason, would he skip and play?
Pleased to the last he crops the flowery food,
And licks the hand just raised to shed his blood.
(I 81–4)

The tenderness of this striking image, and particularly the circum-
stance in the last line, has an artful effect in alleviating the dryness in the argumentative parts of the essay and interesting the reader.

The soul, uneasy and confined from home,
Rests and expatiates in a life to come.
(I 97–8)

In former editions it used to be printed *at home*, but this expression seeming to exclude a future existence (as to speak the plain truth it was intended to do) it was altered to *from home*, not only with great injury to the harmony of the line, but also to the reasoning of the context.

Lo, the poor Indian, whose untutored mind
Sees God in clouds, or hears him in the wind;
His soul proud science never taught to stray
Far as the solar walk, or milky way;
Yet simple nature to his hope has given,
Behind the cloud-topped hill, an humbler heaven;
Some safer world in depth of woods embraced,
Some happier island in the watery waste,
Where slaves once more their native land behold,
No fiends torment, no Christians thirst for gold.
To be, contents his natural desire,
He asks no angel's wing, no seraph's fire;

But thinks, admitted to that equal sky,
His faithful dog shall bear him company.
(I 99–112)

Pope has indulged himself in but few digressions in this piece;
this is one of the most poetical. Representations of undisguised
nature and artless innocence always amuse and delight. The simple
notions which uncivilized nations entertain of a future state are many
of them beautifully romantic and some of the best subjects for poetry.
It has been questioned whether the circumstance of the dog, although
striking at the first view, is introduced with propriety, as it is known
that this animal is not a native of America. The notion of seeing God
in clouds and hearing him in the wind cannot be enough applauded.

From burning suns when livid deaths descend,
When earthquakes swallow, or when tempests sweep
Towns to one grave, whole nations to the deep?
(I 142–4)

I quote these lines as an example of energy of style and of Pope's
manner of compressing together many images without confusion and
without superfluous epithets. Substantives and verbs are the sinews of
language. . . .

All are but parts of one stupendous whole,
Whose body Nature is, and God the soul;
That, changed through all, and yet in all the same,
Great in the earth as in the aethereal frame,
Warms in the sun, refreshes in the breeze,
Glows in the stars, and blossoms in the trees,
Lives through all life, extends through all extent,
Spreads undivided, operates unspent,
Breathes in our soul, informs our mortal part,
As full, as perfect, in a hair as heart;
As full, as perfect, in vile man that mourns,
As the rapt seraph that adores and burns;
To Him on high, no low, no great, no small;
He fills, he bounds, connects, and equals all.
(I 267–80)

Whilst I am transcribing this exalted description of the omni-presence of the Deity, I feel myself almost tempted to retract an assertion in the beginning of this work that there is nothing tran-scendently sublime in Pope. These lines have all the energy and harmony that can be given to rhyme.

From Section X, 'Of the *Moral Essays* in *Five Epistles to Several Persons*'

Like some lone Chartreux stands the good old hall,
Silence without, and fasts within the wall;
No raftered roofs with dance and tabor sound,
No noontide-bell invites the country round;
Tenants with sighs the smokeless towers survey,
And turn th' unwilling steed another way,
Benighted wanderers, the forest o'er,
Curse the saved candle and unopening door;
While the gaunt mastiff, growling at the gate,
Affrights the beggar whom he longs to eat.
(*III*, 189–98)

In the worst inn's worst room, with mat half hung,
The floors of plaster, and the walls of dung,
On once a flock-bed, but repaired with straw,
With tape-tied curtains, never meant to draw,
The George and Garter dangling from that bed,
Where tawdry yellow strove with dirty red,
Great Villiers lies.
(*III*, 299–305)

The use, the force, and the excellence of language certainly consists in raising clear, complete, and circumstantial images and in turning readers into spectators. I have quoted the two preceding passages as eminent examples of this excellence, of all others the most essential in poetry. Every epithet here used paints its object and paints it distinctly. After having passed over the moat full of cresses, do you not actually find yourself in the middle court of this forlorn and solitary mansion overgrown with docks and nettles? And do you not hear the dog that is going to assault you? . . .

Who hung with woods yon mountain's sultry brow?
From the dry rock who bade the waters flow?
Not to the skies in useless columns tossed,
Or in proud falls magnificently lost,
But clear and artless, pouring through the plain
Health to the sick, and solace to the swain.
Whose causeway parts the vale with shady rows?
Whose seats the weary traveller repose?
Who taught that heaven-directed spire to rise?
The Man of Ross, each lisping babe replies.
Behold the marketplace with poor o'erspread!
The Man of Ross divides the weekly bread.
Behold yon alms-house, neat, but void of state,
Where age and want sit smiling at the gate;
Him portioned maids, apprenticed orphans blest,
The young who labour, and the old who rest.
(*III*, 253–68)

These lines, which are eminently beautiful, particularly one of the three last containing a fine prosopopoeia, have conferred immortality on a plain, worthy and useful citizen of Herefordshire, Mr John Kyrle, who spent his long life in advancing and contriving plans of public utility – the Howard of his time who deserves to be celebrated more than all the heroes of Pindar. The particular reason for which I quoted them was to observe the pleasing effect that the use of common and familiar words and objects judiciously managed produces in poetry. Such as are here the words *causeway, seats, spire, marketplace, alms-houses, apprenticed*. A fastidious delicacy and a false refinement in order to avoid meanness have deterred our writers from the introduction of such words, but Dryden often hazarded it and gave by it a secret charm and a natural air to his verses, well knowing of what consequence it was sometimes to soften and subdue his tints and not to paint and adorn every object he touched with perpetual pomp and unremitted splendour.

From Section XIV and Last, 'Of some *Imitations of Horace,* the Miscellanies, Epitaphs, and Prose works'

Thus have I endeavoured to give a critical account, with freedom, but it is hoped, with impartiality, of each of Pope's works, by which review it will appear that the largest portion of them is of the didactic, moral, and satiric kind, and consequently not of the most poetic species of poetry – whence it is manifest that good sense and judgement were his characteristical excellencies rather than fancy and invention; not that the author of *The Rape of the Lock* and *Eloisa* can be thought to want imagination, but because his imagination was not his predominant talent, because he indulged it not, and because he gave not so many proofs of this talent as of the other. This turn of mind led him to admire French models; he studied Boileau attentively, formed himself upon him as Milton formed himself upon the Grecian and Italian sons of fancy. He stuck to describing modern manners, but those manners, because they are familiar, uniform, artificial, and polished, are, in their very nature, unfit for any lofty effort of the Muse. He gradually became one of the most correct, even, and exact poets that ever wrote, polishing his pieces with a care and assiduity that no business or avocation ever interrupted, so that if he does not frequently ravish and transport his reader, yet he does not disgust him with unexpected inequalities and absurd improprieties. Whatever poetical enthusiasm he actually possessed, he withheld and stifled. The perusal of him affects not our minds with such strong emotions as we feel from Homer and Milton, so that no man of a true poetical spirit is master of himself while he reads them. Hence, he is a writer fit for universal perusal, adapted to all ages and stations, for the old and for the young, the man of business and the scholar. He who would think *The Fairy Queen, Palamon and Arcite, The Tempest,* or *Comus* childish and romantic might relish Pope. Surely it is no narrow and niggardly encomium to say he is the great poet of reason, the first of ethical authors in verse. And this species of writing is, after all, the surest road to an extensive reputation. It lies more level to the general capacities of men than the higher flights of more genuine poetry. We all remember when even a Churchill was more in vogue than a Gray. He that treats of fashionable follies and the topics of the day, that describes present persons and recent events, finds many readers whose understandings and whose passions he gratifies. The name of Chesterfield on one hand and of Walpole on the other failed not to make a poem bought up and talked of. And it cannot be doubted that the *Odes* of Horace which celebrated, and the *Satires* which ridiculed, well-known and real characters at Rome were more eagerly read and more frequently cited than the *Aeneid* and the *Georgics* of Virgil.

Where, then, according to the question proposed at the beginning of this essay, shall we with justice be authorized to place our admired Pope? Not, assuredly, in the same rank with Spenser, Shakespeare, and Milton, however justly we may applaud the *Eloisa* and *Rape of the Lock*; but, considering the correctness, elegance, and utility of his works, the weight of sentiment, and the knowledge of man they contain, we may venture to assign him a place next to Milton and just above Dryden. Yet, to bring our minds steadily to make this decision, we must forget for a moment the divine 'Music Ode' of Dryden, and may, perhaps, then be compelled to confess that though Dryden be the greater genius, yet Pope is the better artist.

The preference here given to Pope above other modern English poets, it must be remembered, is founded on the excellencies of his works in general, and taken all together, for there are parts and passages in other modern authors, in Young and in Thomson, for instance, equal to any of Pope, and he has written nothing in a strain so truly sublime as 'The Bard' of Gray.

Oliver Goldsmith

from *The Life of Richard Nash*   1762

... in all his letters, as well as those of Swift, there runs a strain of pride, as if the world talked of nothing but themselves. *Alas*, says he in one of them, *the day after I am dead, the sun will shine as bright as the day before, and the world will be as merry as usual!* Very strange, that neither an eclipse nor an earthquake should follow the loss of a poet!

Adam Smith

from lectures 1762–3 (printed, from students' notes, in
Lectures on Rhetoric and Belles Lettres, 1963)

Two of the most beautiful passages in all Pope's work are those in
which he describes the state of mind of an untaught Indian [*Essay on
Man*, 1 99 ff.], and the other in which he considers the various ranks
and orders of beings in the Universe [1 233–4]. The words 'watery
waste' had been better exchanged for 'ocean' but that the rhyme
required them.

In the latter of these there is not one figurative expression, and the
few there are in the other are no advantage to it.

The ridicule in *The Rape of the Lock* proceeds from the ridiculousness
of the characters themselves, but that of *The Dunciad* is owing
altogether to the circumstances the persons are placed in. Any two
men – Pope and Swift themselves – would look as ridiculous as Curll
and Lintot, if they were described running the same races.

Oliver Goldsmith

from *A History of England in a Series of Letters from a Nobleman
to his Son* 1764

[The age of Queen Anne] . . . of all who have added to the stock of
English poetry Pope perhaps deserves the first place. On him foreigners look as one of the most successful writers of his time; his versification is the most harmonious and his corrections the most remarkable
of all our poets. A noted contemporary of his own [Voltaire?] calls
the English the finest writers on moral topics and Pope the noblest
moral writer of all the English. Mr Pope has somewhere named
himself the last English Muse, and indeed since his time we have
seen scarce any production that can justly claim to immortality. He
carried the language to its highest perfection, and those who have

attempted still farther to improve it, instead of ornament have only caught finery.

William Shenstone

from 'Essays', *Works*, vol. 2   1764

Mr Pope's chief excellence lies in what I would term consolidating or condensing sentences, yet preserving ease and perspicuity. . . .

Pope's talent lay remarkably in what one may naturally enough term the condensation of thoughts. . . .

Pope has made the utmost advantage of alliteration, regulating it by the pause with the utmost success:

Die and endow a college or a cat, *etc., etc.*
(*Moral Essay III*, 98)

It is an easy kind of beauty. Dryden seems to have borrowed it from Spenser.

Philip Dormer Stanhope, Earl of Chesterfield

from a letter to his son   6 October 1770

I content myself with your letters in prose till you are *afflatus lumine* [inspired]. The greatest poets – Dryden, Addison and Pope – have not been always equally inspired any more than you.

Oliver Goldsmith

from *The Life of Dr Parnell*   1770

[Parnell's poetic diction] . . . He found it at that period in which it was brought to its highest pitch of refinement and ever since his time it has been gradually debasing. It is indeed amazing, after what has been done by Dryden, Addison and Pope to improve and harmonize our native tongue, that their successors should have taken so much pains to involve it in pristine barbarity.

Percival Stockdale

from *An Enquiry into the Nature and Genuine Laws of Poetry, including a particular Defence of the Writings and Genius of Mr Pope* 1778

You ask what then is transcendently pathetic and sublime in Pope? One would think the man had lost his senses. Many passages interposed throughout his work: his filial apostrophes to the age and infirmities of an affectionate mother, his *Elegy to the Memory of an Unfortunate Lady*, his Prologue to *Cato*, his *Eloisa to Abelard* are all transcendently pathetic . . . the Epistle from *Eloisa to Abelard* is the warmest, and most affecting, and admirable amorous poem in the world.

If a passage in a poet seems obscure, if it puts the understanding on exertion, either that passage must not be poetry (for poetry must be perspicuous; its effects must be striking, and instantaneous) or the soul of the reader must be torpid and impassive. . . . He who is endowed with good sense and sentiment, who has had no regular education, but is conversant with the English language and with the world, though he has never before opened a poet, will receive great pleasure from reading Pope's *Eloisa to Abelard*, or even his *Essay on Man*.

William Cowper

from *Table Talk*   January 1781

In front of these came Addison. . . .
Then Pope, as harmony itself exact,

In verse well disciplined, complete, compact,
Gave virtue and morality a grace,
That quite eclipsing pleasure's painted face,
Levied a tax of wonder and applause
Even on the fools that trampled on their laws,
But he – his musical finesse was such,
So nice his ear, so delicate his touch –
Made poetry a mere mechanic art,
And every warbler has his tune by heart.

Samuel Johnson

from 'The Life of Pope', *The Lives of the English Poets*   1781
(see Note 1 in Appendix, pp. 490–91).

The same year [1709] was written the *Essay on Criticism*, a work
which displays such extent of comprehension, such nicety of distinction, such acquaintance with mankind, and such knowledge both of
ancient and modern learning, as are not often attained by the maturest
age and longest experience. It was published about two years afterwards, and, being praised by Addison in the *Spectator* with sufficient
liberality, met with so much favour as enraged Dennis,

who (he says) found himself attacked, without any manner of
provocation on his side, and attacked in his person, instead
of his writings, by one who was wholly a stranger to him,
at a time when all the world knew he was persecuted by
fortune – and not only saw that this was attempted in a
clandestine manner, with the utmost falsehood and calumny,
but found that all this was done by a little affected hypocrite,
who had nothing in his mouth at the same time but truth,
candour, friendship, good nature, humanity, and
magnanimity.

How the attack was clandestine is not easily perceived, nor how his
person is depreciated; but he seems to have known something of
Pope's character, in whom may be discovered an appetite to talk too
frequently of his own virtues.

The pamphlet is such as rage might be expected to dictate. He supposes himself to be asked two questions: whether the essay will succeed, and who or what is the author.

Its success he admits to be secured by the false opinions then prevalent; the author he concludes to be 'young and raw'.

First, because he discovers a sufficiency beyond his little ability, and hath rashly undertaken a task infinitely above his force. Secondly, while this little author struts, and affects the dictatorian air, he plainly shows that at the same time he is under the rod, and, while he pretends to give laws to others, is a pedantic slave to authority and opinion. Thirdly, he hath, like schoolboys, borrowed both from living and dead. Fourthly, he knows not his own mind, and frequently contradicts himself. Fifthly, he is almost perpetually in the wrong.

All these positions he attempts to prove by quotations and remarks; but his desire to do mischief is greater than his power. He has, however, justly criticized some passages: in these lines,

There are whom heaven has blessed with store of wit,
Yet want as much again to manage it;
For wit and judgement ever are at strife –
(*Essay on Criticism*, 80–82)

it is apparent that *wit* has two meanings; and that what is wanted, though called *wit*, is, truly, judgement. So far Dennis is undoubtedly right; but, not content with argument, he will have a little mirth, and triumphs over the first couplet in terms too elegant to be forgotten. 'By the way, what rare numbers are here! Would not one swear that this youngster had espoused some antiquated muse, who had sued out a divorce on account of impotence from some superannuated sinner; and, having been poxed by her former spouse, has got the gout, in her decrepit age, which makes her hobble so damnably?' This was the man who would reform a nation sinking into barbarity.

In another place Pope himself allowed that Dennis had detected one of those blunders which are called 'bulls'. The first edition had this line:

What is this wit . . .
Where wanted scorned, and envied where acquired?
(500, 503)

'How,' says the critic, 'can wit be scorned where it is not? Is not this
a figure frequently employed in Hibernian land? The person that
wants this wit may, indeed, be scorned, but the scorn shows the
honour which the contemner has for wit.' Of this remark Pope made
the proper use by correcting the passage.

I have preserved, I think, all that is reasonable in Dennis's criticism;
it remains that justice be done to his delicacy.

For his acquaintance (says Dennis) he names Mr Walsh, who
had by no means the qualification which this author reckons
absolutely necessary to a critic, it being very certain that he
was, like this essayer, a very indifferent poet; he loved to be
well dressed; and I remember a little young gentleman,
whom Mr Walsh used to take into his company, as a double
foil to his person and capacity. Inquire, between Sunninghill
and Oakingham, for a young, short, squab gentleman, the
very bow of the god of love, and tell me whether he be a
proper author to make personal reflections? He may extol
the ancients, but he has reason to thank the gods that he was
born a modern; for had he been born of Grecian parents,
and his father, consequently, had, by law, had the absolute
disposal of him, his life had been no longer than that of one
of his poems, the life of half a day. Let the person of a
gentleman of his parts be never so contemptible, his inward
man is ten times more ridiculous, it being impossible that
his outward form, though it be that of a downright
monkey, should differ so much from human shape as his
unthinking, immaterial part does from human understanding.

Thus began the hostility between Pope and Dennis, which, though it
was suspended for a short time, never was appeased. Pope seems, at
first, to have attacked him wantonly; but, though he always professed to despise him, he discovers, by mentioning him very often,
that he felt his force or his venom.

Of this Essay Pope declared that he did not expect the sale to be quick, because 'not one gentleman in sixty, even of liberal education, could understand it.' The gentlemen, and the education of that time, seem to have been of a lower character than they are of this. He mentioned a thousand copies as a numerous impression.

Dennis was not his only censurer; the zealous papists thought the monks treated with too much contempt, and Erasmus too studiously praised, but to these objections he had not much regard.

The *Essay* has been translated into French by Hamilton, author of the *Comte de Grammont*, whose version was never printed, by Robotham, secretary to the king for Hanover, and by Resnel; and commented by Dr Warburton, who has discovered in it such order and connection as was not perceived by Addison, nor, as is said, intended by the author.

Almost every poem consisting of precepts is so far arbitrary and immethodical that many of the paragraphs may change places with no apparent inconvenience; for of two or more positions, depending upon some remote and general principle, there is seldom any cogent reason why one should precede the other. But for the order in which they stand, whatever it be, a little ingenuity may easily give a reason. 'It is possible,' says Hooker, 'that, by long circumduction, from any one truth all truth may be inferred.' Of all homogeneous truths, at least of all truths respecting the same general end, in whatever series they may be produced, a concatenation by intermediate ideas may be formed, such as, when it is once shown, shall appear natural; but if this order be reversed another mode of connection equally specious may be found or made. Aristotle is praised for naming fortitude first of the cardinal virtues, as that without which no other virtue can steadily be practised; but he might, with equal propriety, have placed prudence and justice before it, since without prudence, fortitude is mad, without justice, it is mischievous.

As the end of method is perspicuity, that series is sufficiently regular that avoids obscurity; and where there is no obscurity, it will not be difficult to discover method.

In the *Spectator* was published the *Messiah*, which he first submitted to the perusal of Steele and corrected in compliance with his criticisms.

It is reasonable to infer from his letters that the verses on the Unfortunate Lady were written about the time when his *Essay* was published. The lady's name and adventures I have sought with fruitless inquiry.

I can, therefore, tell no more than I have learned from Mr Ruffhead [author of the official biography, 1769], who writes with the confidence of one who could trust his information. She was a woman of eminent rank and large fortune, the ward of an uncle who, having given her a proper education, expected, like other guardians, that she should make, at least, an equal match; and such he proposed to her, but found it rejected in favour of a young gentleman of inferior condition.

Having discovered the correspondence between the two lovers, and finding the young lady determined to abide by her own choice, he supposed that separation might do what can rarely be done by arguments, and sent her into a foreign country, where she was obliged to converse only with those from whom her uncle had nothing to fear.

Her lover took care to repeat his vows; but his letters were intercepted and carried to her guardian, who directed her to be watched with still greater vigilance, till of this restraint she grew so impatient that she bribed a woman servant to procure her a sword, which she directed to her heart.

From this account, given with evident intention to raise the lady's character, it does not appear that she had any claim to praise, nor much to compassion. She seems to have been impatient, violent, and ungovernable. Her uncle's power could not have lasted long; the hour of liberty and choice would have come in time. But her desires were too hot for delay, and she liked self-murder better than suspense.

Nor is it discovered that the uncle, whoever he was, is with much justice delivered to posterity as 'a false guardian'; he seems to have done only that for which a guardian is appointed: he endeavoured to direct his niece till she should be able to direct herself. Poetry has not often been worse employed than in dignifying the amorous fury of a raving girl.

Not long after, he wrote *The Rape of the Lock*, the most airy, the most ingenious, and the most delightful of all his compositions, occasioned by a frolic of gallantry, rather too familiar, in which Lord Petre cut off a lock of Mrs [Miss] Arabella Fermor's hair. This, whether stealth or violence, was so much resented that the commerce of the two families, before very friendly, was interrupted. Mr Caryll, a gentleman who, being secretary to King James's queen, had followed his mistress into France, and who, being the author of *Sir Solomon Single*, a comedy, and some translations, was entitled to the notice of a wit, solicited Pope to endeavour a reconciliation by a ludicrous poem, which might bring both the parties to a better temper. In compliance with Caryll's request, though his name was for a long time marked only by the first and last letters, C—l, a poem of two cantos was written (1711), as is said, in a fortnight, and sent to the offended lady, who liked it well enough to show it; and, with the usual process of literary transactions, the author, dreading a surreptitious edition, was forced to publish it.

The event is said to have been such as was desired, the pacification and diversion of all to whom it related, except Sir George Brown, who complained, with some bitterness, that, in the character of Sir Plume, he was made to talk nonsense. Whether all this be true I have some doubt; for at Paris, a few years ago, a niece of Mrs [Miss] Fermor, who presided in an English convent, mentioned Pope's work with very little gratitude, rather as an insult than an honour; and she may be supposed to have inherited the opinion of her family.

At its first appearance it was termed, by Addison, *merum sal* [the perfection of wit]. Pope, however, saw that it was capable of improvement; and, having luckily contrived to borrow his machinery from the Rosicrucians, imparted the scheme with which his head was teeming to Addison, who told him that his work, as it stood, was 'a delicious little thing', and gave him no encouragement to retouch it.

This has been too hastily considered as an instance of Addison's jealousy; for, as he could not guess the conduct of the new design, or the possibilities of pleasure comprised in a fiction of which there had been no examples, he might very reasonably and kindly persuade the author to acquiesce in his own prosperity, and forbear an attempt which he considered as an unnecessary hazard.

Addison's counsel was happily rejected. Pope foresaw the future efflorescence of imagery then budding in his mind, and resolved to spare no art or industry of cultivation. The soft luxuriance of his fancy was already shooting, and all the gay varieties of diction were ready at his hand to colour and embellish it.

His attempt was justified by its success. *The Rape of the Lock* stands forward, in the classes of literature, as the most exquisite example of ludicrous poetry. Berkeley congratulated him upon the display of powers more truly poetical than he had shown before; with elegance of description and justness of precepts, he had now exhibited boundless fertility of invention.

He always considered the intermixture of the machinery with the action as his most successful exertion of poetical art. He, indeed, could never afterwards produce any thing of such unexampled excellence. Those performances which strike with wonder are combinations of skilful genius with happy casualty; and it is not likely that any felicity like the discovery of a new race of preternatural agents should happen twice to the same man. . . .

It cannot be unwelcome to literary curiosity that I deduce . . . minutely the history of the English *Iliad*. It is, certainly, the noblest version of poetry which the world has ever seen; and its publication must, therefore, be considered as one of the great events in the annals of learning. . . .

While the volumes of his Homer were annually published, he collected his former works, 1717, into one quarto volume, to which he prefixed a preface, written with great sprightliness and elegance, which was afterwards reprinted, with some passages subjoined that he at first omitted; other marginal additions of the same kind he made in the later editions of his poems. Waller remarks that poets lose half their praise because the reader knows not what they have blotted. Pope's voracity of fame taught him the art of obtaining the accumulated honour, both of what he had published, and of what he had suppressed. . . .

In the conclusion it is sufficiently acknowledged that the doctrine of the *Essay on Man* was received from Bolingbroke, who is said to have ridiculed Pope, among those who enjoyed his confidence, as having adopted and advanced principles of which he did not perceive the consequence, and as blindly propagating opinions contrary to his own. That those communications had been consolidated into a scheme regularly drawn, and delivered to Pope, from whom it returned only transformed from prose to verse, has been reported, but can hardly be true. The essay plainly appears the fabric of a poet:

what Bolingbroke supplied could be only the first principles; the order, illustration, and embellishments must all be Pope's.

These principles it is not my business to clear from obscurity, dogmatism, or falsehood; but they were not immediately examined; philosophy and poetry have not often the same readers; and the essay abounded in splendid amplifications, and sparkling sentences, which were read and admired with no great attention to their ultimate purpose; its flowers caught the eye, which did not see what the gay foliage concealed, and, for a time, flourished in the sunshine of universal approbation. So little was any evil tendency discovered, that, as innocence is unsuspicious, many read it for a manual of piety. . . .

He afterwards (1734) inscribed to Lord Cobham his *Characters of Men*, written with close attention to the operations of the mind and modifications of life. In this poem he has endeavoured to establish and exemplify his favourite theory of the 'ruling passion', by which he means an original direction of desire to some particular object – an innate affection, which gives all action a determinate and invariable tendency, and operates upon the whole system of life, either openly, or more secretly by the intervention of some accidental or subordinate propension.

Of any passion thus innate and irresistible, the existence may reasonably be doubted. Human characters are by no means constant; men change by change of place, of fortune, of acquaintance; he who is at one time a lover of pleasure is at another a lover of money. Those, indeed, who attain any excellence commonly spend life in one pursuit; for excellence is not often gained upon easier terms. But to the particular species of excellence men are directed, not by an ascendant planet or predominating humour, but by the first book which they read, some early conversation which they heard, or some accident which excited ardour and emulation.

It must be, at least, allowed that this 'ruling passion', antecedent to reason and observation, must have an object independent on human contrivance; for there can be no natural desire of artificial good. No man, therefore, can be born, in the strict acceptation, a lover of money; for he may be born where money does not exist: nor can he be born, in a moral sense, a lover of his country; for society, politically regulated, is a state contradistinguished from a state of nature; and any attention to that coalition of interests which makes the happiness of a country is possible only to those whom inquiry and reflection have enabled to comprehend it. ...

He published, from time to time, between 1730 and 1740, imitations of different poems of Horace, generally with his name, and once [*Sober Advice from Horace*, 1734], as was suspected, without it. What he was upon moral principles ashamed to own, he ought to have suppressed. Of these pieces it is useless to settle the dates, as they had seldom much relation to the times, and perhaps, had been long in his hands.

This mode of imitation, in which the ancients are familiarized, by adapting their sentiments to modern topics, by making Horace say of Shakespeare what he originally said of Ennius, and accommodating his satires on Pantolabus and Nomentanus to the flatterers and prodigals of our own time, was first practised in the reign of Charles the Second, by Oldham and Rochester – at least I remember no instances more ancient. It is a kind of middle composition between translation and original design, which pleases when the thoughts are unexpectedly applicable, and the parallels lucky. It seems to have been Pope's favourite amusement; for he has carried it farther than any former poet.

He published, likewise, a revival, in smoother numbers, of Dr Donne's satires, which was recommended to him by the Duke of Shrewsbury and the Earl of Oxford. They made no great impression on the public. Pope seems to have known their imbecility, and, therefore, suppressed them while he was yet contending to rise in reputation, but ventured them when he thought their deficiencies more likely to be imputed to Donne than to himself.

The *Epistle to Dr Arbuthnot*, which seems to be derived, in its first design, from Boileau's Address *à son Esprit*, was published in January 1735, about a month before the death of him to whom it is inscribed. It is to be regretted that either honour or pleasure should have been missed by Arbuthnot; a man estimable for his learning, amiable for his life, and venerable for his piety. ...

This work [an enlarged *Essay on Man*] in its full extent, being now afflicted with an asthma, and finding the powers of life gradually declining, he had no longer courage to undertake; but, from the materials which he had provided, he added, at Warburton's request, another book to *The Dunciad*, of which the design is to ridicule such studies as are either hopeless or useless, as either pursue what is unattainable, or what, if it be attained, is of no use.

When this book was printed (1742) the laurel had been, for some time, upon the head of Cibber, a man whom it cannot be supposed that Pope could regard with much kindness or esteem, though, in one of the *Imitations of Horace*, he has liberally enough praised *The Careless Husband*. In *The Dunciad*, among other worthless scribblers, he had mentioned Cibber; who, in his *Apology*, complains of the great poet's unkindness as more injurious 'because,' says he, 'I never have offended him.'

It might have been expected that Pope should have been, in some degree, mollified by this submissive gentleness, but no such consequence appeared. Though he condescended to commend Cibber once, he mentioned him afterwards contemptuously in one of his satires, and again in his *Epistle to Arbuthnot*: and, in the fourth book of the *Dunciad*, attacked him with acrimony, to which the provocation is not easily discoverable. Perhaps he imagined, that, in ridiculing the laureate, he satirized those by whom the laurel had been given, and gratified that ambitious petulance with which he affected to insult the great. . . .

From this time, finding his diseases more oppressive, and his vital powers gradually declining, he no longer strained his faculties with any original composition, nor proposed any other employment for his remaining life than the revisal and correction of his former works; in which he received advice and assistance from Warburton, whom he appears to have trusted and honoured in the highest degree.

He laid aside his epic poem, perhaps without much loss to mankind; for his hero was Brutus the Trojan, who, according to a ridiculous fiction, established a colony in Britain. The subject, therefore was of the fabulous age: the actors were a race upon whom imagination has been exhausted, and attention wearied, and to whom the mind will not easily be recalled, when it is invited in blank verse, which Pope had adopted with great imprudence, and, I think, without due consideration of the nature of our language. The sketch is, at least in part, preserved by Ruffhead; by which it appears that Pope was thoughtless enough to model the names of his heroes with terminations not consistent with the time or country in which he places them. . . .

Most of what can be told concerning his petty peculiarities was communicated by a female domestic of the Earl of Oxford, who knew him, perhaps, after the middle of life. He was then so weak as to stand in perpetual need of female attendance; extremely sensible of cold, so that he wore a kind of fur doublet, under a shirt of very coarse warm linen with fine sleeves. When he rose, he was invested in a bodice made of stiff canvas, being scarcely able to hold himself erect till they were laced, and he then put on a flannel waistcoat. One side was contracted. His legs were so slender that he enlarged their bulk with three pair of stockings, which were drawn on and off by the maid; for he was not able to dress or undress himself, and neither went to bed nor rose without help. His weakness made it very difficult for him to be clean. . . .

In all his intercourse with mankind, he had great delight in artifice, and endeavoured to attain all his purposes by indirect and unsuspected methods. 'He hardly drank tea without a stratagem.' If, at the house of his friends, he wanted any accommodation, he was not willing to ask for it in plain terms, but would mention it remotely as something convenient; though, when it was procured, he soon made it appear for whose sake it had been recommended. Thus he teased Lord Orrery till he obtained a screen. He practised his arts on such small occasions that Lady Bolingbroke used to say, in a French phrase, that 'he played the politician about cabbages and turnips.' His unjustifiable impression of the Patriot King, as it can be imputed to no particular motive, must have proceeded from his general habit of secrecy and cunning; he caught an opportunity of a sly trick, and pleased himself with the thought of outwitting Bolingbroke.

In familiar or convivial conversation, it does not appear that he excelled. He may be said to have resembled Dryden, as being not one that was distinguished by vivacity in company. It is remarkable that, so near his time, so much should be known of what he has written, and so little of what he has said; traditional memory retains no sallies of raillery, nor sentences of observation, nothing either pointed or solid, either wise or merry. One apophthegm only stands upon record. When an objection raised against his inscription for Shakespeare was defended by the authority of Patrick, he replied, 'horresco referens' – that he 'would allow the publisher of a dictionary to know the meaning of a single word, but not of two words put together'.

He was fretful and easily displeased, and allowed himself to be capriciously resentful. He would sometimes leave Lord Oxford silently, no one could tell why, and was to be courted back by more letters and messages than the footmen were willing to carry. The table was, indeed, infested by Lady Mary Wortley, who was the friend of Lady Oxford, and who, knowing his peevishness, could by no entreaties be restrained from contradicting him, till their disputes were sharpened to such asperity that one or the other quitted the house.

He sometimes condescended to be jocular with servants or inferiors; but by no merriment, either of others or his own, was he ever seen excited to laughter.

Of his domestic character, frugality was a part eminently remarkable. Having determined not to be dependent, he determined not to be in want, and, therefore, wisely and magnanimously rejected all temptations to expense unsuitable to his fortune. This general care must be universally approved; but it sometimes appeared in petty artifices of parsimony, such as the practice of writing his compositions on the back of letters, as may be seen in the remaining copy of the *Iliad*, by which, perhaps, in five years five shillings were saved; or in a niggardly reception of his friends, and scantiness of entertainment, as, when he had two guests in his house, he would set at supper a single pint upon the table; and, having himself taken two small glasses, would retire, and say, 'Gentlemen, I leave you to your wine.' Yet he tells his friends that he 'has a heart for all, a house for all, and whatever they may think, a fortune for all'.

He sometimes, however, made a splendid dinner, and is said to have wanted no part of the skill or elegance which such performances require. That this magnificence should be often displayed, that obstinate prudence with which he conducted his affairs would not permit; for his revenue, certain and casual, amounted only to about eight hundred pounds a year, of which, however, he declares himself able to assign one hundred to charity. . . .

To charge those favourable representations which men give of their own minds with the guilt of hypocritical falsehood would show more severity than knowledge. The writer commonly believes himself. Almost every man's thoughts, while they are general, are right; and most hearts are pure while temptation is away. It is easy to awaken generous sentiments in privacy; to despise death when there is no danger; to glow with benevolence when there is nothing to be given. While such ideas are formed, they are felt, and self-love does not suspect the gleam of virtue to be the meteor of fancy.

If the letters of Pope are considered merely as compositions, they seem to be premeditated and artificial. It is one thing to write because there is something which the mind wishes to discharge; and another to solicit the imagination because ceremony or vanity requires something to be written. Pope confesses his early letters to be vitiated with 'affectation and ambition'; to know whether he disentangled himself from these perverters of epistolary integrity, his book and his life must be set in comparison.

One of his favourite topics is contempt of his own poetry. For this, if it had been real, he would deserve no commendation; and in this he was certainly not sincere, for his high value of himself was sufficiently observed; and of what could he be proud but of his poetry? He writes, he says, when he 'has just nothing else to do', yet Swift complains that he was never at leisure for conversation, because he had 'always some poetical scheme in his head'. It was punctually required that his writing-box should be set upon his bed before he rose; and Lord Oxford's domestic related that, in the dreadful winter of forty, she was called from her bed by him four times in one night to supply him with paper, lest he should lose a thought. . . .

From this curiosity arose the desire of travelling to which he alludes in his verses to Jervas; and which, though he never found an opportunity to gratify it, did not leave him till his life declined.

Of his intellectual character, the constituent and fundamental principle was good sense, a prompt and intuitive perception of consonance and propriety. He saw immediately, of his own conceptions, what was to be chosen and what to be rejected; and, in the works of other, what was to be shunned and what was to be copied.

But good sense alone is a sedate and quiescent quality, which manages its possessions well, but does not increase them; it collects few materials for its own operations, and preserves safety, but never gains supremacy. Pope had, likewise, genius, a mind active, ambitious, and adventurous, always investigating, always aspiring – in its widest searches still longing to go forward, in its highest flights still wishing to be higher, always imagining something greater than it knows, always endeavouring more than it can do.

To assist these powers, he is said to have had great strength and exactness of memory. That which he had heard or read was not easily lost; and he had before him not only what his own meditation suggested, but what he had found in other writers that might be accommodated to his present purpose. . . .

Pope was not content to satisfy; he desired to excel, and, therefore, always endeavoured to do his best. He did not court the candour, but dared the judgement of his reader, and, expecting no indulgence from others, he showed none to himself. He examined lines and words with minute and puntilious observation, and retouched every part with indefatigable diligence, till he had left nothing to be forgiven.

For this reason he kept his pieces very long in his hands, while he considered and reconsidered them. The only poems which can be supposed to have been written with such regard to the times as might hasten their publication were the two satires of Thirty-eight, of which Dodsley told me that they were brought to him by the author that they might be fairly copied. 'Almost every line,' he said, 'was then written twice over; I gave him a clean transcript, which he sent some time afterwards to me for the press, with almost every line written twice over a second time.'

His declaration that his care for his works ceased at their publication was not strictly true. His parental attention never abandoned them; what he found amiss in the first edition, he silently corrected in those that followed. He appears to have revised the *Iliad*, and freed it from some of its imperfections; and the *Essay on Criticism* received many improvements after its first appearance. It will seldom be found that he altered without adding clearness, elegance, or vigour. Pope had, perhaps, the judgement of Dryden; but Dryden certainly wanted the diligence of Pope.

In acquired knowledge, the superiority must be allowed to Dryden, whose education was more scholastic, and who, before he became an author, had been allowed more time for study, with better means of information. His mind has a larger range, and he collects his images and illustrations from a more extensive circumference of science. Dryden knew more of man in his general nature, and Pope in his local manners. The notions of Dryden were formed by comprehensive speculation, and those of Pope by minute attention. There is more dignity in the knowledge of Dryden, and more certainty in that of Pope.

Poetry was not the sole praise of either; for both excelled likewise in prose; but Pope did not borrow his prose from his predecessor. The style of Dryden is capricious and varied, that of Pope is cautious and uniform. Dryden obeys the motions of his own mind, Pope constrains his mind to his own rules of composition. Dryden is sometimes vehement and rapid; Pope is always smooth, uniform, and gentle. Dryden's page is a natural field, rising into inequalities, and diversified by the varied exuberance of abundant vegetation; Pope's is a velvet lawn, shaven by the scythe, and levelled by the roller.

Of genius, that power which constitutes a poet, that quality without which judgement is cold, and knowledge is inert, that energy which collects, combines, amplifies, and animates, the superiority must, with some hesitation, be allowed to Dryden. It is not to be inferred that of this poetical vigour Pope had only a little, because Dryden had more; for every other writer since Milton must give place to Pope; and even of Dryden it must be said that, if he has brighter paragraphs, he has not better poems. Dryden's performances were always hasty, either excited by some external occasion, or extorted by domestic necessity; he composed without consideration, and published without correction. What his mind could supply at call, or gather in one excursion, was all that he sought, and all that he gave. The dilatory caution of Pope enabled him to condense his sentiments, to multiply his images, and to accumulate all that study might produce, or chance might supply. If the flights of Dryden, therefore, are higher, Pope continues longer on the wing. If of Dryden's fire the blaze is brighter, of Pope's the heat is more regular and constant. Dryden often surpasses expectation, and Pope never falls below it. Dryden is read with frequent astonishment, and Pope with perpetual delight.

This parallel will, I hope, when it is well considered, be found just; and, if the reader should suspect me, as I suspect myself, of some partial fondness for the memory of Dryden, let him not too hastily condemn me; for meditation and inquiry may, perhaps, show him the reasonableness of my determination.

The works of Pope are now to be distinctly examined, not so much with attention to slight faults, or petty beauties, as to the general character and effect of each performance.

It seems natural for a young poet to initiate himself by pastorals, which, not professing to imitate real life, require no experience; and, exhibiting only the simple operation of unmingled passions, admit no subtle reasoning or deep inquiry. Pope's *Pastorals* are not, however, composed but with close thought; they have reference to the times of the day, the seasons of the year, and the periods of human life. The last, that which turns the attention upon age and death, was the author's favourite. To tell of disappointment and misery, to thicken the darkness of futurity, and perplex the labyrinth of uncertainty, has been always a delicious employment of the poets. His preference was probably just. I wish, however, that his fondness had not overlooked a line in which the zephyrs are made 'to lament in silence'. . . .

That the *Messiah* excels the *Pollio* is no great praise, if it be considered from what original the improvements are derived.

The *Verses* on the *Unfortunate Lady* have drawn much attention by the illaudable singularity of treating suicide with respect; and they must be allowed to be written, in some parts, with vigorous animation, and, in others, with gentle tenderness; nor has Pope produced any poem in which the sense predominates more over the diction. But the tale is not skilfully told; it is not easy to discover the character of either the lady or her guardian. History relates that she was about to disparage herself by a marriage with an inferior; Pope praises her for the dignity of ambition, and yet condemns the uncle to detestation for his pride; the ambitious love of a niece may be opposed by the interest, malice, or envy of an uncle, but never by his pride. On such an occasion a poet may be allowed to be obscure, but inconsistency never can be right. . . .

One of his greatest, though of his earliest, works is the *Essay on Criticism*, which, if he had written nothing else, would have placed him among the first critics and the first poets, as it exhibits every mode of excellence that can embellish or dignify didactic composition – selection of matter, novelty of arrangement, justness of precept, splendour of illustration, and propriety of digression. I know not whether it be pleasing to consider that he produced this piece at twenty, and never afterwards excelled it. He that delights himself with observing that such powers may be so soon attained cannot but grieve to think that life was ever after at a stand.

To mention the particular beauties of the *Essay* would be unprofitably tedious; but I cannot forbear to observe that the comparison of a student's progress in the sciences with the journey of a traveller in the Alps is, perhaps, the best that English poetry can show. A simile, to be perfect, must both illustrate and ennoble the subject, must show it to the understanding in a clearer view, and display it to the fancy with greater dignity; but either of these qualities may be sufficient to recommend it. In didactic poetry, of which the great purpose is instruction, a simile may be praised which illustrates, though it does not ennoble; in heroics, that may be admitted which ennobles, though it does not illustrate. That it may be complete, it is required to exhibit, independently of its references, a pleasing image; for a simile is said to be a short episode. To this antiquity was so attentive that circumstances were sometimes added which, having no parallels, served only to fill the imagination, and produced what Perrault ludicrously called 'comparisons with a long tail'. In their similes the greatest writers have sometimes failed; the ship-race, compared with the chariot-race, is neither illustrated nor aggrandized; land and water make all the difference. When Apollo, running after Daphne, is likened to a greyhound chasing a hare, there is nothing gained; the ideas of pursuit and flight are too plain to be made plainer, and a god and the daughter of a god are not represented much to their advantage by a hare and dog. The simile of the Alps has no useless parts, yet affords a striking picture by itself; it makes the foregoing position better understood, and enables it to take faster hold on the attention; it assists the apprehension and elevates the fancy.

Let me, likewise, dwell a little on the celebrated paragraph in which it is directed that 'The sound must seem an echo to the sense' – a precept which Pope is allowed to have observed beyond any other English poet.

This notion of representative metre and the desire of discovering frequent adaptations of the sound to the sense have produced, in my opinion, many wild conceits and imaginary beauties. All that can furnish this representation are the sounds of the words considered singly, and the time in which they are pronounced. Every language has some words framed to exhibit the noises which they express, as *thump, rattle, growl, hiss*. These, however, are but few, and the poet cannot make them more, nor can they be of any use but when sound is to be mentioned. The time of pronunciation was, in the dactylic measures of the learned laguages, capable of considerable variety; but that variety could be accommodated only to motion or duration, and different degrees of motion were, perhaps, expressed by verses rapid or slow without much attention of the writer, when the image had full possession of his fancy; but our language having little flexibility, our verses can differ very little in their cadence. The fancied resembl-ances, I fear, arise sometimes merely from the ambiguity of words; there is supposed to be some relation between a *soft* line and a *soft* couch, or between *hard* syllables and *hard* fortune.

Motion, however, may be in some sort exemplified, and yet it may be suspected that in such resemblances the mind often governs the ear, and the sounds are estimated by their meaning. One of the most successful attempts has been to describe the labour of Sisyphus:

With many a weary step, and many a groan,
Up the high hill he heaves a huge round stone;
The huge round stone, resulting with a bound,
Thunders impetuous down, and smokes along the ground.
(*Odyssey*, XI 735–8; Broome)

Who does not perceive the stone to move slowly upward and roll violently back? But set the same numbers to another sense:

While many a merry tale, and many a song,
Cheered the rough road, we wished the rough road long;
The rough road then, returning in a round,
Mocked our impatient steps, for all was fairy ground.

We have now surely lost much of the delay and much of the rapidity.

But, to show how little the greatest master of numbers can fix the principles of representative harmony, it will be sufficient to remark that the poet who tells us that,

When Ajax strives some rock's vast weight to throw,
The line too labours, and the words move slow;
Not so, when swift Camilla scours the plain,
Flies o'er th' unbending corn, and skims along the main,
(*Essay on Criticism*, 370–73)

when he had enjoyed for about thirty years the praise of Camilla's lightness of foot, he tried another experiment upon *sound* and *time*, and produced this memorable triplet:

Waller was smooth: but Dryden taught to join
The varying verse, the full resounding line,
The long majestic march, and energy divine.
(*Imitations of Horace, Epistles*, II i 267–9)

Here are the swiftness of the rapid race and the march of slow-paced majesty exhibited by the same poet in the same sequence of syllables, except that the exact prosodist will find the line of *swiftness* by one time longer than that of *tardiness*.

Beauties of this kind are commonly fancied, and, when real, are technical and nugatory, not to be rejected and not to be solicited.

To the praises which have been accumulated on *The Rape of the Lock* by readers of every class, from the critic to the waiting-maid, it is difficult to make any addition. Of that which is universally allowed to be the most attractive of all ludicrous compositions let it rather be now inquired from what sources the power of pleasing is derived.

Dr Warburton, who excelled in critical perspicacity, has remarked that the preternatural agents are very happily adapted to the purposes of the poem. The heathen deities can no longer gain attention; we should have turned away from a contest between Venus and Diana. The employment of allegorical persons always excites conviction of its own absurdity: they may produce effects but cannot conduct actions – when the phantom is put in motion it dissolves. Thus,

Discord may raise a mutiny but Discord cannot conduct a march nor besiege a town. Pope brought into view a new race of beings, with powers and passions proportionate to their operation. The sylphs and gnomes act at the toilet and the tea-table what more terrific and more powerful phantoms perform on the stormy ocean or the field of battle; they give their proper help and do their proper mischief.

Pope is said, by an objector [Warton], not to have been the inventor of this petty nation, a charge which might with more justice have been brought against the author of the *Iliad*, who doubtless adopted the religious systems of his country – for what is there but the names of his agents which Pope has not invented? Has he not assigned them characters and operations never heard of before? Has he not, at least, given them their first poetical existence? If this is not sufficient to denominate his work original, nothing original ever can be written.

In this work are exhibited, in a very high degree, the two most engaging powers of an author. New things are made familiar, and familiar things are made new. A race of aerial people, never heard of before, is presented to us in a manner so clear and easy that the reader seeks for no further information, but immediately mingles with his new acquaintance, adopts their interests and attends their pursuits, loves a sylph and detests a gnome.

That familiar things are made new every paragraph will prove. The subject of the poem is an event below the common incidents of common life. Nothing real is introduced that is not seen so often as to be no longer regarded, yet the whole detail of a female-day is here brought before us, invested with so much art of decoration that, though nothing is disguised, everything is striking, and we feel all the appetite of curiosity for that from which we have a thousand times turned fastidiously away.

The purpose of the poet is, as he tells us, to laugh at 'the little unguarded follies of the female sex.' It is therefore without justice that Dennis charges *The Rape of the Lock* with the want of a moral, and for that reason sets it below the *Lutrin*, which exposes the pride and discord of the clergy. Perhaps neither Pope nor Boileau has made the world much better than he found it, but, if they had both succeeded, it were easy to tell who would have deserved most from public gratitude. The freaks and humours and spleen and vanity of women, as they embroil families in discord and fill houses with disquiet, do more to obstruct the happiness of life in a year than the ambition of the clergy in many centuries. It has been well observed that the misery of man proceeds not from any single crush of overwhelming evil but from small vexations continually repeated.

It is remarked by Dennis, likewise, that the machinery is superfluous, that, by all the bustle of preternatural operation, the main event is neither hastened nor retarded. To this charge an efficacious answer is not easily made. The sylphs cannot be said to help or to oppose, and it must be allowed to imply some want of art that their power has not been sufficiently intermingled with the action. Other parts may likewise be charged with want of connection: the game at ombre might be spared, but, if the lady had lost her hair while she was intent upon her cards, it might have been inferred that those who are too fond of play will be in danger of neglecting more important interests. Those, perhpas, are faults; but what are such faults to so much excellence?

The Epistle of *Eloisa to Abelard* is one of the most happy productions of human wit; the subject is so judiciously chosen that it would be difficult, in turning over the annals of the world, to find another which so many circumstances concur to recommend. We regularly interest ourselves most in the fortune of those who most deserve our notice. Abelard and Eloise were conspicuous in their days for eminence of merit. The heart naturally loves truth. The adventures and misfortunes of this illustrious pair are known from undisputed history. Their fate does not leave the mind in hopeless dejection; for they both found quiet and consolation in retirement and piety. So new and so affecting is their story that it supersedes invention, and imagination ranges at full liberty without straggling into scenes of fable.

The story, thus skilfully adopted, has been diligently improved. Pope has left nothing behind him which seems more the effect of studious perseverance and laborious revisal. Here is particularly observable the 'curiosa felicitas', a fruitful soil and careful cultivation. Here is no crudeness of sense, nor asperity of language.

The sources from which sentiments which have so much vigour and efficacy have been drawn, are shown to be the mystic writers by the learned author [Warton] of the *Essay on the Life and Writings of Pope*, a book which teaches how the brow of criticism may be smoothed, and how she may be enabled, with all her severity, to attract and to delight.

The train of my disquisition has now conducted me to that poetical wonder, the translation of the *Iliad*, a performance which no age or nation can pretend to equal. . . .

The chief help of Pope in this arduous undertaking was drawn from the versions of Dryden. Virgil had borrowed much of his imagery from Homer, and part of the debt was now paid by his translator. Pope searched the pages of Dryden for happy combinations of heroic diction; but it will not be denied that he added much to what he found. He cultivated our language with so much diligence and art that he has left in his Homer a treasure of poetical elegancies to posterity. His version may be said to have tuned the English tongue; for, since its appearance, no writer, however deficient in other powers, has wanted melody. Such a series of lines, so elaborately corrected, and so sweetly modulated, took possession of the public ear; the vulgar was enamoured of the poem, and the learned wondered at the translation. . . .

Of the *Odyssey*, nothing remains to be observed; the same general praise may be given to both translations, and a particular examination of either would require a large volume. The notes were written by Broome, who endeavoured, not unsuccessfully, to imitate his master.

Of *The Dunciad*, the hint is confessedly taken from Dryden's *MacFlecknoe*; but the plan is so enlarged and diversified as justly to claim the praise of an original, and affords the best specimen that has yet appeared of personal satire ludicrously pompous.

That the design was moral, whatever the author might tell either his readers or himself, I am not convinced. The first motive was the desire of revenging the contempt with which Theobald had treated his Shakespeare, and regaining the honour which he had lost, by crushing his opponent. Theobald was not of bulk enough to fill a poem, and, therefore, it was necessary to find other enemies with other names, at whose expense he might divert the public.

In this design there was petulance and malignity enough; but I cannot think it very criminal. An author places himself uncalled before the tribunal of criticism, and solicits fame at the hazard of disgrace. Dullness or deformity are not culpable in themselves, but may be very justly reproached when they pretend to the honour of wit or the influence of beauty. If bad writers were to pass without reprehension, what should restrain them? *Impune diem consumpserit ingens Telephus*; and upon bad writers only will censure have much effect. The satire which brought Theobald and Moore into contempt dropped impotent from Bentley, like the javelin of Priam.

All truth is valuable, and satirical criticism may be considered as useful when it rectifies error and improves judgement; he that refines the public taste is a public benefactor.

The beauties of this poem are well known; its chief fault is the grossness of its images. Pope and Swift had an unnatural delight in ideas physically impure, such as every other tongue utters with unwillingness, and of which every ear shrinks from the mention.

But even this fault, offensive as it is, may be forgiven for the excellence of other passages; such as the formation and dissolution of Moore, the account of the traveller, the misfortune of the florist, and the crowded thoughts and stately numbers which dignify the concluding paragraph.

The alterations which have been made in *The Dunciad*, not always for the better, require that it should be published, as in the present collection, with all its variations.

The *Essay on Man* was a work of great labour and long consideration, but certainly not the happiest of Pope's performances. The subject is, perhaps, not very proper for poetry, and the poet was not sufficiently master of his subject; metaphysical morality was to him a new study; he was proud of his acquisitions, and, supposing himself master of great secrets, was in haste to teach what he had not learned. Thus he tells us, in the first epistle, that from the nature of the supreme being may be deduced an order of beings such as mankind, because infinite excellence can do only what is best. He finds out that these beings must be 'somewhere'; and that 'all the question is whether man be in a wrong place'. Surely if, according to the poet's Leibnitzian reasoning, we may infer that man ought to be only because he is, we may allow that his place is the right place, because he has it. Supreme wisdom is not less infallible in disposing than in creating. But what is meant by 'somewhere' and 'place', and 'wrong place', it had been vain to ask Pope, who, probably, had never asked himself.

Having exalted himself into the chair of wisdom, he tells us much that every man knows, and much that he does not know himself; that we see but little, and that the order of the universe is beyond our comprehension; an opinion not very uncommon, and that there is a chain of subordinate beings 'from infinite to nothing', of which himself and his readers are equally ignorant. But he gives us one comfort, which, without her help, he supposes unattainable, in the position 'that though we are fools, yet God is wise'.

This essay affords an egregious instance of the predominance of genius, the dazzling splendour of imagery, and the seductive powers of eloquence. Never were penury of knowledge and vulgarity of sentiment so happily disguised. The reader feels his mind full, though he learns nothing; and, when he meets it in its new array, no longer knows the talk of his mother and his nurse. When these wonder-working sounds sink into sense, and the doctrine of the essay, disrobed of its ornaments, is left to the powers of its naked excellence, what shall we discover? That we are, in comparison with our creator, very weak and ignorant; that we do not uphold the chain of existence; and that we could not make one another with more skill than we are made. We may learn yet more: that the arts of human life were copied from the instinctive operations of other animals; that if the world be made for man, it may be said that man was made for geese. To these profound principles of natural knowledge are added some moral instructions equally new; that self-interest, well understood, will produce social concord; that men are mutual gainers by mutual benefits; that evil is sometimes balanced by good; that human advantages are unstable and fallacious, of uncertain duration and doubtful effect; that our true honour is, not to have a great part, but to act it well; that virtue only is our own; and that happiness is always in our power.

Surely a man of no very comprehensive search may venture to say that he has heard all this before; but it was never till now recommended by such a blaze of embellishment, or such sweetness of melody. The vigorous contraction of some thoughts, the luxuriant amplification of others, the incidental illustrations, and sometimes the dignity, sometimes the softness, of the verses, enchain philosophy, suspend criticism, and oppress judgement by overpowering pleasure.

This is true of many paragraphs; yet if I had undertaken to exemplify Pope's felicity of composition before a rigid critic, I should not select the *Essay on Man*; for it contains more lines unsuccessfully laboured, more harshness of diction, more thoughts imperfectly expressed, more levity without elegance, and more heaviness without strength, than will easily be found in all his other works.

The *Characters of Men* and *Women* are the product of diligent speculation upon human life: much labour has been bestowed upon them, and Pope very seldom laboured in vain. That his excellence may be properly estimated, I recommend a comparison of his *Characters of Women* with Boileau's satire; it will then be seen with how much more perspicacity female nature is investigated, and female excellence selected; and he surely is no mean writer to whom Boileau shall be found inferior. The *Characters of Men*, however, are written with more, if not with deeper, thought, and exhibit many passages exquisitely beautiful. The Gem and the Flower will not easily be equalled. In the women's part are some defects: the character of Atossa is not so neatly finished as that of Clodio, and some of the female characters may be found, perhaps, more frequently among men. What is said of Philomedé was true of Prior.

In the Epistles to Lord Bathurst and Lord Burlington, Dr Warburton has endeavoured to find a train of thought which was never in the writer's head, and, to support his hypothesis, has printed that first which was published last. In one, the most valuable passage is, perhaps, the eulogy on good sense; and the other, the end of the Duke of Buckingham.

The *Epistle to Arbuthnot*, now arbitrarily called the *Prologue to the Satires*, is a performance consisting, as it seems, of many fragments wrought into one design, which, by this union of scattered beauties, contains more striking paragraphs than could probably, have been brought together into an occasional work. As there is no stronger motive to exertion than self-defence, no part has more elegance, spirit or dignity than the poet's vindication of his own character. The meanest passage is the satire upon Sporus.

Of the two poems which derived their names from the year, and which are called the *Epilogue to the Satires*, it was very justly remarked by Savage that the second was, in the whole, more strongly conceived, and more equally supported, but that it had no single passages equal to the contention in the first for the dignity of Vice and the celebration of the triumph of Corruption.

The *Imitations of Horace* seem to have been written as relaxations of his genius. This employment became his favourite by its facility; the plan was ready to his hand, and nothing was required but to accommodate, as he could, the sentiments of an old author to recent facts or familiar images. But what is easy is seldom excellent; such imitations cannot give pleasure to common readers; the man of learning may be sometimes surprised and delighted by an unexpected parallel, but the comparison requires knowledge of the original, which will likewise often detect strained applications. Between Roman images and English manners there will be an irreconcilable dissimilitude, and the work will be generally uncouth and party-coloured — neither original nor translated, neither ancient nor modern.

Pope had, in proportions very nicely adjusted to each other, all the qualities that constitute genius. He had invention, by which new trains of events are formed, and new scenes of imagery displayed, as in *The Rape of the Lock*; and by which extrinsic and adventitious embellishments and illustrations are connected with a known subject, as in the *Essay on Criticism*. He had imagination, which strongly impresses on the writer's mind, and enables him to convey to the reader, the various forms of nature, incidents of life, and energies of passion, as in his *Eloisa, Windsor Forest*, and *Ethic Epistles*. He had judgement, which selects from life or nature what the present purpose requires, and, by separating the essence of things from its concomitants, often makes the representation more powerful than the reality; and he had colours of language always before him, ready to decorate his matter with every grace of elegant expression, as when he accommodates his diction to the wonderful multiplicity of Homer's sentiments and descriptions.

Poetical expression includes sound as well as meaning; 'Music,' says Dryden, 'is inarticulate poetry'. Among the excellencies of Pope, therefore, must be mentioned the melody of his metre. By perusing the works of Dryden, he discovered the most perfect fabric of English verse and habituated himself to that only which he found the best; in consequence of which restraint, his poetry has been censured as too uniformly musical, and as glutting the ear with unvaried sweetness. I suspect this objection to be the cant of those who judge by principles rather than perception; and who would even themselves have less pleasure in his works if he had tried to relieve attention by studied discords, or affected to break his lines and vary his pauses.

But, though he was thus careful of his versification, he did not oppress his powers with superfluous rigour. He seems to have thought, with Boileau, that the practice of writing might be refined till the difficulty should overbalance the advantage. The construction of his language is not always strictly grammatical; with those rhymes which prescription had conjoined he contented himself, without regard to Swift's remonstrances, though there was no striking consonance; nor was he very careful to vary his terminations, or to refuse admission, at a small distance, to the same rhymes.

To Swift's edict for the exclusion of alexandrines and triplets, he paid little regard; he admitted them, but, in the opinion of Fenton, too rarely; he uses them more liberally in his translation than his poems.

He has a few double rhymes; and always, I think, unsuccessfully, except once in *The Rape of the Lock*.

Expletives he very early rejected from his verses; but he now and then admits an epithet rather commodious than important. Each of the six first lines of the *Iliad* might lose two syllables with very little diminution of the meaning; and sometimes, after all his art and labour, one verse seems to be made for the sake of another. In his latter productions the diction is sometimes vitiated by French idoms, with which Bolingbroke had, perhaps, infected him.

I have been told that the couplet by which he declared his own ear to be most gratified, was this:

Lo! where Maeotis sleeps, and hardly flows
The freezing Tanais through a waste of snows.
(*The Dunciad*, III 87–8)

But the reason of this preference I cannot discover.

It is remarked by Watts that there is scarcely a happy combination of words, or a phrase poetically elegant, in the English language which Pope has not inserted into his version of Homer. How he obtained possession of so many beauties of speech it were desirable to know. That he gleaned from authors, obscure as well as eminent what he thought brilliant or useful and preserved it all in a regular collection, is not unlikely. When, in his last years, Hall's *Satires* were shown him, he wished that he had seen them sooner.

New sentiments, and new images, others may produce; but to attempt any farther improvement of versification will be dangerous. Art and diligence have now done their best, and what shall be added will be the effort of tedious toil and needless curiosity.

After all this, it is surely, superfluous to answer the question that has once been asked [by Warton] whether Pope was a poet, otherwise than by asking, in return, if Pope be not a poet, where is poetry to be found? To circumscribe poetry by a definition will only show the narrowness of the definer, though a definition which shall exclude Pope will not easily be made. Let us look round upon the present time and back upon the past; let us inquire to whom the voice of mankind has decreed the wreath of poetry; let their productions be examined and their claims stated, and the pretensions of Pope will be no more disputed. Had he given the world only his version, the name of poet must have been allowed him. If the writer of the *Iliad* were to class his successors, he would assign a very high place to his translator, without requiring any other evidence of genius.

William Cowper

from a letter to William Unwin   5 January 1782

In the last [*Monthly*] *Review*, I mean in the last but one, I saw Johnson's critique upon Prior and Pope. I am bound to acquiesce in his opinion of the latter, because it has always been my own. I could never agree with those who preferred him to Dryden – nor with others (I have known such, and persons of taste and discernment too) who could not allow him to be a poet at all. He was certainly a mechanical maker of verses, and in every line he ever wrote we see indubitable marks of the most indefatigable industry and labour. Writers who find it necessary to make such strenuous and painful exertions are generally as phlegmatic as they are correct, but Pope was in this respect exempted from the common lot of authors of that class. With the unwearied application of a plodding Flemish painter, who draws a shrimp with the most minute exactness, he had all the genius of one of the first masters.

Vicesimus Knox

from *Essays, Moral and Literary*, no. 129 1782

I think it is not difficult to perceive that the admirers of English poetry are divided into two parties. The objects of their love are perhaps of equal beauty, though they greatly differ in their air, their dress, and the turn of their features and their complexion. On one side are the lovers and imitators of Spenser and Milton; and on the other those of Dryden, Boileau and Pope.

Now it happens, unfortunately, that those who are in love with one of these forms are sometimes so blind to the charms of the other as to dispute their existence. The author [Joseph Warton] of the *Essay on Pope*, who is himself a very agreeable poet and of what I call the old school of English poetry, seems to deny the justice of Mr Pope's claim to the title of a true poet and to appropriate to him the subordinate character of a satirical versifier. On the other hand, the authors of the *Traveller* [Goldsmith] and the *Lives of the English Poets* [Johnson] hesitate not to strip the laurels from the brow of the lyric Gray .... I remember to have heard Goldsmith converse, when I was young, on several subjects of literature and make some oblique and severe reflections on the fashionable poetry. I became a convert to his opinion, because I revered his authority. I took up the odes of Gray with unfavourable prepossessions ... [but now] I am not ashamed to retract my former opinion.

Hugh Blair

from *Lectures on Rhetoric and Belles Lettres* 1783

When Mr Pope [*Eloisa to Abelard*] says,

All then is full, possessing and possessed;
No craving void left aching in the brest.
(93–4)

A void may metaphorically be said to *crave*; but can a void be said to *ache*?
(Lecture XV: *Metaphor*)

There is another sort of antithesis, the beauty of which consists in surprising us by the unexpected contrast of things which it brings together. Much wit may be shown in this; but it belongs wholly to pieces of professed wit and humour, and can find no place in grave compositions. Mr Pope, who is remarkably fond of antithesis, is often happy in this use of the figure. So in his *Rape of the Lock* [II 105–10]:

Whether the nymph shall break Diana's law,
Or some frail china jar receive a flaw;
Or stain her honour, or her new brocade,
Forget her prayers or miss a masquerade;
Or lose her heart or necklace at a ball,
Or whether Heaven has doomed that Shock must fall.
(Lecture XVII: *Antithesis*)

. . . In another passage he [Virgil, *Eclogue* III 65] makes a shepherdess throw an apple at her lover:

Tum fugit ad salices et se cupit ante videri.

This is *naïve*, as the French express it, and perfectly suited to pastoral manners. Mr Pope wanted to imitate this passage – and, as he thought, to improve upon it. He does it thus:

The sprightly Sylvia trips along the green;
She runs, but hopes she does not run unseen;
While a kind glance at her pursuer flies,
How much at variance are her feet and eyes!
(*Pastorals*, I 57–60)

This falls far short of Virgil; the natural and pleasing simplicity of the description is destroyed by the quaint and affected turn in the last line ('How much at variance are her feet and eyes!').
(Lecture XXXIX: *Pastoral Poetry*)

Few poets had more wit and at the same time more judgement to direct the proper employment of that wit. . . . His paintings of characters are natural and lively in a high degree, and never was any writer so happy in that concise spirited style which gives animation to satires and epistles. We are never so sensible of the good effects of rhyme in English verse as in reading these parts of his works. We see it adding to the style an elevation which otherwise it could not have possessed, while at the same time he manages it so artfully that it never appears in the least to encumber him but on the contrary serves to increase the liveliness of his manner.

(Lecture XL: *Didactic Poetry*)

Thomas Warton

from the Preface to his edition of Milton's Minor Poems   1785

My father used to relate that when he once at Magdalen College, Oxford, mentioned in high terms this volume [Milton's *Poems*, 1645] to Mr Digby, the intimate friend of Pope, Mr Digby expressed much surprise that he had never heard Pope speak of them, went home and immediately gave them an attentive reading – and asked Pope if he knew anything of this hidden treasure. Pope availed himself of the question, and accordingly we find him soon afterwards sprinkling his *Eloisa to Abelard* with epithets and phrases of a new form and sound, pilfered from *Comus* and the *Penseroso*. It is a phenomenon in the history of English poetry that Pope, a poet not of Milton's pedigree, should be their first copier.

[In the mid-eighteenth century] . . . A visible revolution succeeded in the general cast and character of the national composition. Our versification contracted a new colouring, a new structure and phraseology, and the school of Milton rose in emulation of the school of Pope.

John Hookham Frere

from the *Microcosm*, no. 9
29 January 1787

Pope has fully availed himself of the dear-bought experience of all
who went before him; there is perhaps no poet more entirely free
from this failing. I shall however only cite one instance in which he
may seem to have carried his regard for simplicity so far as to show
himself guilty of inaccuracy and inattention.

The hungry judges soon the sentence sign,
And wretches hang that jurymen may dine.
(*The Rape of the Lock*, III 21–2)

That judges in England never *sign* a sentence is well known, and
hunger, whatever effect it may have had on the jurymen of ancient
days, with those of modern times seems to operate rather as an
incitement to mercy. 'Cliveden's proud alcove' (*Moral Essay* III, 307)
has not at present and probably never had any existence. But the
fault, if any there is, seems rather that of the language than that of the
poet – or perhaps after all it was mere penury of rhyme and a distress
similar to that which made him in another place hunt his poor
dab-chick into a *copse*, where it was never seen but in *The Dunciad*
[I 59].

Henry Headley

from *Select Beauties of Ancient English Poetry* 1787

Pope, Atterbury and Swift, who headed one party, Addison, Congreve
and Steele who led the other in Queen Anne's reign, with their
respective minor adherents, in the general tenor of their writings
addressed the judgement rather than the fancy, and with a Parnassian
sneer peculiar to themselves either neglected or hunted down their
poetical predecessors . . . . Satire and morality they carried to perfection, but the higher regions of poesy received neither extension nor

embellishments from their hands . . . . Compound epithets, which are the life of a language, and in which our own is far from being deficient, they almost totally discarded.

Joseph Weston

from *An Essay on the Superiority of Dryden's Versification over that of Pope and of the Moderns*, prefixed to his translation of John Morfitt's *Philotoxi-Ardenae, The Woodmen of Arden: A Latin Poem* 1788.

The poetry of Pope, though less enriched by classical knowledge and less illumined by vivid imagination, appears, however, at first sight, to greater advantage than that of Dryden, as it is certainly more elaborately correct and more mechanically regular – more delicately polished and more systematically dignified. But are these really advantages? Let us examine.

Does the skilful painter bring all his figures forward on the canvas, and bestow the last hand upon every part of the picture? Does the musician cloy the ear with an eternal succession of harmonious sounds, uncontrasted by the dire but necessary discords? . . . Why then must Poetry adopt a preposterous plan of *equalization* which her sister Muses reject with scorn – and aspire to an imaginary perfection alike unknown to nature and to art.

The question seems to lie in so small a compass, and to be so easy of determination, that one feels inclined to inquire how so absurd a notion could possibly gain a footing and maintain its ground in an age so polished and enlightened as to have acquired the title of Augustan. Great events, 'tis certain, arise sometimes from very trivial causes; but never surely was so important a revolution in the Parnassian realms produced by means so utterly contemptible!

When Dryden's sun was set . . . Pope was beginning to dawn on the poetical hemisphere. . . . among others one Walsh undertook to usher this rising genius into the world: he did more; he affected to point out a way by which his pupil should surpass all who had gone before him. 'Mr Pope,' said he, 'there is one path as yet entirely untrodden – the path of *correctness*: Dryden was a great poet – but he had not leisure to be correct. Seize the glorious opportunity; supply the deficiency, and be immortal!'

In an evil hour did the ambitious young bard hearken to the fatal advice of 'knowing Walsh' (as he somewhere calls him [Epistle to Arbuthnot 136]); and, hoping to supply this supposed deficiency, he began to labour and stiffen and polish and refine – till, having discarded whatever seemed loose or languid or harsh or prosaic, his verse flowed in one equal smooth, mellifluous stream, marked by an almost total want of that variety of pause, accent, cadence and diction so eminently conspicuous in his incomparable predecessor and so absolutely essential to the harmony of true poetry.

The thought is so seldom suffered to stray beyond the bounds of the couplet and so frequently wire-drawn merely to end with it – one part of a line so exactly reflects the other – and there is such a paucity of triplets and of alexandrines (the break too in the latter so regularly at the sixth syllable) – that even the most ingenious allusions, the most striking, beautiful and graceful imagery, the most perspicuous and pointed good sense, and the most elegant and nervous expression – with all their powers united – find it difficult to render the tiresome uniformity of his versification supportable.

To the officious interposition of this same Walsh, then, we are indebted for the contamination of the Heliconian fountain for near a century! *Risum teneatis*?[1]

James Boswell

from *The Life of Samuel Johnson, LL.D.*   1791

It is said that Mr Pope expressed himself concerning it [Johnson's Latin version of Pope's *Messiah*, performed as an undergraduate exercise at Oxford] in terms of strong approbation. Dr Taylor told me that it was first printed for old Mr Johnson, without the knowledge of his son, who was very angry when he heard of it. A *Miscellany of Poems*, collected by a person of the name of Husbands, was published at Oxford in 1731. In that *Miscellany*, Johnson's translation

1 'A bit absurd!' (Horace). [Ed.]

of the *Messiah* appeared, with this modest motto from Scaliger's *Poetics*, 'Ex alieno ingenio poeta, ex suo tantum versificator.' (1728)

Pope, who then filled the poetical throne without a rival, it may reasonably be presumed must have been particularly struck by the sudden appearance of such a poet [Johnson, with his poem *London*]; and to his credit let it be remembered that his feelings and conduct on the occasion were candid and liberal. He requested Mr Richardson, son of the painter, to endeavour to find out who this new author was. Mr Richardson, after some inquiry, having informed him that he had discovered only that his name was Johnson, and that he was some obscure man, Pope said, 'He will soon be *déterré* [unearthed]'. (1738)

After dinner our conversation first turned upon Pope. Johnson said his characters of men were admirably drawn, those of women not so well. He repeated to us, in his forcible, melodious manner, the concluding lines of *The Dunciad*. While he was talking loudly in praise of those lines, one of the company ventured to say, 'Too fine for such a poem – a poem on what?' JOHNSON (with a disdainful look): 'Why, on *dunces*. It was worth while being a dunce then. Ah, sir, hadst *thou* lived in those days! It is not worth while being a dunce now, when there are no wits.' Bickerstaff observed, as a peculiar circumstance, that Pope's fame was higher when he was alive than it was then. Johnson said his *Pastorals* were poor things, though the versification was fine. He told us, with high satisfaction, the anecdote of Pope's inquiring who was the author of his *London*, and saying he will be soon *déterré*. He observed that in Dryden's poetry there were passages drawn from a profundity which Pope could never reach. He repeated some fine lines on love, by the former, which I have now forgotten, and gave great applause to the character of Zimri. Goldsmith said that Pope's character of Addison showed a deep knowledge of the human heart. (1769).

I remember but little of our conversation. I mentioned Shenstone's saying of Pope that he had the art of condensing sense more than anybody. Dr Johnson said, 'It is not true, sir. There is more sense in a line of Cowley than in a page' (or a sentence, or ten lines – I am not quite certain of the very phrase) 'of Pope.' (1778)

We talked of Pope. JOHNSON: 'He wrote his *Dunciad* for fame. That was his primary motive. Had it not been for that, the dunces might have railed against him till they were weary, without his troubling himself about them. He delighted to vex them, no doubt; but he had more delight in seeing how well he could vex them.' (1775)

RAMSAY: 'I am old enough[1] to have been a contemporary of Pope. His poetry was highly admired in his life-time, more a great deal than after his death.' JOHNSON: 'Sir, it has not been less admired since his death; no authors ever had so much fame in their own life-time as Pope and Voltaire; and Pope's poetry has been as much admired since his death as during his life. It has only not been as much talked of; but that is owing to its being now more distant, and people having other writings to talk of. Virgil is less talked of than Pope, and Homer is less talked of than Virgil; but they are not less admired. We must read what the world reads at the moment.' (1778)

Mrs Thrale told us that a curious clergyman of our acquaintance had discovered a licentious stanza, which Pope had originally in his 'Universal Prayer', before the stanza,

What conscience dictates to be done,
  Or warns me not to do, *etc.*

It was this:

Can sins of moment claim the rod
  Of everlasting fires?
And that offend great nature's God
  Which nature's self inspires?

and that Dr Johnson observed, 'it had been borrowed from Guarini.' There are, indeed, in *Pastor Fido* many such flimsy superficial reasonings as that in the last two lines of this stanza.

1 Mr Ramsay was about Johnson's age.

BOSWELL: 'In that stanza of Pope's, "*rod of fires*" is certainly a bad metaphor.' MRS THRALE: 'And "sins of *moment*" is a faulty expression; for its true import is *momentous*, which cannot be intended.' JOHNSON: 'It must have been written "*of moments*". Of *moment* is *momentous*; of *moments*, *momentary*. I warrant you, however, Pope wrote this stanza, and some friend struck it out. Boileau wrote some such thing, and Arnaud struck it out, saying "*Vous gagnerez deux ou trois impies, et perdrez je ne sçais combien d'honnêtes gens.*" These fellows want to say a daring thing, and don't know how to go about it. Mere poets know no more of fundamental principles than –.' Here he was interrupted somehow. Mrs Thrale mentioned Dryden. JOHNSON: 'He puzzled himself about predestination. How foolish was it in Pope to give all his friendship to lords, who thought they honoured him by being with him – and to choose such lords as Burlington, and Cobham, and Bolingbroke! Bathurst was negative, a pleasing man; and I have heard no ill of Marchmont. And then always saying, "I do not value you for being a lord;" which was a sure proof he did.' (1778)

I went home with him, and we had a long quiet conversation.

I read him a letter from Dr Hugh Blair concerning Pope (in writing whose life he was now employed), which I shall insert as a literary curiosity.[1]

1 The Rev. Dr Law, Bishop of Carlisle, in the preface to his valuable edition of Archbishop King's *Essay on the Origin of Evil*, mentions that the principles maintained in it had been adopted by Pope in his *Essay on Man*; and adds, 'The fact, notwithstanding such denial (Bishop Warburton's), might have been strictly verified by an unexceptionable testimony, viz. that of the late Lord Bathurst, who saw the very same system of the το βελτιον (taken from the Archbishop) in Lord Bolingbroke's own hand, lying before Mr Pope, while he was composing his *Essay*.' This is respectable evidence: but that of Dr Blair is more direct from the fountain-head, as well as more full. Let me add to it that of Dr Joseph Warton: 'The late Lord Bathurst repeatedly assured me that he had read the whole scheme of the *Essay on Man*, in the handwriting of Bolingbroke, and drawn up in a series of propositions, which Pope was to versify and illustrate.' – *Essay on the Genius and Writings of Pope*, vol. 2, p. 62.

Dr Blair to Mr Boswell

Broughton Park, 21 September 1779

Dear Sir, – In the year 1763, being at London, I was carried by Dr John Blair, Prebendary of Westminster, to dine at old Lord Bathurst's, where we found the late Mr Mallet, Sir James Porter, who had been ambassador at Constantinople, the late Dr Macaulay, and two or three more. The conversation turning on Mr Pope, Lord Bathurst told us that the *Essay on Man* was originally composed by Lord Bolingbroke in prose; and that Mr Pope did no more that put into it verse; that he had read Lord Bolingbroke's manuscript in his own handwriting; and remembered well that he was at a loss whether most to admire the elegance of Lord Bolingbroke's prose or the beauty of Mr Pope's verse.

When Lord Bathurst told this, Mr Mallet bade me attend, and remember this remarkable piece of information; as, by the course of nature, I might survive his lordship, and be a witness of his having said so. The conversation was indeed too remarkable to be forgotten. A few days after, meeting with you, who were then also at London, you will remember that I mentioned to you what had passed on this subject; as I was much struck with this anecdote. But what ascertains my recollection of it, beyond doubt, is that, being accustomed to keep a journal of what passed when I was at London, which I wrote out every evening, I find the particulars of the above information, just as I have now given them, distinctly marked; and am thence enabled to fix this conversation to have passed on Friday, the 22nd of April 1763.

I remember also distinctly (though I have not for this the authority of my journal) that the conversation going on concerning Mr Pope, I took notice of a report which had been sometimes propagated that he did not understand Greek. Lord Bathurst said to me that he knew that to be false; for that part of the *Iliad* was translated by Mr Pope in his house in the country; and that in the morning when they assembled at breakfast, Mr Pope used frequently to repeat, with great rapture, the Greek lines which he had been translating, and then to give them his version of them, and to compare them together.

If these circumstances can be of any use to Dr Johnson, you have my full liberty to give them to him. I beg you will, at the same time, present to him my most respectful compliments, with best wishes for his success and fame in all his literary undertakings. I am, with great respect, my dearest sir, your most affectionate and obliged humble servant,

Hugh Blair

JOHNSON: 'Depend upon it, sir, this is too strongly stated. Pope may have had from Bolingbroke the philosophic *stamina* of his *Essay*; and admitting this to be true, Lord Bathurst did not intentionally falsify. But the thing is not true in the latitude that Blair seems to imagine; we are sure that the poetical imagery, which makes a great part of the poem, was Pope's own. It is amazing, sir, what deviations there are from precise truth in the account which is given of almost everything'. (1779)

The 'Life of Pope' was written by Johnson *con amore*, both from the early possession which that writer had taken of his mind, and from the pleasure which he must have felt in for ever silencing all attempts to lessen his poetical fame by demonstrating his excellence, and pronouncing the following triumphant eulogium:

After all this, it is, surely, superfluous to answer the question that has once been asked, whether Pope was a poet? otherwise than by asking, in return, if Pope be not a poet, where is poetry to be found? To circumscribe poetry by a definition will only show the narrowness of the definer, though a definition which shall exclude Pope will not easily be made. Let us look round upon the present time, and back upon the past; let us inquire to whom the voice of mankind has decreed the wreath of poetry; let their productions be examined, and their claims stated, and the pretensions of Pope will be no more disputed.

I remember once to have heard Johnson say, 'Sir, a thousand years may elapse before there shall appear another man with a power of versification equal to that of Pope.' That power must undoubtedly be allowed its due share in enhancing the value of his captivating composition. (1781)

Alexander Tytler, Lord Woodhouselee

from *Essay on the Principles of Translation*   1791

A striking example . . . is the translation of that picture in the end of the eighth book of the *Iliad*, which Eustathius [author of Greek commentaries on Homer *c*. 1150] esteemed the finest night-piece that could be found in poetry:

'As when the resplendent moon appears in the serene canopy of the heavens, surrounded with beautiful stars, when every breath of air is hushed, when the high watch-towers, the hills and woods are distinctly seen; when the sky appears to open to the sight in all its boundless extent; and when the shepherd's heart is delighted within him.' How nobly is this picture raised and improved by Mr Pope!

As when the moon refulgent lamp of night,
O'er heaven's clear azure spreads her sacred light,
When not a breath disturbs the deep serene,
And not a cloud o'ercasts the solemn scene;
Around her throne the vivid planets roll,
And stars unnumbered gild the glowing pole,
O'er the dark trees a yellower verdure shed,
And tip with silver every mountain's head;
Then shine the vales, the rocks in prospect rise,
A flood of glory bursts from all the skies.
The conscious swains, rejoicing in the sight,
Eye the blue vault and bless the useful light.
So many flames before proud Ilion blaze,
And lighten glimmering Xanthus with their rays.

The long reflections of the distant fires
Gleam on the walls and tremble on the spires.
A thousand piles the dusky horrors gild,
And shoot a shady lustre o'er the field.
Full fifty guards each flaming pile attend,
Whose umbered arms by fits thick flashes send.
Loud neigh the coursers o'er their heaps of corn,
And ardent warriors wait the rising morn.
(*Iliad* VIII 687–708)

Part Two The Continuing Debate

Introduction

The debate over Pope's place in the hierarchy of English poets reached its peak in the Romantic period. As *the* Augustan poet, he became 'the pivot of a dispute in taste' – as Shelley (one of the few poets who took no part in the controversy) remarked in a letter to Byron of 4 May 1821. Warton's estimate of Pope now found new advocates and, more important, a new 'reading public' which was prepared to accept it in preference to Dr Johnson's. Leigh Hunt – one of the more perceptive critics of his time – traced three main causes of the revolution in taste in his preface to a volume of poems with the characteristic title *Foliage*, published in 1818:

The downfall of the French school of poetry has of late been increasing in rapidity; its cold and artificial compositions have given way, like so many fantastic figures of snow; and imagination breathes again in a more green and genial time. . . .

This has undoubtedly been owing, in the first instance, to the political convulsions of the world, which shook up the minds of men, and rendered them too active and speculative to be satisfied with their commonplaces. A second cause was the revived inclination for our older and great school of poetry, chiefly produced, I have no doubt, by the commentators on Shakespeare, though they were certainly not aware what fine countries they were laying open. The third, and not the least, was the accession of a new school of poetry itself, of which Wordsworth has justly the reputation of being the most prominent ornament, but whose inner priest of the temple perhaps was Coleridge – a man who has been the real oracle of the time in more than one respect.

Hunt goes on to summarize the critical criteria of the new school: 'A sensitiveness to the beauty of the external world, to the unsophisticated impulses of our nature, and above all, imagination, or the power to see, with verisimilitude, what others do not . . . .'

It was because he felt they lacked these qualities that Hazlitt classified Dryden and Pope as 'the great masters of the artificial style of poetry in our language'.

The growing appreciation of the Elizabethans on one hand, and of Wordsworth and Coleridge on the other, gave rise to a new view of literary history. As René Wellek has pointed out, Johnson tended to see the course of English literature as 'one continuous effort towards the establishment of one timeless norm, that of Pope and Dryden'. But with the Romantic revival the Augustan age came to be regarded as a sort of interregnum – a period of French usurpation – between the 'golden age' of the Elizabethans and the reflected glory of their legitimate, if sometimes degenerate, successors of the new school. This is essentially the view put forward by Francis Jeffrey, the influential editor of the *Edinburgh Review*, in his article on John Ford (August 1811). Jeffrey's opinion is especially noteworthy in that he was then, to say the least, no ardent admirer of the Lake Poets. Here was Wordsworth's most indefatigable critic admitting that his poetry belonged to a higher class than Pope's. Jeffrey and his contemporaries did not, however, neglect the Pre-Romantic contribution to the overthrow of the 'school of Pope'. For instance Thomas Love Peacock – in his brilliant and provocative essay 'The Four Ages of Poetry' (1820) – treats the 'return to nature' as part of the general breakdown of intellectual authority in the eighteenth century:

The contemporaries of Gray and Cowper were deep and elaborate thinkers. The subtle scepticism of Hume, the solemn irony of Gibbon, the daring paradoxes of Rousseau, and the biting ridicule of Voltaire, directed the energies of four extra-ordinary minds to shake every portion of the reign of authority. Enquiry was roused, the activity of intellect was excited, and poetry came in for its share of the general result. The changes had been rung on lovely maid and sylvan shade, summer heat

and green retreat, waving trees and sighing breeze, gentle swains
and amorous pains, by versifiers who took them on trust, as
meaning something very soft and tender, without much
caring what: but with this general activity of intellect came a
necessity for even poets to appear to know something of what
they professed to talk of. Thomson and Cowper looked at the
trees and hills which so many ingenious gentlemen had rhymed
about so long without looking at them at all, and the effect
of the operation on poetry was like the discovery of a new
world.

A refusal to take things on trust was, of course, the very basis of
Wordsworth's objection to the poetic diction of the eighteenth
century.

Wordsworth, Coleridge, and Southey all regarded Pope's
translation of Homer as 'the main source of our pseudo-poetic
diction' (to use Coleridge's phrase). The trouble with 'poetic
diction' – as described by Wordsworth in the Preface (1800) and
Appendix (1802) to *Lyrical Ballads* – was that it inevitably betrayed
the poet into false description by focusing his attention on words
rather than things. Speaking of his own style, Wordsworth says,
'I have at all times endeavoured to look steadily at my subject'.
Coleridge, in one of his lectures, appears to have been the first to
point out Pope's failure to look steadily at his subject in rendering
the celebrated 'moonlight scene' in the eighth book of the *Iliad*.
Southey followed with a caustic analysis of the passage in the
Quarterly Review, and Wordsworth went so far as to declare that
'a blind man, in the habit of attending accurately to descriptions
casually dropped from the lips of those around him, might easily
depict these appearances with more truth'. Half a century later
Matthew Arnold made the same point in *On Translating Homer*
(1861). 'Homer', he says, quoting Wordsworth, 'invariably
composes "with his eye on the object"', whether the object be a

moral or a material one: Pope composes with his eye on his style, into which he translates his object, whatever it is.'

The reaction against Pope's style was due, in large measure, to the ease and frequency with which it was imitated. The *locus classicus* is Macaulay's depreciation of the heroic couplet in his essay on Addison (1843). Leigh Hunt took a more direct line of attack in a long note to *The Feast of the Poets* (1814). Simply by marking the caesura with a dash in two celebrated passages, he was able to provide a graphic illustration (later improved on by George Saintsbury) of the monotony of Pope's 'cuckoo-song' versification. Hunt's later comment on the 'see-saw' motion of Pope's antithetically balanced lines was perhaps suggested by Pope's own triplet on Hervey, in the character of Sporus:

His wit all see-saw between *that* and *this*,
Now high, now low, now Master up, now Miss,
And he himself one vile antithesis.

The weakness of this, as of most nineteenth-century criticism of the Popian couplet – Matthew Arnold's *On Translating Homer* is a notable exception – lies in its failure to relate style to subject.

It was, after all, mainly on account of the subject-matter of his most original poems that Pope was relegated to a lower order of poets. The leading critic from this point of view was the Reverend William Lisle Bowles, a minor poet who edited Pope's *Works* in 1806. For the most part Bowles's criticism follows the lines laid down by Warton, though its general tone is less sympathetic and more polemical. Their most significant difference of opinion occurs over *The Rape of the Lock*. Whereas Warton had regarded this as the greatest of Pope's poems ('in which he displayed more imagination than in all his other works taken together'), Bowles consigned it to 'an inferior province of poetry' because it dealt with 'artificial life' and 'local manners'. According to Bowles's 'invariable principles of poetry', Pope's description of the game of ombre was *necessarily* less poetical than Cowper's description of a morning walk. The question whether Nature or Art provided the best materials for poetry was debated *ad nauseam* in the 'Pope controversy' of 1819–26 – which Bowles won after a fashion at the time merely by outlasting all his opponents (Thomas Campbell, Isaac D'Israeli, Byron, and others). Today the winner is more likely to be thought Byron, because Byron interests us so much more than the others – and because his critical prose style is so good:

Away, then with this cant about nature, and 'invariable prin-ciples of poetry'! A great artist will make a block of stone as sublime as a mountain, and a good poet can imbue a pack of cards with more poetry than inhabits the forests of America.

What is not always noticed is that Byron's doctrine is here the opposite of the neo-classic one (which was that an epic, a tragedy or a 'great óde' like Pindar's was alone capable of sublimity). And Bowles, the 'Romantic', Coleridge's schoolboy model, was in fact proposing to reintroduce the genres.

Most Victorian criticism of Pope was coloured to some extent by the critic's view – usually unfavourable – of his personal character. De Quincey and Leslie Stephen, for example, both attributed the weaknesses of Pope's poetry to the defects of his character and an incapacity for sustained thought. According to Macaulay, Pope was 'all stiletto and mask' – an opinion that was confirmed in the 1850s by the literary detective-work of Charles Wentworth Dilke, which revealed the full extent of Pope's duplicity over the publication of his correspondence. Leslie Stephen provides a nice illustration of the Victorian attitude to Dilke's discoveries in his essay 'Pope as a Moralist' (1873): 'Genteel equivocation is not one of the Christian graces; and a gentleman convicted at the present day of practices comparable to those in which Pope indulged so freely might find it expedient to take his name off the books of any respectable club.' Pope's poetry tended to fall under the same cloud as his moral character, sincerity being one of the tests of a poet as well as of a gentleman.

In 1880 Matthew Arnold reopened the old question of Pope's poetic status with his memorable pronouncement that 'Dryden and Pope are not classics of our poetry, they are classics of our prose.' There was, however, no storm of protest. The general feeling seems to have been that the question was no longer worth asking, that everything had now been said. For almost half a century Pope attracted little attention outside the literary histories, and Arnold's dictum went virtually unchallenged.

Robert Southey

from the Preface to *Joan of Arc* 1795

Homer is, indeed, the best of poets, for he is at once dignified and simple; but Pope has disguised him in fop-finery, and Cowper has stripped him naked.

William Wordsworth

from the Appendix to *Lyrical Ballads* 1802

Perhaps in no way, by positive example, could more easily be given a notion of what I mean by the phrase *poetic diction* than by referring to a comparison between the metrical paraphrase which we have of passages in the Old and New Testament, and those passages as they exist in our common translation. See Pope's *Messiah* throughout. . . .

William Lisle Bowles

from 'Memoirs of the Life and Writings of Pope', in his edition of *The Works of Alexander Pope* 1806 (see p. 491)

The anger of Swift was general; the spleen of Pope particular: one was disgusted with the *nature of man*; the other piqued and offended by *individuals*, confining his animosity to the small circle of those who offended him. Swift, politically speaking, was disappointed that the high post in society to which, from his talents, he thought himself entitled to aspire was early wrested from the grasp of his ambition. Pope, attaining a situation, though a private one, much higher than he could have expected, chiefly felt offended when his intellectual superiority was disputed.

Neither had reason to complain; but the acrimony of Swift was directed against man and society; the spleen of Pope against the individuals, Philips, and Dennis, Lord Fanny, and Lady Mary, etc. etc.

William Lisle Bowles

from 'Concluding Observations on the Poetic Character of Pope',
in his edition of *The Works of Alexander Pope* 1806 (see p. 491)

I presume it will readily be granted that 'all images drawn from what
is beautiful or sublime in the works of Nature are more beautiful and
sublime than any images drawn from Art'; and that they are therefore,
per se, more poetical.

In like manner, those passions of the human heart which belong
to Nature in general are, *per se*, more adapted to the higher species
of poetry than those which are derived from incidental and transient
manners. A description of a forest is more poetical than a description
of a cultivated garden; and the passions which are portrayed in the
Epistle of an Eloisa render such a poem more poetical (whatever
might be the difference of merit in point of execution), intrinsically
more poetical, than a poem founded on the characters, incidents, and
modes of artificial life; for instance, *The Rape of the Lock*.

If this be admitted, the rule by which we would estimate Pope's
general poetical character would be obvious.

Let me not, however, be considered as thinking that the subject
alone constitutes poetical excellency. The execution is to be taken
into consideration at the same time; for, with Lord Harvey, we might
fall asleep over the *Creation* of Blackmore, but be alive to the touches
of animation and satire in Boileau.

The subject and the execution, therefore, are equally to be considered
– the one respecting the poetry – the other, the art and powers of the
poet. The poetical subject, and the art and talents of the poet, should
always be kept in mind; and I imagine it is for want of observing
this rule that so much has been said, and so little understood, of the
real ground of Pope's character as a poet. . . .

In speaking of the poetical subject, and the powers of execution;
with regard to the first, Pope cannot be classed among the highest
orders of poets; with regard to the second, none ever was his superior.
It is futile to affect to judge of one composition by the rules of another.
To say that Pope, in this sense, is not a poet is to say that a didactic
poem is not a tragedy, and that a satire is not an ode. Pope must be
judged according to the rank in which he stands among those of the

French school, not the Italian; among those whose delineations are taken more from manners than from Nature. . . .

The career, therefore, which he opened to himself was in the second order in poetry; but it was a line pursued by Horace, Juvenal, Dryden, Boileau; and if in that line he stands the highest, upon these grounds we might fairly say, with Johnson, 'it is superfluous to ask whether Pope were a poet'. . . .

In what has been said, I have avoided the introduction of picturesque description; that is, accurate representations from external objects of Nature: but if the premises laid down in the commencement of these reflections are true, no one can stand pre-eminent as a great poet unless he has not only a heart susceptible of the most pathetic or most exalted feelings of Nature, but an eye attentive to, and familiar with, every external appearance that she may exhibit, in every change of season, every variation of light and shade, every rock, every tree, every leaf, in her solitary places. He who has not an eye to observe these, and who cannot with a glance distinguish every diversity of hue in her variety of beauties, must so far be deficient in one of the essential qualities of a poet.

Here Pope, from infirmities, and from physical causes, was particularly deficient . When he left his own laurel circus at Twicken-ham, he was lifted into his chariot or his barge; and with weak eyes, and tottering strength, it is physically impossible he could be a descriptive bard. Where description has been introduced among his poems, as far as his observation could go, he excelled; more could not be expected. In the description of the cloister, the scenes surrounding the melancholy convent, as far as could be gained by books, or suggested by imagination, he was eminently successful; but even here, perhaps, he only proved that he could not go far: and

The wandering streams that shine between the hills,
The grots that echo to the tinkling rills,
(*Eloisa to Abelard,* 157–8)

were possibly transcripts of what he could most easily transcribe – his own views and scenery.

But how different, how minute is his description, when he describes what he is master of: for instance, the game of ombre in *The Rape of the Lock.* This is from artificial life; and with artificial life, from his infirmities, he must have been chiefly conversant: but if he had been gifted with the same powers of observing outward Nature, I have no doubt he would have evinced as much accuracy in describing the appropriate and peculiar beauties, such as Nature exhibits in in the forest where he lived, as he was able to describe, in a manner so novel, and with colours so vivid, a game of cards. . . .

When he left these regions, to unite the most exquisite machinery of fancy with the descriptions of artificial life, *The Rape of the Lock* will, first and last, present itself – a composition, as Johnson justly observes, the 'most elegant, the most airy', of all his works; a composition to which it will be in vain to compare anything of the kind. He stands alone, unrivalled, and possibly never to be rivalled. All Pope's successful labour of correct and musical versification, all his talents of accurate description, though in an inferior province of poetry, are here consummately displayed; and as far as artificial life, that is, manners, not passions, are capable of being rendered poetical, they are here rendered so, by the fancy, the propriety, the elegance, and the poetic beauty of the Sylphic machinery.

This 'delightful' poem, as I have said, appears to stand conspicuous and beautiful, in that medium where poetry begins to leave Nature, and approximates to local manners. The Muse has, indeed, no longer her great characteristic attributes, pathos or sublimity; but she appears so interesting that we almost doubt whether the garb of elegant refinement is not as captivating as the most beautiful appearances of Nature.

After what I have taken the liberty of suggesting, I hope I shall be excused if I say a few words respecting Pope's versification. . . .

That Pope has made the versification of English couplets infinitely more smooth, I will readily allow. . . .

For myself, I mean merely to say that I should think it the extreme arrogance of folly to make my own ear the criterion of music; but I cannot help thinking that Dryden, and of later days Cowper, are much more harmonious in their general versification than Pope. . . .

Whoever candidly compares these writers together, unless his ear be habituated to a certain recurrence of pauses at the end of a line, will not (though he will give the highest praise for compactness, skill, precision, and force to the undivided couplets of Pope, separately considered), will not, I think, assent to the position that, in versification, 'what he found brick-work, he left marble'.

In variety, and in variety *only*, let it be remembered, I think Pope deficient.

William Wordsworth

from a letter to Walter Scott 18 January 1808

I have a very high admiration of the talents both of Dryden and Pope, and ultimately, as from all good writers of whatever kind, their country will be benefitted greatly by their labours. But thus far I think their writings have done more harm than good. It will require yet half a century completely to carry off the poison of Pope's Homer.

Charles Lamb

in conversation (*c.* 1808), reported in Hazlitt's essay 'Of Persons One Would Wish to have Seen', *New Monthly Magazine* January 1826 (reprinted in *Literary Remains*, 1836)

'I thought,' said A— [the music critic William Ayrton], turning short round upon L— [Lamb], 'that you of the Lake School did not like Pope?' – 'Not like Pope! My dear sir, you must be under a mistake – I can read him over and over for ever!' – 'Why certainly, the *Essay on Man* must be allowed to be a masterpiece.' – 'It may be so, but I seldom look into it.' – 'Oh! then it's his *Satires* you admire?' – 'No, not his *Satires*, but his friendly *Epistles* and his compliments.' – 'Compliments! I did not know he ever made any.' – 'The finest,' said L—, 'that were ever paid by the wit of man. Each of them is worth an estate for life – nay, is an immortality.'

William Blake

from his Notebook *c.* 1808–11

Imitation of Pope: A Compliment to the Ladies

Wondrous the gods, more wondrous are the men,
More wondrous, wondrous still, the cock and hen,
More wondrous still the table, stool and chair;
But ah! more wondrous still the charming fair.

William Blake

from 'Public Address' *c.* 1810

I do not condemn Pope or Dryden because they did not understand imagination, but because they did not understand verse.

Henry Fuseli

in conversation, reported by John Knowles in *The Life and Writings of Henry Fuseli* 1831

Fuseli's acquaintance with English poetry and literature was very extensive. . . . 'England,' he once said, 'has produced only three genuine poets, Shakespeare, Milton, and Dryden.' A friend asked, 'What do you say of Pope?' 'Ay, ay,' he interrupted, 'with Broome, Cawthorne, Yalden, Churchill, Dyer, Sprat, and a long list of contemptibles. These are favourites, I know, and they may be poets to you; but, by Heaven, they are none to me.' Another gentleman who was present maintained the genius of Pope, and thought *The Dunciad* his best production. Fuseli denied this, and added, 'Pope never showed poetic genius but once, and that in *The Rape of the Lock*. A poet is an inventor; and what has Pope invented, except the Sylphs? In *The Dunciad*, he flings dirt in your face every minute. Such a perfomance may be as witty as you please, but can never be esteemed a first-rate poem.' He then called his *Eloisa to Abelard* 'hot ice'.

William Wordsworth

from 'Upon Epitaphs' 1810 (see p. 491)

For the occasion of writing an epitaph is matter of fact in its intensity, and forbids more authoritatively than any other species of composition all modes of fiction, except those which the very strength of passion has created; which have been acknowledged by the human heart, and have become so familiar that they are converted into substantial realities. When I come to the epitaphs of Chiabrera, I shall perhaps give instances in which I think he has not written under the impression of this truth; where the poetic imagery does not elevate, deepen, or refine the human passion, which it ought always to do or not to act at all, but excludes it. In a far greater degree are Pope's epitaphs debased by faults into which he could not I think have fallen if he had written in prose as a plain man and not as a metrical wit. I will transcribe from Pope's Epitaphs the one upon Mrs Corbet (who died of a cancer), Dr Johnson having extolled it highly and pronounced it the best of the collection.

Here rests a woman, good without pretence,
Blest with plain reason and with sober sense;
No conquests she, but o'er herself desired,
No arts essayed, but not to be admired;
Passion and pride were to her soul unknown,
Convinced that Virtue only is our own.
So unaffected, so composed a mind,
So firm yet soft, so strong yet so refined,
Heaven, as its purest gold, by tortures tried;
The saint sustained it, but the woman died.

This *may* be the best of Pope's Epitaphs; but if the standard which we have fixed be a just one, it cannot be approved of. First, it must be observed that in the epitaphs of this writer the true impulse is wanting, and that his motions must of necessity be feeble. For he has no other aim than to give a favourable portrait of the character of the deceased. Now mark the process by which this is performed. Nothing is represented implicitly, that is, with its accompaniment of circumstances, or conveyed by its effects. The author forgets that it is a living creature that must interest us and not an intellectual existence, which a mere character is. Insensible to this distinction the brain of the writer is set at work to report as flatteringly as he may of the mind of his subject; the good qualities are separately abstracted (can it be otherwise than coldly and unfeelingly?) and put together again as coldly and unfeelingly. The epitaph now before us owes what exemption it may have from these defects in its general plan to the excrutiating disease of which the lady died; but it is liable to the same censure, and is, like the rest, further objectionable in this: namely, that the thoughts have their nature changed and moulded by the vicious expression in which they are entangled, to an excess rendering them wholly unfit for the place they occupy.

Here rests a woman, good without pretence,
Blest with plain reason –

from which *sober sense* is not sufficiently distinguishable. This verse and a half, and the one 'So unaffected, so composed a mind', are characteristic, and the expression is true to nature; but they are, if I may take the liberty of saying it, the only parts of the epitaph which have this merit. Minute criticism is in its nature irksome, and, as commonly practised in books and conversation, is both irksome and injurious. Yet every mind must occasionally be exercised in this discipline, else it cannot learn the art of bringing words rigorously to the test of thoughts; and these again to a comparison with things, their archetypes, contemplated first in themselves, and secondly in relation to each other; in all which processes the mind must be skilful, otherwise it will be perpetually imposed upon. In the next couplet the word *conquest* is applied in a manner that would have been displeasing even from its triteness in a copy of complimentary verses to a fashionable beauty; but to talk of making conquests in an epitaph is not to be endured. 'No arts essayed, but not to be admired', are words expressing that she had recourse to artifices to conceal her amiable and admirable qualities; and the context implies that there was a merit in this; which surely no sane mind would allow. But the meaning of the author, simply and honestly given, was nothing more than that she shunned admiration, probably with a more apprehensive modesty than was common; and more than this would have been inconsistent with the praise bestowed upon her – that she had an unaffected mind. This couplet is further objectionable, because the sense of love and peaceful admiration which such a character naturally inspires is disturbed by an oblique and ill-timed stroke of satire. She is not praised so much as others are blamed, and is degraded by the author in thus being made a covert or stalking-horse for gratifying a propensity the most abhorrent from her own nature – 'Passion and pride were to her soul unknown.' It cannot be meant that she had no passions, but that they were moderate and kept in subordination to her reason; but the thought is not here expressed; nor is it clear that a conviction in the understanding that 'virture only is our own', though it might suppress her pride, would be itself competent to govern or abate many other affections and passions to which our frail nature is, and ought in various degrees, to be subject. In fact, the author appears to have had no precise notion of his own meaning. If she was 'good without pretence', it seems unnecessary to say that she was not proud. Dr Johnson, making an exception of the verse, 'Convinced that Virtue only is our own', praises this epitaph for 'containing nothing taken from commonplaces'. Now in fact, as may be deduced from the principles of this discourse, it is not only no fault but a primary requisite in an epitaph that it shall contain thoughts and feelings which are in their substance commonplace, and even trite. It is grounded upon the universal intellectual property of man – sensations which all men have felt and feel in some degree daily and hourly – truths whose very interest and importance have caused them to be unattended to, as things which could take care of themselves. But it is required that these truths should be instinctively ejaculated or should rise irresistibly from circumstances; in a word that they should be uttered in such connection as shall make it felt that they are not adopted, not spoken by rote, but perceived in their whole compass with the freshness and clearness of an original intuition. The writer must introduce the truth with such accompaniment as shall imply that he has mounted to the sources of things, penetrated the dark cavern from which the river that murmurs in everyone's ear has flowed from generation to generation. The line 'Virtue only is our own' is objectionable, not from the commonplaceness of the truth, but from the vapid manner in which it is conveyed. . . . 'So firm yet soft, so strong yet so refined': These intellectual operations (while they can be conceived of as operations of intellect at all, for in fact one half of the process is mechanical, words doing their own work and one half of the line manufacturing the rest) remind me of the motions of a posture-master, or of a man balancing a sword upon his finger, which must be kept from falling at all hazards. 'The saint sustained it, but the woman died.' Let us look steadily at this antithesis: the *saint*, that is her soul strengthened by religion, supported the anguish of her disease with patience and resignation; but the *woman*, that is her body (for if anything else is meant by the word woman, it contradicts the former part of the proposition and the passage is nonsense), was overcome. Why was not this simply expressed; without playing with the reader's fancy, to the delusion and dishonour of his understanding, by a trifling epigrammatic point? But alas! ages must pass away before men will have their eyes open to the beauty and majesty of Truth, and will be taught to venerate Poetry no further than as she is a handmaid pure as her mistress – the noblest handmaid in her train!

I vindicate the rights and dignity of Nature; and as long as I condemn nothing without assigning reasons not lightly given, I cannot suffer any individual, however highly and deservedly honoured by my countrymen, to stand in my way. If my notions are right, the epitaphs of Pope cannot well be too severely condemned; for not only are they almost wholly destitute of those universal feelings and simple movements of mind which we have called for as indispensable, but they are little better than a tissue of false thoughts, languid and vague expressions, unmeaning antithesis, and laborious attempts at discrimination.

Francis Jeffrey, Lord Jeffrey (anonymously)

from an article on *The Dramatic Works of John Ford*, *Edinburgh Review* August 1811 (reprinted in *Contributions to the 'Edinburgh Review'*, 1844)

Pope is a satirist, and a moralist, and a wit, and a critic, and a fine writer, much more than he is a poet. He has all the delicacies and proprieties and felicities of diction – but he has not a great deal of fancy, and scarcely ever touches any of the greater passions. He is much the best, we think, of the classical Continental school; but he is not to be compared with the masters – nor with the pupils – of that old English one from which there had been so lamentable an apostasy. There are no pictures of nature or of simple emotion in all his writings. He is the poet of town life, and of high life, and of literary life; and seems so much afraid of incurring ridicule by the display of natural feeling or unregulated fancy, that it is difficult not to imagine that he thought such ridicule would have been very well directed.

Samuel Taylor Coleridge

from a lecture   28 October 1813 (published in a newspaper report)

Considering only great exquisiteness of language, and sweetness of metre, it is impossible to deny to Pope the title of a delightful writer; whether he be a poet must be determined as we define the word: doubtless if everything that pleases be poetry, Pope's *Satires* and *Epistles* must be poetry.

Isaac D'Israeli

from 'Pope and His Miscellaneous Quarrels', *Quarrels of Authors* 1814

Pope has proudly perpetuated the history of his literary quarrels; and he appears to have been among those authors, surely not forming the majority, who have delighted in, or have not been averse to provoke, hostility. He has registered the title of every book, even to a single paper, or a copy of verses, in which their authors had committed treason against his poetical sovereignty. His ambition seemed gratified in heaping these trophies to his genius, while his meaner passions could compile one of the most voluminous of the scandalous chronicles of literature. We are mortified on discovering so fine a genius in the text humbling itself through all the depravity of a commentary full of spleen, and not without the fictions of satire.

The unhappy influence his literary quarrels had on this great poet's life remains to be traced. He adopted a system of literary politics abounding with stratagems, conspiracies, manoeuvres, and factions.

Pope's literary quarrels were the wars of his poetical ambition, more perhaps than of the petulance and strong irritability of his character. They were some of the artifices he adopted from the peculiarity of his situation.

Thrown out of the active classes of society from a variety of causes sufficiently known, concentrating his passions into a solitary one, his retired life was passed in the contemplation of his own literary greatness. Reviewing the past, and anticipating the future, he felt he was creating a new era in our literature, an event which does not always occur in a century: but eager to secure present celebrity, with the victory obtained in the open field, he combined the intrigues of the cabinet: thus, while he was exerting great means, he practised little artifices. No politician studied to obtain his purposes by more oblique directions, or with more intricate stratagems; and Pope was at once the lion and the fox of Machiavel. A book might be written on the Stratagems of Literature, as Frontinus has composed one on War, and among its subtlest heroes we might place this great poet.

James Henry Leigh Hunt

from Notes on *The Feast of the Poets*   1814

The charge against Pope of a monotonous and cloying versification is not new; but his successors have found the style of too easy and accommodating a description to part with it; and readers in general, it must be confessed, have more than acquiesced in their want of ambition. . . .

I am not here joining the cry of those who affect to consider Pope as no poet at all. He is, I confess, in my judgement, at a good distance from Dryden, and at an immeasurable one from such men as Spenser and Milton; but if the author of *The Rape of the Lock*, of *Eloisa to Abelard*, and of the *Elegy on an Unfortunate Lady* is no poet, then are fancy and feeling no properties belonging to poetry. I am only considering the versification; and upon that point I do not hesitate to say that I regard him, not only as no master of his art, but as a very indifferent practiser, and one whose reputation will grow less and less, in proportion as the lovers of poetry become intimate with his great predecessors, and with the principles of musical beauty in general. Johnson, it is true, objects to those who judge of Pope's versification 'by principles rather than perception', treating the accusation against him as a cant, and suspecting that the accusers themselves 'would have less pleasure in his works, if he had tried to relieve attention by studied discords, and affected to break his lines and vary his pauses.' ...

The truth is that perception has had nothing to do with the matter. The public ear was lulled into a want of thought on the subject; the words *music* and *harmony* came to be tossed about with an utter forgetfulness of their meaning; and so contented and uninquisitive had everybody become on this head, that even those who sat down for the express purpose of calling Mr Pope's admirers to a proper and smaller sense of his merits as a poet were nevertheless equally agreed that as a versifier his pre-eminence was not to be touched. ...

If the attention, however, of more poetical readers is once roused to this point, they will find our author not merely deficient on the score of harmony, but to a degree apparently so obvious and at the same time so surprising, that they will be inclined to wonder how they could have endured so utter a want of variety, and will not be willing, in future, to listen to a poet of any pretensions, who shall come before them without a new stop or two to his lyre. – To come to particulars. – Let the reader take any dozen or twenty lines from Pope at a hazard or, if he pleases, from his best and most elaborate passages, and he will find that they have scarcely any other pauses than at the fourth or fifth syllable, and both with little variation of accent. Upon these the poet is eternally dropping his voice, line after line, sometimes upon only one of them for eight or ten lines together; so that when Voltaire praised him for bringing down the harsh wranglings of the English trumpet to the soft tones of the flute, he should have added that he made a point of stopping every instant upon one or two particular notes. See, for instance, the first twenty lines of *Windsor Forest*, the two first paragraphs of *Eloisa to Abelard*, and that gorgeous misrepresentation of the exquisite moonlight picture in Homer. The last may well be quoted:

As when the moon – refulgent lamp of night,
O'er heaven's clear azure – spreads her sacred light,
When not a breath – disturbs the deep serene,
And not a cloud – o'ercasts the solemn scene;
Around her throne – the vivid planets roll,
And stars unnumbered – gild the glowing pole,
O'er the dark trees – a yellower verdure shed,
And tip with silver – every mountain's head;
Then shine the vales – the rocks in prospect rise,
A flood of glory – bursts from all the skies:
The conscious swains – rejoicing in the sight,
Eye the blue vault – and bless the useful light.
(*Iliad*, VIII 687–98.)

Yet this is variety to the celebrated picture of Belinda in *The Rape of the Lock*:

Not with more glories – in th' ethereal plain
The sun first rises – o'er the purpled main,
Than issuing forth – the rival of his beams
Launched on the bosom – of the silver Thames.
Fair nymphs, and well-dressed youths – around her shone,
But every eye – was fixed on her alone.
On her white breast – a sparkling cross she wore,
Which Jews might kiss – and infidels adore.
Her lively looks – a sprightly mind disclose,
Quick as her eyes – and as unfixed as those.
Favours to none – to all she smiles extends,
Oft she rejects – but never once offends.
Bright as the sun – her eyes the gazers strike,
And like the sun – they shine on all alike.
Yet graceful ease – and sweetness void of pride
Might hide her faults – if belles had faults to hide.
If to her share – some female errors fall,
Look on her face – and you'll forget 'em all.
(II 1–18)

This is a very brilliant description of a drawing-room heroine;
but what are the merits of its versification which are not possessed

by even Sternhold and Hopkins? Out of eighteen lines, we have no less than *thirteen* in *succession* which pause at the fourth syllable – to say nothing of the four *ies* and the six *os* which fall together in the rhymes; and the accent in all is so unskilfully managed, or rather so evidently and totally forgotten, that the ear has an additional monotony humming about it –

Quick as her eyes,
Favours to none,
Oft she rejects,
Bright as the sun.

It does not follow that the critic who objects to this kind of singsong should be an advocate for other extremes and for the *affected* varieties of which Johnson speaks. Let the varieties, like all the other beauties of a poet, be perfectly unaffected: but passion and fancy naturally speak a various language; it is monotony and uniformity alone that are out of nature. When Pope, in one of his happy couplets, ridiculed the old fashion of gardening, he forgot that, on principles common to all the arts, he was passing a satire on himself and his versification; for who can deny that in the walks of his Muse

Grove nods at grove – each alley has a brother,
And half the platform – just reflects the other?
(*Moral Essay IV*, 117–18)

Sir Walter Scott

from 'Memoirs of Jonathan Swift', *The Works of Jonathan Swift*
1814

Pope's character and habits were exclusively literary, with all the hopes, fears, and failings which are attached to that feverish occupation – a restless pursuit of poetical fame. Without domestic society or near relations, separated by weak health and personal disadvantages from the gay, by fineness of mind and lettered indolence from the busy part of mankind, surrounded only by a few friends, who valued these gifts in which he excelled, Pope's whole hopes, wishes, and fears were centred in his literary reputation. To extend his fame, he laboured indirectly, as well as directly; and to defend it from the slightest taint was his daily and nightly anxiety. Hence the restless impatience which he displayed under the libels of dunces, whom he ought to have despised, and the venomed severity with which he retorted their puny attacks.

Robert Southey (anonymously)

from an article on Chalmers's *English Poets*, *Quarterly Review* October 1814

Of Pope's Homer we are, as Englishmen, proud to acknowledge the great and general merits. It must be confessed, however, that amidst every beauty, we find much of that perverse style which is calculated to dazzle and mislead a young writer. True to the maxim of his favourite Boileau,

Le poète s'égaye en mille inventions,
Orne, élève, embellit, agrandit toutes choses.

Whatever Homer has said must, in literal obedience to this doctrine, be ornamented, elevated, embellished, and exaggerated. This is done in very different degrees; sometimes with a delicacy which hardly oversteps the original sentiment, yet oftener with a verboseness and amplification equally adverse to Homer and a just taste. If Homer speaks of blood flowing, Pope tells us that *slaughtered heroes swell the dreadful tide*; if Homer brings Discord into the field, Pope makes her *bathe the purple plain*; if Homer speaks of glittering arms, Pope makes them *lighten all the strand.* . . .

But it is perhaps in the descriptive similes that the perversion of the original is most observable. Boileau advises the poet:

Que de traits surprenants sans cesse il nous réveille!
Qu'il coure dans ses vers de merveille en merveille!

and Pope does indeed surprise those readers who understand what they are reading with marvellous descriptions. He had read of comets, and had seen a sky-rocket; his comet therefore

Shakes the sparkles from its blazing hair.

Lightning also, according to him, appears in sparks, and, what is more wonderful, in streams of sparks; it kindles all the skies, and extends from one pole to another. . . .

In Dr Rees's *Cyclopaedia*, under the article 'Poetry', we are told that Pope has translated the description of Night in the eighth book of the *Iliad* with singular felicity: perhaps no passage in the whole translation has been more frequently quoted and admired. But, as old Henry More says,

– now let's sift the verity
Of this opinion, and with reason rude
Rub, crush, toss, rifle this fine fantasy. . . .

How has Pope rendered this description?

As when the moon, refulgent lamp of night,
O'er heaven's clear azure spreads her sacred light,
When not a breath disturbs the deep serene,
And not a cloud o'ercasts the solemn scene;
Around her throne the vivid planets roll,
And stars unnumbered gild the glowing pole,
O'er the dark trees a yellower verdure shed,
And tip with silver every mountain's head;
Then shine the vales, the rocks in prospect rise,
A flood of glory bursts from all the skies:
The conscious swains, rejoicing in the sight,
Eye the blue vault, and bless the useful light.

Here are the planets rolling round the moon; here is the pole gilt and glowing with stars; here are trees made yellow and mountains tipped with silver by the moonlight; and here is the whole sky in a flood of glory; appearances not to be found either in Homer or in nature; finally these gilt and glowing skies, at the very time when they are thus pouring forth a flood of glory, are represented as a blue vault! The astronomy in these lines would not appear more extraordinary to Dr Herschel than the imagery to every person who has observed moonlight scenes.

Hobbes has said, 'that which giveth a poem the true and natural colour, consisteth in two things, which are, *to know well*, that is, to have images of nature in the memory distinct and clear, and *to know much*'. But images of nature were not in fashion during the prevalence of the French school: from Dryden to Thomson, there is scarcely a rural image drawn from life to be found in any of the English poets, except Gay and Lady Winchilsea; and for the duty of *knowing much* before they begin to write, too many of our poets, and almost all our professional critics, would have done well had they borne in mind the saying of Skelton,

How rivers run not till the spring be full;
Better a dumb mouth than a brainless skull.

William Wordsworth

from 'Essay Supplementary to the Preface', *Poems* 1815

The arts by which Pope, soon afterwards, contrived to procure to himself a more general and a higher reputation than perhaps any English poet ever attained during his lifetime are known to the judicious. And as well known is it to them that the undue exertion of those arts is the cause why Pope has for some time held a rank in literature to which, if he had not been seduced by an over-love of immediate popularity, and had confided more in his native genius, he never could have descended. He bewitched the nation by his melody, and dazzled it by his polished style, and was himself blinded by his own success. Having wandered from humanity in his Eclogues with boyish inexperience, the praise which these compositions obtained tempted him into a belief that Nature was not to be trusted, at least in pastoral poetry. . . .

Now, it is remarkable that, excepting the *Nocturnal Reverie* of Lady Winchilsea and a passage or two in the *Windsor Forest* of Pope, the poetry of the period intervening between the publication of the *Paradise Lost* and *The Seasons* does not contain a single new image of external nature; and scarcely presents a familiar one from which it can be inferred that the eye of the poet had been steadily fixed upon his object, much less that his feelings had urged him to work upon it in the spirit of genuine imagination. To what a low state knowledge of the most obvious and important phenomena had sunk is evident from the style in which Dryden has executed a description of Night in one of his tragedies, and Pope his translation of the celebrated moonlight scene in the *Iliad*. A blind man, in the habit of attending accurately to descriptions casually dropped from the lips of those around him, might easily depict these appearances with more truth. Dryden's lines are vague, bombastic, and senseless; those of Pope, though he had Homer to guide him, are throughout false and contradictory. The verses of Dryden, once highly celebrated, are forgotten; those of Pope still retain their hold upon public estimation – nay, there is not a passage of descriptive poetry which at this day finds so many and such ardent admirers. Strange to think of an enthusiast, as may have been the case with thousands, reciting those verses under the cope of a moonlight sky, without having his raptures in the least disturbed by a suspicion of their absurdity! If these two distinguished writers could habitually think that the visible universe was of so little consequence to a poet that it was scarcely necessary for him to cast his eyes upon it, we may be assured that those passages of the elder poets which faithfully and poetically describe the phenomena of nature were not at that time holden in much estimation, and that there was little accurate attention paid to those appearances.

James Henry Leigh Hunt

from the Preface to *The Story of Rimini* 1816

I do not hesitate to say, however, that Pope and the French school of versification have known the least on the subject of any poets perhaps that ever wrote. They have mistaken mere smoothness for harmony; and, in fact, wrote as they did because their ears were only sensible of a marked and uniform regularity. One of the most successful of Pope's imitators, Dr Johnson, was confessedly insensible to music. In speaking of such men, I allude, of course, only to their style in poetry, and not to their undisputed excellence in other matters. The great masters of modern versification are Dryden ... Spenser ... Milton ... Ariosto ... Shakespeare ... Chaucer .... All these are about as different from Pope, as the church organ is from the bell in the steeple, or, to give him a more decorous comparison, the song of the nightingale, from that of the cuckoo.

Samuel Taylor Coleridge

from *Biographia Literaria*, chapter 1   1817

Among those with whom I conversed, there were, of course, very many who had formed their taste, and their notions of poetry, from the writings of Mr Pope and his followers: or to speak more generally, in that school of French poetry, condensed and invigorated by English understanding, which had predominated from the last century. I was not blind to the merits of this school, yet as from inexperience of the world, and consequent want of sympathy with the general subjects of these poems, they gave me little pleasure, I doubtless undervalued the *kind*, and with the presumption of youth withheld from its masters the legitimate name of poets. I saw that the excellence of this kind consisted in just and acute observations on men and manners in an artificial state of society, as its matter and substance: and in the logic of wit, conveyed in smooth and strong epigrammatic couplets, as its *form*. Even when the subject was addressed to the fancy, or the intellect, as in *The Rape of the Lock*, or the *Essay on Man*; nay, when it was a consecutive narration, as in that astonishing product of matchless talent and ingenuity, Pope's translation of the *Iliad*; still a *point* was looked for at the end of each second line, and the whole was as it were a sorites, or, if I may exchange a logical for a grammatical metaphor, a *conjunction disjunctive*, of epigrams. Meantime the matter and diction seemed to me characterized not so much by poetic thoughts, as by thoughts *translated* into the language of poetry. . . . I was, at that early period, led to a conjecture, which, many years afterwards, was recalled to me from the same thought having been started in conversation, but far more ably, and developed more fully, by Mr Wordsworth; namely, that this style of poetry, which I have characterized above as translations of prose thoughts into poetic language, had been kept up by, if it did not wholly arise from, the custom of writing Latin verses, and the great importance attached to these exercises, in our public schools. Whatever might have been the case in the fifteenth century, when the use of the Latin tongue was so general among learned men that Erasmus is said to have forgotten his native language; yet in the present day it is not to be supposed that a youth can *think* in Latin, or that he can have any other reliance on the force or fitness of his phrases but the authority of the writer from whence he has adopted them. Consequently he must first prepare his thoughts, and then pick out, from Virgil, Horace, Ovid, or perhaps more compendiously from his *gradus*, halves and quarters of lines in which to embody them.

Samuel Taylor Coleridge

from *Biographia Literaria*, note to chapter 2   1817

In the course of one of my lectures, I had occasion to point out the almost faultless position and choice of words in Mr Pope's *original* compositions, particularly in his *Satires* and *Moral Essays*, for the purpose of comparing them with his translation of Homer, which I do not stand alone in regarding as the main souce of our pseudo-poetic diction. And this, by the bye, is an additional confirmation of a remark made, I believe, by Sir Joshua Reynolds, that next to the man who forms and elevates the taste of the public, he that corrupts it is commonly the greatest genius. Among other passages, I analysed sentence by sentence, and almost word by word, the popular lines,

As when the moon, refulgent lamp of night, *etc.*
   [see p. 161–2 above]

much in the same way as has been since done in an excellent article on Chalmers's *British Poets* in the *Quarterly Review*. [See pp. 184–5 above.] The impression on the audience in general was sudden and evident: and a number of enlightened and highly educated persons, who at different times afterwards addressed me on the subject, expressed their wonder, that truth so obvious should not have struck them *before*; but at the same time acknowledged (so much had they been accustomed, in reading poetry, to receive pleasure from the separate images and phrases successively, without asking themselves whether the collective meaning was sense or nonsense) that they might in all probability have read the same passage again twenty times with undiminished admiration. . . .

John Keats

from 'Sleep and Poetry', *Poems* 1817

Yes, a schism

Nurtured by foppery and barbarism,
Made great Apollo blush for this his land.
Men were thought wise who could not understand
His glories: with a puling infant's force
They swayed about upon a rocking horse,
And thought it Pegasus. Ah dismal souled!
The winds of heaven blew, the ocean rolled
Its gathering waves – ye felt it not. The blue
Bared its eternal bosom, and the dew
Of summer nights collected still to make
The morning precious: beauty was awake!
Why were ye not awake? But ye were dead
To things ye knew not of – were closely wed
To musty laws lined out with wretched rule
And compass vile: so that ye taught a school
Of dolts to smooth, inlay, and clip, and fit,
Till, like the certain wands of Jacob's wit,
Their verses tallied. Easy was the task:
A thousand handicraftsmen wore the mask
Of Poesy. Ill-fated, impious race!
That blasphemed the bright Lyrist to his face,
And did not know it – no, they went about,
Holding a poor, decrepid standard out
Marked with most flimsy mottos, and in large
The name of one Boileau!
(181–206)

John Keats

from a letter to B. R. Haydon 10 May 1817

Truth is I have been in such a state of mind as to read over my lines and hate them ... yet when Tom [Keats] who meets with some of Pope's Homer in Plutarch's *Lives* reads some of those to me they seem like mice to mine.

James Henry Leigh Hunt (anonymously)

from a review of Keats's *Poems*, *Examiner* 1 June 1817

It is no longer a new observation that poetry has of late years undergone a very great change, or rather, to speak properly, poetry has undergone no change, but something which was not poetry has made way for the return of something which is. The school which existed till lately since the restoration of Charles the Second was rather a school of wit and ethics in verse than anything else; nor was the verse, with the exception of Dryden's, of the best order. The authors, it is true, are to be held in great honour. Great wit there certainly was, excellent satire, excellent sense, pithy sayings; and Pope distilled as much real poetry as could be got from the drawing-room world in which the art then lived – from the flowers and luxuries of artificial life – into that exquisite little toilet-bottle of essence, *The Rape of the Lock*. But there was little imagination of a higher order, no intense feeling of nature, no sentiment, no real music or variety.

James Henry Leigh Hunt

from the Preface to *Foliage* 1818

The consequence of this re-awakening of the poetical faculty is not, as some imagine, a *contempt* for Pope and the other chief writers of the French school. It justly appreciates their wit, terseness, and acuteness; but it can neither confound their monotony with a fine music, nor recognize the real spirit of poetry in their town habits, their narrow sphere of imagination, their knowledge of manners rather than natures, and their gross mistake about what they called classical, which was Horace and the Latin breeding, instead of the elementary inspiration of Greece.

William Hazlitt

from 'On Dryden and Pope', *Lectures on the English Poets,* lecture 4 1818

Dryden and Pope are the great masters of the artificial style of poetry in our language, as the poets of whom I have already treated, Chaucer, Spenser, Shakespeare, and Milton, were of the natural; and though this artificial style is generally and very justly acknowledged to be inferior to the other, yet those who stand at the head of that class ought, perhaps, to rank higher than those who occupy an inferior place in a superior class. They have a clear and independent claim upon our gratitude, as having produced a kind and degree of excellence which existed equally nowhere else. What has been done well by some later writers of the highest style of poetry is included in, and obscured by, a greater degree of power and genius in those before them: what has been done best by poets of an entirely distinct turn of mind stands by itself, and tells for its whole amount. Young, for instance, Gray, or Akenside only follow in the train of Milton and Shakespeare: Pope and Dryden walk by their side, though of an unequal stature, and are entitled to a first place in the lists of fame. This seems to be not only the reason of the thing, but the common sense of mankind, who, without any regular process of reflection, judge of the merit of a work, not more by its inherent and absolute worth, than by its originality and capacity of gratifying a different faculty of the mind, or a different class of readers; for it should be recollected that there may be readers (as well as poets) not of the highest class, though very good sort of people, and not altogether to be despised.

The question whether Pope was a poet has hardly yet been settled, and is hardly worth settling; for if he was not a great poet, he must have been a great prose writer, that is, he was a great writer of some sort. He was a man of exquisite faculties, and of the most refined taste; and as he chose verse (the most obvious distinction of poetry) as the vehicle to express his ideas, he has generally passed for a poet, and a good one. If, indeed, by a great poet we mean one who gives the utmost grandeur to our conceptions of nature, or the utmost force to the passions of the heart, Pope was not in this sense a great poet; for the bent, the characteristic power of his mind, lay the clean contrary way; namely, in representing things as they appear to the indifferent observer, stripped of prejudice and passion, as in his Critical Essays; or in representing them in the most contemptible and insignificant point of view, as in his *Satires*; or in clothing the little with mock-dignity, as in his poems of Fancy; or in adorning the trivial incidents and familiar relations of life with the utmost elegance of expression, and all the flattering illusions of friendship or self-love, as in his *Epistles*. He was not then distinguished as a poet of lofty enthusiasm, of strong imagination, with a passionate sense of the beauties of nature, or a deep insight into the workings of the heart; but he was a wit, and a critic, a man of sense, of observation, and the world, with a keen relish for the elegances of art, or of nature when embellished by art, a quick tact for propriety of thought and manners as established by the forms and customs of society, a refined sympathy with the sentiments and habitudes of human life, as he felt them within the little circle of his family and friends. He was, in a word, the poet, not of nature, but of art; and the distinction between the two, as well as I can make it out, is this – The poet of nature is one who, from the elements of beauty, of power, and of passion in his own breast, sympathizes with whatever is beautiful, and grand, and impassioned in nature, in its simple majesty, in its immediate appeal to the senses, to the thoughts and hearts of all men; so that the poet of nature, by the truth, and depth, and harmony of his mind, may be said to hold communion with the very soul of nature; to be identified with and to foreknow and to record the feelings of all men at all times and places, as they are liable to the same impressions; and to exert the same power over the minds of his readers that nature does. He sees things in their eternal beauty, for he sees them as they are; he feels them in their universal interest, for he feels them as they affect the first principles of his and our common nature. Such was Homer, such was Shakespeare, whose works will last as long as nature, because they are a copy of the indestructible forms and everlasting impulses of nature, welling out from the bosom as from a perennial spring, or stamped upon the senses by the hand of their maker. The power of the imagination in them is the representative power of all nature. It has its centre in the human soul, and makes the circuit of the universe.

Pope was not assuredly a poet of this class, or in the first rank of it. He saw nature only dressed by art; he judged of beauty by fashion; he sought for truth in the opinions of the world; he judged of the feelings of others by his own. The capacious soul of Shakespeare had an intuitive and mighty sympathy with whatever could enter into the heart of man in all possible circumstances: Pope had an exact knowledge of all that he himself loved or hated, wished or wanted. Milton has winged his daring flight from heaven to earth, through Chaos and old Night. Pope's Muse never wandered with safety, but from his library to his grotto, or from his grotto into his library back again. His mind dwelt with greater pleasure on his own garden than on the garden of Eden; he could describe the faultless whole-length mirror that reflected his own person better than the smooth surface of the lake that reflects the face of heaven – a piece of cut glass or a pair of paste buckles with more brilliance and effect than a thousand dew-drops glittering in the sun. He would be more delighted with a patent lamp than with 'the pale reflex of Cynthia's brow', that fills the skies with its soft silent lustre, that trembles through the cottage window, and cheers the watchful mariner on the lonely wave. In short, he was the poet of personality and of polished life. That which was nearest to him was the greatest; the fashion of the day bore sway in his mind over the immutable laws of nature. He preferred the artificial to the natural in external objects, because he had a stronger fellow-feeling with the self-love of the maker or proprietor of a gewgaw than admiration of that which was interesting to all mankind. He preferred the artificial to the natural in passion, because the involuntary and uncalculating impulses of the one hurried him away with a force and vehemence with which he could not grapple; while he could trifle with the conventional and superficial modifications of mere sentiment at will, laugh at or admire, put them on or off like a masquerade dress, make much or little of them, indulge them for a longer or a shorter time, as he pleased; and because while they amused his fancy and exercised his ingenuity, they never once disturbed his vanity, his levity, or indifference. His mind was the antithesis of strength and grandeur; its power was the power of indifference. He had none of the enthusiasm of poetry; he was in poetry what the sceptic is in religion.

It cannot be denied that his chief excellence lay more in diminishing than in aggrandizing objects; in checking, not in encouraging our enthusiasm; in sneering at the extravagances of fancy or passion, instead of giving a loose to them; in describing a row of pins and needles, rather than the embattled spears of Greeks and Trojans; in penning a lampoon or a compliment, and in praising Martha Blount.

. . . His Muse was on a peace establishment, and grew somewhat effeminate by long ease and indulgence. He lived in the smiles of fortune, and basked in the favour of the great. In his smooth and polished verse we meet with no prodigies of nature, but with miracles of wit; the thunders of his pen are whispered flatteries; its forked lightnings pointed sarcasms; for 'the gnarled oak', he gives us 'the soft myrtle': for rocks, and seas, and mountains, artificial grass-plats, gravel-walks, and tinkling rills; for earthquakes and tempests, the breaking of a flowerpot, or the fall of a china jar; for the tug and war of the elements, or the deadly strife of the passions, we have

Calm contemplation and poetic ease.

Yet within this retired and narrow circle how much, and that how exquisite, was contained! What discrimination, what wit, what delicacy, what fancy, what lurking spleen, what elegance of thought, what pampered refinement of sentiment! It is like looking at the world through a microscope, where everything assumes a new character and a new consequence, where things are seen in their minutest circumstances and slightest shades of difference; where the little becomes gigantic, the deformed beautiful, and the beautiful deformed. The wrong end of the magnifier is, to be sure, held to everything, but still the exhibition is highly curious, and we know not whether to be most pleased or surprised. Such, at least, is the best account I am able to give of this extraordinary man, without doing injustice to him or others. It is time to refer to particular instances in his works. *The Rape of the Lock* is the best or most ingenious of these.

It is the most exquisite specimen of *filigree* work ever invented. It is admirable in proportion as it is made of nothing. . . . It is made of gauze and silver spangles. The most glittering appearance is given to everything, to paste, pomatum, billet-doux, and patches. Airs, languid airs, breathe around – the atmosphere is perfumed with affectation. A toilette is described with the solemnity of an altar raised to the Goddess of vanity, and the history of a silver bodkin is given with all the pomp of heraldry. No pains are spared, no profusion of ornament, no splendour of poetic diction, to set off the meanest things. The balance between the concealed irony and the assumed gravity is as nicely trimmed as the balance of power in Europe. The little is made great, and the great little. You hardly know whether to laugh or weep. It is the triumph of insignificance, the apotheosis of foppery and folly. It is the perfection of the mock-heroic! . . .

The Rape of the Lock is a double-refined essence of wit and fancy, as the *Essay on Criticism* is of wit and sense. The quality of thought and observation in this work, for so young a man as Pope was when he wrote it, is wonderful: unless we adopt the supposition, that most men of genius spend the rest of their lives in teaching others what they themselves have learned under twenty. The conciseness and felicity of the expression are equally remarkable. . . .

There is a cant in the present day about genius, as everything in poetry: there was a cant in the time of Pope about sense, as perform-ing all sorts of wonders. It was a kind of watchword, the shibboleth of a critical party of the day. As a proof of the exclusive attention which it occupied in their minds, it is remarkable that in the *Essay on Criticism* (not a very long poem) there are no less than half a score successive couplets rhyming to the word *sense*. . . .

I have mentioned this the more for the sake of those critics who are bigoted idolizers of our author, chiefly on the score of his correctness. These persons seem to be of opinion that 'there is but one perfect writer, even Pope'. This is, however, a mistake: his excellence is by no means faultlessness. If he had no great faults, he is full of little errors. His grammatical construction is often lame and imperfect. . . . Pope's rhymes are constanly defective, being rhymes to the eye instead of the ear; and this to a greater degree, not only than in later, but than in preceding writers. The praise of his versification must be confined to its uniform smoothness and harmony. In the translation of the *Iliad*, which has been considered as his masterpiece in style and execution, he continually changes the tenses in the same sentence for the purposes of the rhyme, which shows either a want of technical resources, or great inattention to punctilious exactness. . . .

The *Essay on Man* is not Pope's best work. It is a theory which Bolingbroke is supposed to have given him, and which he expanded into verse. But 'he spins the thread of his verbosity finer than the staple of his argument'. All that he says, 'the very words, and to the selfsame tune', would prove just as well that whatever is is *wrong*, as that whatever is is *right*. *The Dunciad* has splendid passages, but in general it is dull, heavy, and mechanical. . . .

His *Satires* are not in general so good as his *Epistles*. His enmity is effeminate and petulant from a sense of weakness, as his friendship was tender from a sense of gratitude. I do not like, for instance, his character of Chartres, or his characters of women. His delicacy often borders upon sickliness; his fastidiousness makes others fastidious. . . .

The finest piece of personal satire in Pope (perhaps in the world) is his character of Addison; and this, it may be observed, is of a mixed kind, made up of his respect for the man, and a cutting sense of his failings. . . .

And shall we cut ourselves off from beauties like these with a theory? Shall we shut up our books, and seal up our senses, to please the dull spite and inordinate vanity of those 'who have eyes, but they see not – ears, but they hear not – and understandings, but they understand not' – and go about asking our blind guides, whether Pope was a poet or not? It will never do. Such persons, when you point out to them a fine passage in Pope, turn it off to something of the same sort in some other writer. Thus they say that the line, 'I lisped in numbers, for the numbers came', is pretty, but taken from that of Ovid – *Et quum conabar scribere, versus erat.* They are safe in this mode of criticism: there is no danger of anyone's tracing their writings to the classics. . . .

Dryden was a better prose writer, and a bolder and more varied versifier than Pope. He was a more vigorous thinker, a more correct and logical declaimer, and had more of what may be called strength of mind than Pope; but he had not the same refinement and delicacy of feeling. Dryden's eloquence and spirit were possessed in a higher degree by others, and in nearly the same degree by Pope himself;

but that by which Pope was distinguished was an essence which he alone possessed, and of incomparable value on that sole account. . . .

MacFlecknoe is the origin of the idea of *The Dunciad*; but it is less elaborately constructed, less feeble, and less heavy. The difference between Pope's satirical portraits and Dryden's appears to be this in a good measure, that Dryden seems to grapple with his antagonists, and to describe real persons; Pope seems to refine upon them in his own mind, and to make them out just what he pleases, till they are not real characters, but the mere drivelling effusions of his spleen and malice. Pope describes the thing, and then goes on describing his own description till he loses himself in verbal repetitions. Dryden recurs to the object often, takes fresh sittings of nature, and gives us new strokes of character as well as of his pencil.

Samuel Taylor Coleridge

from a lecture   17 February 1818

In Massinger, as in all our poets before Dryden, in order to make harmonious verse in the reading it is absolutely necessary that the meaning should be understood; when the meaning is once seen, then the harmony is perfect. Whereas in Pope and in most of the writers who followed his school, it is the mechanical metre which determines the sense.

Samuel Taylor Coleridge

from a lecture   13 March 1818

In them [the principal writers before the Restoration] the precise intended meaning of a word can never be mistaken; whereas in the later writers, as especially in Pope, the use of words is for the most part purely arbitrary, so that the context will rarely show the true specific sense, but only that something of the sort is designed.

Thomas Campbell

from 'Essay on English Poetry', *Specimens of the British Poets*   1819
(see p. 491)

Pope gave our heroic couplet its strictest melody and tersest expression.

D'un mot mis en sa place il enseigne le pouvoir.

If his contemporaries forgot other poets in admiring him, let him
not be robbed of his just fame on pretence that a part of it was
superfluous. The public ear was long fatigued with repetitions of his
manner; but if we place ourselves in the situation of those to whom
his brilliancy, succinctness, and animation were wholly new, we
cannot wonder at their being captivated to the fondest admiration. In
order to do justice to Pope, we should forget his imitators, if that
were possible; but it is easier to remember than to forget by an effort —
to acquire associations than to shake them off. Every one may recollect
how often the most beautiful air has palled upon his ear, and grown
insipid from being played or sung by vulgar musicians. It is the same
thing with regard to Pope's versification. That his peculiar rhythm
and manner are the very best in the whole range of our poetry need
not be asserted. He has a gracefully peculiar manner, though it is not
calculated to be an universal one; and where, indeed, shall we find
the style of poetry that could be pronounced an exclusive model for
every composer? His pauses have little variety, and his phrases are
too much weighed in the balance of antithesis. But let us look to the
spirit that points his antithesis, and to the rapid precision of his thoughts,
and we shall forgive him for being too antithetic and sententious. . . .

Mr Bowles . . . lays great stress upon the argument that Pope's
images are drawn from art more than from nature. That Pope was
neither so insensible to the beauties of nature, nor so indistinct in
describing them as to forfeit the character of a genuine poet,
is what I mean to urge, without exaggerating his picturesqueness. But
before speaking of that quality in his writings, I would beg leave to
observe, in the first place, that the faculty by which a poet luminously
describes objects of art is essentially the same faculty which enables
him to be a faithful describer of simple nature; in the second place,
that nature and art are to a greater degree relative terms in poetical

description than is generally recollected; and, thirdly, that artificial objects and manners are of so much importance in fiction as to make the exquisite description of them no less characteristic of genius than the description of simple physical appearances. The poet is 'creation's heir'. He deepens our social interest in existence. It is surely by the liveliness of the interest which he excites in existence, and not by the class of subjects which he chooses, that we most fairly appreciate the genius or the life of life which is in him. It is no irreverence to the external charms of nature to say that they are not more important to a poet's study than the manners and affections of his species. Nature is the poet's goddess; but, by nature, no one rightly understands her mere inanimate face – however charming it may be – or the simple landscape painting of trees, clouds, precipices, and flowers. Why then try Pope, or any other poet, exclusively by his powers of describing inanimate phenomena? Nature, in the wide and proper sense of the word, means life in all its circumstances – nature moral as well as external. As the subject of inspired fiction, nature includes artificial forms and manners. Richardson is no less a painter of nature than Homer. Homer himself is a minute describer of works of art; and Milton is full of imagery derived from it. . . .

. . . Pope's discrimination lay in the lights and shades of human manners, which are at least as interesting as those of rocks and leaves. In moral eloquence he is for ever *densus et instans sibi*. The mind of a poet employed in concentrating such lines as these descriptive of creative power, which

Builds life on death, on change duration founds,
And gives th' eternal wheels to know their rounds,
(*Moral Essay III*, 169–70)

might well be excused for not descending to the minutely picturesque. The vindictive personality of his satire is a fault of the man, and not of the poet. But his wit is not all his charm. He glows with passion in the Epistle of Eloisa, and displays a lofty feeling much above that of the satirist and the man of the world in his Prologue to *Cato*, and his *Epistle to Lord Oxford*. I know not how to designate the possessor of such gifts but by the name of a genuine poet.

William Lisle Bowles

from *The Invariable Principles of Poetry, in a Letter Addressed to Thomas Campbell, Esq.* 1819 (see p. 491)

The plain course of my argument was simply this: First. *Works of nature*, speaking of those *more* beautiful and sublime, are *more* sublime and beautiful than works of art, therefore more poetical. Second. The passions of the human heart, which are the same in all ages, and which are the causes of the sublime and pathetic in sentiment, are more *poetical* than *artificial manners*. Third. The great poet of human passions is the most consummate master of his art; and the heroic, the lofty, and the pathetic, as belonging to this class, are distinguished. Fourth. If these premises be true, the descriptive poet, who paints from an intimate knowledge of external nature, is more poetical, supposing the fidelity and execution equal, *not* than the painter of human passions, but the painter of external circumstances in *artificial life*; as Cowper paints a morning walk, and Pope a game of cards!!

George Gordon Byron, Baron Byron

from 'Some Observations upon an Article in *Blackwood's Magazine*' 15 March 1820 (see p. 491–2)

There will be found as comfortable metaphysics, and ten times more poetry in the *Essay on Man* than in *The Excursion*. If you search for passion, where is it to be found stronger than in the epistle from *Eloisa to Abelard*, or in *Palamon and Arcite*? Do you wish for invention, imagination, sublimity, character? seek them in *The Rape of the Lock*, the *Fables* of Dryden, the *Ode on Saint Cecilia's Day*, and *Absalom and Achitophel*: you will discover in these two poets only *all* for which you must ransack innumerable metres, and God only knows how many *writers* of the day, without finding a tittle of the same qualities – with the addition, too, of wit, of which the latter have none. . . . I will say nothing of the harmony of Pope and Dryden in comparison, for there is not a living poet (except Rogers, Gifford, Campbell, and Crabbe) who can write an heroic couplet. The fact is that the exquisite beauty of their versification has withdrawn the public attention from their other excellences, as the vulgar eye will rest more upon the splendour of the uniform than the quality of the troops. It is this very harmony, particularly in Pope, which has raised the vulgar and atrocious cant against him – because his versification is perfect, it is assumed that it is his only perfection; because his truths are so clear, it is asserted that he has no invention; and because he is always intelligible, it is taken for granted that he has no genius. We are sneeringly told that he is the 'Poet of Reason', as if this was a reason for his being no poet. Taking passage for passage, I will undertake to cite more lines teeming with *imagination* from Pope than from any *two* living poets, be they who they may.

Isaac D'Israeli (anonymously)

from a review of Spence's *Anecdotes* and Bowles's *Invariable Principles of Poetry*, *Quarterly Review* July 1820 (see p. 491)

It is clear to us that a theory which, frequently admitting everything the votary of Pope could desire to substantiate the high genius of his master, yet terminates in excluding the poet from 'the highest order of poets', must involve some fallacy; and this we presume we have discovered in the absurd attempt to raise 'a criterion of poetical talents'. Such an artificial test is repugnant to the man of taste who can take enlarged views, and to the experience of the true critic. In the contrast of human tempers and habits, in the changes of circumstances in society, and the consequent mutations of tastes, the objects of poetry may be different in different periods; pre-eminent genius obtains its purpose by its adaptation to this eternal variety; and on this principle, if we would justly appreciate the creative faculty, we cannot see why Pope should not class, at least in file, with Dante, or Milton. It is probable that Pope could not have produced an *Inferno*, or a *Paradise Lost*, for his invention was elsewhere: but it is equally probable that Dante and Milton, with their cast of mind, could not have so exquisitely touched the refined gaiety of *The Rape of the Lock*.

It has frequently been attempted to raise up such arbitrary standards and such narrowing theories of art; and these 'criterions' and 'invariable principles' have usually been drawn from the habitual practices and individual tastes of the framers; they are a sort of concealed egotism, a stratagem of self-love. When Mr Bowles informs us that one of the *essential* qualities of a poet 'is to have *an eye attentive to* and *familiar with*' (for so he strengthens his canons of criticism) 'every external appearance of nature, every change of season, every variation of light and shade, every rock, every tree, every leaf, every diversity of hue, etc.', we all know who the poet is that Mr Bowles so fondly describes. ... It happened, however, that Pope preferred *indoor* to *outdoor* nature; but did this require inferior skill or less of the creative faculty than Mr Bowles's *Nature*? In Pope's *artificial life* we discover a great deal of *nature*; and in Mr Bowles's *nature*, or poetry, we find much that is *artificial*.

George Gordon Byron, Baron Byron

from a letter to John Murray   4 November 1820 (see p. 491)

They support Pope, I see, in the *Quarterly*. Let them continue to do so: it is a sin, and a shame, and a *damnation* to think that *Pope*!! should require it – but he does. Those miserable mountebanks of the day, the poets, disgrace themselves and deny God, in running down Pope, the most faultless of poets, and almost of men.

George Gordon Byron, Baron Byron

from *Letter to* ********** [John Murray], *Esq. on the Rev. W. L. Bowles's Strictures on the Life and Writings of Pope* 1821 (see p. 491)

To the question, 'Whether the description of a game of cards be as poetical, supposing the execution of the artists equal, as a description of a walk in a forest?' it may be answered that the materials are certainly not equal; but that 'the artist', who has rendered the 'game of cards poetical', is by far the greater of the two. But all this 'ordering' of poets is purely arbitrary on the part of Mr B. There may or may not be, in fact, different 'orders' of poetry, but the poet is always ranked according to his execution, and not according to his branch of the art.

Tragedy is one of the highest presumed orders. Hughes has written a tragedy, and a very successful one; Fenton another; and Pope none. Did any man, however – will even Mr B. himself – rank Hughes and Fenton as poets above Pope? . . .

The depreciation of Pope is partly founded upon a false idea of the dignity of his order of poetry, to which he has partly contributed by the ingenious boast,

That not in fancy's maze he wandered long,
But *stooped* to truth, and moralized his song.
(*Epistle to Dr Arbuthnot*, 340–41)

He should have written 'rose to truth'. In my mind, the highest of all poetry is ethical poetry, as the highest of all earthly objects must be moral truth. . . . What made Socrates the greatest of men? His moral truth – his ethics. What proved Jesus Christ the Son of God hardly less than his miracles? His moral precepts. And if ethics have made a philosopher the first of men, and have not been disdained as an adjunct to his Gospel by the Deity himself, are we to be told that ethical poetry, or didactic poetry, or by whatever name you term it, whose object is to make men better and wiser, is not the very first order of poetry; and are we to be told this too by one of the priesthood? It requires more mind, more wisdom, more power, than all the 'forests' that ever were 'walked for their description', and all the epics that ever were founded upon fields of battle. . . .

It is the fashion of the day to lay great stress upon what they call 'imagination' and 'invention', the two commonest of qualities: an Irish peasant with a little whisky in his head will imagine and invent more than would furnish forth a modern poem. If Lucretius had not been spoiled by the Epicurean system, we should have had a far superior poem to any now in existence. As mere poetry, it is the first of Latin poems. What then has ruined it? His ethics. Pope has not this defect; his moral is as pure as his poetry is glorious. . . .

The attempt of the poetical populace of the present day to obtain an ostracism against Pope is as easily accounted for as the Athenian's shell against Aristides; they are tired of hearing him always called 'the Just'. They are also fighting for life; for, if he maintains his station, they will reach their own – by falling. They have raised a mosque by the side of a Grecian temple of the purest architecture; and, more barbarous than the barbarians from whose practice I have borrowed the figure, they are not contented with their own grotesque edifice, unless they destroy the prior, and purely beautiful fabric which preceded, and which shames them and theirs for ever and ever. I shall be told that amongst those I *have* been (or it may be still *am*) conspicuous – true, and I am ashamed of it. I *have* been amongst the builders of this Babel, attended by a confusion of tongues, but *never* amongst the envious destroyers of the classic temple of our predecessor. I have loved and honoured the fame and name of that illustrious and unrivalled man, far more than my own paltry renown, and the trashy jingle of the crowd of 'Schools' and upstarts, who pretend to rival or even surpass him. Sooner than a single leaf should be torn from his laurel, it were better that all which these men, and that I, as one of their set, have ever written, should

Clothe spice, line trunks, or, fluttering in a row,
Befringe the rails of Bedlam and Soho!
(*Imitations of Horace, Epistles*, II i 418–19)

There are those who will believe this, and those who will not. You, sir, know how far I am sincere, and whether my opinion, not only in the short work intended for publication, and in private letters which can never be published, has or has not been the same. I look upon this as the declining age of English poetry; no regard for others, no selfish feeling, can prevent me from seeing this, and expressing the truth. There can be no worse sign for the taste of the times than the depreciation of Pope. It would be better to receive for proof Mr Cobbett's rough but strong attack upon Shakespeare and Milton than to allow this smooth and 'candid' undermining of the reputation of the most perfect of our poets, and the purest of our moralists. Of his power in the passions, in description, in the mock heroic, I leave others to descant. I take him on his strong ground as an ethical poet: in the former, none excel; in the mock heroic and the ethical, none equal him; and, in my mind, the latter is the highest of all poetry, because it does that in verse which the greatest of men have wished to accomplish in prose. If the essence of poetry must be a lie, throw it to the dogs, or banish it from your republic, as Plato would have done. He who can reconcile poetry with truth and wisdom is the only true 'poet' in its real sense, 'the maker', 'the creator' – why must this mean the 'liar', the 'feigner', the 'tale-teller'? A man may make and create better things than these.

I shall not presume to say that Pope is as high a poet as Shakespeare and Milton, though his enemy, Warton, places him immediately under them. I would no more say this than I would assert in the mosque (once St Sophia's) that Socrates was a greater man than Mahomet. But if I say that he is very near them, it is no more than has been asserted of Burns, who is supposed

To rival all but Shakespeare's name below.

... If any great national or natural convulsion could or should over-whelm your country in such sort as to sweep Great Britain from the kingdoms of the earth, and leave only that, after all, the most living of human things, a dead language, to be studied and read, and imitated by the wise of future and far generations, upon foreign shores; if your literature should become the learning of mankind, divested of party cabals, temporary fashions, and national pride and prejudice – an Englishman, anxious that the posterity of strangers should know that there had been such a thing as a British epic and tragedy, might wish for the preservation of Shakespeare and Milton; but the surviving world would snatch Pope from the wreck, and let the rest sink with the people. He is the moral poet of all civilization; and as such, let us hope that he will one day be the national poet of mankind. He is the only poet that never shocks; the only poet whose faultlessness has been made his reproach. Cast your eye over his productions; consider their extent, and contemplate their variety – pastoral, passion, mock heroic, translation, satire, ethics – all excellent, and often perfect. If his great charm be his melody, how comes it that foreigners adore him even in their diluted translations?

George Gordon Byron, Baron Byron

from a letter to John Murray   March 1821 (see p. 491)

Whether I have made out the case for Pope, I know not; but I am very sure that I have been zealous in the attempt. If it comes to the proofs, we shall beat the blackguards. I will show more imagery in twenty lines of Pope than in any equal length of quotation in English poesy, and that in places where they least expect it: for instance, in his lines on Sporus [*Epistle to Dr Arbuthnot*, 305–33] – now, do just read them over – the subject is of no consequence (whether it be satire or epic) – we are talking of poetry and imagery from Nature and Art. Now, mark the images separately and arithmetically –

1. The thing of silk.
2. Curd of ass's milk.
3. The butterfly.
4. The wheel.
5. Bug with gilded wings.
6. Painted child of dirt.
7. Whose buzz.
8. Well-bred spaniels.
9. Shallow streams run dimpling.
10. Florid impotence.
11. Prompter. Puppet squeaks.
12. The ear of Eve.
13. Familiar toad.
14. Half froth, half venom, spits himself abroad.
15. Fop at the toilet.
16. Flatterer at the board.
17. Amphibious thing.
18. Now trips a lady.
19. Now struts a lord.
20. A cherub's face.
21. A reptile all the rest.
22. The Rabbins.
23. Pride that licks the dust. . . .

Now, is there a line of all the passage without the most forcible imagery (for his purpose)? Look at the variety, at the poetry, of the passage – at the imagination: there is hardly a line from which a painting might not be made, and *is*. But this is nothing in comparison with his higher passages in the *Essay on Man*, and many of his other poems, serious and comic. There never was such an unjust outcry in this world as that which these scoundrels are trying against Pope.

George Gordon Byron, Baron Byron

from 'Observations upon "Observations": A Second Letter to John Murray, Esq. on the Rev. W. L. Bowles's Strictures on the Life and Writings of Pope' 25 March 1821 (first published in Byron's *Works*, 1832–3) (see p. 491)

Neither time, nor distance, nor grief, nor age can ever diminish my veneration for him who is the great moral poet of all times, of all climes, of all feelings, and of all stages of existence. The delight of my boyhood, the study of my manhood, perhaps (if allowed to me to attain it) he may be the consolation of my age. His poetry is the Book of Life. Without canting, and yet without neglecting religion, he has assembled all that a good and great man can gather together of moral wisdom clothed in consummate beauty. Sir William Temple observes 'that of all the numbers of mankind that live within the compass of a thousand years, for one man that is born capable of making a great poet, there may be a thousand born capable of making as great generals and ministers of state as any in story'. Here is a statesman's opinion of poetry: it is honourable to him, and to the art. Such a 'poet of a thousand years' was Pope. A thousand years will roll away before such another can be hoped for in our literature. But it can *want* them – he himself is a literature.

William Hazlitt (anonymously)

from 'Pope, Lord Byron, and Mr Bowles', *London Magazine*
June 1821 (reprinted in *Lectures on the English Poets,* 1841) (see p. 491)

The controversy, as it is carried on between the chief combatants, is much like a dispute between two artists, one of whom should maintain that blue is the only colour fit to paint with, and the other that yellow alone ought ever to be used. Much might be said on both sides, but little to the purpose. Mr Campbell leads off the dance, and launches a ship as a beautiful and poetical artificial object. But he so loads it with patriotic, natural, and foreign associations, and the sails are 'so perfumed that the winds are love-sick', that Mr Bowles darts upon and seizes it as contraband to art, swearing that it is no longer the work of the shipwright, but of Mr Campbell's lofty poetic imagination; and dedicates its stolen beauty to the right owners, the sun, the winds, and the waves. Mr Campbell, in his eagerness to make all sure, having overstepped the literal mark, presses no farther into the controversy; but Lord Byron, who is 'like an Irishman in a row, *anybody's customer*', carries it on with good polemical hardihood, and runs a very edifying parallel between the ship without the sun, the winds, and waves – and the sun, the winds, and waves without the ship. 'The sun,' says Mr Bowles, 'is poetical, by your lordship's admission.' We think it would have been so without it. But his lordship contends that 'the sun would no longer be poetical, if it did not shine on ships, or pyramids, or fortresses, and other works of art' ... to which Mr Bowles replies that let the sun but shine, and 'it is poetical *per se*', in which we think him right. ... By *art* and *artificial*, as these terms are applied to poetry or human life, we mean those objects and feelings which depend for their subsistence and perfection on the will and arbitrary conventions of man and society; and by nature, and natural subjects, we mean those objects which exist in the universe at large, without, or in spite of, the interference of human power and contrivance, and those interests and affections which are not amenable to the human will. That we are to exclude art, or the operation of the human will, from poetry altogether is what we do not affirm; but we mean to say that where this operation is the most complete and manifest, as in the creation of given objects, or regulation of certain feelings, there the spring of poetry, i.e. of passion and imagination, is proportionably and much impaired. We are masters of Art, Nature is our master; and it is to this greater power that we find working above, about, and within us that the genius of poetry bows and offers up its highest homage. . . . Pope says, in Spence's *Anecdotes*, that 'a lady of fashion would admire a star because it would remind her of the twinkling of a lamp on a ball-night'. This is a much better account of his own poetry than his noble critic has given. It is a clue to a real solution of the difficulty. What is the difference between the feelings with which we contemplate a gas-light in one of the squares and the crescent moon beside it, but this – that though the brightness, the beauty perhaps, to the mere sense, is the same or greater; yet we know that when we are out of the square we shall lose sight of the lamp, but that the moon will lend us its tributary light wherever we go; it streams over green valley or blue ocean alike; it is hung up in air, a part of the pageant of the universe; it steals with gradual, softened state into the soul, and hovers, a fairy apparition, over our existence! It is this which makes it a more poetical object than a patent lamp, or a Chinese lanthorn, or the chandelier at Covent Garden, brilliant as it is, and which, though it were made ten times more so, would still only dazzle and scorch the sight so much the more; it would not be attended with a mild train of reflected glory; it would 'denote no foregone conclusion', would touch no chord of imagination or the heart; it would have nothing romantic about it. A man can make anything, but he cannot make a sentiment! It is a thing of inveterate prejudice, of old association, of common feelings, and so is poetry, as far as it is serious. A 'pack of cards', a silver bodkin, a paste buckle, 'may be imbued' with as much mock poetry as you please, by lending false associations to it; but real poetry, or poetry of the highest order, can only be produced by unravelling the real web of associations, which have been wound round any subject by nature, and the unavoidable conditions of humanity.

John Clare

from his Journal 26 October 1824

Looked into Pope. I know not how it is but I cannot take him up often or read him long together; the uninterrupted flow of the verses wearies the ear. There are some fine passages in the *Essay on Man*. The *Pastorals* are nicknamed so, for daffodils breathing flutes, beachen bowls, silver crooks, purling brooks, and such like everlasting sing-song does not make pastorals. His prologue to the *Satires* is good; but that celebrated *Epitaph on Gay* ends burlesquely.

John Henry Newman (anonymously)

from an article on *The Theatre of the Greeks, London Review*
January 1829 (reprinted as 'Poetry, with Reference to
Aristotle's *Poetics*' in *Essays Critical and Historical*, 1872)

A talent for composition, then, is no essential part of poetry, though indispensable to its exhibition. Hence it would seem that attention to the language, for its own sake, evidences not the true poet, but the mere artist. Pope is said to have tuned our tongue. We certainly owe much to him – his diction is rich, musical, and expressive: still he is not on this account a poet; he elaborated his composition for its own sake. If we give him poetical praise on that acount, we may as appropriately bestow it on a tasteful cabinet-maker. This does not forbid us to ascribe the grace of his verse to an inward principle of poetry, which supplied him with archetypes of the beautiful and splendid to work by. But a similar gift must direct the skill of every fancy-artist who subserves the luxuries and elegances of life.

William Wordsworth

from a letter to Alexander Dyce 12 January 1829

These three writers, Thomson, Collins, and Dyer, had more poetic imagination than any of their contemporaries, unless we reckon

Chatterton as of that age – I do not name Pope, for he stands alone – as a man most highly gifted – but unluckily he took the plain, when the heights were within his reach.

William Wordsworth

from a letter to Alexander Dyce   10 May 1830

Pope, in that production of his boyhood, the *Ode to Solitude*, and his *Essay on Criticism*, has furnished proofs that at one period of his life he felt the charm of a sober and subdued style, which he afterwards abandoned for one that is to my taste at least too pointed and ambitious, and for a versification too timidly balanced.

Thomas Babington Macaulay, Baron Macaulay (anonymously)

from 'Moore's Life of Lord Byron', *Edinburgh Review*   June 1831 (reprinted in *Critical and Historical Essays*, 1843)

Wherein especially does the poetry of our times differ from that of the last century? Ninety-nine persons out of a hundred would answer that the poetry of the last century was correct, but cold and mechanical, and that the poetry of our time, though wild and irregular, presented far more vivid images, and excited the passions far more strongly, than that of Parnell, of Addison, or of Pope. In the same manner we constantly hear it said that the poets of the age of Elizabeth had far more genius, but far less correctness, than those of the age of Anne. It seems to be taken for granted that there is some incompatibility, some antithesis between correctness and creative power. We rather suspect that this notion arises merely from an abuse of words, and that it has been the parent of many of the fallacies which perplex the science of criticism.

What is meant by correctness in poetry? If by correctness be meant the conforming to rules which have their foundation in truth and in the principles of human nature, then correctness is only another name for excellence. If by correctness be meant the conforming to rules purely arbitrary, correctness may be another name for dullness and absurdity.

A writer who describes visible objects falsely and violates the propriety of character, a writer who makes the mountains 'nod their drowsy heads' at night, or a dying man take leave of the world with a rant like that of Maximin, may be said, in the high and just sense of the phrase, to write incorrectly. He violates the first great law of his art. His imitation is altogether unlike the thing imitated. . . .

In the sense in which we are now using the word correctness, we think that Sir Walter Scott, Mr Wordsworth, Mr Coleridge, are far more correct poets than those who are commonly extolled as the models of correctness, Pope, for example, and Addison. The single description of a moonlight night in Pope's *Iliad* contains more inaccuracies than can be found in all *The Excursion*. . . .

. . . We can discover no eternal rule, no rule founded in reason and in the nature of things, which Shakespeare does not observe much more strictly than Pope. But if by correctness be meant the conforming to a narrow legislation which, while lenient to the *mala in se*, multiplies, without a shadow of a reason, the *mala prohibita*, if by correctness be meant a strict attention to certain ceremonious observances, which are no more essential to poetry than etiquette to good government, or than the washings of a Pharisee to devotion, then, assuredly, Pope may be a more correct poet than Shakespeare; and, if the code were a little altered, Colley Cibber might be a more correct poet than Pope. But it may well be doubted whether this kind of correctness be a merit, nay, whether it be not an absolute fault.

Edward FitzGerald

from a letter to W. M. Thackeray   11 October 1831

Pope I admire more and more for his sense. As to his poetry, I don't know of much. But still it is prose more beautifully and tastefully dressed than anyone has ever made it – and he has given even epigrams the appearance of poetry.

James Henry Leigh Hunt

from the Preface to *Poetical Works*   1832

Inferior indeed as Pope's versification is to Dryden's, upon every principle both of power and music, nobody can deny that it admirably suits the nicer point of his genius, and the subjects on which it was exercised. Dryden had a trenchant sword, which demanded stoutness in the sheath. Pope's weapon was a lancet enclosed in pearl.

Samuel Taylor Coleridge

from *Table Talk*   6 August 1832

You will find this a good gauge or criterion of genius – whether it progresses and evolves, or only spins upon itself. Take Dryden's Achitophel and Zimri – Shaftesbury and Buckingham; every line adds to or modifies the character, which is, as it were, a-building up to the very last verse; whereas, in Pope's Timon, etc., the first two or three couplets contain all the pith of the character, and the twenty or thirty lines that follow are so much evidence or proof of overt acts of jealousy, or pride, or whatever it may be that is satirized.

Samuel Taylor Coleridge

from *Table Talk*   18 August 1833

His [Claudian's] power of pleasingly reproducing the same thought in different language is remarkable, as it is in Pope.

Samuel Taylor Coleridge

from marginal notes on Donne

To read Dryden, Pope, etc., you need only count syllables; but to read Donne you must measure *time*, and discover the time of each word by the sense of passion.

Samuel Taylor Coleridge

from Notebook 17

Pope like an old lark who, though he leaves off soaring and singing in the heights, yet has his *spurs* grow longer and sharper, the older he grows.

Robert Southey

from 'Life of Cowper', *The Works of William Cowper* 1835–7

The age of Pope was the golden age of poets – but it was the pinch-beck age of poetry. They flourished in the sunshine of public and private patronage; the art meantime was debased, and it continued to be so as long as Pope continued lord of the ascendant. More injury was not done to the taste of his countrymen by Marino in Italy, nor by Gongora in Spain, than by Pope in England. The mischief was effected not by his satirical and moral pieces, for these entitle him to the highest place among the poets of his class; it was by his Homer. There have been other versions as unfaithful; but none were ever so well executed in as bad a style; and no other work in the language so greatly vitiated the diction of English poetry. Common readers (and the majority must always be such) will always be taken by glittering faults, as larks are caught by bits of looking-glass: and in this meretricious translation, the passages that were most unlike the original, which were most untrue to nature, and therefore most false in taste, were precisely those which were most applauded, and on which critic after critic dwelt with one cuckoo note of admiration. They who found nothing imitable in Dryden could imitate this. The art of poetry, or rather the art of versification, which was now the same thing, was 'made easy to the meanest capacity'.

Thomas De Quincey

from 'Pope', *Encyclopaedia Britannica*, seventh edition   1842

... that Pope is to be classed as an inferior poet has arisen purely from a confusion between the departments of poetry which he cultivated and the merit of his culture. The first place must undoubtedly be given for ever – it cannot be refused – to the impassioned movements of the tragic, and to the majestic movements of the epic, muse. We cannot alter the relations of things out of favour to an individual. But in his own department, whether higher or lower, that man is supreme who has not yet been surpassed; and such a man is Pope. . . . It is not from superior correctness that Pope is esteemed more correct, but because the compass and sweep of his performances lie more within the range of ordinary judgements. Many questions that have been raised upon Milton or Shakespeare, questions relating to so subtle a subject as the flux and reflux of human passion, lie far above the region of ordinary capacities; and the indeterminateness or even carelessness of the judgement is transferred by a common confusion to its objects. But, waiving this, let us ask what is meant by 'correctness'? Correctness in what? In developing the thought? In connecting it, or effecting the transitions? In the use of words? In the grammar? In the metre? Under every one of these limitations of the idea, we maintain that Pope is *not* distinguished by correctness; nay, that, as compared with Shakespeare, he is eminently incorrect. . . . take the *Essay on Criticism*: it is a collection of independent maxims, tied together into a fasciculus by the printer, but having no natural order or logical dependency: generally so vague as to mean nothing: like the general rules of justice, etc., in ethics, to which every man assents; but, when the question comes about any practical case, *is* it just? The opinions fly assunder far as the poles. And, what is remarkable, many of the rules are violated by no man so often as by Pope, and by Pope nowhere so often as in this very poem. As a single instance, he proscribes monosyllabic lines; and in no English poem of any pretensions are there so many lines of that class as in this. We have counted above a score, and the last line of all is monosyllabic.

Not, therefore, for superior correctness, but for qualities the very same as belong to his most distinguished brethren, is Pope to be considered a great poet: for impassioned thinking, powerful description, pathetic reflection, brilliant narration. His characteristic difference is simply that he carried these powers into a different field, and moved chiefly amongst the social paths of men, and viewed their characters as operating through their manners. And our obligations to him arise chiefly on this ground – that, having already, in the persons of earlier poets, carried off the palm in all the grander trials of intellectual strength, for the majesty of the epopee and the impassioned vehemence of the tragic drama, to Pope we owe it that we can now claim an equal pre-eminence in the sportive and aerial graces of the mockheroic and satiric muse; that in *The Dunciad* we possess a peculiar form of satire, in which (according to a plan unattempted by any other nation) we see alternatively her festive smile and her gloomiest scowl; that the grave good sense of the nation has here found its brightest mirror; and, finally, that through Pope the cycle of our poetry is perfected and made orbicular – that from that day we might claim the laurel equally, whether for dignity or grace.

Thomas Babington Macaulay, Baron Macaulay (anonymously)

from 'The Life and Writings of Addison', *Edinburgh Review* July 1843 (reprinted in *Critical and Historical Essays*, 1850)

At this time Addison seemed inclined to devote himself to poetry. He published a translation of part of the fourth *Georgic*, Lines to King William, and other performances of equal value, that is to say, of no value at all. But in those days, the public was in the habit of receiving with applause pieces which would now have little chance of obtaining the Newdigate prize or the Seatonian prize. And the reason is obvious. The heroic couplet was then the favourite measure. The art of arranging words in that measure, so that the lines may flow smoothly, that the accents may fall correctly, that the rhymes may strike the ear strongly, and that there may be a pause at the end of every distich, is an art as mechanical as that of mending a kettle or shoeing a horse, and may be learned by any human being who has sense enough to learn anything. But, like other mechanical arts, it was gradually improved by means of many experiments and many failures. It was reserved for Pope to discover the trick, to make himself complete master of it, and to teach it to every body else. From the time when his *Pastorals* appeared, heroic versification became matter of rule and compass; and, before long, all artists were on a level. Hundreds of dunces who never blundered on one happy thought or expression were able to write reams of couplets which, as far as euphony was concerned, could not be distinguished from those of Pope himself, and which very clever writers of the reign of Charles the Second, Rochester, for example, or Marvell, or Oldham, would have contemplated with admiring despair.

Ben Jonson was a great man, Hoole a very small man. But Hoole, coming after Pope, had learned how to manufacture decasyllable verses, and poured them forth by thousands and tens of thousands, all as well turned, as smooth, and as like each other as the blocks which have passed though Mr Brunel's mill in the dockyard at Portsmouth.

Thomas Babington Macaulay, Baron Macaulay

marginal note on Pope's *Imitations of Horace*

Horace had perhaps less wit than Pope, but far more humour, far more variety, more sentiment, more thought. But that to which Horace chiefly owes his reputation is his perfect good sense and self-knowledge, in which he exceeded all men. He never has attempted anything for which his powers did not qualify him. There is not one disgraceful failure in all his poems. The case with Pope was widely different. He wrote a moral didactic poem. He wrote odes. He tried his hand at comedy. He meditated an epic. All these were failures. Horace would never have fallen into such mistakes.

James Henry Leigh Hunt

from 'An Answer to the Question, What is Poetry?',
Imagination and Fancy   1844

The following is the boasted melody of the nevertheless exquisite
poet of *The Rape of the Lock* – exquisite in his wit and fancy, though
not in his numbers. The reader will observe that it is literally *see-saw*,
like the rising and falling of a plank, with a light person at one end
who is jerked up in the briefer time, and a heavier one who is set
down more leisurely at the other. It is in the otherwise charming
description of the heroine of that poem. [see p.182.]

James Henry Leigh Hunt

from *Wit and Humour, Selected from the English Poets*   1846

Besides being an admirable wit and satirist, and a man of the most
exquisite good sense, Pope was a true poet; and though in all probability his entire nature could never have made him a great one (since
the whole man contributes to form the genius, and the very weakness
of his organization was in the way of it), yet in a different age the boy
who wrote the beautiful verses

Happy the man whose wish and care . . .
(*Ode on Solitude*)

would have turned out, I think, a greater poet than he was. He had
more sensibility, thought, and fancy than was necessary for the
purposes of his school; and he led a sequestered life with his books
and his grotto, caring little for the manners he drew, and capable
of higher impulses than had been given him by the wits of the time
of Charles the Second. It was unlucky for him (if indeed it did not
produce a lucky variety for the reading world) that Dryden came
immediately before him. Dryden, a robuster nature, was just great
enough to mislead Pope; and French ascendancy completed his fate.
Perhaps, after all, nothing better than such a honey and such a sting
as this exquisite writer developed could have been got out of his little

delicate pungent nature; and we have every reason to be grateful for what they have done for us. Hundreds of greater pretentions in poetry have not attained to half his fame, nor did they deserve it; for they did not take half his pains. Perhaps they were unable to take them, for want of as good a balance of qualities. Success is generally commensurate with its grounds.

Pope, though a genius of a less masculine order than Dryden, and not possessed of his numbers or his impulsiveness, had more delicacy and fancy, has left more passages that have become proverbial, and was less confined to the region of matter of fact. Dryden never soared above earth, however nobly he walked it. The little fragile creature had wings; and he could expand them at will, and ascend, if to no great imaginative height, yet to charming fairy circles just above those of the world about him, disclosing enchanting visions at the top of drawing rooms, and enabling us to see the spirits that wait on coffee-cups and hoop-petticoats.

Thomas De Quincey

from 'Schlosser's Literary History of the Eighteenth Century', *Tait's Edinburgh Magazine* September–October 1847 (reprinted in *Essays, Sceptical and Anti-Sceptical*, 1858)

[The *Essay on Criticism*] is the feeblest and least interesting of Pope's writings, being substantially a mere versification, like a metrical multiplication table, of commonplaces the most mouldy with which criticism has baited its rat-traps . . . .

Thomas De Quincey (anonymously)

from an article on Roscoe's edition of Pope, *North British Review* August 1848 (reprinted in *Leaders in Literature*, 1858)

In making a revaluation of Pope as regards some of his principal works, we should have been glad to examine more closely than we shall be able to do some popular errors affecting his whole intellectual position, and especially these two: first, that he belonged to what is idly called the *French* School of our literature; secondly, that he was specially distinguished from preceding poets by *correctness*. . . . In every nation first comes the higher form of passion, next the lower. This is the mere order of nature in governing the movements of human intellect, as connected with social evolution; this is, therefore, the universal order, that in the earliest stages of literature men deal with the great elementary grandeurs of passion, of conscience, of the will in self-conflict; they deal with the capital struggle of the human race in raising empires, or in overthrowing them – in vindicating their religion (as by crusades), or with the more mysterious struggles amongst spiritual races allied to our own, that have been dimly revealed to us. . . . Expanding social intercourse in towns, multiplied and crowded more and more, banishes those gloomier and grander phases of human history from literature. The understanding is quickened; the lower faculties of the mind – fancy, and the habit of minute distinction – are applied to the contemplation of society and manners. Passion begins to wheel in lower flights, and to combine itself with interests that in part are addressed to the insulated understanding – observing, refining, reflecting. This may be called the *minor* key of literature in opposition to the *major*, as cultivated by Shakespeare, Spenser, Milton. But this key arises spontaneously in *every* people, and by a necessity as sure as any that moulds the progress of civilization. Milton and Spenser were *not* of any Italian school. Their Italian studies were the result and not the cause of the determination given to their minds by nature working in conjunction with their social period. It is equally childish to say of Dryden and Pope that they belonged to any French school. That thing which they did they *would* have done though France had been at the back of China. The school to which they belonged was a school developed at a certain stage of progress in all nations alike by the human heart as modified by the human understanding; it is a school depending on the peculiar direction given to the sensibilities by the reflecting faculty, and by the new phases of society. Even as a fact (though a change as to the fact could not make any change at all in the philosophy of the case), it is not true that either Dryden or Pope was even slightly influenced by French literature. Both of them had a very imperfect acquaintance with the French language. Dryden openly ridiculed French literature; and Pope, except for some purposes connected with his Homeric translations, read as little of it as convenience would allow. . . .

It is an error equally gross, and an error in which Pope himself participated, that his plume of distinction from preceding poets consisted in *correctness*. Correctness in what? Think of the admirable qualifications for settling the scale of such critical distinctions which that man must have had who turned out upon this vast world the single oracular word 'correctness' to shift for itself, and explain its own meaning to all generations. Did he mean logical correctness in maturing and connecting thoughts? But of all poets that have practised reasoning in verse, Pope is the one most inconsequential in the deduction of his thoughts, and the most severely distressed in any effort to effect or to explain the dependency of their parts. There are not ten consecutive lines in Pope unaffected by this infirmity. All his thinking proceeded by insulated and discontinuous jets; and the only resource for *him*, or chance of even seeming correctness, lay in the liberty of stringing his aphoristic thoughts like pearls, having no relation to each other but that of contiguity. To *set* them like diamonds was for Pope to risk distraction; to systematize was ruin. On the other hand, if this elliptical word *correctness*, for elliptical it must be until its subject of control is assigned, is to be understood with such a complimentary qualification as would restrict it to Pope's use of *language*, that construction is even more untenable than the other – more conspicuously untenable – for many are they who have erred by illogical thinking, or by distracted evolution of thoughts: but rare is the man amongst classical writers in any language who has disfigured his meaning more remarkably than Pope by imperfect expressions. We do not speak of plebeian phrases, of exotic phrases, of slang, from which Pope was not free, though *more* free than many of his contemporaries. From vulgarism indeed he was shielded, though imperfectly, by the aristocratic society he kept; *they* being right, *he* was right: and he erred only in the cases where they misled him: for even the refinement of that age was oftentimes coarse and vulgar. His grammar, indeed, is often vicious; preterites and participles he constantly confounds, and registers this class of blunders for ever by the cast-iron index of rhymes that never *can* mend. But worse than this mode of viciousness is his syntax, which is so bad as to darken his meaning at times, and at other times to defeat it. But these were errors cleaving to his times; and it would be unfair to exact from Pope a better quality of diction than belonged to his contemporaries. Still it is indisputable that a better model of diction and of grammar prevailed a century before Pope. In Spenser, in Shakespeare, in the Bible of King James's reign, and in Milton, there are very few grammatical errors. But Pope's defect in language was almost peculiar to himself. It lay in an inability, nursed doubtless by indolence, to carry out and perfect the expression of the thought he wishes to communicate. The language does not realize the idea: it simply suggests or hints it. Thus, to give a single illustration –

Know, God and Nature only are the same:
In man, the judgement shoots at flying game.
(*Moral Essay I*, 154–5)

The first line one would naturally construe into this: that God and Nature were in harmony, whilst all other objects were scattered into incoherency by difference and disunion. Not at all; it means nothing of the kind; but that God and Nature only are exempted from the infirmities of change. *They* only continue uniform and self-consistent. This *might* mislead many readers; but the second line *must* do so: for who would not understand the syntax to be, that the judgement, as it exists in man, shoots at flying game? But, in fact, the meaning is that the judgement, in aiming its calculations at man, aims at an object that is still on the wing, and never for a moment stationary. We give this as a specimen of a fault in diction, the very worst amongst all that are possible; to write bad grammar or colloquial slang does not necessarily obscure the sense; but a fault like this is a treachery, and hides the true meaning under the cloud of a conundrum: nay worse; for even a conundrum has fixed conditions for determining its solution, but this sort of mutilated expression is left to the solutions of conjecture.

There are endless varieties of this fault in Pope, by which he sought relief for himself from half an hour's labour, at the price of utter darkness to his reader. . . .

Amongst the early poems of Pope, the *Eloisa to Abelard* has a special interest of a double order: first, it has a *personal* interest as the poem of Pope, because indicating the original destination of Pope's intellect, and the strength of his native vocation to a class of poetry in deeper keys of passion than any which he systematically cultivated. For itself also, and abstacting from its connection with Pope's natural destination, this poem has a *second* interest, an intrinsic interest, that will always make it dear to impassioned minds. The self-conflict – the flux and reflux of the poor agitated heart – the spectacle of Eloisa now bending penitentially before the shadowy austerities of a monastic future, now raving upon the remembrances of the guilty past – one moment reconciled by the very anguish of her soul to the grandeurs of religion and of prostrate adoration, the next moment revolting to perilous retrospects of her treacherous happiness – the recognition by shining gleams through the very storm and darkness evoked by her earthly sensibilities, of a sensibility deeper far in its ground, and that trembled towards holier objects – the lyrical tumult of the changes, the hope, the tears, the rapture, the penitence, the despair – place the reader in tumultuous sympathy with the poor distracted nun. . . .

The *Satires* of Pope, and what under another name *are* satires, viz. his *Moral Epistles*, offer a second variety of evidence to his voluptuous indolence. They offend against philosophic truth more heavily than the *Essay on Man*; but not in the same way. The *Essay on Man* sins chiefly by want of central principle, and by want therefore of all coherency amongst the separate thoughts. But taken *as* separate thoughts, viewed in the light of fragments and brilliant aphorisms, the majority of the passages have a mode of truth; not of truth central and coherent, but of truth angular and splintered. The *Satires*, on the other hand, were of false origin. They arose in a sense of talent for caustic effects, unsupported by any satiric heart. Pope had neither the malice (except in the most fugitive form) which thirsts for leaving wounds, nor, on the other hand, the deep moral indignation which burns in men whom Providence has from time to time armed with scourges for cleansing the sanctuaries of truth or justice. He was contented enough with society as he found it: bad it might be, but it was good enough for *him*: and it was the merest self-delusion if at any moment the instinct of glorying in his satiric mission (the *magnificabo apostolatum meum*) persuaded him that in *his* case it might be said – *Facit indignatio versum.* The indignation of Juvenal was not always very noble in its origin, or pure in its purpose: it was sometimes mean in its quality, false in its direction, extravagant in its expression: but it was tremendous in the roll of its thunders, and as withering as the scowl of a Mephistopheles. Pope having no such internal principle of wrath boiling in his breast, being really (if one must speak the truth) in the most pacific and charitable frame of mind towards all scoundrels whatever, except such as might take it into their heads to injure a particular Twickenham grotto, was unavoidably a hypocrite of the first magnitude when he affected (or sometimes really conceited himself) to be in a dreadful passion with offenders as a body. It provokes fits of laughter, in a man who knows Pope's real nature, to watch him in the process of brewing the storm that spontaneously will not come; whistling, like a mariner, for a wind to fill his satiric sails; and pumping up into his face hideous grimaces in order to appear convulsed with histrionic rage. Pope should have been counselled never to write satire, except on those evenings when he was suffering horribly from indigestion. By this means the indignation would have been ready-made. The rancour against all mankind would have been sincere; and there would have needed to be no extra expense in getting up the steam. As it is, the short puffs of anger, the uneasy snorts of fury in Pope's satires, give one painfully the feeling of a locomotive-engine with unsound lungs. Passion of any kind may become in some degree ludicrous, when disproportioned to its exciting occasions. But it is never entirely ludicrous, until it is self-betrayed as counterfeit. Sudden collapses of the manufactured wrath, sudden oblivion of the criminal, announce Pope's as *always* counterfeit. . . .

Truth, even of the most appreciable order, truth of history, goes to wreck continually under the perversities of Pope's satire applied to celebrated men; and as to the higher truth of philosophy, it was still less likely to survive amongst the struggles for striking effects and startling contrasts. But worse by far are Pope's satiric sketches of women, as carrying the same outrages on good sense to a far greater excess. . . .

It is painful to follow a man of genius through a succession of inanities descending into absolute nonsense, and of vulgar fictions sometimes terminating in brutalities. These are harsh words, but not harsh enough by half as applied to Pope's gallery of female portraits. What is the key to his failure? It is simply that, throughout this whole satiric section, not one word is spoken in sincerity of heart, or with any vestige of self-belief. The case was one of those so often witnessed, where either the indiscretion of friends, or some impulse of erring vanity in the writer, had put him upon undertaking a task in which he had too little natural interest to have either thought upon it with originality, or observed upon it with fidelity. . . . 'Most women,' he says, 'have no character at all'; yet, for all that, finding himself pledged to treat this very subject of female characters, he introduces us to a museum of monsters in that department, such as few fancies could create, and no logic can rationally explain. What was he to do? He had entered upon a theme, he had pledged himself to a chase, on which, as the result has shown, he had not one solitary thought – good, bad, or indifferent. Total bankruptcy was impending. Yet he was aware of a deep interest connected with this section of his satires; and, to meet this interest, he invented what was pungent, when he found nothing to record which was true.

It is a consequence of this desperate resource – this plunge into absolute fiction – that the true objection to Pope's satiric sketches of the other sex ought not to arise amongst women, as the people that suffered by his malice, but amongst readers generally, as the people that suffered by his fraud. He has promised one thing, and done another. He has promised a chapter in the zoology of nature, and he gives us a chapter in the fabulous zoology of the herald's college. A tigress is not much within ordinary experience, still there *is* such a creature; and in default of a better choice, that is, of a choice settling on a more familiar object, we are content to accept a good description of a tigress. We are reconciled; but we are *not* reconciled to a description, however spirited, of a basilisk. A viper might do; but not, if you please, a dragoness or a harpy. The describer knows, as well as any of us the spectators know, that he is romancing; the *incredulus odi* overmasters us all; and we cannot submit to be detained by a picture which, according to the shifting humour of the poet, angry or laughing, is a lie where it is not a jest, is an affront to the truth of nature where it is not confessedly an extravagance of drollery. In a playful fiction, we can submit with pleasure to the most enormous exaggerations; but then they must be offered as such. These of Pope's are not *so* offered, but as serious portraits; and in that character they affect us as odious and malignant libels. The malignity was not real – as indeed nothing was real, but a condiment for hiding insipidity. . . .

If the question were asked, What ought to have been the best among

Pope's poems? most people would answer the *Essay on Man*. If the question were asked, What *is* the worst? all people of judgement would say, the *Essay on Man*. Whilst yet in its rudiments, this poem claimed the first place by the promise of its subject; when finished, by the utter failure of its execution, it fell into the last. . . . It may seem odd – but it is not so – that a man's social position should over-rule his intellect. The scriptural denunciation of riches, as a snare to any man that is striving to rise above worldly views, applies not at all less to the intellect, and to any man seeking to ascend by some aerial arch of flight above ordinary intellectual efforts. Riches are fatal to those continuities of energy without which there is no success of that magnitude. Pope had £800 a year. *That* seems not so much. No, certainly not, supposing a wife and six children: but by accident Pope had no wife and no children. He was luxuriously at his ease: and this accident of his position in life fell in with a constitutional infirmity that predisposed him to indolence. Even his religious faith, by shutting him out from those public employments which else his great friends would have been too happy to obtain for him, aided his idleness, or sometimes invested it with a false character of conscientious self-denial. He cherished his religion too certainly as a plea for idleness. The result of all this was that in his habits of thinking and of study (if *study* we can call a style of reading so desultory as *his*) Pope became a pure dilettante; in his intellectual eclecticism he was a mere epicure; toying with the delicacies and varieties of literature; revelling in the first bloom of moral speculations, but sated immediately; fastidiously retreating from all that threatened labour, or that exacted continuous attention; fathoming, throughout all his vagrancies amongst books, no foundation; filling up no chasms; and with all his fertility of thought expanding no germs of new life.

This career of luxurious indolence was the result of early luck which made it possible, and of bodily constitution which made it tempting. And when we remember his youthful introduction to the highest circles in the metropolis, where he never lost his footing, we cannot wonder that, without any sufficient motive for resistance, he should have sunk passively under his constitutional propensities, and should have fluttered amongst the flower-beds of literature or philosophy far more in the character of a libertine butterfly for casual enjoyment than of a hard-working bee pursuing a premeditated purpose.

Such a character, strengthened by such a situation, would at any rate have disqualified Pope for composing a work severely philosophic, or where philosophy did more than throw a coloured light of pensiveness upon some sentimental subject. If it were necessary that the philosophy should enter substantially into the very texture of the poem, furnishing its interest and prescribing its movement, in that case Pope's combining and theorizing faculty would have shrunk as from the labour of building a pyramid. And woe to him where it did *not*, as really happened in the case of the *Essay on Man*. For his faculty of execution was under an absolute necessity of shrinking in horror from the enormous details of such an enterprise, to which so rashly he had pledged himself. He was sure to find himself, as find himself he did, landed in the most dreadful embarrassment upon reviewing his own work. A work which, when finished, was not even begun; whose arches wanted their key-stones; whose parts had no coherency; and whose pillars, in the very moment of being thrown open to public view, were already crumbling into ruins.

James Henry Leigh Hunt

from *Autobiography*, chapter 4   1850

This reminds me that I could make as little of Pope's Homer, which a schoolfellow of mine was always reading, and which I was ashamed of not being able to like. It was not that I did not admire Pope; but the words in his translation always took precedence in my mind of the things, and the unvarying sweetness of his versification tired me before I knew the reason. This did not hinder me afterwards from trying to imitate it; nor from succeeding; that is to say, as far as everybody else succeeds, and writing smooth verses. It is Pope's wit and closeness that are the difficult things, and that make him what he is: a truism which the mistakes of critics on divers sides have rendered it too warrantable to repeat.

Charles Augustin Sainte-Beuve

from 'Qu'est-ce qu'un classique?', *Causeries du lundi*   21 October 1850

And when we come to the modern world, what shall we say? The greatest names that we perceive at the beginnings of literatures are those which most disturb and shock certain restricted ideas which have been enunciated upon the beautiful and the fitting in poetry. Was Shakespeare, for example, a classic? Yes, he is so today for England and for the world; but in Pope's time he was not so. Pope and his friends were the only classics *par excellence*; they seemed to be definitely so on the morrow of their death. Today they are still classics, and they deserve to be, but they are classics of the second order, and you see them for ever overshadowed and put back in their right place by the man who has resumed his own on the heights of the horizon.

It is not for me indeed to speak ill of Pope, nor of his excellent disciples, especially when they have the charm and naturalness of Goldsmith; next to the greatest, they are the most pleasing perhaps among writers and poets, and the most capable of giving a charm to life. One day when Lord Bolingbroke was writing to Doctor Swift, Pope added a postscript to the letter, in which he said: 'I imagine that if we three were to spend only three years together, there might result some advantage for our century.' No, we should never speak lightly of men who were entitled to say such things of themselves without any boasting; we should rather envy the happy and favoured ages when men of talent could propose such unions, which were not a chimera in their day. Those ages, whether we call them by the name of Louis XIV or that of Queen Anne, are the only true classical ages in the moderate sense of the word, the only ones that offer to finished talent a propitious climate and a shelter. We know it only too well, we others, in our disconnected epochs when talents, equal to them perhaps, are wasted and dissipated by the uncertainties and inclemencies of the weather. However, let us allow his due credit and superiority to every great man. The true and supreme men of genius triumph over difficulties which cause others to come to grief; Dante, Shakespeare and Milton attained their full height and produced their imperishable works, in spite of obstacles, oppressions and storms.

Thomas De Quincey

from 'Lord Carlisle on Pope', *Tait's Edinburgh Magazine*
April–July 1851 (reprinted in *Speculations, Literary
and Philosophic*, 1858)

I admire Pope in the very highest degree; but I admire him as a
pyrotechnic artist for producing brilliant and evanescent effects out
of elements that have hardly a moment's life within them. There is
a flash and a startling explosion, then there is a dazzling coruscation,
all purple and gold; the eye aches under the suddenness of a disp'ay
that, springing like a burning arrow out of darkness, rushes back into
darkness with arrowy speed, and in a moment all is over. Like festal
shows, or the hurrying music of such shows—

It *was*, and it is not.

Untruly, therefore, was it ever fancied of Pope that he belonged by
his classification to the family of the Drydens. Dryden had within him
a principle of continuity which was not satisfied without lingering
upon his own thoughts, brooding over them, and oftentimes pursuing
them through their unlinkings with the *sequaciousness* (pardon a
Coleridgian word) that belongs to some process of creative nature,
such as the unfolding of a flower. But Pope was all jets and tongues
of flame; all showers of scintillation and sparkle. Dryden followed,
genially, an impulse of his healthy nature. Pope obeyed, spasmodically,
an overmastering febrile paroxysm.

John Ruskin

from a letter to his father　14 September 1851 (see p. 492)

I have brought my little volume of Pope's poems with me; which
I shall read carefully. I hardly know which is most remarkable, the
magnificent power and precision of mind, or the miserable corruption
of the entire element in which it is educated, and the flatterings, false-
nesses, affectations, and indecencies which divert the purpose and waste

the strength of the writer, while his natural perception of truth and his carefully acquired knowledge of humanity still render his works of inestimable value. I see he was first educated by a Roman Catholic, and then in *Twickenham* classicism. I am glad to find my term is exactly what I wanted it to be. Pope is the purest example, as well as the highest, of the Cockney classic.

William Makepeace Thackeray

from 'Prior, Gay, and Pope', *The English Humourists of the Eighteenth Century*, lecture 4   1853

We are now come to the greatest name on our list – the highest among the poets, the highest among the English wits and humourists with whom we have to rank him. If the author of *The Dunciad* be not a humourist, if the poet of *The Rape of the Lock* be not a wit, who deserves to be called so? Besides that brilliant genius and immense fame, for both of which we should respect him, men of letters should admire him as being the greatest literary *artist* that England has seen. He polished, he refined, he thought; he took thoughts from other works to adorn and complete his own; borrowing an idea or a cadence from another poet as he would a figure or a simile from a flower, or a river, stream, or any object which struck him in his walk, or contemplation of Nature. . . .

Without the utmost sensibility, Pope could not have been the poet he was; and through his life, however much he protested that he disregarded their abuse, the coarse ridicule of his opponents stung and tore him. One of Cibber's pamphlets coming into Pope's hands, whilst Richardson the painter was with him, Pope turned round and said, 'These things are my diversions': and Richardson, sitting by whilst Pope perused the libel, said he saw his features 'writhing with anguish'. How little human nature changes! Can't one see that little figure? Can't one fancy one is reading Horace? Can't one fancy one is speaking of today?

The tastes and sensibilities of Pope, which led him to cultivate the society of persons of fine manners, or wit, or taste, or beauty, caused him to shrink equally from that shabby and boisterous crew which formed the rank and file of literature in his time: and he was as unjust to these men as they to him. The delicate little creature sickened at habits and company which were quite tolerable to robuster men: and in the famous feud between Pope and the Dunces, and without attributing any peculiar wrong to either, one can quite understand how the two parties should so hate each other. As I fancy, it was a sort of necessity that, when Pope's triumph passed, Mr Addison and his men should look rather contemptuously down on it from their balcony; so it was natural for Dennis and Tibbald, and Welsted and Cibber, and the worn and hungry press-men in the crowd below, to howl at him and assail him. And Pope was more savage to Grub Street than Grub Street was to Pope. The thong with which he lashed them was dreadful; he fired upon that howling crew such shafts of flame and poison, he slew and wounded so fiercely, that, in reading *The Dunciad* and the prose lampoons of Pope, one feels disposed to side against the ruthless little tyrant, at least to pity those wretched folks upon whom he was so unmerciful. It was Pope, and Swift to aid him, who established among us the Grub Street tradition. He revels in base descriptions of poor men's want; he gloats over poor Dennis's garret, and flannel night-cap, and red stockings; he gives instructions how to find Curll's authors, the historian at the tallow-chandler's under the blind arch in Petty France, the two translators in bed together, the poet in the cock-loft in Budge Row, whose landlady keeps the ladder. It was Pope, I fear, who contributed, more than any man who ever lived, to depreciate the literary calling. It was not an unprosperous one before that time, as we have seen; at least there were great prizes in the profession which had made Addison a minister, and Prior an ambassador, and Steele a commissioner, and Swift all but a bishop. The profession of letters was ruined by that libel of *The Dunciad*. If authors were wretched and poor before, if some of them lived in haylofts, of which their landladies kept the ladders, at least nobody came to disturb them in their straw; if three of them had but one coat between them, the two remained invisible in the garret, the third, at any rate, appeared decently at the coffee-house, and paid his twopence like a gentleman. It was Pope that dragged into light all this poverty and meanness, and held up those wretched shifts and rags to public ridicule. It was Pope that has made generations of the reading world (delighted with the mischief, as who would not be that reads it?) believe that author and wretch, author and rags, author and dirt, author and drink, gin, cow-heel, tripe, poverty, duns, bailiffs, squalling children and clamorous landladies, were always associated together. The condition of authorship began to fall from the days of *The Dunciad*: and I believe in my heart that much of that obloquy which has since pursued our calling was occasioned by Pope's libels and wicked wit. Everybody read those. Everybody was familiarized with the idea of the poor devil, the author. The manner is so captivating that young authors practise it, and begin their career with satire. It is so easy to write, and so pleasant to read! to fire a shot that makes a giant wince, perhaps; and fancy one's self his conqueror. It is easy to shoot – but not as Pope did – the shafts of his satire rise sublimely: no poet's verse ever mounted higher than that wonderful flight with which *The Dunciad* concludes. . . .

In these astonishing lines Pope reaches, I think, to the very greatest height which his sublime art has attained, and shows himself the equal of all poets of all times. It is the brightest ardour, the loftiest assertion of truth, the most generous wisdom, illustrated by the noblest poetic figure, and spoken in words the aptest, grandest, and most harmonious. It is heroic courage speaking: a splendid declaration of righteous wrath and war. It is the gage flung down, and the silver trumpet ringing defiance to falsehood and tyranny, deceit, dullness, superstition. It is Truth, the champion, shining and intrepid, and fronting the great world-tyrant with armies of slaves at his back. It is a wonderful and victorious single combat, in that great battle, which has always been waging since society began.

In speaking of a work of consummate art one does not try to show what it actually is, for that were vain; but what it is like, and what are the sensations produced in the mind of him who views it. And in considering Pope's admirable career, I am forced into similitudes drawn from other courage and greatness, and into comparing him with those who achieved triumphs in actual war. I think of the works of young Pope as I do of the actions of young Bonaparte or young Nelson. In their common life you will find frailties and meannesses, as great as the vices and follies of the meanest men. But in the presence of the great occasion, the great soul flashes out, and conquers transcendent. In thinking of the splendour of Pope's young victories, of his merit, unequalled as his renown, I hail and salute the achieving genius, and do homage to the pen of a hero.

Thomas De Quincey

from 'Pope's Retort upon Addison', *The Note Book of an English Opium Eater* 1855

Pope alleges it as a palliation of his satiric malice that it had been forced from him in the way of retaliation; forgetting that such a plea wilfully abjures the grandest justification of a satirist, viz. the deliberate assumption of the character as something corresponding to the prophet's mission amongst the Hebrews. It is no longer the *facit indignatio versum*. Pope's satire, where even it was most effective, was personal and vindictive, and upon that argument alone could not be philosophic.

Walter Bagehot (anonymously)

from 'William Cowper', *National Review* July 1855 (reprinted in *Estimates of Some Englishmen and Scotchmen*, 1858).

As a poet, Cowper belongs, though with some differences, to the school of Pope. Great question, as is well known, has been raised whether that very accomplished writer was a poet at all; and a second-ary and equally debated question runs side by side, whether, if a poet, he were a great one. With the peculiar genius and personal rank of Pope we have in this article nothing to do. But this much may be safely said, that according to the definition which has been ventured of the poetical art, by the greatest and most accomplished master of the other school, his works are delicately-finished specimens of artistic excellence in one branch of it. 'Poetry,' says Shelley, who was surely a good judge, 'is the expression of the imagination,' by which he meant of course not only the expression of the interior sensations accompanying the faculty's employment, but likewise, and more emphatically, the exercise of it in the delineation of objects which attract it. Now society, viewed as a whole, is clearly one of those objects. There is a vast assemblage of human beings, of all nations, tongues, and languages each with ideas and a personality and a cleaving mark of its own, yet each having somewhat that resembles something of all, much that resembles a part of many – a motley regiment, of various forms, of a million impulses, passions, thoughts, fancies, motives, actions; a 'many-headed monster thing'; a Bashi Bazouk array; a clown to be laughed at; a hydra to be spoken evil of; yet, in fine, our all – the very people of the whole earth. There is nothing in nature more attractive to the fancy than this great spectacle and congregation. Since Herodotus went to and fro to the best of his ability over all the earth, the spectacle of civilization has ever drawn to itself the quick eyes and quick tongues of seeing and roving men. Not only, says Goethe, is man ever interesting to man, but 'properly there is nothing else interesting'. There is a distinct subject for poetry – at least according to Shelley's definition – in selecting and working out, in idealizing, in combining, in purifying, in intensifying the great features and peculiarities which make society, as a whole, interesting, remarkable, fancy-taking. No doubt it is not the object of poetry to versify the works of the eminent narrators, 'to prose', according to a disrespectful description, 'o'er books of travelled seamen', to chill you with didactic icebergs, to heat you with torrid sonnets. The difficulty of reading such local narratives is now great – so great that a gentleman in the reviewing department once wished 'one man would go everywhere and say everything', in order that the limit of his labour at least might be settled and defined. And it would certainly be much worse if palm trees were of course to be in rhyme, and the dinner of the migrator only recountable in blank verse. We do not wish this. We only maintain that there are certain principles, causes, passions, affections, acting on and influencing communities at large, permeating their life, ruling their principles, directing their history, working as a subtle and wandering principle over all their existence. These have a somewhat abstract character, as compared with the soft ideals and passionate incarnations of purely individual character, and seem dull beside the stirring lays of eventful times, in which the earlier and bolder poets delight. Another cause co-operates. The tendency of civilization is to pare away the oddness and licence of personal character, and to leave a monotonous agreeableness as the sole trait and comfort of mankind. This obviously tends to increase the efficacy of general principles, to bring to view the daily efficacy of constant causes, to suggest the hidden agency of subtle abstractions. Accordingly as civilization augments and philosophy grows, we commonly find a school of 'common-sense poets', as they may be called, arise and develop, who proceed to depict what they see around them, to describe its *natura naturans*, to delineate its *natura naturata*, to evolve productive agencies, to teach subtle ramifications. Complete, as the most characteristic specimen of this class of poets, stands Pope. He was, someone we think has said, the sort of person we cannot even conceive existing in a barbarous age. His subject was not life at large, but fashionable life. He described the society in which he was thrown – the people among whom he lived. His mind was a hoard of small maxims, a quintessence of petty observations. When he described character, he described it, not dramatically, nor as it is in itself; but observantly and from without, calling up in the mind not so much a vivid conception of the man, of the real, corporeal, substantial being, as an idea of the idea which a metaphysical bystander might refine and excruciate concerning him. Society in Pope is scarcely a society of people, but of pretty little atoms, coloured and painted with hoops or in coats – a miniature of metaphysics, a puppet-show of sylphs. He elucidates the doctrine that the tendency of civilized poetry is towards an analytic sketch of the existing civilization. Nor is the effect diminished by the pervading character of keen judgement and minute intrusive sagacity; for no great painter of English life can be without a rough sizing of strong sense, or he would fail from want of sympathy with his subject.

John Ruskin

from 'Of the Pathetic Fallacy', *Modern Painters*, vol. 3, part 4, chapter 12   1856 (see p. 492)

Simply bad writing may almost always . . . be known by its adoption of these fanciful metaphorical expressions, as a sort of current coin; yet there is even a worse, at least a more harmful, condition of writing than this, in which such expressions are not ignorantly and feeling-lessly caught up, but, by some master, skilful in handling, yet insincere, deliberately wrought out with chill and studied fancy; as if we should try to make an old lava stream look red-hot again, by covering it with dead leaves, or white-hot, with hoar-frost.

When Young is lost in veneration, as he dwells on the character of a truly good and holy man, he permits himself for a moment to be overborne by the feeling so far as to exclaim:

Where shall I find him? angels, tell me where.
You know him; he is near you; point him out.
Shall I see glories beaming from his brow,
Or trace his footsteps by the rising flowers?

This emotion has a worthy cause, and is thus true and right. But now hear the cold-hearted Pope say to a shepherd girl:

Where'er you walk, cool gales shall fan the glade,
Trees, where you sit, shall crowd into a shade, . . .
Your praise the birds shall chant in every grove,
And winds shall waft it to the powers above.
But would you sing, and rival Orpheus' strain,
The wondering forests soon should dance again,
The moving mountains hear the powerful call,
And headlong streams hang listening in their fall!
(Pastorals, II 73–4, 79–84)

This is not, nor could it for a moment be mistaken for, the language of passion. It is simple falsehood, uttered by hypocrisy; definite absurdity, rooted in affectation, and coldly asserted in the teeth of nature and fact. Passion will indeed go far in deceiving itself; but it must be a strong passion, not the simple wish of a lover to tempt his mistress to sing.

George Gilfillan (anonymously)

from 'Satire and Satirists', *Scottish Review* January 1856
(reprinted in *A Gallery of Literary Portraits*, 1909)

Pope belonged in some measure to the same school as Swift, but the
feminine element which was in him mellowed and modified his
feelings. He had little truth of nature, but he had some tenderness of
heart. He was also more successful (according to his idea of success)
and a happier man than Swift. He was very much smaller too in
soul as well as in body, and his gall organ was proportionable.
Swift's feeling to humanity was a black malignity, Pope's a tiny malice.
Swift was a man, nay a monster of misanthropy. Pope always reminds
us of an injured and pouting hero of Lilliput, 'doing well to be angry'
under the gourd of a pocket-flap, or squealing out his griefs from the
centre of an empty snuff-box. In minute and microscopic vision of
human infirmities, Pope excels even Swift, but then you always
conceive Swift leaning down – a giant, although a gnarled stature – to
behold them, while Pope is on their level, and has only to look
straight before him. It is curious to notice how both are stung by
their very different degrees of satirical feeling into poetry. But how
different the poetry of Swift from that of Pope! Swift's, which comes
out only in his most vehement prose, is more fierce and terrible than
even Juvenal's, it is 'black fire and horror' – think of his description
of war and of statesmanship in the last parts of Gulliver's travels –
description in which, working with the barest and coldest words, he
produces the effects of poetry, as though a hot furnace should be
fuelled with snow. Pope, again, never waxes so lofty and so poetical
as when he has lashed himself, with long struggle, and after many
unsuccessful efforts, into an enthusiasm of moral fury. Whether this
be simulated or not, and we are afraid it often is, it is then and then
only that he soars above the mere satirist and artist, and becomes the
poet. In polish and delicate strokes, in damning hints and annihilating
whispers, where 'more is meant than meets the ear', Pope excels all
satirists.

George Eliot (anonymously)

from 'Worldliness and Other-Worldliness: The Poet Young',
Westminster Review   January 1857 (reprinted in *Essays and Leaves from a Notebook*, 1884)

Young is not a satirist of a high order. His satire has neither the terrible vigour, the lacerating energy of genuine indignation, nor the humour which owns loving fellowship with the poor human nature it laughs at; nor yet the personal bitterness which, as in Pope's characters of Sporus and Atticus, ensures those living touches by virtue of which the individual and particular in Art becomes the universal and immortal. . . . He has none of those felicitous epithets, none of those pregnant lines, by which Pope's *Satires* have enriched the ordinary speech of educated men. . . .

Like Pope, whom he imitated, he sets out with a psychological mistake as the basis of his satire, attributing all forms of folly to one passion – the love of fame, or vanity – a much grosser mistake, indeed, than Pope's exaggeration of the extent to which the 'ruling passion' determines conduct in the individual. . . .

Young's satires on women are superior to Pope's, which is only saying that they are superior to Pope's greatest failure.

John Ruskin

from 'Claude and Poussin', *Modern Painters*, vol. 5, part 9, chapter 5   1860 (see p, 492)

It is not possible that the classical spirit should ever take possession of a mind of the highest order. Pope is, as far as I know, the greatest man who ever fell strongly under its influence; and though it spoiled half his work, he broke through it continually into true enthusiasm and tender thought.[1]

1 Cold-hearted I have called him. [See p. 237 above.] He was so in writing the *Pastorals*, of which I then spoke; but in after life his errors were those of his time, his wisdom was his own; it would be well if we also made it ours.

Matthew Arnold

from *On Translating Homer*, lecture 1   1861

It is well known how conscientiously literal is Cowper in his translation of Homer. It is well known how extravagantly free is Pope . . .
yet, on the whole, Pope's translation of the *Iliad* is more Homeric
than Cowper's, for it is more rapid.

Pope's movement, however, though rapid, is not of the same kind
as Homer's; and here I come to the real objection to rhyme in a
translation of Homer. It is commonly said that rhyme is to be abandoned in a translation of Homer, because 'the exigences of rhyme',
to quote Mr Newman, 'positively forbid faithfulness', because 'a just
translation of any ancient poet in rhyme', to quote Cowper, 'is
impossible'. This, however, is merely an accidental objection to
rhyme. If this were all, it might be supposed that if rhymes were more
abundant, Homer could be adequately translated in rhyme. But this is
not so; there is a deeper, a substantial objection to rhyme in a
translation of Homer. It is that rhyme inevitably tends to pair lines
which in the original are independent, and thus the movement of
the poem is changed. . . .

Rhyme certainly, by intensifying antithesis, can intensify separation,
and this is precisely what Pope does; but this balanced rhetorical
antithesis, though very effective, is entirely un-Homeric. And this is
what I mean by saying that Pope fails to render Homer, because he
does not render his plainness and directness of style and diction.
Where Homer marks separation by moving away, Pope marks it by
antithesis. . . .

One feels that Homer's thought has passed through a literary and
rhetorical crucible, and come out highly intellectualized; come out
in a form which strongly impresses us, indeed, but which no longer
impresses us in the same way as when it was uttered by Homer. . . .

A literary and intellectualized language is, however, in its own way
well suited to grand matters; and Pope, with a language of this kind
and his own admirable talent, comes off well enough as long as he
has passion, or oratory, or a great crisis, to deal with. Even here, as
I have been pointing out, he does not render Homer; but he and his
style are in themselves strong. It is when he comes to level passages,

passages of narrative or description, that he and his style are sorely tried, and prove themselves weak. A perfectly plain direct style can of course convey the simplest matter as naturally as the grandest; indeed, it must be harder for it, one would say, to convey a grand matter worthily and nobly than to convey a common matter, as alone such a matter should be conveyed, plainly and simply. But the style of *Rasselas* is incomparably better fitted to describe a sage philosophizing than a soldier lighting his camp-fire. The style of Pope is not the style of *Rasselas*; but it is equally a literary style, equally unfitted to describe a simple matter with the plain naturalness of Homer.

Every one knows the passage at the end of the eighth book of the *Iliad*, where the fires of the Trojan encampment are likened to the stars. It is very far from my wish to hold Pope up to ridicule, so I shall not quote the commencement of the passage, which in the original is of great and celebrated beauty, and in translating which Pope has been singularly and notoriously unfortunate. But the latter part of the passage, where Homer leaves the stars, and comes to the Trojan fires, treats of the plainest, most matter-of-fact subject possible, and deals with this, as Homer always deals with every subject, in the plainest and most straightforward style. 'So many in number, between the ships and the streams of Xanthus, shone forth in front of Troy the fires kindled by the Trojans. There were kindled a thousand fires in the plain; and by each one there sat fifty men in the light of the blazing fire. And the horses, munching white barley and rye, and standing by the chariots, waited for the bright-throned Morning.'

In Pope's translation, this plain story becomes the following:

So many flames before proud Ilion blaze,
And lighten glimmering Xanthus with their rays.
The long reflections of the distant fires
Gleam on the walls and tremble on the spires.
A thousand piles the dusky horrors gild,
And shoot a shady lustre o'er the field.
Full fifty guards each flaming pile attend,
Whose umbered arms by fits thick flashes send.
Loud neigh the coursers o'er their heaps of corn,
And ardent warriors wait the rising morn.

It is for passages of this sort, which, after all, form the bulk of a narrative poem, that Pope's style is so bad. In elevated passages he is powerful, as Homer is powerful, though not in the same way; but in plain narrative, where Homer is still powerful and delightful, Pope, by the inherent fault of his style, is ineffective and out of taste. Wordsworth says somewhere that wherever Virgil seems to have composed 'with his eye on the object', Dryden fails to render him. Homer invariably composes 'with his eye on the object', whether the object be a moral or a material one: Pope composes with his eye on his style, into which he translates his object, whatever it is. That, therefore, which Homer conveys to us immediately, Pope conveys to us through a medium. He aims at turning Homer's sentiments pointedly and rhetorically; at investing Homer's description with ornament and dignity. A sentiment may be changed by being put into a pointed and oratorical form, yet may still be very effective in that form; but a description, the moment it takes its eyes off that which it is to describe, and begins to think of ornamenting itself, is worthless.

Therefore, I say, the translator of Homer should penetrate himself with a sense of the plainness and directness of Homer's style; of the simplicity with which Homer's thought is evolved and expressed. He has Pope's fate before his eyes, to show him what a divorce may be created even between the most gifted translator and Homer by an artificial evolution of thought and a literary cast of style.

Hippolyte Adolphe Taine

from *Histoire de la littérature anglaise* 1863

However, a poet exists in Pope, and to discover him we have only to read him by fragments; if the whole is, as a rule wearisome or shocking, the details are admirable. It is so at the close of every literary age. Pliny the younger, and Seneca, so affected and so stiff, are charming in small bits; each of their phrases, taken by itself, is a master-piece; each verse in Pope is a masterpiece when taken alone. At this time, and after a hundred years of culture, there is no movement, no object, no action, which poets cannot describe. Every aspect of nature was observed; a sunrise, a landscape reflected in the water, a breeze amid the foliage, and so forth. Ask Pope to paint in verse an eel, a perch, or a trout; he has the exact phrase ready; we might glean from him the contents of a Gradus. He gives the features so exactly that at once we think we see the thing; he gives the expression so copiously, that our imagination, however obtuse, will end by seeing it. . . .

After all is there anything in the lines just quoted [*Essay on Man*, II 1–18] but decoration? Translate them literally into prose, and of all those beauties there remains not one. If the reader dissects Pope's arguments, he will hardly be moved by them; he would instinctively think of Pascal's *Pensées*, and remark upon the astonishing difference between a versifier and a man. A good epitome, a good bit of style, well worked out, well written, he would say, and nothing further. Clearly the beauty of the verses arose from the difficulty overcome, the well-chosen sounds, the symmetrical rhythms; this was all, and it was not much. A great writer is a man who, having passions, knows his dictionary and grammar; Pope thoroughly knew his dictionary and his grammar, but stopped there.

People will say that this merit is small, and that I do not inspire them with a desire to read Pope's verses. True; at least I do not counsel them to read many. I would add, however, by way of excuse, that there is a kind in which he succeeds, that his descriptive and oratorical talents find in portraiture matter which suits them, and that in this he frequently approaches La Bruyère; that several of his portraits, those of Addison, Lord Hervey, Lord Wharton, the Duchess of Marlborough, are medals worthy of finding a place in the cabinets of the curious, and of remaining in the archives of the human race; that when he chisels one of these heads, the comprehensive images, the unlooked for connections of words, the sustained and multiplied contrasts, the perpetual and extraordinary conciseness, the incessant and increasing impulse of all the strokes of eloquence brought to bear upon the same spot, stamp upon the memory an impress which we never forget. It is better to repudiate these partial apologies, and frankly to avow that, on the whole, this great poet, the glory of his age, is wearisome – wearisome to us. 'A woman of forty,' says Stendhal, 'is only beautiful to those who have loved her in their youth.' The poor muse in question is not forty years old for us;

she is a hundred and forty. Let us remember, when we wish to judge her fairly, the time when we made French verses like our Latin verse. Taste became transformed an age ago, for the human mind has wheeled round; with the prospect the perspective has changed; we must take this change of place into account. Nowadays we demand new ideas and bare sentiments; we care no longer for the clothing, we want the thing. Exordium, transitions, peculiarities of style, elegances of expression, the whole literary wardrobe, is sent to the old-clothes shop; we only keep what is indispensable; we trouble ourselves no more about adornment but about truth. The men of the preceding century were quite different. This was seen when Pope translated the *Iliad*; it was the *Iliad* written in the style of the *Henriade*: by virtue of this travesty the public admired it. They would not have admired it in the simple Greek guise; they only consented to see it in powder and ribbons. It was the costume of the time, and it was very necessary to put it on. Dr Johnson in his commercial and academical style affirms even that the demand for elegance had increased so much that pure nature could no longer be borne.

Good society and men of letters made a little world by themselves, which had been formed and refined after the manner and ideas of France. They adopted a correct and noble style at the same time as fashion and fine manners. They held by this style as by their coat; it was a matter of propriety or ceremony; there was an accepted and unalterable pattern; they could not change it without indecency or ridicule; to write, not according to the rules, especially in verse, effusively and naturally, would have been like showing oneself in the drawing-room in slippers and a dressing-gown. Their pleasure in reading verse was to try whether the pattern had been exactly followed; originality was only permitted in details; a man might adjust here a lace, there some embroided stripe, but he was bound scrupulously to preserve the conventional form, to brush everything minutely, and never to appear without new gold lace and glossy broadcloth. The attention was only bestowed on refinements; a more elaborate braid, a more brilliant velvet, a feather more gracefully arranged; to this were boldness and experiment reduced; the smallest incorrectness, the slightest incongruity, would have offended their eyes; they perfected the infinitely little. Men of letters acted like these coquettes, for whom the superb goddesses of Michelangelo and Rubens are but milkmaids, but who utter a cry of pleasure at the sight of a ribbon at twenty francs a yard. A division, a displacing of verses, a metaphor delighted them, and this was all which could still charm them. They went on day by day embroidering, bedizening, narrowing the bright classic robe, until at last the human mind, feeling fettered, tore it, cast it away, and began to move. Now that this robe is on the ground the critics pick it up, hang it up in their museum of ancient curiosities, so that everybody can see it, shake it, and try to conjecture from it the feelings of the fine lords and of the fine speakers who wore it.

Gerard Manley Hopkins

from a letter to A. W. M. Baillie   10 September 1864

When one reads Pope's Homer with a critical eye one sees, artificial as it is, in every couplet that he was a great man, but no doubt to an uncritical humour and an uncritical flippant modernist it does offer a great handle.

John Ruskin

from 'The Relation of Art to Morals', *Lectures on Art*, lecture 3 1870 (see p. 492)

And of yet greater importance is it deeply to know that every beauty possessed by the language of a nation is significant of the innermost laws of its being. Keep the temper of the people stern and manly; make their associatations grave, courteous, and for worthy objects; occupy them in just deeds; and their tongue must needs be a grand one. Nor is it possible, therefore – observe the necessary reflected action – that any tongue should be a noble one, of which the words are not so many trumpet-calls to action. All great languages invariably utter great things, and command them; they cannot be mimicked but by obedience; the breath of them is inspiration because it is not only vocal, but vital; and you can only learn to speak as these men spoke by becoming what these men were.

Now for direct confirmation of this, I want you to think over the relation of expression to character in two great masters of the absolute art of language, Virgil and Pope. You are perhaps surprised at the last name; and indeed you have in English much higher grasp and melody of language from more passionate minds, but you have nothing else, in its range, so perfect. I name, therefore, these two men, because they are the two most accomplished *artists*, merely as such, whom I know in literature; and because I think you will be afterwards interested in investigating how the infinite grace in the words of the one, and the severity in those of the other, and the precision in those of both, arise wholly out of the moral elements of their minds – out of the deep tenderness in Virgil which enabled him to write the stories of Nisus and Lausus; and the serene and just benevolence which placed Pope, in his theology, two centuries in advance of his time, and enabled him to sum the law of noble life in two lines which, so far as I know, are the most complete, the most concise, and the most lofty expression of moral temper existing in English words –

Never elated, while one man's oppressed;
Never dejected, while another's blessed.
(*Essay on Man*, IV 323–4)

I wish you also to remember these lines of Pope, and to make yourselves entirely masters of his system of ethics; because, putting Shakespeare aside as rather the world's than ours, I hold Pope to be the most perfect representative we have, since Chaucer, of the true English mind; and I think *The Dunciad* is the most absolutely chiselled and monumental work 'exacted' in our country. You will find, as you study Pope, that he has expressed for you, in the strictest language and within the briefest limits, every law of art, of criticism, of economy, of policy, and, finally, of a benevolence, humble, rational, and resigned, contented with its allotted share of life, and trusting the problem of its salvation to Him in whose hand lies that of the universe.

Whitwell Elwin

from his Introduction to *An Essay on Criticism*, in his edition of
The Works of Alexander Pope, vol. 2 1871 (see p. 492)

Almost anybody may convert ordinary prose into defective verse,
and much of the verse in the *Essay on Criticism* is of a low order. The
phraseology is frequently mean and slovenly, the construction
inverted and ungrammatical, the ellipses harsh, the expletives feeble,
the metre inharmonious, the rhymes imperfect. Striving to be poetical,
Pope fell below bald and slip-shod prose.

James Russell Lowell

from 'Pope', *North American Review* January 1871 (reprinted in
My Study Windows, 1871)

It will hardly be questioned that the man who writes what is still
piquant and remembrable, a century and a quarter after his death,
was a man of genius. But there are two modes of uttering such things
as cleave to the memory of mankind. They may be said or sung. I do
not think that Pope's verse anywhere sings, but it should seem that
the abiding presence of fancy in his best work forbids his exclusion
from the rank of poet. The atmosphere in which he habitually dwelt
was an essentially prosaic one, the language habitual to him was that
of conversation and society, so that he lacked the help of that fresher
dialect which seems like inspiration in the elder poets. His range of
associations was of that narrow kind which is always vulgar, whether
it be found in the village or the court. Certainly he has not the force
and majesty of Dryden in his better moods, but he has a grace, a
finesse, an art of being pungent, a sensitiveness to impressions, that
would incline us to rank him with Voltaire (whom in many ways he
so much resembles), as an author with whom the gift of writing was
primary, and that of verse secondary. No other poet that I remember
ever wrote prose which is so purely prose as his; and yet, in any
impartial criticism, *The Rape of the Lock* sets him even as a poet far

above many men more largely endowed with poetic feeling and insight than he.

A great deal must be allowed to Pope for the age in which he lived, and not a little, I think, for the influence of Swift. In his own province he still stands unapproachably alone. If to be the greatest satirist of individual men, rather than of human nature, if to be the highest expression which the life of the court and the ball-room has ever found in verse, if to have added more phrases to our language than any other but Shakespeare, if to have charmed four generations make a man a great poet – then he is one. He was the chief founder of an artificial style of writing, which in his hands was living and powerful, because he used it to express artificial modes of thinking and an artificial state of society. Measured by any high standard of imagination, he will be found wanting; tried by any test of wit, he is unrivalled.

Mark Pattison (anonymously)

from 'Pope and His Editors', *British Quarterly Review*   April 1872 (reprinted in *Essays*, 1889)

Taking the test of value proposed before, viz. fullness of representation of contemporary life and feeling, his *Satires and Epistles* are his most valuable production. Indeed, it is no paradox to say that these Imitations of Horace are the most original of his writings. From this point of view the *Essay on Man* is the least valuable. Its point of view is indistinct. A good representation of the thoughts of that age on the great questions of natural theology would be always worth preserving. But Pope's is far from being such a representation. . . .

Mr Elwin spends many pages of careful writing in a furious denunciation of the *Essay* as shallow metaphysics, a tissue of incoherence and inconsistency. This, again, is a charge which no one can attempt to deny, and which, we may add, no one need have attempted to prove. It is understood by everyone who reads the *Essay*. But, we would ask, why is the *Essay on Man* still read, when many a volume of the same age, of the same shallow metaphysics, is forgotten? It is much to be lamented that Pope attempted philosophy. He was very ignorant; ignorant of everything except the art of versification. Of philosophy he knew nothing beyond the name. In 1739, he told Warburton he had never read a line of Leibniz, nor knew there was such a term as 'pre-established harmony', till he saw it in Crousaz's review of himself. It were to be wished that he had always kept to what he calls 'ethical epistles, in the Horatian way', and had never written either a *Dunciad* or an *Essay on Man*. In the selection of his subject, he was determined against the bent of his own genius by the direction in which the curiosity of his reading public happened to be running. His ambition as a poet led him beyond his powers. Unless he was to be content to be the poet of social life, and to be read only by 'the town', he must apply himself to the larger argument which was then absorbing the attention of all serious minds. He had no interest in the subject. Though a great reader, 'he only skimmed literature to pick up sentiments that could be versified, and to learn attractive forms of composition'. He quarried his stone anywhere. But what he was engaged in building was a beautifully contrived and adorned piece of verse, not a philosophical system. The want of reflection his works discover 'was the fault of an intellect unconscious of its weakness. To him the disjointed bits of philosophy presented no gaps. He had no conception of philosophical thought, no glimmer of the combination of philosophical ideas into an integral design.' These are Mr Elwin's words, and we unhesitatingly subscribe to their truth. But surely they are incompatible with Mr Elwin's own theory, that Pope was engaged in a conspiracy with Bolingbroke to propagate Bolingbroke's system of 'irreligious metaphysics'.

Matthew Arnold

from his Introduction to *The English Poets*, edited by
T. H. Ward   1880 (reprinted as 'The Study of Poetry' in
Essays in Criticism, Second Series, 1888)

Are Dryden and Pope poetical classics? Is the historic estimate, which represents them as such, and which has been so long established that it cannot easily give way, the real estimate? Wordsworth and Coleridge, as is well known, denied it; but the authority of Wordsworth and Coleridge does not weigh much with the young generation, and there are many signs to show that the eighteenth century and its judgements are coming into favour again. Are the favourite poets of the eighteenth century classics?

It is impossible within my present limits to discuss the question fully. And what man of letters would not shrink from seeming to dispose dictatorially of the claims of two men who are, at any rate, such masters in letters as Dryden and Pope; two men of such admirable talent, both of them, and one of them, Dryden, a man, on all sides, of such energetic and genial power? And yet, if we are to gain the full benefit from poetry, we must have the real estimate of it. I cast about for some mode of arriving, in the present case, at such an estimate without offence. And perhaps the best way is to begin, as it is easy to begin, with cordial praise.

When we find Chapman, the Elizabethan translator of Homer, expressing himself in his preface thus: 'Though truth in her very nakedness sits in so deep a pit that from Gades to Aurora and Ganges few eyes can sound her, I hope yet those few here will so discover and confirm that, the date being out of her darkness in this morning of our poet, he shall now gird his temples with the sun' – we pronounce that such a prose is intolerable. When we find Milton writing: 'And long it was not after, when I was confirmed in this opinion, that he, who would not be frustrate of his hope to write well hereafter in laudable things, ought himself to be a true poem' – we pronounce that such a prose has its own grandeur, but that it is obsolete and inconvenient. But when we find Dryden telling us: 'What Virgil wrote in the vigour of his age, in plenty and at ease, I have undertaken to translate in my declining years; struggling with wants, oppressed with sickness, curbed in my genius, liable to be misconstrued in all I write' – then we exclaim that here at last we have the true English prose, a prose such as we would all gladly use if we only knew how. Yet Dryden was Milton's contemporary.

But after the Restoration the time had come when our nation felt the imperious need of a fit prose. So, too, the time had likewise come when our nation felt the imperious need of freeing itself from the absorbing preoccupation which religion in the Puritan age had exercised. It was impossible that this freedom should be brought about without some negative excess, without some neglect and impairment of the religious life of the soul; and the spiritual history of the eighteenth century shows us that the freedom was not achieved without them. Still, the freedom was achieved; the preoccupation, an undoubtedly baneful and retarding one if it had continued, was got rid of. And as with religion amongst us at that period, so it was also with letters. A fit prose was a necessity; but it was impossible that a fit prose should establish itself amongst us without some touch of frost to the imaginative life of the soul. The needful qualities for a fit prose are regularity, uniformity, precision, balance. The men of letters, whose destiny it may be to bring their nation to the attainment of a fit prose must of necessity, whether they work in prose or in verse, give a predominating, an almost exclusive attention to the qualities of regularity, uniformity, precision, balance. But an almost exclusive attention to these qualities involves some repression and silencing of poetry.

We are to regard Dryden as the puissant and glorious founder, Pope as the splendid high priest, of our age of prose and reason, of our excellent and indispensable eighteenth century. For the purposes of their mission and destiny their poetry, like their prose, is admirable. Do you ask me whether Dryden's verse, take it almost where you will, is not good?

A milk-white hind, immortal and unchanged,
Fed on the lawns and in the forest ranged.

I answer: Admirable for the purposes of the inaugurator of an age of prose and reason. Do you ask me whether Pope's verse, take it almost where you will, is not good?

To Hounslow Heath I point, and Banstead Down;
Thence comes your mutton, and these chicks my own.
(*Imitations of Horace, Satires*, II ii 143–4)

I answer: Admirable for the purposes of the high priest of an age of prose and reason. But do you ask me whether such verse proceeds from men with an adequate poetic criticism of life, from men whose criticism of life has a high seriousness, or even, without that high seriousness, has poetic largeness, freedom, insight, benignity? Do you ask me whether the application of ideas to life in the verse of these men, often a powerful application, no doubt, is a powerful *poetic* application? Do you ask me whether the poetry of these men has either the matter or the inseparable manner of such an adequate poetic criticism; whether it has the accent of

Absent thee from felicity awhile . . .

or of

And what is else not to be overcome . . .

or of

O martyr souded in virginitee!

I answer: It has not and cannot have them; it is the poetry of the builders of an age of prose and reason. Though they may write in verse, though they may in a certain sense be masters of the art of versification, Dryden and Pope are not classics of our poetry, they are classics of our prose.

Matthew Arnold

from 'Thomas Gray', *The English Poets*, edited by T. H. Ward 1880 (reprinted in *Essays in Criticism, Second Series*, 1888)

The difference between genuine poetry and the poetry of Dryden, Pope, and all their school, is briefly this; their poetry is conceived and composed in their wits, genuine poetry is conceived and composed in the soul. The difference between the two kinds of poetry is immense. They differ profoundly in their modes of language, they differ profoundly in their modes of evolution. The poetic language of our eighteenth century in general is the language of men composing *without their eye on the object*, as Wordsworth excellently said of Dryden; language merely recalling the object, as the common language of prose does, and then dressing it out with a certain smartness and brilliancy for the fancy and understanding. This is called 'splendid diction'. The evolution of the poetry of our eighteenth century is likewise intellectual; it proceeds by ratiocination, antithesis, ingenious turns and conceits. This poetry is often eloquent, and always, in the hands of such masters as Dryden and Pope, clever; but it does not take us much below the surface of things, it does not give us the emotion of seeing things in their truth and beauty. The language of genuine poetry, on the other hand, is the language of one composing with his eye on the object; its evolution is that of a thing which has been plunged in the poet's soul until it comes forth naturally and necessarily. This sort of evolution is infinitely simpler than the other, and infinitely more satisfying; the same thing is true of the genuine poetic language likewise. But they are both of them, also, infinitely harder of attainment; they come only from those who, as Emerson says, 'live from a great depth of being'.

Mark Pattison

from 'Alexander Pope', *The English Poets*, edited by
T. H. Ward   1880

Pope at once took the lead in the race of writers because he took more pains than they. He laboured day and night to form himself for his purpose, that viz. of becoming a writer of finished verse. To improve his mind, to enlarge his view of the world, to store up knowledge – these were things unknown to him. Any ideas, any thoughts, such as custom, chance, society or sect may suggest, are good enough, but each idea must be turned over till it has been reduced to its neatest and most epigrammatic expression. . . .

In two directions, in that of condensing and pointing his meaning, and in that of drawing the utmost harmony of sound out of the couplet, Pope carried versification far beyond the point at which it was when he took it up. Historical parallels are proverbially misleading. Yet the analogy between what Virgil did for the Latin hexameter as he received it from Lucretius, and Pope's maturing the ten-syllable couplet which he found as Dryden left it, is sufficiently close to be of use in aiding us to realize Pope's merit. Because, after Pope, his trick of versification became common property, and 'every warbler had his tune by heart', we are apt to overlook the merit of the first invention.

But epigrammatic force and musical flow are not the sole elements of Pope's reputation. The matter which he worked up into his verse has a permanent value, and is indeed one of the most precious heirlooms which the eighteenth century has bequeathed us. And here we must distinguish between Pope when he attempts general themes, and Pope when he draws that which he knew, viz. the social life of his own day. When in the *Pastorals* he writes of natural beauty, in the *Essay on Criticism* he lays down the rules of writing, in the *Essay on Man* he versifies Leibnizian optimism, he does not rise above the herd of eighteenth-century writers, except in so far as his skill of language is more accomplished than theirs. *The Rape of the Lock* and *The Dunciad* have a little more interest, because they treat of contemporary manners. But even in these poems, because the incidents are trivial and the personages contemptible, Pope is not more than pretty in *The Rape of the Lock*, and forcible, where force is ludicrously mis-placed, in *The Dunciad*. It is where he comes to describe the one thing which he knew, and about which he felt sympathy and antipathy, viz. the court and town of his time, in the *Moral Essays*, and the *Satires and Epistles*, that Pope found the proper material on which to lay out his elaborate workmanship. And even in these capital works we must distinguish between Pope's general theorems and his particular portraits. Where he moralizes, or deduces general principles, he is superficial, second-hand, and onesided as the veriest scribbler. For example: in the splendid lines on the Duke of Wharton (*Moral Essay I*, 174) we must separate the childish theory of 'the ruling passion' from the telling accumulation of epigram on epigram which follows under that spurious rubric. . . .

In short, Pope, wherever he recedes from what was immediately close to him, the manners, passions, prejudices, sentiments, of his own day, has only such merit – little enough – which wit divorced from truth can have. He is at his best only where the delicacies and subtle felicities of his diction are employed to embody some transient phase of contemporary feeling. Pope has small knowledge of books. Though he was, as Sir W. Hamilton says, 'a curious reader', he read for style, not for facts. Of history, of science, of nature, of anything except 'the town' he knows nothing. He just shares the ordinary prejudices of the ordinary 'wit' of his day. He was a Tory-Catholic, like any other Tory-Catholic of George II's day. His sentiments reflect the social medium in which he lived. The complex web of society, with its indefinable shades, its minute personal affinities and repulsions, is the world in which Pope lived and moved, and which he has drawn in a few vivid lines, with the keenness and intensity of which there is nothing in our literature that can compare. Clarendon's portraits in his gallery of characters are more complete and discriminating, and infinitely more candid. But they do not flash the personage, or the situation, upon the imagination, and fix it in the memory, as one of Pope's incisive lines does. Like all the greatest poets, Pope is individual and local. He can paint with his full power only what he sees. When he attempts abstract truth, general themes, past history, his want of knowledge makes itself felt, in feeble and distorted views.

Leslie Stephen

from 'Epistles and Satires', *Alexander Pope*, chapter 8   1880

I fancy that under Pope's elaborate masks of hypocrisy and mystification there was a heart always abnormally sensitive. Unfortunately it was as capable of bitter resentment as of warm affection, and was always liable to be misled by the suggestions of his strangely irritable vanity. And this seems to me to give the true key to Pope's poetical as well as to his personal characteristics.

To explain either, we must remember that he was a man of impulses; at one instant a mere incarnate thrill of gratitude or generosity, and in the next of spite or jealousy. A spasm of wounded vanity would make him for the time as mean and selfish as other men are made by a frenzy of bodily fear. He would instinctively snatch at a lie even when a moment's reflection would have shown that the plain truth would be more convenient, and therefore he had to accumulate lie upon lie, each intended to patch up some previous blunder. Though nominally the poet of reason, he was the very antithesis of the man who is reasonable in the highest sense: who is truthful in word and deed because his conduct is regulated by harmonious and invariable principles. Pope was governed by the instantaneous feeling. His emotion came in sudden jets and gushes, instead of a continuous stream. The same peculiarity deprives his poetry of continuous harmony or profound unity of conception. His lively sense of form and proportion enables him indeed to fill up a simple framework (generally of borrowed design) with an eye to general effect, as in *The*

Rape of the Lock or the first *Dunciad*. But even there his flight is short; and when a poem should be governed by the evolution of some profound principle or complex mood of sentiment, he becomes incoherent and perplexed. But on the other hand he can perceive admirably all that can be seen at a glance from a single point of view. Though he could not be continuous, he could return again and again to the same point; he could polish, correct, eliminate superfluities, and compress his meaning more and more closely, till he has constructed short passages of imperishable excellence. This microscopic attention to fragments sometimes injures the connection, and often involves a mutilation of construction. He corrects and prunes too closely. He could, he says, in reference to the *Essay on Man*, put things more briefly in verse than in prose; one reason being that he could take liberties of this kind not permitted in prose writing. But the injury is compensated by the singular terseness and vivacity of his best style. Scarcely anyone, as is often remarked, has left so large a proportion of quotable phrases, and, indeed, to the present he survives chiefly by the current coinage of that kind which bears his image and superscription.

This familiar remark may help us to solve the old problem whether Pope was, or rather in what sense he was, a poet. Much of his work may be fairly described as rhymed prose, differing from prose not in substance or tone of feeling, but only in the form of expression. Every poet has an invisible audience, as an orator has a visible one, who deserve a great part of the merit of his works. Some men may write for the religious or philosophic recluse, and therefore utter the emotions which come to ordinary mortals in the rare moments when the music of the spheres, generally drowned by the din of the commonplace world, becomes audible to their dull senses. Pope, on the other hand, writes for the wits who never listen to such strains, and moreover writes for their ordinary moods. He aims at giving us the refined and doubly distilled essence of the conversation of the statesmen and courtiers of his time. The standard of good writing always implicitly present to his mind is the fitness of his poetry to pass muster when shown by Gay to his duchess, or read after dinner to a party composed of Swift, Bolingbroke, and Congreve. That imaginary audience is always looking over his shoulder, applauding a good hit, chuckling over allusions to the last bit of scandal, and

ridiculing any extravagance tending to romance or senti-
mentalism. . . .

Pope's best writing, I have said, is the essence of conversation. It has
the quick movement, the boldness and brilliance, which we suppose
to be the attributes of the best talk. Of course the apparent facility is
due to conscientious labour. In the Prologue and Epilogue and the
best parts of the *Imitations of Horace*, he shows such consummate
mastery of his peculiar style that we forget the monotonous metre.
The opening passage, for example, of the Prologue is written apparently with the perfect freedom of real dialogue; in fact, it is of course
far more pointed and compressed than any dialogue could ever be.
The dramatic vivacity with which the whole scene is given shows that
he could use metre as the most skilful performer could command a
musical instrument. Pope, indeed, shows in the *Essay on Criticism* that
his views about the uniformity of sound and sense were crude enough;
they are analogous to the tricks by which a musician might decently
imitate the cries of animals or the murmurs of a crowd; and his art
excludes any attempt at rivalling the melody of the great poets who
aim at producing harmony quite independent of the direct meaning
of their words. I am only speaking of the felicity with which he can
move in metre, without the slightest appearance of restraint, so as to
give a kind of idealized representation of the tone of animated verbal
intercourse. Whatever comes within this province he can produce
with admirable fidelity. . . .

A genuine report of even the best conversation would be
intolerably prosy and unimaginative. But imagine the very pith and
essence of such talk brought to a focus, concentrated into the smallest
possible space with the infinite dexterity of a thoroughly trained hand,
and you have the kind of writing in which Pope is unrivalled;
polished prose with occasional gleams of genuine poetry – the *Epistle
to Arbuthnot* and the *Epilogue to the Satires*.

One point remains to be briefly noticed. The virtue on which Pope
prided himself was correctness; and I have interpreted this to mean the
quality which is gained by incessant labour, guided by quick feeling,
and always under the strict supervision of common sense. The next
literary revolution led to a depreciation of this quality. Warton (like
Macaulay long afterwards) argued that, in a higher sense, the Elizabethan poets were really as correct as Pope. Their poetry embodied

a higher and more complex law, though it neglected the narrow cut-and-dried precepts recognized in the Queen Anne period. The new school came to express too undiscriminating a contempt for the whole theory and practice of Pope and his followers. Pope, said Cowper, and a thousand critics have echoed his words –

Made poetry a mere mechanic art,
And every warbler has his tune by heart.

Without discussing the wider question, I may here briefly remark that this judgement, taken absolutely, gives a very false impression of Pope's artistic quality. Pope is undoubtedly monotonous. Except in one or two lyrics, such as the *Ode on St Cecilia's Day*, which must be reckoned amongst his utter failures, he invariably employed the same metre. The discontinuity of his style, and the strict rules which he adopted, tend to disintegrate his poems. They are a series of brilliant passages, often of brilliant couplets, stuck together in a conglomerate; and as the inferior connecting matter decays, the interstices open and allow the whole to fall into ruin. To read a series of such couplets, each complete in itself, and each so constructed as to allow of a very small variety of form, is naturally to receive an impression of monotony. Pope's antitheses fall into a few common forms, which are repeated over and over again, and seem copy to each other. And, in a sense, such work can be very easily imitated. A very inferior artist can obtain most of his efforts, and all the external qualities of his style. One ten-syllabled rhyming couplet, with the whole sense strictly confined within its limits, and allowing only of such variety as follows from changing the pauses, is undoubtedly very much like another. And accordingly one may read in any collection of British poets innumerable pages of versification which – if you do not look too close – are exactly like Pope. All poets who have any marked style are more or less imitable. ... That which makes the imitations of Pope prominent is partly the extent of his sovereignty; the vast number of writers who confined themselves exclusively to his style; and partly the fact that what is easily imitable in him is so conspicuous an element of the whole. The rigid framework which he adopted is easily definable with mathematical precision. The difference between the best works of Pope and the ordinary work of his followers is confined within narrow limits, and not easily perceived at a glance.

The difference between blank verse in the hands of its few masters and in the hands of a third-rate imitator strikes the ear in every line. Far more is left to the individual idiosyncrasy. But it does not at all follow, and in fact it is quite untrue that the distinction which turns on an apparently insignificant element is therefore unimportant. The value of all good work ultimately depends on touches so fine as to elude the sight. And the proof is that although Pope was so constantly imitated, no later and contemporary writer succeeded in approaching his excellence. . . . The explanation is – if the phrase explains anything – that he was a man of genius, or that he brought to a task, not of the highest class, a keenness of sensibility, a conscientious desire to do his very best, and a capacity for taking pains with his work, which enabled him to be as indisputably the first in his own peculiar line, as our greatest men have been in far more lofty undertakings.

Algernon Charles Swinburne

from 'A Century of English Poetry', *Fortnightly Review*
October 1880 (reprinted in *Miscellanies*, 1886)

Mr Leslie Stephen has indicated, with equally fautless instinct and fearless intelligence, the fact which even yet may seem something of a paradox, and which in other days would hardly have found utterance or hoped to find a hearing – that, 'though nominally the poet of reason', when he failed most gravely as a writer or erred most gravely as a man, he erred mainly if not merely through excess of irrational impulse. For those of course must be accounted the gravest failures of a great writer, which are made in his own proper field. Pope's lyrical collapse and pastoral imbecility need not be weighed at the weight of a feather or the worth of a straw against the worth and weight of his claims as a great writer and an admirable poet. Such matters are as much out of the question as they are now beyond and below the cognizance of serious criticism. But his faults as a moralist or a satirist, an ethical or a philosophic poet, are as clearly as ever were the faults of Byron or of Burns the natural and unavoidable errors of a temperament or an intellect in which instinct or impulse had practically the upper hand of principle and of reason. The instincts of a deformed invalid, with a bitter wit and most irritable nerves, are of course more likely than the impulses of a strong man, with healthy blood and hot passions, to seem rather intellectual than physical energies or infirmities; yet in Pope's case the body was perhaps as liable to misguide the mind, and emotion to get the start of reflection, as in the case of any hot-brained lyrist – even of any brainless athlete. Anger, if not malice also in many cases, is surely after all no less properly definable as a sensual passion than lust or gluttony. . . .

To Pope as to Dryden the general instinct of criticism has hardly been unjust, which fixes in either case upon some few detached passages as samples or as tests of their genius at its highest rather than on any whole single poem or class of poems. For it is not usually of the *Essay on Man* or the *Religio Laici*, full as these poems are of grave and careful excellence, that we all think at once when we think of Charles the Second's poet laureate or Queen Anne's poet regent. It is not of *The Hind and the Panther*, opulent and superb in august eloquence and passionate humour as is that unrivalled masterpiece of polemical poetry; perhaps it is hardly even of *The Rape of the Lock*, blameless in its beauty and perfect in its charm as is that sovereign flower of social satire. Achitophel and Zimri, Atticus and Atossa, Doeg and Og, Sporus and Bufo, rise first and clearest on our recollection, weigh last and heaviest in our judgement. As long as these great and splendid studies are familiar to all students of English literature – in other words, as long as English literature may hope to find students at all – men different in temper and tone of mind, if equally rational and capable, will agree to differ in their preference of one master to the other. My own verdict, as may probably be evident enough, would stand unhesitatingly and emphatically in favour of the elder. But I must have failed indeed of my purpose if it is not now equally evident that few if any can rate higher or relish more keenly the faultless and peerless accomplishment of his more fortunate successor. Whatever Pope has left us is 'as round and smooth as Giotto's O'; whatever Dryden has left us is liable to come short of this especial and surely precious praise. The strength of Dryden never wholly fails him; but the skill of Pope never fails him at all. He is none of the greater gods; but he is at least, in Massinger's phrase, a 'godling'; or a libellous parasite of his own day might have likened him, in Shakespeare's phrase, to 'that giant dwarf', the cunning sharpshooter of Olympus. As humorist rather than as poet, Pope is to Dryden what Sheridan is to Congreve; less deep, less rich, less naturally strong of hand; more considerate, more cautious, more 'obvious' if not 'obtrusive', in the method of his workmanship and the presentation of his talent. But Congreve on the whole must be ranked far higher above Sheridan than Dryden can properly be ranked above Pope.

Alfred Tennyson, Baron Tennyson

in conversation (*c.* 1880–83), reported in Hallam Tennyson, *Alfred Lord Tennyson: A Memoir*, 1897

He felt what Cowper calls the 'musical finesse' of Pope, and admired single lines and couplets very much; but he found the 'regular da da, da da' of his heroic metre monotonous. He quoted

What dire offence from amorous causes springs.
(*The Rape of the Lock*, I I)

'"Amrus causiz springs!" Horrible! I would sooner die than write such a line!! ...
'Pope here and there has a real insight into Nature, for example about the spider, which

Feels at each thread and lives along the line.
(*Essay on Man*, I 217)

His lancet touches are very fine.

Now night descending, the proud scene was o'er
But lived in Settle's numbers one day more.
(*The Dunciad*, I 89–90)

'What a difference,' he would add, 'between Pope's little poisonous barbs, and Dryden's strong invective! And how much more real poetic force there is in Dryden!
'Look at Pope:

He said, observant of the blue-eyed maid,
Then in the sheath returned the shining blade.
(*Iliad*, 1 291–2)

'Then at Dryden:

He said; with surly faith observed her word,
And in the sheath reluctant plunged the sword.

'The *Elegy on the Unfortunate Lady* is good, but I do not find much human feeling in him, except perhaps in *Eloisa to Abelard*.'

George Saintsbury

from 'Pope and the Later Couplet',
A History of English Prosody, vol. 2   1908

The Popian couplet is, in its own way, a Quintessence, an Entelechy; and nothing *qui tient de la Quinte* arrives at perfection at once. Whether he composed his works as early as he said he did, or as early as we know he did, they are still remarkably precocious, and it was not to be supposed that he would at once discard the easements and licences which Dryden had permitted and transmitted. Yet, as we see from Garth's *Dispensary*, there was already a tendency to reject both the alexandrine and the triplet, and it was one of Pope's special character-istics to be sensitive to such perhaps not quite skyey influences, and to express them early, forcibly, and in a way finally. He laughed at the alexandrine before he practically abandoned it: except in very early work he never seems to have been much given to Dryden's triplet, though he never quite abandoned this either, using it occasion-ally with an obvious desire for special – generally for comic – effect. In the case of these two poets the style certainly was 'de l'homme même', as the probably better reading of Buffon's maxim runs. Not merely the range of Dryden's interests, and the weight and vigour of his understanding, but a certain *bonhomie* which distinguished him, are reflected in his metre; Pope's narrower accomplishment, and his slightly viperish disposition, find their natural utterance in his. But accomplishment is a very delightful thing, and the viper, though a formidable, is really a beautiful beast. It is very interesting to watch the gradual, though by no means tardy, polishing and lightening, and in the process the necessary whittling or filing away, of the measure. With the discard of the alexandrine and the triplet, or their very unfrequent use, not only is an approach made to the imaginary 'purity' of the style, but another and still close one is also made to its uniformity, and yet another, closest of all, to its maximum swiftness. This latter desideratum is further secured by a certain not easily describable but most perceptible lightening of the rhymes – a large proportion of Pope's final words are monosyllabic – and an avoidance, not prudish, but evident, of long and heavy vocables in the interior of the lines themselves. The first line is allowed to run into the second in sense, though there is generally reserved a perceptible halt in sound to mark it; but one couplet is never allowed to run into another except for some special purpose, and seldom at all. The pause is kept as nearly as possible to the three charmed centre syllables, fourth, fifth, and sixth; and though antithesis in the halves is seldom as striking as it sometimes is in Dryden, it is perhaps more uniformly present; while that between line and line, or between both halves of both lines, is not uncommon.

One drastic but dangerous device for securing the undulating penetration of the line had been obvious from the very first in Fairfax, and much more in Waller; while, though avoided to a great extent by Dryden's masculine strength and his fertility of ideas, it had become very prominent in Garth and was never relinquished by Pope. In fact, it is probable that to his dealing with it is due the popularity of some of his most popular passages. This is the use, either at one place in the line or at corresponding ones towards its two ends, of the 'gradus epithet', the filling or padding, the cheville as the French call it, which, when overdone, is perhaps the worst blemish of the style. There are passages . . . in The Dispensary and The Rape of the Lock where you can convert the decasyllable into the octosyllable for several lines together without detriment to sense or poetry, by simply taking out these specious superfluities. No doubt, in Pope himself especially, there are others where you cannot; but the temptation is a besetting one, and the second-rate poets fall into it almost to a man.

With Pope, however, as with other poets majorum gentium, we must trace the successive shapings of this famous instrument. Let us take

his word for it that the *Pastorals*, though not published till 1709, were
written five years earlier, in their author's sixteenth year. The first
six lines will well illustrate the process above outlined; but if space
would permit, the illustration might be extended to the whole piece –

First in these fields I try the *sylvan* strains,
Nor blush to sport on Windsor's *blissful* plains.
Fair Thames, flow gently from thy *sacred* spring,
While on thy banks *Sicilian* Muses sing;
Let *vernal* airs through *trembling* osiers play,
And Albion's cliffs resound the *rural* lay.

   Now this, by the omission of some of the *gradus* epithets, becomes –

First in these fields I try the strains,
Nor blush to sport on Windsor's plains.
Fair Thames, flow gently from thy spring,
While on thy banks [the] Muses sing;
Let vernal airs through osiers play,
And Albion's cliffs resound the lay –

where, if anybody prefers it, the fifth line may run –

Let airs through trembling oisiers play;

for 'vernal' and 'trembling' are equally good illustrations of that
antithetic epithet with no antithesis in it, which is the curse of the
style, and which Pope, though he often avoided it later, did not
always, even then, avoid.

   This sample, purposely cut short in order not to take an unfair
advantage, shows at once, but I think without appeal, the intensely
artificial character of this versification, and its attendant diction.
Poetry becomes an abacus, where a certain but limited number of
beads can be slipped on or off, arranged in corresponding groups to
suit taste and demand. Dictionaries of phrase and rhyme become, as
they were in the 'Maronolatrous' period of the Renaissance, allow-
able and almost indispensable, and the Temple of Apollo is a sort of
poetic exchange or clearing-house.

   Yet in these, and in their professed companions the *Messiah* and the
First Part of *Windsor Forest*, it would be either idle or uncatholic to

deny an extraordinary dexterity at the game, such as it is. The wonderful *nerve* of Dryden (which Pope was hardly ever to reach, except perhaps in the really magnificent close of *The Dunciad*) is not there; and the matter is *publica materies* enough. But the 'careless verses', which Langton in a tell-tale phrase complained of (as Boswell tells us) in Glorious John, are absent likewise – the whole is swept, garnished, polished (furniture-polished?) to a miraculous degree. . . .

If we turn to the *Essay on Criticism*, said to have been written some four or five years later than this group, it is interesting to find something of a declension from this rigid playing of the game, not an advance in it. The alexandrine is indeed stigmatized in the famous verse that exemplifies it;[1] but there are numerous triplets, which is explained by the fact that the poem is argumentative, and that, in consequence, the author not merely feels the twenty-syllable cramp much more sharply than in descriptive and imitated substance, but naturally recurs to the licence allowed himself by the greatest master, except Lucretius, of argumentative poetics. The constraint and the pattern are both removed in *The Rape of the Lock*; and the triplet accordingly disappears. But the *gradus* epithet and its antithetic distribution appear more than ever – for equally obvious reasons. Point and sparkle, which they supply at a tolerably cheap rate, are especially necessary; and there is another subtle influence which may be seen in operation from Chaucer downwards in almost all our greater poets except Milton, Wordsworth, Shelley, and Tennyson, in whom the sense of humour was weak or intermittent, and Byron, in whom it was kept down by egotism and affectation. The poet, to what extent consciously it is difficult to say, caricatures himself and his methods as a means of adding zest to the caricature of other things and persons. This may seem to be considering too curiously as to the cause; the effect is certain. The famous and, in its rococo way, really beautiful opening of the second canto exhibits it in a fashion which a few italics ought to bring out sufficiently; while the other fashion in which the verses 'split' right down the paragraph – like a bit of starch when you drop water on it – and the odd ridge-backed appearance

1 It is only fair to Pope to remind the reader, again, that he also fully admitted and illustrated its merits in the line on his and its great master—

> The long majestic march, and energy divine.

(*Imitations of Horace, Epistles*, II i 269)

which they present, may be pardonably illustrated by a very slight violence to their typographical arrangement in a note.[1]

The diagram, I think, does not bring out unfairly the curious jointed-doll character of the metre. Hardly even Johnson's prose antitheses are more exactly proportioned than these: 'ethereal', 'purpled', and 'silver' in different lines; 'white' and 'sparkling', 'Jews' and 'Infidels', in the same; while the way in which the verse runs up the hill, halts, and then runs down again, is positively acrobatic in its deftness of mechanic agility. For the subject nothing could be better: nothing, at least in a poem of any length, could well be so good: but then the subject is – the subject.

The *Elegy on an Unfortunate Lady* answers the objection started in the final words of the last paragraph, and shows once for all *qualis artifex* Pope was, and how ridiculous it is to ask the question 'Whether he was a poet?' (I do not say that it is ridiculous to ask 'What sort of a poet was he?'). The general scheme of verse is the same; but it is altered with marvellous ingenuity to suit the particular matter. It is an enormous confession, though one made quite safely to the immediate readers – who did not in the least apprehend it – and perhaps even made unconsciously by the poet, that the double arrangement – the centred *crease* – of every line is largely given up. There are lines, and

1

Not with more glories in th' *ethereal* plain
The sun first rises o'er the *purpled* main,
Than issuing forth the rival of his beams
Launched on the bosom of the *silver* Thames.
Fair nymphs, and well-dressed youths around her shone,
But every eye was fixed on her alone.
On her *white* breast a *sparkling* cross she wore,
Which *Jews* might kiss and *infidels* adore.
Her *lively* looks a *sprightly* mind disclose,
Quick as her eyes and as unfixed as those.
Favours to none to all she *smiles* extends,
Oft she rejects but never *once* offends.
Bright as the sun her eyes the gazers strike,
And like the sun they shine on all alike.
Yet graceful ease and sweetness void of pride
Might hide her faults if belles had faults to hide.
If to her share some female errors fall,
Look on her face and you'll forget 'em all.

many of them, which have hardly more middle pause than in Shakespeare, save a fictitious one. The *gradus* epithet and its antithetic use are not absent; but they are rarer and subdued, as if purposely. Old rhetorical devices – epanaphora especially – are brought in to heighten the style; to be 'sources of the sublime', as Longinus says. The piece has always been something of a puzzle, and all the exertions of the commentator as to 'Mrs W.' have not quite cleared that puzzle up. But it remains Pope's best serious thing, untinged by satire – for this last appears even in *The Dunciad* 'curtain'. And it would have been interesting to see whether, if he had made larger practice in the language of the heart, instead of that of the head and the spleen, he could have given yet further range and timbre to his poetic speech.

It is only necessary to turn to the other piece which is sometimes coupled with it, *Eloisa to Abelard*, to see the return from the piano to the pianola. Here too, of course, old Mr Pope would have been justified in saying 'these are good rhymes', but perhaps nobody would be justified in saying much more. That the artificiality which is the curse of the couplet can be vanquished has just been admitted: it is proved not merely by *The Unfortunate Lady* and *The Dunciad* close in Pope, but in Johnson by the almost equally magnificent and much more certainly sincere termination of *The Vanity of Human Wishes* (where, however, there is a strong infusion of Dryden), by Tickell's splendid 'Cadogan' epicede, and elsewhere. But it has always got to do everything that it knows to keep the art from being too obviously uppermost, and too suggestively exclusive. *Eloisa to Abelard* . . . does not do this. Its last line,

He best can paint 'em who shall feel 'em most

is unlucky in more than its apostrophes. The painting of the poem is admirable, but of the feeling it is impossible to say much; and this extends to the most as well as to the least mechanical part of the execution. The undoubted truth, and still more undoubted *pointe*,

All is not Heaven's while Abelard has part,

or

Nor wished an angel whom I loved a man –

the frequent tags from Dryden, which only bring out the difference of method, the 'roseate bowers' and 'trances ecstatic' and the rest – leave us sadly cold. It is very neat – very neat indeed; but neatness is not exactly poetry. . . .

It is, however, most interesting, and should supply a fresh evidence of Pope's craftsmanship, to find that though his thirteen years' practice in translation is in a sense a 'loop' – that though he comes back at the end of it to his old style like a giant refreshed, he has not been pursuing that style with slavish exactness or constancy inviolable meanwhile. The fact is that, like a wise man, he evidently had consulted Dryden's translations afresh before he attempted his own, and that he to some extent recurs to the Drydenian model rather than to his own. He is, perhaps, rather more faithful; and this fidelity itself keeps out the antithetic *gradus* epithet – to some extent only. In the same way, Homer does not so very frequently admit, and certainly never invites, the antithetic or 'ridge-backed' division of the line itself. On the other hand, he does invite the alexandrine; and Pope finds this by no means 'needless', and manages to make it by no means 'slow'.

Still, the whole medium, deft as it is, has much more monotony than Dryden's, and its peculiar character is almost sufficiently indicated by the well-known fact that there is really very little difference between the work of Pope's coadjutors and his own – a fact which ought to be taken in conjunction with the anticipations of Garth and Young, and the 'tune by heart' of all the couplet-warblers of the rest of the century. The Popian line is indeed so thoroughly 'standardized' – its parts are, like those of a cheap watch, made so perfectly interchangeable, that in its mere prosodic influence there is hardly any secret effect left possible. . . . The rosin as well as the fiddle is within the reach of Hoole as well as of Pope. There is, of course, a difference, and a vast one, between Pope and Hoole; but that wants a different simile. The glass is the same glass almost exactly; but the wine poured in is very different.

The quality of the wine which Pope poured out for his guests in the *Essays* and *Satires* is well known. People may call it amontillado or absinthe, vermouth or vitriol, as they like; in fact, it, at different times, deserves well enough each of the four descriptions. But we are here concerned with this wine only in connection with its glass. It is certain (to drop the metaphor) that no other form of verse has ever been devised which would have suited the matter so well; while there is no other example, in all literature, of a single metre (except perhaps the Lucretian hexameter) in such absolute adaptation to the temper and mood of the poet. Pope may have lisped in numbers: he certainly thought in couplets. Moreover, now that he was free from translation, he went back, naturally enough, to his own more special form, and brought that form closer and closer to its highest – or lowest – terms. Here you may turn pages and pages without finding a triplet; while the alexandrine is never used unless for some very special purpose. There is hardly such a thing as a rough, a loose, or a limping line. We think most naturally of the purple patches: the 'Atticus' libel, written earlier no doubt, but polished and published now; the *Dunciad* conclusion; the scores of passages only less famous, and the hundreds or thousands of couplets, lines, or phrases, which are (or recently were) part of the language of every educated Englishman. But this is in a way unjust; for the difficulty – not quite the impossibility – would be to find anything that is not perfect according to its own standard of perfection.

Francis Thompson

from 'Pope', *A Renegade Poet and Other Essays*   1910

The Dunciad De Quincey ranked even above *The Rape of the Lock*. At my peril I venture to question a judgement backed by all the ages. The superb satire of parts of the poem I admit; I admit the exceedingly fine close, in which Pope touched a height he never touched before or after; I admit the completeness of the scheme. But from that completeness comes the essential defect of the poem. He adapted the scheme from Dryden's *MacFlecknoe*. But Dryden's satire is at once complete and succinct: Pope has built upon the scheme an edifice greater than it will bear; has extended a witty and ingenious idea to a portentous extent at which it ceases to be amusing. The mock solemnity of Dryden's idea becomes a very real and dull solemnity when it is extended to liberal epic proportions. A serious epic is apt to nod, with the force of a Milton behind it; an epic satire fairly goes to sleep. A pleasantry in several books is past a pleasantry. And it is bolstered out with a great deal which is sheer greasy scurrility. The mock-heroic games of the poets are in large part as dully dirty as the water into which Pope makes them plunge.

If the poem had been half as long, it might have been a masterpiece. As it is, unless we are to reckon masterpieces by avoirdupois weight, or to assign undue value to mere symmetry of scheme, I think we must look for Pope's satirical masterpiece elsewhere. Not in the satire on women, where Pope seems hardly to have his heart in his work; but in the imitations from Horace, those generally known as Pope's *Satires*. Here he is at his very best and tersest. They are as brilliant as anything in *The Dunciad*, and they are brilliant right through; the mordant pen never flags. It matters not that they are imitated from Horace. They gain by it: their limits are circumscribed, their lines laid down, and Pope writes the better for having these limits set him, this tissue on which to work. Not a whit does he lose in essential originality: nowhere is he so much himself. It is very different from Horace, say the critics. Surely that is exactly the thing for which to thank poetry and praise Pope. It has not the pleasant urbane good humour of the Horatian spirit. No, it has the spirit of Pope – and satire is the gainer. Horace is the more charming companion; Pope is the greater satirist. In place of an echo of Horace (and no verse translation was every anything but feeble which attempted merely to echo the original), we have a new spirit in satire; a fine series of English satirical poems, which in their kind are unapproached by the Roman, and in his kind wisely avoid the attempt to approach him. *Satires after Horace* would have been a better title than *Imitations*; for less imitative poems in essence were never written. These and *The Rape of the Lock* are Pope's finest title to fame. . . .

On the whole, it is as a satirist we must think of him, and the second greatest in the language. The gods are in pairs, male and female; and if Dryden was the Mars of English satire, Pope was the Venus – a very eighteenth-century Venus, quite as conspicuous for malice as for elegance. If a woman's satire were informed with genius, and cultivated to the utmost perfection of form by lifelong and exclusive literary practice, one imagines it would be much like Pope's. His style seems to me feminine in what it lacks; the absence of any geniality, any softening humour to abate its mortal thrust. It is feminine in what it has, the malice, the cruel dexterity, the delicate needle point which hardly betrays its light and swift entry, yet stings like a bee. Even in his coarseness – as in *The Dunciad* – Pope appears to me female. It is the coarseness of the fine ladies of that material time, the Lady Maries and the rest of them. Dryden is a rough and thick-natured man, cudgelling his adversaries with coarse speech in the heat and brawl and the bluntness of his sensibilities; a country squire, who is apt at times to use the heavy end of his cutting whip; but when Pope is coarse he is coarse with effort, he goes out of his way to be nasty, in the evident endeavour to imitate a man. It is a girl airing the slang of her schoolboy brother.

The one thing, perhaps, which differentiates him from a woman, and makes it possible to read his verse with a certain pleasure, without that sense of unrelieved cruelty which repels one in much female satire, is his artist's delight in the exercise of his power.

J. C. Squire

from 'How They Would Have Done It', *Tricks of the Trade*   1917

If Pope Had Written 'Break, Break, Break'

Fly, Muse, thy wonted themes, nor longer seek
The consolations of a powder'd cheek;
Forsake the busy purlieus of the Court
For calmer meads where finny tribes resort.
So may th' Almighty's natural antidote
Abate the worldly tenour of thy note,
The various beauties of the liquid main
Refine thy reed and elevate thy strain.

See how the labour of the urgent oar
Propels the barks and draws them to the shore.
Hark! from the margin of the azure bay
The joyful cries of infants at their play.
(The offspring of a piscatorial swain,
His home the sands, his pasturage the main.)
Yet none of these may soothe the mourning heart,
Nor fond alleviation's sweets impart;

Nor may the pow'rs of infants that rejoice
Restore the accents of a former voice,
Nor the bright smiles of ocean's nymphs command
The pleasing contact of a vanished hand.
So let me still in meditation move,
Muse in the vale and ponder in the grove,
And scan the skies where sinking Phoebus glows
With hues more rubicund than Cibber's nose. . . .

(*After which the Poet gets into his proper stride.*)

T. S. Eliot (anonymously)

from 'John Dryden', *The Times Literary Supplement* 9 June 1921
(reprinted in *Homage to John Dryden*, 1924)

Much of Dryden's unique merit consists in his ability to make the small into the great, the prosaic into the poetic, the trivial into the magnificent. In this he differs not only from Milton, who required a canvas of the largest size, but from Pope, who required one of the smallest. If you compare any satiric 'character' of Pope with one of Dryden, you will see that the method and intention are widely divergent. When Pope alters, he diminishes; he is a master of miniature. The singular skill of his portrait of Addison, for example, in the *Epistle to Arbuthnot*, depends upon the justice and reserve, the apparent determination not to exaggerate. The genius of Pope is not for caricature. But the effect of the portraits of Dryden is to transform the object into something greater.

Lytton Strachey

from *Pope* 1925

Pope, we are told, was not only without 'high seriousness'; he lacked no less an 'adequate poetic criticism of life'. What does this mean? The phrase is ambiguous; it signifies at once too much and too little. If we are to understand – as the context seems to imply – that, in

Matthew Arnold's opinion, no poetic criticism of life can be adequate unless it possesses largeness, freedom, and benignity, we must certainly agree that Pope's poetic criticism of life was far from adequate; for his way of writing was neither large nor free, and there was nothing benignant about him. But the words will bear another interpretation; and in this sense it may turn out that Pope's poetic criticism of life was adequate to an extraordinary degree.

Let us examine for a moment the technical instrument which Pope used – I mean the heroic couplet. . . .

Perhaps the most characteristic of all the elements in the couplet is antithesis. Ordinary regularity demands that the sense should end with every line – that was a prime necessity; but a more scrupulous symmetry would require something more – a division of the line itself into two halves, whose meanings should correspond. And yet a further refinement was possible: each half might be again divided, and the corresponding divisions in the two halves might be so arranged as to balance each other. The force of neatness could no further go; and thus the most completely evolved type of the heroic line is one composed of four main words arranged in pairs, so as to form a double antithesis.

Willing to wound, and yet afraid to strike
(*Epistle to Dr Arbuthnot*, 203)

is an example of such a line, and Pope's poems are full of them. With astonishing ingenuity he builds up these exquisite structures, in which the parts are so cunningly placed that they seem to interlock spontaneously, and, while they are all formed on a similar model, are yet so subtly adjusted that they produce a fresh pleasure as each one appears. But that is not all. Pope was pre-eminently a satirist. He was naturally drawn to the contemplation of human beings, their conduct in society, their characters, their motives, their destinies; and the feelings which these contemplations habitually aroused in him were those of scorn and hatred. Civilization illumined by animosity – such was his theme; such was the passionate and complicated material from which he wove his patterns of balanced precision and polished clarity. Antithesis penetrates below the structure; it permeates the whole conception of his work. Fundamental opposites clash, and are reconciled. The profundities of persons, the futilities of existence, the rage and spite of genius – these things are mixed together, and presented to our eyes in the shape of a Chinese box. The essence of all art is the accomplishment of the impossible. This cannot be done, we say; and it *is* done. What has happened? A magician has waved his wand. It is impossible that Pope should convey to us his withering sense of the wretchedness and emptiness of the fate of old women in society, in five lines, each containing four words, arranged in pairs, so as to form a double antithesis. But the magician waves his wand, and there it is –

See how the world its veterans rewards!
A youth of frolics, an old age of cards;
Fair to no purpose, artful to no end,
Young without lovers, old without a friend;
A fop their passion, but their prize a sot;
Alive, ridiculous, and dead, forgot!
(*Moral Essay II*, 243–8)

And now, perhaps, we have discovered what may truly be said to have been Pope's 'poetic criticism of life'. His poetic criticism of life was, simply and solely, the heroic couplet.

Virginia Woolf

from *Orlando: A Biography*, chapter 4   1928

For about the third time Orlando went there [to one of Lady R.'s assemblies] a certain incident occurred. She was still under the illusion that she was listening to the most brilliant epigrams in the world, though, as a matter of fact, old General C. was only saying, at some length, how the gout had left his left leg and gone to his right, while Mr L. interrupted when any proper name was mentioned, 'R.? Oh! I know Billy R. as well as I know myself. S.? My dearest friend. T.? Stayed with him a fortnight in Yorkshire' – which, such is the force of illusion, sounded like the wittiest repartee, the most searching comment upon human life, and kept the company in a roar; when the door opened and a little gentleman entered whose name Orlando did not catch. Soon a curiously disagreeable sensation came over her. To judge from their faces, the rest began to feel it as well. One

gentleman said there was a draught. The Marchioness of C. feared a
cat must be under the sofa. It was as if their eyes were being slowly
opened after a pleasant dream and nothing met them but a cheap
wash-stand and a dirty counterpane. It was as if the fumes of some
delicious wine were slowly leaving them. Still the General talked and
still Mr L. remembered. But it became more and more apparent how
red the General's neck was, how bald Mr L.'s head was. As for what
they said – nothing more tedious and trivial could be imagined.
Everybody fidgeted and those who had fans yawned behind them.
At last Lady R. rapped with hers upon the arm of her great chair.
Both gentlemen stopped talking.

> Then the little gentleman said,
> He said next,
> He said finally,[1]

Here, it cannot be denied, was true wit, true wisdom, true profundity,
The company was thrown into complete dismay. One such saying was
bad enough; but three, one after another, on the same evening! No
society could survive it.

'Mr Pope,' said old Lady R. in a voice trembling with sarcastic
fury, 'you are pleased to be witty.' Mr Pope flushed red. Nobody
spoke a word. They sat in dead silence some twenty minutes. Then,
one by one, they rose and slunk from the room. That they would
ever come back after such an experience was doubtful.
(182–3)

Allen Tate

'Mr Pope', from *Mr Pope and Other Poems* 1928

When Alexander Pope strolled in the city
Strict was the glint of pearl and gold sedans.
Ladies leaned out more out of fear than pity
For Pope's tight back was rather a goat's than man's.

---

1 These sayings are too well known to require repetition, and besides, they
are all to be found in his published works.

Often one thinks the urn should have more bones
Than skeletons provide for speedy dust,
The urn gets hollow, cobwebs brittle as stones
Weave to the funeral shell a frivolous rust.

And he who dribbled couplets like a snake
Coiled to a lithe precision in the sun
Is missing. The jar is empty; you may break
It only to find that Mr Pope is gone.

What requisitions of a verity
Prompted the wit and rage between his teeth
One cannot say. Around a crooked tree
A moral climbs whose name should be a wreath.

Edith Sitwell

from 'Some Notes on Pope's Poetry', *Alexander Pope*,
chapter 18   1930

It is generally believed, by those whose appreciation of verse is a
platonic one, that poetry springs from the poet's head, as Minerva
sprang from the head of Jove. That is an easy explanation of the birth
of our goddess, but it is not one which satisfies me. If we were to ask
any of the poets of the past, we should without doubt be told that
poetry is just as much a matter of physical aptitude as of spiritual.
The poet feels, with his poetry, the same certainty yet excitement as
a jockey feels with a racehorse. He has sensitive hands that feel the
horse's mouth, that understand all the variations of speed, he has a
body that is supremely fitted to ride the horse, a body that is light
and that seems like part of his polished and victorious speed.

I believe that a poem begins in the poet's head, and then grows in
his blood, as a rose grows among its dark leaves.

The poet feels the poem in the palm of his sensitive hands, understanding its exact weight (a most necessary part of the growth of the
poem) letting the poem grow in his veins. He strokes it with his long
fingers, as a sculptor divines the shape within the snow-cold, or sea-
cold, marble that will soon discard, with his aid, all its outer sleep-

wrappings, and stand revealed in its age-long beauty, one of a people of smiling statues, looking across an eternal and youthful sea.

The poet knows, through his sensitive hands, the difference between the sea-cold marble of the Ode, with all its divine variation of ivy-dark veins (cold as the satyrine forests) – veins with the shape of the Aegean waves within them, veins full of the light – the difference between this and the hot velvet petals of that rose the lyric – whose sound and whose music with its air-subtle variation makes the listener

Die of a rose in aromatic pain.
(*Essay on Man*, I 200)

He feels in the veins of his hand, the shape and the texture of the poem before it has grown.

Poetry, too, is not only a result of this sensitiveness, but the form of the poem is dependent, very largely, on muscle. It is nearly always possible to judge of the poet's physique from his technique. Blanks, for instance, would have been impossible to a poet of Pope's tiny and weak body; but the stopped heroic couplet, with its sustaining rhymes, its outward cage (though that cage holds within it all the waves, and the towers and the gulfs of the world), this was born to be his measure. And it was because of his physical pain and weak physique that he, so wisely, perfected himself in the use of the couplet (the perfection is more miraculous, perhaps, than that of any other poetry), instead of attempting other and less suitable forms. He must, I think, have had strong and sensitive hands, otherwise he would not have attained to his supreme mastery of texture – that texture and under-standing of the accumulation of quantities to which his extraordinary variation is due.

Professor Saintsbury has written so fully of the heroic couplet that it would be a mere impertinence for one of so little learning as myself to discuss the couplet; but I would like, however, to examine the charge of monotony that has been brought against Pope.

Sir Leslie Stephen, in his *Life of Pope*, complains of the monotony of Pope's technique – as though the heroic couplet, with its infinite and subtle variation (especially in the hands of Pope) – were all of one depth, of one height, of one texture. How, for instance, can one compare the deep, sleepy richness, like that of some heavily-perfumed dark rose, of Keats' enjambed couplets, with the bucolic clumsiness of Chaucer's heroic couplets (as yet an unperfected form), or with the sylph-woven nets of dew of *The Rape of the Lock*, and the murky and hellish beauty of *The Dunciad*? . . .

The heroic couplet which is kept strictly within the limits of its outward structure is as variable within those limits, as waves, as the air, with its light variations of wind, indeed, as variable as the earth itself, with its mountains and plains, its snows and gardens, towers, and gulfs. The reason why, to an insensitive ear, the heroic couplet seems monotonous is because structure alone, and not texture, has been regarded as the maker of rhythm. In reality, both are the parents of rhythm in poetry; and variations in speed are certainly the result, not only of structure, but also of texture. Prosodists have been unable, for obvious reasons, to discuss *all* the infinitely subtle variations and fluctuations of rhythm, and people of a coarse ear or taste in poetry have seized upon this silence as to these minute fluctuations and variations, as an excuse for denying or ignoring that the variations were there. Yet half the beauty and variation of English poetry is due to the prosodists' cunning and pretended deafness to the slightest of these fluctuations.

How faint they are, yet how significant – faint as the little air which comes to us from the feathers of the swan's wings, as he floats upon the lake. How slight, and how subtle are the changes of speed, or of depth, due to the difference in texture, and due to the fact that the English, in their cunning over the matter of poetry, have adopted the idea of equivalent syllables, that system which produces more variation than any other device. For is it really to be supposed that two words of one syllable each equal in speed one word of two syllables? The two-syllabled words, if unweighted by heavy consonants, move far more quickly. The system, therefore, of equivalent syllables gives variation to our poetry. Think, too, of the difference in speed caused by texture, by the use of heavy consonants, and especially the enormous effect on rhythm obtained by the variable use of rhyme.

I think I am right in saying that the rhythm and speed of a skilful and beautiful *un*rhymed poem differs from the rhythm and speed of a rhymed poem containing the same number and arrangement of feet, and that both the rhymed and unrhymed poems differ slightly in these respects from a poem ending with dissonances or with assonances, yet still containing the same number and arrangement of feet. It is a fact, too, that if assonances and dissonances are put at different places within the lines, and intermingled with equally skilfully placed internal rhymes, this has an intense effect both upon rhythm and in controlling and heightening speed; and the effect on rhythm and sometimes, though not always, on speed, is different to that of lines containing elaborately schemed internal rhymes without assonances or dissonances.

The truth is that the texture of a poem has, in the past, been regarded as merely a matter of fatness or leanness – has been acknowledged only as producing richness, or sweetness, or harshness, in the poem; but the fact that texture is largely responsible for rhythm, for variations in the speed of the poem, that has not been acknowledged....

As an example of Pope's so-called monotony, let us take the difference between *The Rape of the Lock*, with its infinite variations, and *The Dunciad*, with its enormous variations of height and depth, speed, and heavy consciously-dulled sloth. *The Rape of the Lock*, this miraculous poem, which has been most foolishly described as a work in silver filigree, is light, variable and enchanting as a little summer wind blowing down the golden spangles of the dew from the great faunal trees – the whole poem might have been woven by the air-thin golden fingers of Pope's sylphs. This thin and glittering texture, how did it ever come into being? The lines differ in no wise from the wings of the sylphs, as they float above the barge:

Some to the sun their insect-wings unfold,
Waft on the breeze, or sink in clouds of gold.
Transparent forms, too fine for mortal sight,
Their fluid bodies half dissolved in light.
Loose to the wind their airy garments flew,
Thin glitt'ring textures of the filmy dew;
Dipped in the richest tincture of the skies,
Where light disports in ever-mingling dyes,
While every beam new transient colours flings,
Colours that change whene'er they wave their wings.
(II 59–68)

Those lines are the only fitting description of the poem itself; it is impossible to describe it in other terms. And yet Pope has been held to be deficient in beauty!

The only touch of shadow in those lines is the word 'waft', but I imagine that not in any other poem in the English language could such complete and dazzling control of texture be found, with the light and lovely liquids of the earlier lines, and the richer colour of the last two couplets. Compare the lines quoted above, with the description of the card-party, in the third canto, with the velvety softness, and depth and shade – like the shadow cast by a great tree on some hot afternoon.

And particoloured troops, a shining train,
Draw forth to combat on the velvet plain.
The skilful nymph reviews her force with care;
Let spades be trumps! she said, and trumps they were.
Now move to war her sable Matadores,
In show like leaders of the swarthy Moors.
Spadillio first, unconquerable lord!
Led off two captive trumps, and swept the board.
(III 43–50)

Compare this with the early morning whiteness of the first canto, and see how far the charge of monotony can be brought against Pope. . . .

It has been the fashion to regard only the tempests of fury, and not the strange murky and Tartarean beauty of *The Dunciad*, although it is one of the greatest poems in our language. Yet it is just as beautiful in its own way, and just as strange, as *The Ancient Mariner*. It has been held not to be, only because it is a satire, and people whose liking for poetry is a purely sentimental one are unable to believe that beauty is not dependent upon subject alone.

How enormous are the opening lines, with the thick, muffled, dull thud of the alliterating *m*s:

The mighty mother, and her son who brings
The Smithfield muses to the ears of kings.

The sound is thick, gross, and blind as stupidity itself. Then take the lines:

Fate in their dotage this fair idiot gave,
Gross as her sire, and as her mother grave,

Laborious, heavy, busy, bold, and blind,
She ruled, in native anarchy, the mind.
(l 13–16)

The *g* sounds in the first and last word of the second line give a
designedly unwieldy lumbering gait to the line, a gait indicative
of the subject; the next line, with its appalling deafening blows,
caused by the alliterative *b*s, placed so close together, has an overwhelming effect of power.

If we compare those varying lines with those I have quoted from
The Rape of the Lock, I do not see how it is possible, for any but the
most insensitive, to uphold that Pope is monotonous.

A. E. Housman

from *The Name and Nature of Poetry* 1933

His great successor, whose *Iliad* was a more dazzling and seductive
example of the false manner than any work of Dryden's own, and
became, as Coleridge said, 'the main source of our pseudo-poetic
diction' – Pope, though he threw open to others the wide gate, did
not long keep them company on the broad way, which led them to
destruction. He came to recognize, and for the last twenty years of his
life he steadily followed, the true bent of his genius, in satire or
disputation: into these he put no larger quantity and no rarer quality
of poetry than they would assimilate, and he made no more ascents
in the balloon. Pope has less of the poetic gifts than Dryden; in
common with his contemporaries he drew from a poorer vocabulary;
and his versification, though more evenly good, did not reach the
buoyant excellence of Dryden's at its best. What lifts him nearest to
true poetry is sincere inward ardour. Pope had a soul in his body, an
aery and fiery particle, where Dryden had nothing but a lump of
clay, and he can be nobler than Dryden can. But not even in the
Elegy to the Memory of an Unfortunate Lady does the fire burn clear of
smoke, and truth of emotion do itself full justice in naturalness and
purity of diction.

Nuns fret not at their convent's narrow room, and the eighteenth
century, except for a few malcontents, was satisfied with what its

leading poets provided. 'It is surely superfluous,' says Johnson, 'to answer the question that has once been asked, whether Pope was a poet, otherwise than by asking in return, if Pope be not a poet, where is poetry to be found?' It is to be found, Dr Johnson, in Dr Watts.

Soft and easy is thy cradle;
   Coarse and hard thy Saviour lay,
When his birthplace was a stable
   And his softest bed was hay.

That simple verse, bad rhyme and all, is poetry beyond Pope. It is to be found again, Samuel, in your namesake Benjamin, as tough a piece of timber as yourself.

What gentle ghost, besprent with April dew,
Hails me so solemnly to yonder yew,
And beckoning woos me, from the fatal tree,
To pluck a garland for herself or me?

When Pope imitated that, he got no nearer than this:

What beckoning ghost, along the moonlight shade
Invites my step, and points to yonder glade?
'Tis she! – but why that bleeding bosom gored, *etc.*
(*Elegy to the Memory of an Unfortunate Lady*, 1–3)

When I hear anyone say, with defiant emphasis, that Pope was a poet, I suspect him of calling in ambiguity of language to promote confusion of thought. That Pope was a poet is true; but it is one of those truths which are beloved of liars, because they serve so well the cause of falsehood. That Pope was not a poet is false; but a righteous man, standing in awe of the last judgement and the lake which burneth with fire and brimstone, might well prefer to say it.

It is impossible to admire such poetry as Pope's so whole-heartedly as Johnson did, and to rest in it with such perfect contentment, without losing the power to appreciate finer poetry or even to recognize it when met.

Part Three Modern Views

Introduction

The fluctuations of Pope's reputation have been more extreme than in the case of any other comparable English poet, except perhaps Tennyson. During his life-time, though his personal character was often – and rightly – under attack, the excellence of his verse was not denied even by his enemies (with the one exception of John Dennis). And by 1740, to men of such wide general culture as Chesterfield and Fielding, he was already a classic, a poet comparable to Virgil or Horace, to Tasso or Boileau – one of the then very few English literary classics. The reaction with Wordsworth and Coleridge, and the Romantics generally (except Byron), was equally excessive. Their ultimate literary criterion was 'sincerity', and judged by this test Pope's poetry was, with some justice, dismissed as a continual falsetto. But, as the nineteenth century proceeded, the Romantic reaction gradually worked itself out. In the criticism of such representative figures as George Saintsbury, Edmund Gosse, Leslie Stephen and Austin Dobson, for example, a much more sympathetic if still rather superficial attitude is already discernible.

The almost sub-critical interest common to the Edwardians was transmitted in due course to the Bloomsbury group who dominated the London literary scene throughout the 1920s. Virginia Woolf, the daughter of Leslie Stephen, and her friend and ally Lytton Strachey, are its representative figures. Both were Popians, but in a fanciful and sub-critical way, as was also Edith Sitwell, who between her poems managed to write an eccentric, enthusiastic and very inaccurate life of Pope.

The more recent attitude to Pope is at its best both more critical and more scholarly. Indeed, it is the convergence of these two approaches that has been the most significant development since 1930. A crucial influence from one side has been William Empson's *Seven Types of Ambiguity* (1930), a book that is the source and fountain-head of all modern 'close reading', 'practical criticism', and 'explication' of poetry – techniques Empson has demonstrated

to be particularly fruitful for a proper reading of Pope. A simple
example of Empsonian subtlety is the familiar 'zeugma' about
Hampton Court in *The Rape of the Lock*, in which the one word
'take' is used in two different senses according to the verb's object:

There thou, great Anna, whom three realms obey
Dost sometimes counsel take and sometimes tea.[1]

Empson's comment on these lines is that 'the effect of limited
comprehensiveness, of a unity in variety mirrored from the real
world, is obtained by putting together two of the innumerable
meanings of the word "take"' – which in a single sentence
transmutes a rhetorical trick into a comment on the relationship
between language and phenomenal reality.

The protagonist and hero in the reform of Pope scholarship in
our time has been George Sherburn, professor successively at
Chicago and Harvard, whose elegant English prose style might
nevertheless have emanated from Oxford or Cambridge. Sherburn's
The Early Career of Alexander Pope (1934) is a model biography in
which a mass of factual material, much of it new, is organized into
a lucid and eminently readable story. Its only fault is that it stops
at 1727. The history of Pope's later life, which begins with the first
version of *The Dunciad*, still awaits a comparable treatment, though
Sherburn's successor will have the benefit of Sherburn's meticulous
edition of *The Correspondence of Alexander Pope* (5 vols., 1956) to
build on.

While Sherburn and his colleagues, English and American, were
busy on their respective biographical and editorial labours, the
younger scholar-critics whom they had trained were writing
articles in the learned or semi-learned journals on different aspects
of Pope's poetry and life. Maynard Mack, who edited the *Essay on
Man* for the collaborative Twickenham edition, and also supervised
its *Iliad* and *Odyssey*, has assembled what he calls *Essential Articles*

1 Then pronounced as in the French *thé*.

for the Study of Alexander Pope (1965), none of which is earlier than
1935. If it is difficult to agree that all of the forty-four articles are
'essential', most of them are at least well worth looking at. The
most searching criticism of Pope that is now being written will be
found in such articles and studies, and the serious reader of Pope
will be well advised to keep a watchful eye on the current issues of
the standard journals. His point of departure will presumably be
the one-volume edition into which John Butt, the general editor of
the series, abbreviated the separate 'Twickenham' volumes (except
the *Iliad* and the *Odyssey*).

All in all Pope is more popular today, at least among lovers and
students of poetry, than he has been at any time since the days of
Dr Johnson. No one is likely to deny that. But a critical caveat must
be added. The success of Empson and his fellow-explicators and of
Sherburn and his fellow-scholars has carried with it a possible
danger. Granted, as we must, the special success of the new methods
in the case of Pope's poetry, may there not be a risk that its value
as aesthetic artifact has been proportionately overrated? May not
the reaction against Matthew Arnold's pooh-poohs have gone too
far? Perhaps the new enthusiasm is sometimes more a fact about
ourselves – and the critical and scholarly techniques that we have
perfected – than about the poems that Pope actually wrote?

Is Pope, in the final analysis, a *major* or a *minor* poet? That was
the essential question that Joseph Warton posed in 1756, and it is
still one we have to answer today. For Warton the problem could
be reduced to the genres in which Pope excelled. The neo-classic
assumption was that satire was one of the lower genres; Pope was
a good satirist . . . yes, but not capable of the sublimity and pathos
that were the *sine qua non* of the highest of the literary kinds, such
as the epic, tragedy and the 'great' or Pindaric ode. It followed,
according to Warton, that Pope could not be considered a major
poet. The demotion was a technical, almost a logical, necessity.
With the advent of the Romantics the genres have lost their earlier

hierarchical prestige. A modern Warton – we can take Robert
Graves as our twentieth-century equivalent – is more concerned
with the quality of the writing. Does Pope use the best words in
the best order? Is 'the naked thew and sinew of the English
language' that Gerard Manley Hopkins praised in Dryden to be
found to an equal degree in Pope? The questions have been
answered in an emphatic negative by Robert Graves in the analysis
to which he submits six lines selected 'at random' (they are in fact
from the second *Epilogue to the Satires*) in his *The Crowning Privilege*
(1955):

Let Envy howl, while Heaven's whole chorus sings,
And bark at honour not conferred by kings;
Let Flattery sickening see the incense rise,
Sweet to the world and grateful to the skies.
Truth guards the poet, sanctifies the line,
And makes immortal verse as mean as mine.

The passage, we may agree, is thoroughly typical of Pope's mature
verse – and not least in its *complacency*, that distressing habit Pope
had of patting himself on the back. But Graves, a scrupulous verbal
technician in his own verse, is not concerned with Pope's moral
obliquities and concentrates entirely upon a certain shoddiness in the
writing. As he puts it, the passage 'should have been carried
through three more drafts at least'. On the first line ('Let Envy
howl while Heaven's whole chorus sings') his comment is '*Envy*
and *Heaven*, like *howl*, *while* and *whole*, are too close in sound to
occur decently in the same line. *Howl*, *Heaven* and *whole* are
over-alliterative. *Chorus sings* is not as tuneful as the sense requires.'
This may seem niggling, but the criteria that Graves invokes are
those that Pope himself preached both in the *Essay on Criticism* and
in his letters and conversation – and that he continued to practise
intermittently to the end of his poetic career. And they can hardly
be ignored in *any* poem if Coleridge was correct in his 'homely

definition' of poetry: 'Prose = words in their best order; poetry = the *best* words in the best order.'

'Let Envy howl while Heaven's whole chorus sings', is decidedly a tongue-twister, a line difficult, though not impossible, to read aloud. Moreover its various repetitions of sound seem quite functionless. The general rule in English poetry is to *vary* the vowels – and as far as possible the consonants too – unless a special effect is aimed at. If it is said that the howling of envy requires dissonance (and perhaps achieves it in *howl*), the objection only lends point to Graves's complaint that *chorus sings* 'is not as tuneful as the sense requires'.

We need not proceed through Graves's indictment point by point. Some of his criticisms are unfair and even incorrect, but he registers several other palpable technical hits, as when he points out that Pope's *s*'s have got quite out of hand[1] in the second couplet, that at one point there are five *the*'s in nineteen words ('Pope could never control his definite article'), and that 'makes immortal verse as mean as mine' is over-alliterative. (Three *m*'s would have been alright, four *m*'s vulgarize the effect.)

The case *for* Pope, on the other hand, has been made with especial persuasiveness in the essays by F. R. Leavis, Cleanth Brooks and Maynard Mack, all of which are included in this collection. But four points may be added to Graves's short criticism – if only as a stimulus to the reader's considered disagreement – to complete the modern case *against* Pope. Unlike those of the Victorian critics, which are essentially ethical, they are primarily concerned with Pope's craftsmanship.[2]

1 Tennyson had made the same complaint about the sibilants in the first line of *The Rape of the Lock:* 'Amrus causiz springs'! Horrible! I would sooner die than write such a line' (see p. 261 above).
2 Most of these points were made by me at a meeting of the American Modern Language Association, which was attended by most ardent American Popians. To my surprise, little or no attempt was made to defend their hero against my charges.

1. Pope's habit of revising and then re-revising his poems was in
effect a confession that many whole passages, or at least isolated
couplets or single words and phrases, had not reached their
perfected form when they were originally published. That he often
kept on fiddling with the same passage in edition after edition
points to his own consciousness of an erratic stylistic sense. At his
best he could eventually find *le mot juste*, but he could not count
on finding it as a Milton, a Marvell or a Dryden normally could.
There is an intermittent coarseness of the verbal texture even in
Pope's most brilliant passages.

The description of the young English nobleman's grand tour in
Dunciad IV will serve as a text. It combines in typical Popian
fashion brilliant phrasing and sheer verbal insensitivity. The young
hopeful proceeds, it will be remembered,

To isles of fragrance, lily-silvered vales,
Diffusing languor in the panting gales.

Which is very pretty (too pretty, perhaps, for the satiric context).
But what diffused the languor? The lilies (tuberoses according to
the Pope-Warburton note)? But the lilies have just been compared
to silver, which is odourless. And can even poetic *gales* pant? Didn't
Pope really mean 'panting *air*'? The tyranny of rhyme here is
evident again in the couplet on Venice which follows almost
immediately:

Where, eased of fleets, the Adriatic main
Wafts the smooth eunuch and enamoured swain.

The *Adriatic main* means the Adriatic; the *enamoured swain* means
the *inamorato*. The rhyme-words are superfluous and even, because
they call attention to themselves so emphatically, actually
misleading. The Adriatic is not the *main* but an inland sea that is
part of another inland sea; this lover, too, because of the
conjunction with *eunuch*, cannot surely be a pastoral *swain*. There

are no eunuchs in neo-classic or rococo pastoral. (Grammatically, anyhow, the line ought to mean that the swain is enamoured of the eunuch.)

It is the stylistic *uncertainty* that is the special embarrassment. Pope is continually setting a standard in one couplet that the next couplet cannot meet. He is then hoist with his own petard. Thus the couplet preceding the *main-swain* one is superb:

But chief her shrine where naked Venus keeps,
And Cupids ride the lion of the deeps.

To descend from poetry of such superb pictorial concentration to the mere padding of *main-swain* is disconcerting.

Dryden hardly ever lets the reader down in this way. Some of the subjects he tackled are unsympathetic to us, but the actual writing is 'all of a piece throughout'. 'How much more real poetic force there is in Dryden', Tennyson is reported to have said (see pp. 261–2 above), illustrating the point by comparing Pope's and Dryden's version of *Iliad* I 220–21.

Look at Pope:

He said, observant of the blue-eyed maid,
Then in the sheath returned the shining blade.

Then at Dryden:

He said; with surly faith believed her word,
And in the sheath reluctant plunged the sword.

Tennyson did not go on to analyse the nature of Dryden's superiority. But 'surly faith' and 'reluctant plunged the sword' speak for themselves. In comparison Pope's is schoolboy stuff: 'observant', 'the blue-eyed maid' (for Athene!), 'shining blade'. This is no better than the tired poetic diction which is the staple of Pope's hack collaborators in the *Odyssey*.

2. The intermittent coarseness of the verbal texture reflects a poverty of vocabulary and syntactic device. Dryden writes, as T. S. Eliot has said, with the whole of the English language. Pope, on the other hand, is selective, partly on principle but partly because he doesn't know, can't use, the whole of the English language. Since each passage shows its author at his best, it is fair to compare the first ten lines of *Absalom and Achitophel* and of the *Epistle to Dr Arbuthnot*. In his ten lines Dryden has sixty-nine words, with the ratio of polysyllables to monosyllables approximately one to *two*: Pope has eighty-six words in his ten lines, with a ratio of polysyllables to monosyllables of about one to *six*. In *An Essay on Criticism* Pope had specifically condemned monosyllabic poetry ('And ten low words oft creep in one dull line'), but in this passage from *An Epistle to Dr Arbuthnot* he commits one himself ('What walls can guard me, or what shades can hide'), and in general he is over-monosyllabic. Moreover, Dryden uses only eight of his words more than once, whereas Pope repeats thirteen, the definite article occurring seven times to Dryden's once (this incidentally confirms Graves's charge that 'Pope could never control his definite article'). Dryden has almost twice as many nouns as verbs (twenty-two to twelve), which is the Indo-European norm; Pope has exactly the same number of nouns and verbs (twenty-one of each). Finally, Dryden's ten lines constitute a single sentence with five subordinate clauses and two main verbs. Pope's lines, on the other hand, contain eleven separate sentences and no subordinate clauses at all (he has eighteen main verbs). In these two passages, then, Pope has noticeably less verbal density and variety, and what he has to say is not articulated syntactically but consists of a series of separate paratactic statements.

The verbal poverty and syntactic monotony are the signs of a certain inventive deficiency in Pope. His frequent borrowings or plagiarisms from other poets are usually intelligently done, but they too point to a sluggish linguistic imagination. An especially curious feature of his work is the number of times he repeats or half-repeats himself. Thus the fourth line of the passage analysed by Graves:

Sweet to the world, and grateful to the skies

is identical with *The Temple of Fame*, line 377. No allusion can possibly be intended; and most of the other self-quotations are equally perfunctory. Pope's habit of working in detached epigrams or discarded passages from his earlier poems illustrates the same creative poverty. The contrast with Dryden's exuberant verbal inventiveness is striking. Two lines in the description of Timon's villa in the *Epistle to Burlington* (*Moral Essay IV*), which are only some forty lines apart, may be taken as typical of Pope:

As brings all Brobdignag before your thought
(104)

And bring all Paradise before your eye
(148)

Both are mechanically echoing *Il Penseroso*, line 166:

And bring all Heaven before mine eyes.

No doubt other poets repeat themselves, but not surely to the degree that Pope does. Or if parallel cases can be found it will be in general among the good minor writers – a Collins or a Goldsmith.

3. The stylistic uncertainty and the frequent poverty of the linguistic imagination seem to be the outward and visible signs of a certain philistinism, an intermittent coarseness of the whole moral and spiritual fibre. *Eloisa to Abelard* is really inexcusable; Henry Fuseli found the right words for it when he called it 'hot ice'. And in our own time W. H. Auden has regretted that Pope did not

'spare' us it and its 'bogus classicalism'. The conflict in Eloisa of the 'hot' of sexual love and the 'ice' of Christian chastity is vulgarized intolerably by the emphasis on Abelard's emasculation. This is shame-making stuff – Hollywood in its most Technicolor mood. And the *Elegy to the Memory of an Unfortunate Lady*, if less slick, is almost equally crude.

Pope was almost without any tragic sense. The optimism of 'Whatever is, is RIGHT' necessarily precluded it, as it precluded the savage indignation of the greatest satire. With everything for the best in the best of all possible worlds it was difficult for Pope to get worked up, except factitiously, about Grub Street dunces, or City crooks, or even Sir Robert Walpole. The *Essay on Man* is explicit:

If plagues or earthquakes break not Heaven's design
Why then a Borgia or a Catiline?
(I 155–6)

And South Sea swindlers or publishers like Curll were small beer after all compared to Lucius Sergius Catilina or Pope Alexander VI.

The *Imitations of Horace* are Pope's most satisfying poems because Horace was not an intermittent philistine. Here too, infected by his model's *curiosa felicitas*, most of Pope's verbal uncertainties disappear. The revisions are significantly much fewer. (In the eleven *Imitations* the average of stylistic revision per one hundred lines is only three, whereas in the *Moral Essays* the average is sixteen per one hundred lines.) With Horace as his mentor Pope can even skirt the edges of pornography without embarrassing us with the occasional silly smut which turns up in *The Rape of the Lock* and *Eloisa to Abelard*. But to the last when Pope is on his own – as in the *Epistle to Dr Arbuthnot* – the commonplaceness of his mind is a continuous liability. Pope couldn't *think*. Is there a single memorable *aperçu* in all his letters? The contrast with Gray, or Keats, or even Hopkins, is glaring.

4. The later English poets, almost without exception, have all preferred Dryden: Gray, Johnson, Cowper, Wordsworth, Coleridge, Keats, Tennyson, Hopkins, Housman, T. S. Eliot, Robert Graves.... It is an impressive list. Even the anonymous hack, presumably Robert Shiels, who compiled the life of Pope in *The Lives of the Poets of Great Britain and Ireland* (vol. 5, 1753), and also seems to have initiated in it the Dryden–Pope comparison as a critical exercise, had no doubt about the relative status of the two poets:

This great man [Pope], is allowed to have been one of the first rank amongst the poets of our nation, and to acknowledge the superiority of none but Shakespeare, Milton and Dryden.

The first rank is a nicely elastic Poets' Corner. For Matthew Arnold, who edited *The Six Chief Lives from Johnson's 'Lives of the Poets'*, Pope and Gray just scrape into it – 'if, without seeking a close view of individual differences, we form a large and liberal first class among English writers. . . .' A large and liberal first class will certainly include Pope. We shall all, on those terms, be happy to let Pope in. But Number Five in the whole hierarchy of English poetry, as some American critics have recently suggested, the inferior only of Chaucer, Shakespeare, Milton and Wordsworth, is surely to overstate his claims. Because he was underrated in the nineteenth century is not an adequate excuse for overrating Pope today. A critical balance needs to be struck. Is the best of Pope as good as the best of Donne, say, or Marvell, Dryden, Blake, Coleridge or Keats? And if not, where are we to rank him? The issue is still undecided; the reader is free to make up his own mind without surrendering his right of choice to any editor or critical big-wig. Nor can the question of Pope's personal character be omitted altogether. No doubt our ideal Poets' Corner contains some very doubtful characters – criminals like Villon, government spies like Marlowe, rakes and drug-addicts like Rochester and

Coleridge. And no doubt in the end we excuse them. But the
moral issue cannot be evaded altogether. The American so-called
'New Critics', whose most persuasive prophet has been W. K.
Wimsatt, the author of the 'Intentional Fallacy' (in collaboration
with Monroe Beardsley), have tried to exclude 'author psychology'
altogether from literary criticism. The passages included in the
following pages from Cleanth Brooks's *The Well-Wrought Urn*
(1947), and Wimsatt's *The Verbal Icon* (1954) and Maynard Mack's
Wit and Poetry and Pope (1949) demonstrate how successful such an
approach can be when applied to Pope. But by excluding Pope's
psychology, the criticism of these Yale Formalists, as they have
been called (they are all Professors of English literature at Yale),
remains artificial and incomplete. Something fundamental has been
left out. The author *cannot* be excluded altogether from his artifact.
What is wrong with *Eloisa to Abelard* is, at least in part, what was
humanly defective in Pope's feelings about Lady Mary Wortley
Montagu, to whom the last lines of the poem are addressed; what
is wrong with the later satires is typified by the inexcusable lines on
Sappho (whose identity with Lady Mary was immediately apparent
to their contemporaries). Pope's 'love' for Lady Mary had turned
to hatred, and the psychological revolution naturally affected the
kind of poetry he wrote about her. A criticism of Pope that ignores
such elementary facts is incomplete and misleading. It is because
Dr Johnson, was at all times prepared to combine technical
considerations with the human content within which they operated
that his *Life of Pope* is still – in spite of some eccentric passages – the
most judicious criticism of Pope's poetry that we have had. The
runner-up is probably Empson. But the nineteenth-century critics.
for all their superficiality, have something to teach us, too, in their
emphasis on Pope the man as well as Pope the poet. The two
aspects ultimately coincide.

And the little wasp of Twickenham had a tenderer side, which is
just as much a part of the 'meaning' of his poetry as his acidities.

Lamb is the best witness to Pope's humanity – perhaps because his testimony is so unexpected, so totally disinterested. The conversation recorded by Hazlitt in *On Persons One Would Wish to have Seen* (part of which will be found on page 173 above) continues with Lamb reciting, 'with a slight hectic on his cheek and his eye glistening', the lines from the *Epistle to Dr Arbuthnot* (135–46) which list Pope's friends who had insisted on his publishing his poems:

But why then publish? . . .
Well-natured Garth inflamed with early praise,
And Congreve loved and Swift endured my lays . . .
And St John's self, great Dryden's friends before,
With open arms received one poet more . . .

As Lamb reached the end of the passage, Hazlitt says 'his voice totally failed him'. 'Do you think,' Lamb demanded, 'I would not wish to have been friends with such a man as this?' The question was left unanswered. Old Mrs Reynolds, the mother of Keats's friend, abruptly changed the subject: 'I would rather have seen him talking with Patty Blount'. Perhaps we would, too. Patty, Martha Blount's nickname, brought out all that was best in Pope – from the early *Epistle to Miss Blount on her Leaving Town after the Coronation* (though this may have been meant for Martha's elder sister) to the delicious *To a Lady (Moral Essay II)*. Martha was almost certainly Pope's mistress for some years. The wasp was, after all, human, in spite of his diminutive stature and his vindictive habits.

William Empson

from *Seven Types of Ambiguity* 1930

How loved, how honoured once, avails thee not,
To whom related, or by whom begot;
A heap of dust alone remains of thee;
'Tis all thou art, and all the proud shall be!
(*Elegy to the Memory of an Unfortunate Lady* 71–4)

The two parts of the second line make a claim to be alternatives which
is not obviously justified, and this I think implies a good deal. If the
antithesis is to be serious, *or* must mean 'one of her relations was grand
but her father was humble,' or the other way about; thus one would
take *how* to mean 'whether much or little' (it could mean 'though
you were so greatly'), and the last line to contrast her with the *proud*,
so as to imply that she is humble (it could unite her with the *proud*,
and deduce the death of all of them from the death of one). This
obscurity is part of the 'Gothic' atmosphere that Pope wanted: 'her
birth was high, but there was a mysterious stain on it'; or 'though
you might not think it, her birth was high'; or 'her birth was high,
but not higher than births to which I am accustomed'. Here, however,
the false antithesis is finding another use, to convey the attitude of
Pope to the subject. 'How simple, how irrelevant to the merits of the
unfortunate lady, are such relationships; everybody has had both a
relation and a father; how little I can admire the arrogance of great
families on this point; how little, too, the snobbery of my reader,
who is unlikely to belong to a great family; to how many people this
subject would be extremely fruitful of antitheses; how little fruitful
of antitheses it seems to an independent soul like mine.' What is
important about such devices is that they leave it to the reader vaguely
to invent something, and make him leave it at the back of his
mind. . . .

The eighteenth-century ambiguity was essentially easy and colloquial;
it was concerned to exploit, as from a rational and sensible mental
state, the normal resources of the spoken language.

   Its possible grace and slightness may be shown by a fine detail from
The Rape of the Lock. When Belinda wins at cards

The nymph, exulting, fills with shouts the sky;
The walks, the woods, and long canals reply.
O thoughtless mortals, ever blind to fate,
Too soon dejected, and too soon elate!
Sudden these honours shall be snatched away,
And cursed for ever this victorious day.
(III 99–104)

Reply may be transitive or intransitive. It is the poet who makes these classical reflections, but, as far as the grammar is concerned, the speaker may as well be the environs of Hampton Court, accustomed as they are to the fall of favourites and the brevity of human glory.

Such a use of the verb may be insisted upon by prepositions or adverbs placed where the different meanings are wanted; this needs no illustration, and my example is intended chiefly to show in how small a compass these typical devices may be employed.

Oh! if to dance all night, and dress all day,
Charmed the smallpox, or chased old age away,
Who would not scorn what huswife's cares produce,
Or who would learn one earthly thing of use?
(*The Rape of the Lock*, v 19 ff.)

Here *charmed* at first means 'fascinated,' so as to make it sit still and do no harm, as one would do to snakes or one's husband; and then, because *chased* insists on the activity of this process, and because *away* is in a prominent position at the end of the line, *charmed* takes on a new meaning as *charmed away*, 'removed entirely even when it had already arrived,' no doubt by some apparently unreasonable incantation, as one does warts. It is these slight variations of suggestion, I think, that give vivacity to the line.

In the same way, the lyrical outburst of good sense that follows on from this plays continually on the border-line between the first and second types of ambiguity.

But since, alas! frail beauty must decay,

This insists it is reasonable by being a tautology: 'in so far as beauty is frail it is exposed to decay'; but *frail* from its setting also carries a suggestion of moral as well as physical fragility, which continues to haunt the verses.

Curled or uncurled, since locks will turn to grey;

Locks may have been *curled* by art (or *uncurled* for that matter), or have been, to start with, (naturally) *curled*; so that we have now three ways of dividing up women – chaste susceptible, from the first line; beautiful-ugly if *uncurled* hair is out of fashion, and artificial-natural, from the second. *Will turn to grey* is in part a simple and inexorable future tense, the statement of Nature or the poet, and in part the metre makes it a statement of the lady; 'It *will* turn to grey, the nasty stuff, I *can't* stop it.'

Since painted, or not painted, all shall fade

Artificial-natural, with its associate susceptible-chaste, is now strengthened against beautiful-ugly as the distinction in question, but not left in possession of the field; *painted* might be applied to 'meads' in Pope's dialect, and had not quite lost the sense of 'coloured from whatever cause.'

The verb is now only future, as the place of the ambiguous *will* at the place of emphasis has been taken by *all*. But these changes help the crescendo.

And she who scorns a man must die a maid;

The wave as it breaks returns to tautology, from which the original beautiful-ugly criterion seems to have faded out. It may combine artificial-natural with wanton-chaste; 'modesty and virtue are no security, because if you don't make the most of yourself you won't get a husband'; or may oppose them to one another; 'artificiality and virtue are no security, because if you think yourself too fine for any of the available men you won't get a husband either.' The tautology chiefly breaks down in its tenses, and thus implies that 'you may not want a husband now, whether because you are too humble or too fanciful, too chaste or too gay, but in the end, every woman must admit it was what she needed.' In this roundabout way, by not defining the relation between two criteria and leaving a loophole in a tautology, Pope arrives, as did Chaucer in flat sentences, at what may indeed be the fundamental commonplace of poetry, a statement of the limitations of the human situation. 'Seeing then the inherent crudity of all possible earthly happiness, considering the humility of those demands which can alone hope to be satisfied . . .'

What then remains, but well our power to use,
And keep good humour still whate'er we lose?

Well may mean 'thoroughly' or 'with moderation,' and thus implies a sort of humility and *good humour* in deciding which of them is best in any particular situation. *Still* may mean that we must always keep our balance, always be prepared to laugh at the absurdity of the world and our own nature, or *keep* it *still* may mean that we must be careful not to laugh too publicly, to give ourselves away by not insisting on our dignity or our rights.[1] Reviewing, finally, the three sets of opposites, we may *lose* beauty, refinement, or virginity, the lover we had desired, the privacy we had built up, or the husband it would have been wise to obtain.

Where Bentley late tempestuous wont to sport
In troubled waters, but now sleeps in port.
(*The Dunciad*, IV 201–2)

The pun is sustained into an allegory by the rest of the couplet; *tempestuous* and *sport* are satirical in much the same way as the last word. But here, I grant, we have a simply funny pun; its parts are united by derivation indeed, but too accidentally to give dignity; it jumps out of its setting, yapping, and bites the Master in the ankles. . . .

So far I have dealt with the ambiguity of this type which talks about several things at once; there is also the ambiguity which talks about one thing and implies several ways of judging or feeling about it. This tends to be less rational and self-conscious, therefore less strictly fitted to the third type; it is more dramatic and more aware of the complexities of human judgement. Pope continually makes use of it; partly because, though himself a furious partisan (or rather because of

1 [Empson added a note here in the second edition:] The idea that the rival idiom 'keep still' pokes up, I now think, was a folly on my part. It would suggest 'Keep good humour from acting,' and Pope would not intend to contradict himself flatly in a moral sentiment. But *still* ('even then') does, I think, enrich itself a little with the idea 'calm'.

it, so as to pretend he is being fair), he externalizes his remarks very completely into statements of fact such as must always admit of two judgements; partly because his statements are so compact, and his rhythmic unit so brief, that he has not always room for an unequivocal expression of feeling. The word 'equivocal' is a good one here; much of the force of his satire comes from its pretence of equity. He stimulates the reader's judgement by leaving an apparently unresolved duality in his own – 'this is the truth about my poor friend, and you may laugh if you will'. The now fashionable attitude to the eighteenth century rather tends to obscure this point; it is true the humour of the period is often savage, but that does not show that the judgements with which it is concerned are crude.

Is Pope sneering or justifying, for instance, in one of the best known of these spare but widely buttressed constructions?

... who, high in Drury Lane,
Lulled by soft zephyrs through the broken pane,
Rhymes ere he wakes, and prints before term ends,
Obliged by hunger and request of friends.
(*Epistle to Dr Arbuthnot*, 41–4)

No one can deny that these words ridicule, but: *obliged by hunger*: I am not sure that they titter; it is only after you have been faced with the dignity of human need that you are moved on to see the grandeur of human vanity. Much recent apologetic for Pope has contented itself with saying how clever it was of the little fellow to be so rude; but to suppose this line means merely 'the man must have been a fool as well as a bore, since he was hungry,' is not merely an injustice to Pope's humanity, it is a failure to understand the tone he adopts towards his readers.

Soft were my numbers, who could take offence
While pure description held the place of sense? ...
Yet then did Gildon draw his venal quill.
I wished the man a dinner, and sat still.
(*Epistle to Dr Arbuthnot*, 147–8, 151–2)

Good, sympathetic Mr Pope, one is to think; he has a profound knowledge of human nature. The situation in these two examples is the same; the first stresses his contempt, the second his magnanimity;

but in neither can one be sure what proportions are intended. A more verbal expression for this doubt is given in the line about the Goddess of Dullness:

Where, in nice balance, truth with gold she weighs,
And solid pudding against empty praise.
(*The Dunciad*, I 53–4)

Neither *truth* nor *gold*, neither *praise* nor *pudding*, are to be despised, and the pairs may be connected in various ways. A poet is *praised* by posterity for attending to what Pope called *truth*; whereas *gold* and *pudding* are to be gained by flattery. *Gold* may be the weights of the balance with which *truth* is *weighed*, so that the poet will tell any lie that he decides will pay; or all four things may be alike, and equally desirable, so that, though the author is hungry and sensible, he is also *truthful* and anxious for his reputation; his proportion of *praise* and *pudding* has to be worked out with honest care. This spectacle, in its humble way, is taken to be charming; so that this version is contemptuous but without the bitterness of the first one. For these versions, *praise* is that of good critics, and it is *empty* beside *pudding* in a sense that would sympathize with the poet's hunger, or as an imagined quotation from him so as to bring him into contempt. But it might be *empty* as unjustified, as being the *praise* of (that is, from or to) the rich patrons who had bought the compliments; *gold* then takes on the suggestion of contempt, never far from it in Pope's mind, and means 'shoddy poetical ornament'; *pudding* is paired with *truth*, in the natural order of the antitheses, and means either the cheap food which is all he would be able to buy, or the *solid* reality of his dull but worthy writings. At any rate, the epithets *solid* and *empty* contradict the antithesis 'venal' and 'genuine'; it is gay and generous of Pope to have so much sympathy with *pudding*; and it is this detachment from either judgement in the matter (the *truth* such men could tell, the *praise* they could win, is nothing for Pope to be excited about) which makes the act of *weighing* them seem so absurd.

This process of interpretation may evidently be applied to the feelings a reader imposes on the material; there may be an interest due to the contrast between the stock response and the response demanded by the author. I think myself, in the following border-line case, that I am describing the attitude of Pope, but such an analysis would have achieved its object if it described the attitude only of the majority of his readers. It is that description of a great eighteenth-century mansion in which Pope is apparently concerned only to make its grandeur seem vulgar and stupid.

> ... his building is a town,
> His pond an ocean, his parterre a down.
> Who but must laugh, the master when he sees,
> A puny insect, shivering at a breeze!

> My lord advances with majestic mien,
> Smit with the mighty pleasure to be seen.

> But hark! the chiming clocks to dinner call;
> A hundred footsteps scrape the marble hall.

> Is this a dinner? this a genial room?
> No, 'tis a temple, and a hecatomb.
> (*Moral Essay IV*, 105–8, 127–8, 151–2, 155–6)

All this is great fun; but before concluding that Pope's better judgement really disapproved of the splendour that he evidently envied, one must remember the saying that as Augustus found Rome, so Dryden found English 'brick, and left it marble'; that the Augustans minded about architecture and what Augustus did; that a great part of the assurance and solidity of their attitude to life depended on solid contemporary evidences of national glory. When Pope prophesies the destruction of the building his language takes on a grandeur which reflects back and transfigures it:

> Another age shall see the golden ear
> Embrown the slope and nod on the parterre,
> Deep harvests bury all his pride has planned,
> And laughing Ceres re-assume the land.

These lines seem to me to convey what is called an intuitive intimacy with nature; one is made to see a cornfield as something superb and as old as humanity, and breaking down dykes irresistibly, like the sea. But, of course, it *embrowns* as with further, more universal, *gilding*, and *nods on the parterre* like a duchess; common things are made dignified by a mutual comparison which entirely depends on the dignity of Canons. The glory is a national rather than a personal one; democracy will *bury* the oligarch; but the national glory is now centred in the oligarch; and if the whole people has been made great, it is through the greatness of the Duke of Chandos.

This seems to me rather a curious example of the mutual comparison which elevates both parties; in this case, it is the admiration latent in a sneer which becomes available as a source of energy for these subsidiary uses: and also an example of how the Wordsworthian feeling for nature can be called forth not by an isolated and moping interest in nature on her own account, but by a conception of nature in terms of human politics. I hope, at any rate, you agree with me that the lines convey this sort of sympathy intensely; that there is some sense of the immensity of harvest through a whole country; that the relief with which the cripple for a moment identifies himself with something so strong and generous gives these two couplets an extra-ordinary scale. . . .

A much fainter example of the sort of ambiguity in question is supplied by one of Pope's great passages about dowagers, which possesses in a high degree the sensuous beauty that is supposed to have been beyond his powers:

As hags hold sabbaths, less for joy than spite,
So these their merry, miserable night;
Still round and round the ghosts of beauty glide,
And haunt the places where their honour died.
See how the world its veterans rewards!
A youth of frolics, an old age of cards;
Fair to no purpose, artful to no end,
Young without lovers, old without a friend;
A fop their passion, but their prize a sot;
Alive, ridiculous, and dead, forgot!
(*Moral Essay II*, 239–48)

An impression of febrile and uncontrollable hatred is given to the terrible climax of this passage by the flat, indifferent little words, *fop*, *sot*, which, if they are to fill our the line, to give it weight, as its meaning and position demand, cannot be dropped with the analytical contempt with which they appear on the printed page; must be hurled at a person conceived as in front of you, to whom you know they are intolerable. Never was the couplet more of a rocking-horse if each line is considered separately; but all the inertia of this flatness is needed to give him strength; never was the couplet given more delicacy of modulation than is here imposed by the mere weight and passion of the sense conveyed. What is so compelling about the passage is the combination within it of two sharply distinguished states of mind; the finicking precision with which the subject-matter is handled; the pity, bitterness, and terror with which the subject-matter must be conceived.

In the third type, two such different moods would both be included, laid side by side, made relevant as if by a generalization; in the fourth type they react with one another to produce something different from either, and here the reaction is an explosion.

I spoke of 'sensuous beauty', thinking of the second couplet quoted, to which a more verbal analysis can be applied. The dowagers may *glide round and round* because they are still dancing, or merely, since they are fixed to the card-table in the next couplet, because they go on and on, in rotation, to the same drawing-rooms. In this way they may at once be conceived as still dancing and yet as at an age when, in those days, they would have had to stop. They are first spoken of as *ghosts* of their dead *beauty*, and will then be thought of as still dancing, since such *ghosts* would still be echoing what they had done in life; but in the next line they are *ghosts* of their dead *honour*, *haunting* a *place* only, and that not so much the ballroom as the card-table. (These *places*, however, are practically the same, so there is an independent ambiguity as to whether they lost their *honour* by cheating at the card-table or making assignations in the ballroom.) The result of this is that the two lines cannot run as simply as they claim to do; *ghosts* means something different for each line, and you must in each case translate the line back into something said about old ladies, or the transitions will not work. But one is accustomed to this process of immediate translation only in verses of flowery and graceful ornament, so that it is a parody of the manner in which a gallant compliment would have been paid to the ladies, and has a ghastly air of being romantic and charming.

I must not deny that the *ghost* of a dead *beauty* might haunt the place where her *honour* had died, as she might haunt the place where anything that interested her had happened. If you read it like this, there is a touch of that form of wit which caps a sentence with the unexpected word; 'you might think she was most distressed at losing her beauty; but no, it's her conscience that troubles the old woman, and well it may'. However, I find it very difficult to read the lines like this; they stand too completely parallel and apart, and read like one blow after another.

Or you may say from this parallelism that *beauty* and *honour* are treated as necessary corollaries of one another, the two names being used in the two lines only for variety (as if from the old dictionary interest in synonyms); so that *ghosts of beauty* are the same as *ghosts of honour*, and had necessarily to lose their properties in the same place. Beauty and honour, then, are identical, so that we find ourselves, to our justifiable surprise, in Spenser's fairy-story world of sensuous idealism. There is a sort of subterranean resonance in the verses from the clash of this association; with a feverish anger, like the screws of a liner racing above water, Pope finds himself indeed hag-ridden by these poor creatures; they excite in him feelings irrelevantly powerful, of waste, of unavoidable futility, which no bullying of its object can satisfy.

Aldous Huxley

from *Texts and Pretexts* 1932

In the worst inn's worst room, with mat half hung,
The floors of plaster and the walls of dung,
On once a flock-bed, but repaired with staw,
With tape-tied curtains, never meant to draw,
The George and Garter dangling from that bed,
Where tawdry yellow strove with dirty red,
Great Villiers lies – alas, how changed from him,
That life of pleasure, and that soul of whim!
Gallant and gay in Cliveden's proud alcove,
The bower of wanton Shrewsbury and love;
Or just as gay, at council, in a ring
Of mimicked statesmen, and their merry king.

No wit to flatter left of all his store!
No fool to laugh at, which he valued more.
There, victor of his health, of fortune, friends,
And fame, this lord of useless thousands ends.

The theorists of 'Classicism' decreed that all poetical description
should be couched in general terms. In spite of which, this admirable
purple passage from the *Epistle to Lord Bathurst* [*Moral Essay III*, 299–
314] is full of the most accurate particularities.

I remember, the first time I read Pope's lines, being profoundly
impressed by those walls of dung. Indeed, they still disturb my
imagination. They express, for me, the Essential Horror. A floor of
dung would have seemed almost normal, acceptable. But *walls* – Ah,
no, no!

Ezra Pound

from *ABC of Reading*   1934

A great deal has been written about Pope's bitterness in attacks by
people who neglect to note, or at any rate neglect to mention, that
these attacks coincided with expressions of respect to the better authors
(as Dryden and Swift, for example) whom he attempts to weed out
from writers who were nuisances in his day and who are now so
forgotten that his work needs footnotes longer than the text itself. . . .

The Dunciad in large chunks is very hard reading simply because
we have the very greatest possible difficulty in beating up ANY
interest whatever in the bores he is writing about. Even if one does
remember a particularly lively crack, it is almost too much trouble to
find it again (confession of present author, looking for a few lines he
would like to quote). Nevertheless, Pope should be given credit for
his effort at drainage.

He is constantly fishing out the better writers. See *Dunciad*, II 124:
Congreve, Addison and Prior, 127: Gay, sieved out from seven
authors now completely forgotten. . . .

Book Two, along about line 270, gets up a momentum and I find
it possible to run on for a while without skipping. But I am a

specialist, getting on toward my fiftieth year, with a particular and matured interest in writing and even in literary criticism. I think it would be sheer idiocy to try to force this kind of reading on the general reader, and nothing could dry up the interest of a young student more quickly than telling him he must, should, or ought to BE INTERESTED in such pages. Such reading is not even training for writers. It is a specialized form of archaeology.

The root of the dullness is in the fact that a good deal of Pope isn't informative! We don't really know anything more about his gilded bug that stinks and stings after reading of him than we did before. We do get a few points on the state of scholarship, journalism, etc. . . .

'Give up Cicero to C or K'

Hibernian politics, O Swift, thy fate!
And Pope's, ten years to comment and translate.

Geoffrey Tillotson (anonymously)

from 'Alexander Pope', *The Times Literary Supplement*
25 October 1934 (reprinted in *Essays in Criticism and Research*, 1942)

Pope may be considered to exemplify, especially as a young poet, certain qualities of two other London-born poets, the Milton of the Horton period and the young Keats. Pope's early conception of the poet is as much as Keats's one of enthusiasm. The ideal poet as he frets through the surface of the *Essay on Criticism* is a bold and fiery spirit with some of the qualities which Pope in the preface to his *Iliad* saw in Homer. A poem for Pope is one

Where nature moves, and rapture warms the mind;
(*Essay on Criticism*, 236)

and in *Windsor Forest* there is the apostrophe:

Ye sacred Nine! that all my soul possess,
Whose raptures fire me, and whose visions bless. . . .
(259–60)

And Pope and Keats both did their poetic reading in the same spirit: Pope

Glows while he reads, but trembles as he writes,
(*Essay on Criticism*, 198).

he confesses. The sonnet on Chapman's Homer sprang from a similar glow and, to take one of Pope's two senses, was written with similar trembling. Pope differs from the young Keats by having a much more continuous regard for orderliness. A poem must be bold but regular. The poet must know when to let fly and when to hold the poem tight. This sense of structure is a rare and valuable thing in English poetry. *Endymion* lacked it, fatally by any high standard. And Pope very nearly produced his own *Endymions*. He told Spence that he 'had some thoughts of writing a Persian fable', in which he would 'have given a full loose to description and imagination. It would have been a very wild thing. . . .' And these thoughts were amplified in a letter to Judith Cowper:

I have long had an inclination to tell a fairy tale, the more
wild and exotic the better; therefore a *vision*, which is confined
to no rules of probability, will take in all the variety and
luxuriancy of description you will.

There is a strong element of wildness in *The Temple of Fame*, but it is restrained, and wisely restrained.

Like Keats and the young Milton, Pope was a country poet before he was a town poet. We have heard too exclusively of Pope's urban preoccupation with morals and satire. His world of experience was as extensive as that of any other poet. Pope is held to be deficient in a sense of beauty, in the amount of beauty he experienced and in the quality of that experience. Actually he was as sensitive to aesthetic experience as the young Milton, and probably as sensitive to it as the young Keats. Spence preserved some important fragments of his aesthetics. He shows Pope on the Thames receiving 'That Idea of the Picturesque, from the swan just gilded with the sun amidst the shade of a tree over the water'. And another remark, almost Wordsworthian in imputing to education the spoiling of the natural instincts:

A tree is a nobler object than a prince in his coronation
robes. . . . Education leads us from the admiration of beauty
in natural objects, to the admiration of artificial (or customary)
excellence. . . . I don't doubt but that a thoroughbred lady
might admire the stars, *because* they twinkle like so many
candles at a birth-night.

Pope is seen in the second chapter (1705–15) [of George Sherburn's
The Early Career of Alexander Pope (1934)] to be as completely
environed with lane, wood and field as Milton was in the vacations
and after leaving Cambridge, and as Keats liked to be. Gay in 1713
inscribed his *Rural Sports* to Pope – to

You, who the sweets of rural life have known,
[And] despise th' ungrateful hurry of the town.

In the *Pastorals* and *Windsor Forest*, Pope is as warmly in love with
natural sights and sounds as any of those pastoralists and country-
drawn poets who are always breaking into seventeenth-century
poetry with their sunny landscapes. Pope asks for:

. . . sequestered scenes,
The bowery mazes and surrounding greens;
. . . Thames's banks, which fragrant breezes fill,
Or where ye Muses sport on Cooper's Hill. . . .
I seem through consecrated walks to rove,
I hear soft music die along the grove.
Led by the sound, I roam from shade to shade,
By god-like poets venerable made.
(*Windsor Forest*, 261–4, 267–70)

Pope made the most of the usual training for a poet, things of
acknowledged beauty to see, things of acknowledged beauty to read.
The thoroughbred lady might like stars because of candles. Pope
preferred stars, but had his aesthetic use for candlelight. He carried his
sense of beauty further than any previous poet by taking it indoors
with him and employing it on anything made by the inspired hand
of man. This was one of the easy means of transition to 'town' poetry.
In the work of utilitarian silversmith or carver Pope took a delight
which is new and valuable for English poetry. George Herbert,

Herrick and Waller had touched part of this new area for poetry, but Pope is the first poet who shows himself worthy of looking at the work of the anonymous Inigo Joneses and Grinling Gibbonses of the silver workshops. Pope provides a logical extension of one aspect of Renaissance humanism. The Elizabethans were fond of describing their dolphin chambers. Pope sees the things on a sophisticated table to be lovely, man's hand being god-like even in the common-place –

For lo! the board with cups and spoons is crowned,
The berries crackle, and the mill turns round.
On shining altars of Japan they raise
The silver lamp; the fiery spirits blaze.
From silver spouts the grateful liquors glide,
While China's earth receives the smoking tide. . . .
(*The Rape of the Lock*, III 105–10)

It is part of the way that everything for Pope is centralized in man, in men, in human character and the visible instruments upon which human character orchestrates its fine or broken music. Pope is often laughing at man-made beauty since it is so often misused by man, since it so often exemplifies the proud canker in his soul. But in itself he finds it beautiful.

This experience of indoor beauty – or of beauty contrived by man out of doors, in gardens, for instance – was included no doubt under 'plains' in Wordsworth's famous remark about Pope's neglecting the heights; Wordsworth allowed that the heights were within Pope's reach. But it is what one sees in the plains that matters, as it is equally what one sees in the heights. One might as well quarrel with Manet for wasting time with the bar of the Folies Bergères, when there were mountains sawing the skies, as quarrel with Pope for the Hampton Court interior. . . .

Pope's sense of beauty is almost always incorporated into his sense of interest. He sees meaning among things. This is one of the several seventeenth-century elements in his poetry, and its presence forbids him to discard entirely the metaphysical process. Not that Pope's meaning is of the same kind as that of Donne or Herbert. His process, however, is often theirs. The sensuous world is as important to him as it is to them because it coordinates itself with the strength of his meaning. This is often the explanation of his similes. They are seldom decorations for their own sake, even when they are parodies of epic similes. They are usually sudden and surprising intricacies of the external world which an intricate meaning has magnetized to itself. They are the same in kind as the fine 'homely' similes in the *Biographia Literaria*. The material of these similes may be beautiful or unpleasant, but whether it is one or the other is irrelevant, accident. The meaning has been sufficiently intense and defined to amalgamate itself with that detail of the external world which is, so to speak, the sole example of its law.:

For wit and judgement often are at strife,
Though meant each other's aid, like man and wife.
(*Essay on Criticism*, 82–3)

Or the law may have two manifestations:

Or, if to wit a coxcomb make pretence,
Guard the sure barrier between that and sense;
Or quite unravel all the reasoning thread,
And hang some curious cobweb in its stead!
As, forced from wind-guns, lead itself can fly,
And ponderous slugs cut swiftly through the sky;
As clocks to weight their nimble motion owe,
The wheels above urged by the load below. . . .
(*The Dunciad*, IV 177–84)

Pope uses his acquaintance with beauty or 'interest' where it is needed. And so with every other element in his poetry. One of the most subtle things in poetry is the way in which a poem by Pope is multiple in its layers of significance. Pope is usually doing several things at once. He is writing what he wants to say on his theme. This, of course, is what any author is doing; but for Pope the saying of what he had to say entailed the saying of it in an intensive manner which has seldom been completely that of any other poet. Shenstone said that, more than any other writer, Pope had the art of condensing sense, though Dr Johnson, sitting wet through in a hut in Scotland, did not agree with him. Then Pope was concerning himself with the fine mechanics of his verse. Again, every poet must, of course, be attentive on this point. But Pope was unusually attentive. He distinguished, he told Spence, between sweetness and softness in versification, which will serve to indicate the gradations of his sensitiveness to sound. Then, usually he was writing in imitation of some poet or poetic form. *The Rape of the Lock* and *The Dunciad* are miniature epic poems, and the detailed tallying is effected by a technical mastery which recalls Mozart. The speech of Clarissa, added in the 1717 version of *The Rape*, is a close parody of Pope's own earlier translation of the speech of Sarpedon to Glaucus in the *Iliad*. The *Imitations of Horace* show the poet bound hand and foot and yet dancing as if free. These do not exhaust the sum of his activities. Pope is always eager to adapt the phrases of earlier poets. It was almost a principle with him. As an example of this one might take the line:

[Till] *Alma mater* lie dissolved in port.
(*The Dunciad*, III 338)

This expression derives in the first place from Ovid. Line 612 of Book XIII of the *Metamorphoses* reads:

Quo cubat ipse deus, membris languore solutis.

Sandys translates by:

Here lay the lazy god, dissolved in rest.

When Dryden came to the same line in his translation he avoided the literal perfection of Sandys, and wrote:

       . . . where lay the god
And slept supine, his limbs displayed abroad.

But he remembered the phrase when translating the story of Cymon and Iphigenia from Boccaccio, and at line 550 spoke of

. . . Men dissolved in ease.

So far, in Sandys and Dryden, the phrase has remained virtually static. Pope provides it with its culmination. His line requires the co-operation of the reader's memory for all its juices to be at their most piquant. This kind of imitation was as important for Pope's verse as any other element. And finally, added to all these, there was his continuous attempt to control his poem into shapeliness.

Since all these activities are usually found working together in a poem of Pope's, this is the best answer for anyone who considers a simple cause like ill-nature to have accounted for this satiric poetry. Pope had his hatreds as his contemporaries had theirs for him. But his sense of the strenuous requirements of his verse promoted the personal grudge into a larger emotional context, the disinfecting context of hard work, and finally of great poetry. When one reads the character of Sporus, one's eyes are not on Hervey. It is as much as they can do to receive the fire of the words. Hervey's character is for Pope an entrance into a brilliantly sensuous world every atom of which is vital, a world as exciting to the aesthetic sense as those of the *Nun's Priest's Tale* or of *Lamia*.

Moreover, hatred as an inspiration for Pope's satire has been overstated in importance. The emotion of pity is often as powerfully at work:

Who would not weep, if Atticus were he?
(*Epistle to Dr Arbuthnot*, 214)

Or this from *Of the Characters of Women*:

Ashamed to own they gave delight before,
Reduced to feign it, when they give no more;
As hags hold sabbaths, less for joy than spite,
So these their merry, miserable night;
Still round and round the ghosts of beauty glide,
And haunt the places where their honour died.
(*Moral Essay II*, 237–42)

Satiric poetry such as this affects the primary human emotions, even in Matthew Arnold's sense which limited the meaning to the nobler of those emotions. The terms 'moral' and 'satiric' poetry have put off readers for too long. One's face, if it responded to this poetry (and the face is apt to respond privately to Pope), would wear a complicated solemn intensity. Hazlitt, the profoundest of all critics on *The Rape*, did not know whether to laugh or to weep over the poem. Pope added a 'moral' to it in the 1717 edition:

Oh! if to dance all night, and dress all day,
Charmed the smallpox, or chased old age away,

Who would not scorn what huswife's cares produce,
Or who would learn one earthly thing of use?
To patch, nay ogle, might become a saint,
Nor could it sure be such a sint to paint.
But since, alas! frail beauty must decay,
Curled or uncurled, since locks will turn to grey;
Since painted, or not painted, all shall fade,
And she who scorns a man must die a maid;
What then remains, but well our power to use,
And keep good humour still whate'er we lose?
(v 19-30)

This is indeed (to use a phrase that comes twice in his poetry) 'the language of his heart'. And that language is habitual with him. No other poet has found his sense of beauty so closely and continuously allied to his sense of human values. No other poet has put or answered the question how to live with tenderer concern and more pointed wisdom. In his trembling eye a virtue was as dear a flower.

F. R. Leavis

from 'Pope', *Revaluation: Tradition and Development in
English Poetry*, chapter 3   1936

It is time now to turn to the satirist. . . . For, granting Pope to be pre-eminently a satirist and to enjoy as such what favour he does enjoy, one cannot easily find good reasons for believing that an intelligent appreciation of satiric poetry is much commoner today that it was among the contemporaries of Matthew Arnold. Elementary things still need saying. Such terms as 'venom', 'envy', 'malice' and 'spite' are, among modern connoisseurs, the staple of appreciation (it is, at any rate, difficult to find anything on Pope in other terms): '. . . we are in the happy position of being able, quite imperturbably, to enjoy the fun. . . . We sit at our ease, reading those *Satires* and *Epistles*, in which the verses, when they were written, resembled nothing so much as spoonfuls of boiling oil, ladled out by a fiendish monkey at an upstairs window upon such of the passers-by whom the wretch had a grudge against – and we are delighted' [Strachey]. The Victorians disapproved; Bloomsbury approves: that is the revolution of taste.

It is, in some ways, a pity that we know so much about Pope's life. If nothing had been known but the works, would 'envy', 'venom', 'malice', 'spite' and the rest have played so large a part in the commentary? There is, indeed, evidence in the satires of strong personal feelings, but even – or, rather, especially – where these appear strongest, what (if we are literate) we should find most striking is an intensity of art. To say, with Leslie Stephen and Lytton Strachey, that in the character of Sporus Pope 'seems to be actually screaming with malignant fury' is to betray an essential inability to read Pope.

But one has to conclude from published criticism that the nature of Pope's art is very little understood. Just as I reach this point there comes to hand the following, by an American critic:[1] 'A familiar charge often brought against Shelley is lack of discipline, but in such charges one must always know what the poet is trying to control. If, as in the case of Pope, it is the mere perfection of a regulated line of verse, the problem becomes one of craftsmanship.' A 'mere perfection of a regulated line of verse' is not anything as clearly and precisely indicated as the critic, perhaps, supposes; but that he supposes Pope's technique ('craftsmanship' being plainly depreciatory) to be something superficial, some mere skill of arranging a verbal surface, is confirmed by what he goes on to say: Pope's 'recitation of the dogmas of his day is hollow', and 'in his day as in ours it is a relatively simple matter to accept a ritual of devotion as a substitute for an understanding of basic moral values. . . .'

When Pope contemplates the bases and essential conditions of Augustan culture his imagination fires to a creative glow that produces what is poetry even by Romantic standards. His contemplation is religious in its seriousness. The note is that of these lines, which come in *Moral Essay III*, 165–70, not long after a vigorous satiric passage and immediately before another:

Ask we what makes one keep and one bestow?
That power who bids the ocean ebb and flow,
Bids seed-time, harvest, equal course maintain,
Through reconciled extremes of drought and rain,

1 Horace Gregory, 'A Defense of Poetry', *New Republic*, 11 October 1933.

Builds life on death, on change duration founds,
And gives th' eternal wheels to know their rounds.

The order of Augustan civilization evokes characteristically in
Pope, its poet, when he is moved by the vision of it, a profound
sense of it as dependent on and harmonious with an ultimate inclusive
order. The sense of order expressed in his art when he is at his best
(and he is at his best more than most poets) is nothing merely conventional or superficial, explicable in terms of social elegance and a
pattern of verse. His technique, concerned as it is with arranging
words and 'regulating' movements, is the instrument of a fine
organization, and it brings to bear pressures and potencies that can
turn intense personal feelings into something else. 'His "poetic
criticism of life",' says Lytton Strachey, gibbering solemn fatuity,
'was simply and solely the heroic couplet.' Pope would have found
it hard to determine what precisely this means, but he certainly would
not have found the fatuity Arnold's, and if the Augustan idiom in
which he expressed much the same commonplaces as Arnold's differed
from the Victorian, it was not in being less solemn.

Ask you what provocation I have had?
The strong antipathy of good to bad
(*Epilogue to the Satires, Dialogue II*, 197–8)

– we may not accept this as suggesting adequately the moral basis
of Pope's satire, but it is significant that Pope could offer such an
account: his strength as a satirist was that he lived in an age when such
an account could be offered.

The passages of solemnly exalted imagination like those adduced
above come without incongruity in the midst of the satire – the
significance of this needs no further insisting on. What does need
insisting on is that with this capacity for poised and subtle variety
goes a remarkable command of varied satiric tones.[1] The politeness
of the Atticus portrait is very different from that of *The Rape of the
Lock* (a work that, in my opinion, has enjoyed more than justice);
the intense destructive vivacity of the Sporus portrait is different from
that of the attack on Timon; the following (which is very far from

1 See Note (pp. 322–5 below).

an exception) is enough to dispose of the judgement that 'Pope was witty but not humorous' – the theme is Paper Credit:

Had Colepepper's whole wealth been hops and hogs,
Could he himself have sent it to the dogs?
His Grace will game: to White's a bull be led,
With spurning heels and with a butting head.
To White's be carried, as to ancient games,
Fair coursers, vases, and alluring dames.
Shall then Uxurio, if the stakes he sweep,
Bear home six whores, and make his lady weep?
(*Moral Essay III*, 53–60)

The story of Sir Balaam at the end of *Moral Essay III* is, again, quite different – but one cannot by enumerating, even if there were room, do justice to Pope's variety. Indeed, to call attention to the satiric variety as such is to risk a misleading stress.

Even Mr Eliot, in *Homage to John Dryden*, manages to limit Pope very unjustly. Some accidental unfair suggestion one might expect in such casual reference. But there is decidedly more than that to complain of. For instance:

But the effect of the portraits of Dryden is to transform the
object to something greater, as were transformed the verses
of Cowley quoted above.

A fiery soul, which working out its way,
Fretted the pigmy body to decay:
And o'er informed the tenement of clay.

These lines are not merely a magnificent tribute. They create
the object which they contemplate; the poetry is purer than
anything in Pope except the last lines of *The Dunciad*.

This is a judgement that Matthew Arnold would have understood – or thought he understood; for one knows that Mr Eliot is not appealing here to the prejudices that it is the general aim of his essay to destroy. Yet the judgement is perplexing. The end of *The Dunciad* was admired in the Victorian age as approaching nearer to 'pure poetry' than Pope does characteristically; but no one could have better pointed out than Mr Eliot its strength and subtlety of wit. The passage seems to me finer than anything in Dryden; decidedly finer, for instance, than the comparable part of *MacFlecknoe*. It has a greater intensity (an intensity that Dryden, with his virtues of good humour and good nature, was incapable of), and this is manifest in the very much tauter and more sensitive verse, the finer life of the movement.

As for 'comic creation,' it seems to me easy to find passages of Pope that have a like advantage over the lines of Dryden quoted by Mr Eliot:

The country rings around with loud alarms,
And raw in fields the rude militia swarms;
Mouths without hands – maintained at vast expense,
In peace a charge, in war a weak defence;
Stout once a month, they march, a blust'ring band,
And ever, but in times of need, at hand;
This was the morn, when issuing on the guard,
Drawn up in rank and file they stood prepared
Of seeming arms to make a short essay,
Then hasten to be drunk, the business of the day.

Repeated re-readings of both passages only convince me the more that this of Dryden's is much inferior to the following, which starts twenty lines before the final paragraph of *The Dunciad*:

More had she spoke, but yawned – all nature nods:
What mortal can resist the yawn of gods?
Churches and chapels instantly it reached
(St James's first, for leaden Gilbert preached);
Then catched the Schools; the Hall scarce kept awake;
The Convocation gaped, but could not speak.
Lost was the nation's sense, nor could be found,
While the long solemn unison went round:
Wide, and more wide, it spread o'er all the realm;
Ev'n Palinurus nodded at the helm.
The vapour mild o'er each Committee crept;
Unfinished treaties in each office slept;
And chiefless armies dozed out the campaign,
And navies yawned for orders on the main.

Dryden, says Mr Eliot, 'bears a curious antithetical resemblance to Swinburne. Swinburne was also a master of words, but Swinburne's words are all suggestion and no denotation; if they suggest nothing, it is because they suggest too much. Dryden's words, on the other hand, are precise, they state immensely, but their suggestiveness is almost nothing.' These lines of Pope seem to me to have all the strength of Dryden's, and to have, in addition, a very remarkable potency of suggestion.

We feel the enveloping, thickening, drowsy vapour spread irresistibly and take on, even, something of a rich Romantic glamour – a quality concentrated in

Ev'n Palinurus nodded at the helm.

This is certainly poetic creation, even by Romantic standards, and yet it is, at the same time, 'comic creation'. The suggestive richness is blended with something quite un-Romantic:

Lost was the nation's sense, nor could be found,
While the long solemn unison went round.

The effect of the first of these lines is, to nineteenth-century taste, intrinsically unpoetical, but in the second line the 'long solemn unison' is, though ludicrous, at the same time truly solemn. The 'chiefless armies' doze in an immensely fantastic dream-comedy, and the navies yawn vastly on an enchanted sea.

Beside the passage of *MacFlecknoe* in which Dryden uses Cowley may be set, not to Pope's disadvantage, this from the fourth book of *The Dunciad*:

When Dullness, smiling – 'Thus revive the Wits!
But murder first, and mince them all to bits;
As erst Medea (cruel, so to save!)
A new edition of old Aeson gave;
Let standard-authors, thus, like trophies born,
Appear more glorious as more hacked and torn,
And you, my critics! in the chequered shade,
Admire new light through holes yourselves have made.
Leave not a foot of verse, a foot of stone,
A page, a grave, that they can call their own.'
(119–28)

A commentary like that which Mr Eliot makes on Dryden's borrowings ('only a poet could have made what Dryden made of them') is applicable to Pope's, except that there seems to be even more point in Pope's use of his, and a greater intensity of surprise in his poetry. The ragged squalor of the critics in their dark garrets ('battered and decayed') is ironically enhanced by contrast with Milton's

> many a youth and many a maid
Dancing in the chequered shade.

But it is the use of Waller that is most felicitous:

The soul's dark cottage, battered and decayed,
Lets in new light through chinks that time hath made.

There is nothing merely flippant in Pope's sardonic play upon 'light'; the solemnity of Waller's theme is present in the indignant observation that it was not time that made these holes. Indeed, the seriousness of the original is intensified, for Waller is rather easily conventional in his solemn sentiment. The weight makes itself felt in the next couplet, the last of those quoted:

Leave not a foot of verse, a foot of stone,
A page, a grave, that they can call their own.

The recognition of inevitable death, decay and oblivion charges the bitterness of this – of the pun in the first line and the sardonic concentration of the second.

The Metaphysical descent here is plain, but no plainer than in abundance of other passages. . . .

But illustration might go on indefinitely. A representative selection of passages would fill a great many pages. A selection of all Pope that one would wish to have by one for habitual re-reading would fill a great many more. It is necessary to disclaim the suggestion that he is fairly represented in short extracts. No one, I imagine, willingly reads through the *Essay on Man* (Pope piquing himself on philosophical or theological profundity and acumen is intolerable, and he cannot, as Dryden can, argue interestingly in verse); but to do justice to him one must read through not merely the *Moral Essays*, but, also as a unit, the fourth book of *The Dunciad*, which I am inclined to think the most striking manifestation of his genius. It is certainly satire, and I know of nothing that demonstrates more irresistibly that satire can be great poetry.

An adequate estimate of Pope would go on to describe the extraordinary key-position he holds, the senses in which he stands between the seventeenth and the eighteenth centuries. Communications from the Metaphysicals do not pass beyond him; he communicates forward, not only with Johnson, but also (consider, for instance, *Eloisa to Abelard*) with Thomson and Gray. It was not for nothing that he was so interested in Milton.

Note

Pope's Satiric Modes

One can say without discomfort of mind fairly simple things about the method and manner of Dryden's satire as one cannot of Pope's. Nearly every piece of Pope one comes to seems to demand a different account. The Atticus portrait, upon which generalizations about Pope are sometimes based, may be called, pre-eminently, polite. The manner is that of urbane speech; it is remarkable how, while exploiting the pattern of balance and antithesis to the extreme, Pope appears to be talking with the ease and freedom of the coffee-house:

Damn with faint praise, assent with civil leer,
And, without sneering, teach the rest to sneer;
Willing to wound, and yet afraid to strike,
Just hint a fault, and hesitate dislike.
(*Epistle to Dr Arbuthnot*, 201–4)

There is no apparent animus; Pope is saying what he might have said in any company, provided Addison were not present. As an account of Addison the character may be unfair, but for us it is a piece of observation – Atticus certainly exists: the satire lies in the acuteness of the analysis as registered in the witty precision of the statement.

The opening of *Moral Essay IV* (*Of the Use of Riches*, to Richard Boyle, Earl of Burlington) is also polite in tone, but politeness here is the ironical edge upon explicit critical animus:

'Tis strange the miser should his cares employ
To gain those riches he can ne'er enjoy.
Is it less strange the prodigal should waste

His wealth to purchase what he ne'er can taste?
Not for himself he sees, or hears, or eats;
Artists must choose his pictures, music, meats;
He buys for Topham drawings and designs,
For Pembroke statues, dirty gods, and coins.

The appreciation of satire for us here is the appreciation of wittily
effective malice. True, there is presentment of type, the report of
observation, but the focus of interest is not there – is not upon
analysis and precision of statement. The keyword is that 'dirty' in
line eight; our interest lies in the adroit combination of animus and
urbanity. We note, too, that Pope is appealing to the Augustan
prejudice against the Virtuoso.

The Sporus character offers an extreme contrast with either of these
two passages. It is frankly an indulgence in personal feeling, the effect
depending upon a rejection of all the demands of politeness and
social discretion – for the tone is not that of polite sociality but of the
intimate *tête-à-tête*, the confidant representing a restraint that is
offered to be rejected:

Satire or sense, alas! can Sporus feel?
Who breaks a butterfly upon a wheel?
(*Epistle to Dr Arbuthnot*, 305–14)

The manner of this is much more poetic, there being a vivacious
play of imagery. The images are in the Metaphysical descent, their
force being a matter of wittily felicitous analogy. But it is a matter
also of the intense feeling they express, for they have sensuous value
– a sensuous value the nature of which may be represented by 'this
painted child of dirt' (the element of beauty contributes to a total
effect of repugnance).

The aesthtically pleasing can, in Pope's satire, be offered (and taken)
for its own sake. In the following, in fact, though the human objects
of ironic contemplation are stock Augustan butts, aesthetic pleasure
seems to determine the tone of the whole. After the fourth line, with
its characteristically employed sensuous contrasts –

A nest, a toad, a fungus, or a flower

– there is no touch of animus; it is as if Pope were saying, meaning
strictly what he says: 'How exquisitely silly!'

Then thick as locusts blackening all the ground,
A tribe, with weeds and shells fantastic crowned,
Each with some wondrous gift approached the power,
A nest, a toad, a fungus, or a flower.
(*The Dunciad*, IV 397 ff.)

The pleasure that Pope shares *with* the floriculturist and the butterfly-hunter has, of course, a good deal to do with the total effect. . . .

Poetic creation as the nineteenth century understood it is often in Pope the essential means to a destructive satiric effect. It is so in the passage about Bentley (*Dunciad*, IV 199 ff.), which is complex and varied in satiric method:

As many quit the streams that murmuring fall
To lull the sons of Margaret and Clare Hall,
Where Bentley late tempestuous wont to sport
In troubled waters, but now sleeps in port. . . .

The famous pun on *port* is a truly poetic pun, depending for its rich effect on the evocative power of the first couplet: the streams are really lulling as if they had been Tennyson's, with the result that, after 'tempestuous,' the 'troubled waters' are to the imagination a stormy sea as well as a metaphorical cliché, and Bentley is both the Leviathan resting in sheltered waters after majestic play and the befuddled don dozing. The satiric effect depends upon his being really felt as impressive. . . .

The story of Sir Balaam from the end of *Moral Essay III* (*Of the Use of Riches*, to Allen Lord Bathurst) is in a satiric manner quite different from any yet represented:

The Devil was piqued such saintship to behold,
And longed to tempt him like good Job of old:
But Satan now is wiser than of yore,
And tempts by making rich, not making poor.
Roused by the Prince of Air, the whirlwinds sweep
The surge, and plunge his father in the deep;
Then full against his Cornish lands they roar,
And two rich shipwrecks bless the lucky shore.
Sir Balaam now, he lives like other folks,

He takes his chirping pint, and cracks his jokes:
'Live like yourself,' was soon my lady's word;
And lo! two puddings smoked upon the board.

Quotation cannot suggest the *tempo*, the masterly economy, of the story. In sixty lines we have a representative life of the age; the career of a merchant who rises by trade and speculation to a knighthood and Parliament and at last overreaches himself. It is a magnificent piece of work – hardly characteristic of Pope, and yet only Pope could have done it. . . .

The use of the pun in the Bentley passage is representative. Pope's puns are rarely mere puns; they appear to be a distinctly personal and period development out of the metaphysical conceit. By them 'the most heterogeneous ideas are yoked by violence together' – the most diverse feelings and associations are brought into co-presence. The nearest to the mere pun is illustrated by the following double instance:

See! still thy own, the heavy cannon roll,
And metaphysic smokes involve the pole.
(*Dunciad*, IV 247–8)

'Port' in the Bentley passage completes and fuses a complex and richly poetic effect. In the passage examined on p. 321, the play on 'foot' –

Leave not a foot of verse, a foot of stone,
A page, a grave, that they can call their own

– marks the completed transition from flippant irony to tragic indignation. . . .

The analogies and images in these varied and surprising lines work together (there is both a response of the critical intelligence, admiring the ingenuity of the wit, and a response of feeling) to produce a complex harmony.

Arthur O. Lovejoy

from 'Eighteenth-Century Thought', in *The Great Chain of Being: A Study of the History of an Idea* 1936

Addison, while he finds matter for pride in man's position as the *nexus utriusque mundi*, the link between the animal and the intellectual natures, nevertheless concludes his reflections on the subject thus:

So that he who, in one respect, is associated with angels and archangels, and may look upon a being of Infinite Perfection as his Father, and the highest order of Spirits as his brethren, may, in another respect, say to Corruption, Thou art my Father, and to the worm, Thou art my Sister.

Arguing specifically from the principle of continuity, Bolingbroke also was diligent in the effort to lower man's too high conceit of himself – though he thought that some had gone too far in racial self-disparagement. Man is, indeed, 'the principal inhabitant of this planet, a being superior to all the rest', But his superiority is only one of degree, and of a very slight degree.

The whole chorus of theistical philosophers and divines boast it [reason] to be the distinguishing gift of God to man, that which gives him a pre-eminence and a right of command over his fellow creatures. . . . There have been those who have thought, that the human is a portion of the divine soul. Others have been more modest, and have allowed that the former is a created being, . . . but a being of so high an order, that there is none superior, except the Supreme Being. . . .

There is a middle point between these extremes, where the truth lies; and he who seeks it may find it. . . . He will find . . . many such degrees of comparison between the human intelligence and that of various animals. He may be induced, perhaps, to think that intellectual faculties and corporeal senses, of the same and of different kinds, are communicated in some proportion or other to the whole race of animals. . . .

Man is connected by his nature, and therefore, by the design of the Author of all Nature, with the whole tribe of animals,

and so closely with some of them, that the distance between
his intellectual faculties and theirs, which constitutes as really,
though not so sensibly as figure, the difference of species,
appears, in many instances, small, and would probably appear
still less, if we had the means of knowing their motives, as we
have of observing their actions.

Pope, when he translated these reflections into verse, heightened
the emphasis on the more edifying aspect of Bolingbroke's *via media*:

Far as Creation's ample range extends,
The scale of sensual, mental powers ascends:
Mark how it mounts to man's imperial race,
From the green myriads in the peopled grass. . . .
How instinct varies in the grovelling swine,
Compared, half-reasoning elephant, with thine!
'Twixt that, and reason, what a nice barrier,
For ever separate, yet for ever near!
Remembrance and reflection how allied!
What thin partitions sense from thought, divide!
And middle natures, how they long to join,
Yet never pass th' insuperable line!
Without this just gradation, could they be
Subjected these to those, or all to thee?
The powers of all subdued by thee alone,
Is not thy reason all these powers in one?
(*Essay on Man*, I 2707–10, 221–32)

In spite of Pope's reversion to a more conventional strain in these
last lines, he elsewhere attributes man's lapse from the 'state of
Nature', which was 'the reign of God', to the sin of pride – not that
which caused man's fall in the biblical narrative, but a pride which
led him to separate himself unduly from the other animals:

Pride then was not, nor arts that pride to aid;
Man walked with beast, joint tenant of the shade. . . .
(*Essay on Man*, III 151–6)

W. H. Auden

'Alexander Pope', in Bonamy Dobrée (ed.) *From Anne to Victoria:
Essays by Various Hands* 1937

About 1705 Wycherley's visitors began to 'meet a little Aesopic sort
of animal in his own cropped hair and dress agreeable to the forest
he came from – probably some tenant's son of Wycherley's making
court for continuance in his lease on the decease of his rustic parent –
and were surprised to learn that he was poetically inclined and writ
tolerably smooth verses'. As is so often the case, just as Proust was
a Jew, and Hitler is an Austrian. the man who was to epitomize
Augustan culture was not of it by birth. The invalid self-educated son
of a Roman Catholic linen merchant – it was not a very promising
beginning for the man who was to become the friend of dukes, the
gardener and gourmet, the poet whom a mayor was to offer £4000
for a single couplet.

If Pope's social advantages were few his physical charms were even
less. Only four feet six in height, he was already a sufferer from
Pott's disease, 'the little Alexander whom the women laugh at', and
in middle age was to become really repulsive.

. . . so weak as to stand in perpetual need of female attendance;
extremely sensible of cold, so that he wore a kind of fur
doublet, under a shirt of very coarse warm linen with fine
sleeves. When he rose, he was invested in a bodice made of
stiff canvas, being scarce able to hold himself erect till they
were laced, and he then put on a flannel waistcoat. One side
was contracted. His legs were so slender that he enlarged
their bulk with three pair of stockings, which were drawn on
and off by the maid; for he was not able to dress or undress
himself, and neither went to bed nor rose without help. His
weakness made it very difficult for him to be clean. His hair
had fallen almost all away. . . .

Nor, it must be admitted, even if not as sublimely odious as Addison,
was he a prepossessing character. He was a snob and a social climber,
who lied about his ancestry and cooked his correspondence; he was
fretful and demanded constant attention, he was sly, he was mean,

he was greedy, he was vain, touchy, and worldly while posing as being indifferent to the world and to criticism; he was not even a good conversationalist.

As a poet, he was limited to a single verse form, the end-stopped couplet; his rare attempts at other forms were failures. To limitation of form was added limitation of interest. He had no interest in nature as we understand the term, no interest in love, no interest in abstract ideas, and none in Tom, Dick and Harry. Yet his recognition was immediate, and his reputation never wavered during his lifetime.

If we are to understand his contemporary success, if we are to appreciate the nature of his poetry and its value, we must understand the age in which he lived.

At the beginning of the eighteenth century, although one quarter of the population was in receipt of occasional parish relief, England was the most prosperous country in Europe. According to Gregory King, out of a population of about five million, the two largest classes were cottagers and paupers, and the labouring people and outservants, both of which the Act of Settlement of the Poor prevented from leaving the parishes in which they were born; about a quarter were tenant farmers or freeholders; an eighty-seventh small landed gentry with an income of from £250 to £450 a year; and the remainder the large landowners. One tenth of the population lived in London, which was more than fifteen times larger than her nearest rival, Bristol. The relative prosperity of the country was due, partly to colonies and Britain's favourable position on the Atlantic seaboard, partly to her export of cloth to Europe, partly to her free internal trade and partly to the comparative lack of friction, compared, for example, with France, between the landed aristocracy and business. Though the former professed to look down on the latter, they were ready to profit from them; the younger sons of the poorer gentry were frequently apprentices to business houses, and successful business men could and did become landed genty. The Act of Toleration prevented religious difference from interfering with trade; and the establishment of the Bank of England and the National Debt drew financial and political interests close together.

The dependence on air and water for motive power preserved the balance between town and country; indeed, through the wish to escape obsolete borough restrictions, industry was less urban than in earlier times. There was therefore no emotional demand for 'nature' poetry.

If a large number of the population were illiterate if, by our modern liberal standards, their amusements of drinking, gambling, and cock-fighting were crude, their sanitation primitive, their politics virulent and corrupt, there had nevertheless been an improvement. There were more educated people than ever before, a greater interest in education – charity schools were being built everywhere – and England's increasing importance in, and ties with, Europe gave her culture a breadth and balance hitherto unknown. The arts have hitherto flourished best where cultured society was large enough to provide variety and small enough to be homogeneous in taste. The eighteenth century in England fulfilled both these conditions. There was a growing consciousness of the value of refinement and good manners – a society for the Reformation of Manners is a symptom of a social rather than a puritan conscience – and the age saw the development of these typical modern amusements – smoking – tea-and-coffee-drinking – shooting birds on the wing instead of sitting – horse-racing – and cricket. Whether intentional or not, the wearing of wigs helped to delouse the upper classes, and in politics bribery may not be desirable but it is an improvement upon imprisonment and political murder.

You have, then, a society which, in spite of very wide variations in income and culture varying from the cottager with his bible and pedlar's ballads, through the small squire with his *Hudibras* and Foxe's *Book of Martyrs*, through the Squire Westerns and the Sir Roger de Coverleys, up to the Duke with his classical library, his panelled room, his landscape garden, his china and mahogany furniture, and his round of London, Bath and his country estate, was at no point fundamentally divided in outlook and feeling. Owing to the fusing of landed and trade interests, owing to the fact that England was still rural, was a genuine economic unit and rising in power, there was little clash between politics and economics, no apparent class conflict.

In studying the ideas and art of this period, therefore, we are studying firstly those of any rising class which has recently won power and security for itself – (perhaps the surest sign of victory in a political struggle is the removal of the Censorship; this happened in 1695) – and secondly those of a particular example of such a class in a small

European island shortly before the Industrial Revolution. In consequence we may find certain characteristics which seem likely to recur through history, and others which are peculiar to the particular circumstance of the time, and can never happen again.

To take the more universal characteristics first; what should we expect to find? Those who have risen from a subordinate to a dominant position are, firstly, pleased with themselves, and, secondly, anxious to preserve the status quo. No one is so ready to cry Pax and All's well as he who has just got what he wants. They are optimistic, full of vitality, pacific, within their circle, and conservative.

All nature is but art, unknown to thee;
All chance, direction, which thou canst not see;
All discord, harmony not understood;
All partial evil, universal good;
And, spite of pride, in erring reason's spite,
One truth is clear, WHATEVER IS, IS RIGHT.
(*Essay on Man*, I 289–94)

Secondly, they bring with them a sense of social inferiority; they are anxious to possess and develop the culture and social refinements of the class they have replaced. Contempt for art and manners is a symptom of a rising class that has not yet won power. When they have, they will welcome and reward handsomely art which teaches them refinement, and proves them refined. Because they have been successful, they are interested in themselves. The art of their choice will celebrate their activities, flatter their virtues, and poke fun at their foibles.

Certain qualities of Augustan poetry, then, its air of well being, its gusto, its social reference,

Correct with spirit, eloquent with ease,
(*Essay on Man*, IV 381)

are those which might occur after any social revolution. Others are more unique.

The Reformation split the conception of a God who was both immanent and transcendental, a God of faith and works, into two, into the Inner Light to be approached only through the private conscience, and the Divine Architect and Engineer of the Physical

Universe and the laws of Economics, whose operations could be understood but not interfered with. The religious life tended to become individualized, and the social life secularized. The evil effects of what a Catholic writer has described as

Sundering the believer from his laicized body
Sundering heaven from an earth evermore hireling,
    secularized, enslaved,
tied down to the manufacture of the useful

are more apparent now than then, but of the importance of such an attitude to nature and historical law in the development of the physical sciences, there can be no doubt, and the secularization of education hastened the growth of culture among others than those in orders, and the creation of a general reading public.

At first the emphasis was all on the liberty of the individual conscience, and the Renaissance glorification of the individual, on anti-authoritarianism and anti-popery. But when those who believed in private illumination gained political and public power, they became, as they were bound to become, tyrants. After the Restoration, there-fore, there was a swing over to the other pole, to a belief, equally one-sided, in reason against inspiration, in the laws of nature against enthusiastic private illumination, in society against the individual fanatic.

For forms of government let fools contest;
Whate'er is best administered is best.
For modes of faith let graceless zealots fight;
His can't be wrong whose life is in the right;
In faith and hope the world will disagree,
But all mankind's concern is charity.
All must be false that thwart this one great end;
And all of God, that bless mankind or mend.
(*Essay on Man*, III 303–10)

Anti-popery remained, reinforced by the events of 1688, Louis XIV's power in Europe, and his persecution of the Huguenots, but to it was added Anti-Dissent. Neither were violent enough to lead to real persecution or to prevent social intercourse; they were the natural distrust that people who are doing very nicely as they are have for those who might interfere with them, with their social order, their pleasures, and their cash, but are in point of fact powerless.

The appreciation of law extended itself naturally enough to literature, and literary criticism became for the first time a serious study. Suspicious of enthusiasm and inspiration, Dryden and his successors based their psychology of creative work on Hobbes:

Time and education beget experience.
Experience begets Memory.
Memory begets Judgement and Fancy.
Memory is the world in which the Judgement, the severer
sister, busieth herself in a grave and rigid examination of all
the parts of Nature, and in registering by letters their order,
causes, uses, differences, and resemblances; whereby the
Fancy, when any work of Art is to be performed, finding
her materials at hand and prepared for her use, needs no
more than a swift motion over them.
    Imagination is nothing else but sense decaying or weakened
by the absence of the object.

Such a theory reduces imagination to a recording device and makes creative work a purely conscious activity. It has no place for the solar plexus or the Unconscious of modern writers, nor for the divine inspiration of the Ancients. Poetry becomes a matter of word-painting of the objective world.

The difference is apparent if we compare Pope's invocation at the beginning of his philosophical poem with those of a Catholic like Dante, or a Puritan like Milton.

O good Apollo . . .
Into my bosom enter thou, and so breathe as when thou
    drewest
Marsyas from out what sheathed his limbs.

And chiefly thou, O spirit, that dost prefer
Before all temples the upright heart and pure,
Instruct me, for thou knowst . . .
                        . . . What in me is dark
Illumine; what is low, raise and support.

Awake, my St John! leave all meaner things
To low ambition and the pride of kings.
Let us (since life can little more supply
Than just to look about us and to die)
Expatiate free o'er all this scene of man;
A mighty maze! but not without a plan.

But it would be a mistake to say that the best poetry of Dryden or Pope or any of the Augustans was deliberately written to their theories. The writing of poetry is always a more complex thing than any theory we may have about it. We write first and use the theory afterwards to justify the particular kind of poetry we like and the particular things about poetry in general which we think we like. Further, like most theories, it has its points. We, who have been brought up in the Romantic tradition, are inclined to think that whenever the Augustans wrote bad poetry, they were using their own recipe, and whenever they wrote good poetry they were using the Romantic recipe by mistake. This is false. Without their ideas on nature and the heroic poem, we should miss *The Rape of the Lock* and *The Dunciad* just as much as we should be spared *Eloisa to Abelard* or Darwin's *Loves of the Plants*. The gusto, objectivity and perfection of texture of the one owe quite as much to their theories, as does the bogus classicism of the other.

All theories are one-sided generalizations; and are replaced by their opposite half-truths. When society has become too big to manage, when there is a class of persons whose incomes are drawn from investments without responsibilities of landowners or employers, when the towns are congested, we shall hear other voices. Instead of Hobbes's psychology, we shall have Blake's 'Natural objects deaden and weaken imagination in me.' Instead of Pope's modest intention to please, the poets will proclaim themselves , and be believed in so far as they are listened to at all, as the Divine legislators of the world.

We, again, fancy we know better now; that the writing of poetry is a matter of neither a purely unconscious inspiration, nor purely conscious application, but a mixture of the two, in proportions which vary with different kinds of verse; that it is rarely the tortured madness which some of the Romantics pretended it was, and certainly never the effortless and thoughtless excitement the cinema public imagines it to be.

If the Augustans had the defects of their qualities, so did the Romantics. If the former sometimes came down, according to the late Professor Housman, to 'singing hymns in the prison chapel', the latter sometimes went off into extempore prayers in the county asylum.

And on the whole, yes, on the whole, I think we agree with Byron 'Thou shalt believe in Milton, Dryden and Pope. Thou shalt not set up Wordsworth, Coleridge and Southey'. But then we know better now.

During the two centuries preceding Pope, the literary language had undergone change. We cannot tell how far Shakespeare's conversation in *The Merry Wives of Windsor* is a realistic transcript, but it is remote from us in a way that the dialogue of the Restoration dramatists is not. In Dryden's essay on *The Dramatic Poesy of The Last Age* he gives as the reason, 'the greatest advantage of our century, which proceeds from *conversation*. In the age wherein these poets lived, there was less of gallantry than in ours; neither did they keep the best company of theirs.'

The change in social status is important. It is doubtful if the Elizabethan dramatists would have been received in the best drawing-rooms. The poets of a later age certainly were, and if poetry lost that complete unity of language and sensation which the Elizabethans at their best achieved, Shakespeare's 'in her strong toil of grace' for example, the rise of the writer into society was at least partly responsible. A classical education and the company of ladies and gentlemen may have advantages, but they make an instinctive vocabulary very difficult.

But it is the mark of a great writer to know his limitations. Had Dryden attempted to continue the Elizabethan traditions, he would have been no greater than Massinger. Instead, he did what Nature has usually done in evolutionary changes, he turned to a form which, though it had once been important, during the last age had played second fiddle to blank verse.

The couplet had nevertheless had a continuous history, parallel to and influenced by blank verse. The couplet of Chaucer's time degenerated with the dropping of the final 'e', and with the exception of Dunbar's *Freiris of Berwick* is hardly seen, till it turns up again in Spenser's *Mother Hubbard's Tale*.

To such delight the noble wits had led
Which him relieved as their vain humours fed
With fruitless follies and unsound delights.

Its principal use was for narrative, as in Marlowe and Chapman's *Hero and Leander*, with enjambement and spreading of sentences over several couplets, a feature which developed in Donne and Cowley to a point where the feeling of the couplet is almost lost.

Seek true religion, O where? Mirreus,
Thinking her unhoused here and fled from us,
Seeks her at Rome, there, because he doth know
That she was there a thousand years ago;
And loves the rags so, as we here obey
The state-cloth where the prince sate yesterday.
Crants to such brave loves will not be enthrall'd,
But loves her only who at Geneva's call'd
Religion, plain, simple, sullen, young,
Contemptuous yet unhandsome; as among
Lecherous humours, there is one that judges
No wenches wholesome, but coarse country drudges.
Graius stays still at home here, and because
Some preachers, vile ambitious bawds, and laws,
Still new, like fashions, bid him think that she
Which dwells with us, is only perfect, he
Embraceth her, whom his godfathers will
Tender to him, being tender; as wards still
Take such wives as their guardians offer, or
Pay values. Careless Phrygius doth abhor
All, because all cannot be good; as one,
Knowing some women whores, dares marry none.

But side by side with this, through the use of rhyming tags to round off dramatic scenes, through the conclusions of the sonnets, and occasional addresses, there is a development of the end-stopped epigrammatical couplet. Lytton Strachey in his essay on Pope has drawn attention to a series of couplets in *Othello*, ending,

She was a wight if ever such wight were
To suckle fools and chronicle small beer.

And there are plenty of other instances. Fairfax's Tasso and Sandys's *Metamorphoses* were no sudden new developments.

The evolution of the end-stopped couplet from Spenser through Drayton to them and Waller and Denham, and on to Dryden and Pope is continuous. It is only the pace of the development that alters.

The choice of a verse form is only half conscious. No form will express everything, as each form is particularly good at expressing something. Forms are chosen by poets because the most important part of what they have to say seems to go better with that form than any other; there is generally a margin which remains unsaid, and then, in its turn, the form develops and shapes the poet's imagination so that he says things which he did not know he was capable of saying, and at the same time those parts of his imagination which once had other things to say dry up from lack of use.

The couplet was not Dryden's only instrument – the *Ode on St Cecilia's Day*, *Annus Mirabilis*, the *Threnodia Augustalis* succeed in expressing things that the couplet could not have expressed – but it *was* Pope's.

Nor is the heroic couplet the only tune of the eighteenth century. There are the octosyllabics of Swift, the blank verse of Thomson, the odes of Gray and Collins. There is Prior:

Now let us look for Louis' feather,
That used to shine so like a star:
The generals could not get together,
Wanting that influence, great in war.

There is Gay, forestalling Byron.

See generous Burlington with goodly Bruce
  (But Bruce comes wafted in a soft sedan),
Dan Prior next, beloved by every Muse,
  And friendly Congreve, unreproachful man!
(Oxford by Cunningham hath sent excuse;)
  See hearty Watkins come with cup and can,

And Lewis who has never friend forsaken,
　And Laughton whispering asks 'Is Troytown taken?'

or Dr Johnson, forestalling Housman,

All that prey on vice and folly
　Joy to see their quarry fly
There the gamester light and jolly,
　There the lender grave and sly.

and a host of popular songs and hymns.

Come cheer up, my lads, 'tis to glory we steer
To add something more to this wonderful year.

　No, the poetry of the eighteenth century is at least as varied as that
of any other, but Pope is labelled as the representative Augustan poet,
and as he confined himself to the couplet, the couplet is labelled as
the medium of Augustan poetry. As far as Pope personally was
concerned, his limitation of form – he even denied himself the
variety of an occasional alexandrine – had its advantages. 'Of this
uniformity the certain consequence was readiness and dexterity. By
perpetual practice, language had in his mind a systematical arrangement, having always the same use for words, he had words so selected
and combined as to be ready at his call.'

　With this limit of form went a limit of interest. Pope was interested
in three things – himself and what other people thought of him, his
art, and the manners and characters of society. Not even Flaubert or
Mallarmé was more devoted to his craft. 'What his nature was
unfitted to do, circumstance excused him from doing'; and he was
never compelled to write to order, or to hurry over his work. He
missed nothing. If he thought of something in the midst of the night,
he rang for the servant to bring paper; if something struck him during
a conversation, he would immediately write it down for future use.
He constantly altered and rewrote, and always for the better. The
introduction of sylphs and gnomes into *The Rape of the Lock*, and the
conclusion of *The Dunciad* were not first thoughts.

Let there be darkness (the dread power shall say),
All shall be darkness, as it ne'er were day:

To their first chaos wit's vain works shall fall
And universal dullness cover all.
No more the monarch could such raptures bear;
He waked, and all the vision mixed with air...
(1728)

Lo! the great anarch's ancient reign restored
Light dies before her uncreating word . . . .
Thy hand, great dullness! lets the curtain fall,
And universal darkness covers all.
Enough! enough! the raptured monarch cries;
And through the ivory gate the vision flies.
(1729)

and finally,

Lo! thy dread empire, Chaos! is restored;
Light dies before thy uncreating word.
Thy hand, great anarch! lets the curtain fall;
And universal darkness buries all.

The beauties and variety of his verse have been so brilliantly displayed by others, notably Miss Sitwell, that I shall confine myself to considering two popular ideas about Pope. That his language is either falsely poetic, or 'a classic of our prose', and that his poetry is cold and unemotional. The question of poetic diction was the gravamen of the Romantic's charge. The answer is that Pope and his contemporaries were interested in different fields of experience, in a different 'nature'. If their descriptions of cows and cottages and birds are vague, it is because their focus of interest is sharp elsewhere, and equal definition over the whole picture would spoil its proportion and obscure its design. They are conventional, not because the poets thought that 'the waterpudge, the pilewort, the petty chap, and the pooty' were unpoetic in their naked nature and must be suitably dressed, but because they are intended to be conventional, a backcloth to the more important human stage figures. When Pope writes in his preface[1] to the *Odyssey*, 'There is a real beauty in an easy, pure, perspicuous description even of a *low action*', he is saying something which he both believes and practises.

1 Really postscript. [Ed.]

To compass this, his building is a town,
His pond an ocean, his parterre a down.
Who but must laugh, the master when he sees,
A puny insect, shivering at a breeze!
Lo, what huge heaps of littleness around!
The whole, a laboured quarry above ground.
Two Cupids squirt before; a lake behind
Improves the keenness of the northern wind.
His gardens next your admiration call;
On every side you look, behold the wall!
No pleasing intricacies intervene,
No artful wildness to perplex the scene;
Grove nods at grove, each alley has a brother,
And half the platform just reflects the other.
The suffering eye inverted nature sees,
Trees cut to statues, statues thick as trees;
With here a fountain, never to be played;
And there a summer-house, that knows no shade;
Here Amphitritë sails through myrtle bowers;
There gladiators fight, or die, in flowers;
Un-watered see the drooping sea-horse mourn,
And swallows roost in Nilus' dusty urn.
(*Moral Essay IV*, 105–26)

Now lap-dogs give themselves the rousing shake,
And sleepless lovers, just at twelve, awake;
Thrice rung the bell, the slipper knocked the ground,
And the pressed watch returned a silver sound.
(*The Rape of the Lock*, I 15–18)

There is no vagueness here. These are the images of contemporary
life. This poetry, not Wordsworth's, is the ancestor of 'the patient
etherized on the table', of Baudelaire's

On entend ça et là les cuisines siffler,
Les théâtres glapir, les orchestres ronfler;
Les tables d'hôte, dont le jeu fait les délices,
S'emplissent de catins et d'escrocs, leur complices,
Et les voleurs, qui n'ont ni trève ni merci,

Vont bientôt commencer leur travail, eux aussi,
Et forcer doucement les portes et les caisses
Pour vivre quelques jours et vêtir leurs maîtresses.

Those who complain of Pope's use of periphrasis, of his refusal to call a spade a spade, cannot have read him carefully. When he chooses he is as direct as you please.

So morning insects that in muck begun
Shine, buzz, and flyblow in the setting sun.
(*Moral Essay II*, 27–8)

And when he does use a periphrasis, in his best work at least, it is because an effect is to be gained by doing so.

While China's earth receives the smoking tide.
(*The Rape of the Lock*, III 110)

To say that Pope was afraid to write, as Wordsworth might have written,

While boiling water on the tea was poured

is nonsense. To the microscopic image of tea-making is added the macroscopic image of a flood, a favourite device of Pope's, and the opposite kind of synthesis to Dante's 'A single moment maketh a deeper lethargy for use than twenty and five centuries have wrought on the emprise that erst threw Neptune in amaze at Argo's shadow.'

There are places in Pope, as in all poets, where his imagination is forced, where one feels a division between the object and the word, but at his best there are few poets who can rival his fusion of vision and language.

Chicane in furs, and casuistry in lawn
(*The Dunciad*, IV 28)

Bare the mean heart that lurks beneath a star.
(*Imitations of Horace, Satires* II i 108)

How hints, like spawn, scarce quick in embryo lie,
How new-born nonsense first is taught to cry,
Maggots half-formed in rhyme exactly meet,
And learn to crawl upon poetic feet.
Here one poor word an hundred clenches makes,

And ductile Dullness new meanders takes;
There motley images her fancy strike,
Figures ill paired, and similes unlike.
She sees a mob of metaphors advance,
Pleased with the madness of the mazy dance;
How tragedy and comedy embrace;
How farce and epic get a jumbled race;
How time himself stands still at her command,
Realms shift their place, and ocean turns to land.
Here gay description Egypt glads with showers,
Or gives to Zembla fruits, to Barca flowers;
Glittering with ice here hoary hills are seen,
There painted valleys of eternal green;
In cold December fragrant chaplets blow,
And heavy harvests nod beneath the snow.
(*The Dunciad*, I 59–78)

You will call this Fancy and Judgement if you are an Augustan, and the Imagination if you are a Romantic, but there is no doubt about it.

Like Dante, Pope had a passionate and quite undonnish interest in classical literature. The transformation of the heroic epic into *The Rape of the Lock* and *The Dunciad* is not cheap parody; it is the vision of a man who can see in Homer, in eighteenth-century society, in Grub Street, similarities of motive, character and conduct whereby an understanding of all is deepened. Rams and young bullocks are changed to folios and Birthday Odes, and

Could all our care elude the gloomy grave,
Which claims no less the fearful than the brave,
For lust of fame I should not vainly dare
In fighting fields, nor urge thy soul to war
(*Iliad*, XII 387–90)

becomes

Oh! if to dance all night, and dress all day,
Charmed the smallpox, or chased old age away,
Who would not scorn what huswife's cares produce,
Or who would learn one earthly thing of use?
(*The Rape of the Lock*, V 19–22)

Literature and life are once more happily married. We laugh and we love. Unlike Dryden, Pope is not a dramatic poet. He is at his best only when he is writing directly out of his own experience. I cannot feel that his Homer is anything but a set task, honourably executed; the diction gives it away. But show him the drawing-rooms where he longed to be received as a real gentleman, let him hear a disparaging remark about himself, and his poetry is beyond praise. The *Essay on Man* is smug and jaunty to a degree, until we come to Happiness and Fame

All that we feel of it begins and ends
In the small circle of our foes or friends;
To all beside as much an empty shade,
An Eugene living, as a Caesar dead.
(IV 241-4)

Pope knew what it was to be flattered and libelled, to be ambitious, to be snubbed, to have enemies, to be short, and ugly, and ill and unhappy, and out of his knowledge he made his poetry – succeeded, as Rilke puts it, in

transmuting himself into the words.
Doggedly, as the carver of a cathedral
Transfers himself to the stone's constancy.

and won his reward as he perceived

... how fate may enter into a verse
And not come back, how, once in, it turns image
And nothing but image, nothing but ancestor,
Who sometimes, when you look at him in his frame
Seems to be like you and again not like you.

Cyril Connolly

from 'Imitations of Horace', *New Statesman and Nation*
29 July 1939 (reprinted in *The Condemned Playground*, 1945)

What did the imitators of Horace imitate? It is clear from reading Rochester, Roscommon, Dryden, Cowley, that what appealed to them was sophistication, the new possibilities of personal relations, the improvement in critical values, the discoveries in Taste, which were afforded by the increased security, wealth, artificiality, and centralization of the London of Wren and the Court of Charles II, a civilization which owed much to France, to Saint-Evremond, Boileau, Molière. They were fascinated by the mechanism of clique life, conversation without brawls, disinterested friendship, criticism without duels, unpunished sex. They were modern in the sense in which Pepys is modern; early products of an urban culture, with a newly developed city sense, and an interest in the more mundane ethics, in friendship, or the use of riches, in the value of moderation of the follies and rewards of youth and age. In Rochester the freshness of these discoveries gives to his adaptations a vitality, a clumsy naïvety, which is lacking in Pope, and which is the difference between the Londons of Charles II and George II; and Dryden, being both a lyric poet and a genius, is also a greater translator, because he comprehends diversities of the original which escape his more talented, but more limited successor. His translation ('Descended from an Ancient Line') is one of the great poems in English. But it is not in translation that the influence of a writer is felt so much as in work indirectly inspired by him, and it is in Pope's *Moral Essays* especially in the *Epistle to Lord Burlington* and the *Characters of Women*, that his debt to Horace is repaid, repaid by the depth and variety of observation, the perfection of form, and by that manliness which was the Roman contribution to poetry, and which, present for so long in English verse, has in our time degenerated into heartiness, and now disappeared.

When Pope comes to translate Horace, in spite of his enormous verbal felicity (no tight rope has been more delicately walked), one is conscious of three defects which intrude themselves. One because the heroic couplet is not the natural medium for translating the hexameter, and hence, although the colloquial and broken conversational effects of Horace are exquisitely done, there arises a certain reproach as one compares the splended and sullen force of the original with Pope's urbane numbers. Another and graver defect is that, while we take Horace's estimate of himself on trust, we cannot do the same with Pope, for while Pope in these poems is in love with his own moderation, loyalty, and devotion to virtue, these qualities appear illusions which sharply engender an awareness of their opposite, when we compare them with the rude avowals of the original. Moreover, Horace, although eighteenth-century in much of his thought, was an ancient Roman, and Pope seems too anxious to fit him, as he fitted Doctor Donne, into the *dixhuitième* mould. On the lecherous, irritable, and prematurely bald man of genius the periwig does not quite fit, and it is his lyricism which must suffer.

W. K. Wimsatt

from 'One Relation of Rhyme to Reason', *Modern Language Quarterly*, vol. 5 1944 (reprinted in *The Verbal Icon*, 1954)

We come then to rhyme, the subject of our argument. And first it must be admitted that in certain contexts a high degree of parallel in sense may be found even in rhyme. Even identical words may rhyme. In the sestina, for example, the same set of rhyme words is repeated in six different stanzas. But here the order changes, and so does the relation of each rhyme word to the context. That is the point of the sestina. Somewhat the same may be said for a refrain when it does not rhyme with any other line of the context. In the broadest sense, difference of meaning in rhyme words includes difference of syntax. In fact, words have no character as rhymes until they become points in a syntactic succession. Hence rhyme words (even identical ones) can scarcely appear in a context without showing some difference of meaning. The point of this essay is therefore not to prove that rhyme words must exhibit difference of meaning, but to discuss the value of the difference and to show how a greater degree of difference harmonizes with a certain type of verse structure.

Under certain conditions (much more common than the sestina or refrain mentioned above) the opportunity and the demand for difference of meaning in rhyme may be slight.

Scogan, that knelest at the stremes hed
Of grace, of alle honour and worthynesse,
In th'ende of which strem I am dul as ded,
Forgete in solitarie wildernesse –
Yet, Scogan, thenke on Tullius kyndenesse.

The three identical 'nesse' rhymes could be mere prosy homoeo-oteleuton if the three words occurred in position of nearly parallel logic or syntax. But Chaucer's sense, meandering like the stream through the stanza, makes no great demand upon these rhymes, and, weak though they are, they are strong enough. Even in Chaucer's couplets the same continuity of sense through the verse may be discovered, and the same tendency in rhyming, as we shall illustrate in the comparison which follows.

Pope is the English poet whose rhyming shows perhaps the clearest contrast to Chaucer's. Chaucer found, even in Middle English, a 'skarsete' of rhyme. There would come a day when an even greater scarcity of easy rhymes would create a challenge to the English poet and at the same time indicate one of his most subtle opportunities. In the course of three hundred years English lost many of its easy rhymes, stressed Germanic and Romance endings (y, ing, ere, esse, and able, age, al, aunce, aile, ain, esse, oun, ous, ure), so that Pope perforce rhymed words differing more widely in meaning. The characteristics of Pope's couplet, as opposed to Chaucer's, are, of course, its closure or completeness, its stronger tendency to parallel, and its epigram-matic, witty, intellectual point. One can hardly imagine such a couplet rhyming 'wildernesse' and 'kyndenesse', or 'worthynesse' and 'hethenesse', as Chaucer does in one couplet of the Knight's portrait.

Most likely it is neither feasible nor even desirable to construct a scale of meaning differences to measure the cleverness of rhyme. The analysis which I intend is not in the main statistical. But an obvious, if rude, basis for classification is provided by the parts of speech. It may be said, broadly, that difference in meaning of rhyme words can be recognized in difference of parts of speech and in differ-ence of functions of the same part of speech, and that both of these differences will be qualified by the degree of parallel or of obliquity appearing between the two whole lines of a rhyming pair. The tenor of the comparison which follows will be to suggest that Pope's rhymes are characterized by difference in parts of speech or in function of the same parts of speech, the difference in each case being accentu-ated by the tendency of his couplets to parallel structure.

A large number of rhymes in both Pope and Chaucer, or indeed in any English poet, are rather neutral to our inquiry.

Whan that Aprille with his shoures soote
The droghte of March hath perced to the roote.

Here the rhyme makes its contribution to difference of sense against equality of verse, but because the oblique phrases themselves make a fundamental contrast to the metrically equal lines, and the rhyming parts of speech are a function of the phrases, the rhyme is not likely to be felt as a special element of variation. There is a higher proportion of such rhymes in Chaucer than in Pope. In general Chaucer relies for variation more on continuous sense and syntax than on rhyme, and when his rhyme words are the same part of speech, he is apt to give us a dullish rhyme:

Me thynketh it acordaunt to resoun
To telle you al the condicioun.

In similar constructions Pope is apt to find some quaint minor contrast in length and quality of words:

What guards the purity of melting maids,
In courtly balls, and midnight masquerades?
(*The Rape of the Lock*, 1 71–2)

It is in couplets of parallel structure, however, that the rhyming of Pope is seen to best advantage. More of these couplets in Pope have rhymes of different parts of speech than in Chaucer, and their effect is more pronounced in Pope because the parallel within the closed couplet of Pope is likely to be smarter. Chaucer will write:

And everemoore he hadde a sovereyn prys:
And though that he were worthy, he was wys.

Pope will write:

Oft when the world imagine women stray,
The Sylphs through mystic mazes guide their way.
(*The Rape of the Lock*, 1 91–2)

When Florio speaks, what virgin could withstand,
If gentle Damon did not squeeze her hand?
(1 97–8)

In these two examples, though the syntax is oblique, the sense is parallel and antithetic. Pope's couplets, no matter what their syntax, tend to hover on the verge of antithesis and hence to throw a stress upon whatever difference of meaning appears in the rhyme words.

One might expect to find that a parallel both of general sense and of rhyming parts of speech would produce a quality of flatness, a sort of minimum rhyme such as we found in St Augustine – 'Lingua clamat, cor amat' – only the first step beyond homoeoteleuton. One thing that may prevent this and may lend the rhyme a value of variation is that through some irregularity or incompleteness of parallel the rhyming words have oblique functions. Thus Chaucer:

No deyntee morsel passed thurgh hir throte;
Hir diete was accordant to hir cote.

And Pope:

From each she nicely culls with curious toil,
And decks the goddess with the glittering spoil.
(*The Rape of the Lock*, 1 131–2)

There are more of these couplets in Pope than in Chaucer, and with Pope the rhyme difference is more likely to seem the result of some deft twist or trick.

Some are bewildered in the maze of schools,
And some made coxcombs nature meant but fools.
(*Essay on Criticism*, 26–7)

There is a kind of inversion (from pupils to schools and back to the pupils in a new light) which in some couplets appears more completely as chiasmus, an effect concerning which I shall have more to say.

The two types of rhyme difference which characterize Pope's poetry (that of different parts of speech and that of the same part of speech in different functions) are a complement, as I have suggested, of his tendency to a parallel of lines. To recognize this may affect our opinion about how deliberately or consciously Pope strove for difference of rhyme, but it should not diminish the impression which the actual difference of rhyme makes upon us. Such rhyme difference may be felt more clearly as a characteristic of Pope if we examine the rhymes in a passage where the parallel is somewhat like that which Chaucer at times employs. It is difficult to find passages of sustained parallel in Chaucer. The usual narrative movement of his couplets is the oblique forward movement of actions in a sequence. But in the character sketches of the *Canterbury Prologue* a kind of loose parallel often prevails for ten or twenty lines, as one feature of a pilgrim after another is enumerated. The sense is continuous, in that the couplets tend to be incomplete, but the lines are all members of a parallel bundle. A clear example may be seen in the Yeoman's portrait.

And he was clad in cote and hood of grene,
A sheef of pecock arwes, bright and kene,
Under his belt he bar ful thriftily
(Wel coude he dresse his takel yemanly):
. . . .
Upon his arm he baar a gay bracer,
And by his syde a swerde and a bokeler,
And on that oother syde a gay daggere
Harneised wel and sharp as point of spere;
A Christopher on his brest of silver sheene,
A horn he bar, the bawdryk was of grene.

'Thriftily' and 'yemanly', 'bracer' and bokeler', 'sheene' and 'grene', rhymes like these (aside even from the use of final syllables, 'ly' and 'er') I should call tame rhymes because the same parts of speech are used in closely parallel functions. To see the difference in this respect between Chaucer and Pope we may turn to the classic lines of another portrait:

Blest with each talent and each art to please,
And born to write, converse, and live with ease;
Should such a man, too fond to rule alone,
Bear, like the Turk, no brother near the throne;
View him with scornful, yet with jealous eyes,
And hate for arts that caused himself to rise;
Damn with faint praise, assent with civil leer,
And, without sneering, teach the rest to sneer;
Willing to wound, and yet afraid to strike,
Just hint a fault, and hesitate dislike;
Alike reserved to blame or to commend,
A timorous foe, and a suspicious friend.

The parallel of lines is continuous, but the rhymes are always different parts of speech. The portrait continues:

Dreading ev'n fools; by flatterers besieged,
And so obliging that he n'er obliged;
Like Cato, give his little Senate laws,
And sit attentive to his own applause.
(*Epistle to Dr Arbuthnot*, 195–210)

Here the same parts of speech are rhymed, but one verb is passive, one active; one noun is plural, one singular. The functions are different, in each case what he does being set against what he receives.

It is to be noted that in the yeoman's portrait such rhymes as 'grene' and 'kene', 'thriftily' and 'yemanly' are of the sort which we described above as minimum rhyme, only one step away from homoeoteleuton. Rhymes of this type often escape the extreme, as we saw, by some irregularity of parallel. But it is significant to add now that even when Pope does not escape the extreme he has resources of piquancy. Here and there he will be guilty of a certain flatness:

Each motion guides, and every nerve sustains;
Itself unseen, but in th' effects remains.
(*Essay on Criticism*, 78–9)

Often, however, he conveys some nice contrast in the parallel.

True wit is nature to advantage dressed,
What oft was thought, but ne'er so well expressed.
(Ibid., 297–8)

Here the two rhyme verbs are not merely parallel examples. One is literal, one is figurative, and in being matched with each other they express in brief the metaphor on which this classic critical doctrine is based, that to express is to dress.

Th' adventurous Baron the bright locks admired;
He saw, he wished, and to the prize aspired.
(*The Rape of the Lock*, II 29–30)

Here the difference between 'admired' and 'aspired', the swift ascent of the Baron's aspiration, is precisely the point.

One speaks the glory of the British Queen,
And one describes a charming Indian screen.
(Ibid., III 13–14)

Do thou, Crispissa, tend her fav'rite lock;
Ariel himself shall be the guard of Shock.
(Ibid., II 115–16)

From 'British Queen' to 'Indian screen', from 'lock' to 'Shock',
here is the same bathos he more often puts into one line – 'When
husbands, or when lap-dogs breathe their last.'

What I conceive to be the acme of variation occurs in a construction
to which I have already alluded, chiasmus. The basis of chiasmus will
be a high degree of parallel, often antithetic. The rhyme may be of
the same part of speech or of different parts. If it is of the same part,
the chiastic variation will be a special case of the 'schools'–'fools'
rhyme already quoted, where a twist in the meaning gives different
functions to the rhyme words. If the rhyme is of different parts, the
variation will be a special case of that already discussed, where different
parts of speech rhyme in parallel lines.

Whether the nymph shall break[1] Diana's law,[2]
Or some frail china jar[2'] receive a flaw.[1']
(II 105–6)

In the first line the breakage, then the fragile thing (the law); in the
second line, another fragile thing (the jar) and then its breaking (the
flaw). The parallel is given a kind of roundness and completeness;
the intellectual lines are softened into the concrete harmony of 'law'
and 'flaw'. The meaning is locked in a pattern of inevitability.

What dire offence from amorous causes[1] springs,[2]
What mighty contests rise[2'] from trivial things.[1']
(I 1–2)

Love, hope, and joy, fair pleasure's[1] smiling train,[2]
Hate, fear, and grief, the family[2'] of pain.[1']
(Essay on Man, II 117–18)

Fear[1] to the statesman,[2] rashness[1] to the child,[2]
To kings[2'] presumption,[1'] and to crowds[2'] belief.[1']
(*Essay on Man*, II 243–4)

Thus critics of less judgement[1] than caprice,[2]
Curious,[2'] not knowing,[1'] not exact,[1] but nice.[2]
(*Essay on Criticism*, 285–6)

In the last example the antithesis is tripled, and the order being successively chiastic, returns upon itself, which is sufficient complication to make 'caprice' and 'nice' a surprise. Then one is an adjective and one a noun, and 'caprice' has two syllables.

The contemplation of chiastic rhyme, the most brilliant and complex of all the forms of rhyme variation, leads me to make a brief general remark upon the degree of Pope's reputation for rhyme. I have relied heavily upon examples of rhyme from Pope because he takes such clear and frequent advantage of the rhyming quality with which I am concerned. To that extent, and it seems to me an important extent, he is one of the finest English rhymers. Yet a critic of Pope's rhyme has spoken of 'true' rhymes and 'false' rhymes and 'rhymes to the eye' and has been concerned to discover that of 7,874 rhymes in Pope 1,027 are 'false'. Another has approved of Pope's 'correctness' in excluding polysyllables from his rhymes, but has found Pope's repeated use of the same rhyme words 'monotonous in a high degree and a very serious artistic defect'. The same critic has actually spoken of Pope's 'poverty of rhyme'. One of the purposes of my argument is to cut the ground from under such judgements. They can spring only from a limited view of rhyme as a form of phonetic harmony – to be described and appraised in terms of phonetic accuracy, complexity, and variety – in other words, from a failure to connect rhyme with reason.

We have so far considered rhyme as it makes variation against the parallels of verse. If we think now of the meaning of the words as the basis of comparison, thus beginning with variation or difference, we can discuss the sameness of the rhyme-sound as a binding force. Rhyme is commonly recognized as a binder in verse structure. But where there is need for binding there must be some difference or separation between the things to be bound. If they are already close together, it is supererogatory to emphasize this by the maneuvre of rhyme. So we may say that the greater the difference in meaning between rhyme words the more marked and the more appropriate will be the binding effect. Rhyme theorists have spoken of the 'surprise' which is the pleasure of rhyme, and surely this surprise is not merely a matter of coming upon a similarity which one has not *previously* anticipated. It cannot be a matter of time. Even after the discovery, when the rhyme is known by heart, the pleasurable surprise remains. It must depend on some incongruity or unlikelihood inherent in the coupling. It is a curious thing that 'queen' should rhyme with 'screen', they are very unlike objects. But Pope has found a connection between them, has classified them as topics of chat, and then the parallel of sound comes to his aid as a humorous binder.

The hero William, and the martyr Charles,
One knighted Blackmore, and one pensioned Quarles.
(*Imitations of Horace*, II i 386–7)

'Charles' did not actually pension 'Quarles', but we are well on the way to believing that he did; the rhyme at least is a *fait accompli*.

The most extreme examples of this kind of humour are the extravagant double or triple rhymes of a Butler, a Swift, a Byron, or a Browning. One stanza from Byron will do.

He was a Turk, the colour of mahogany;
And Laura saw him, and at first was glad,
Because the Turks so much admire philogyny,
Although their usage of their wives is sad;
'Tis said they use no better than a dog any
Poor woman, whom they purchase like a pad:
They have a number, though they ne'er exhibit 'em,
Four wives by law, and concubines 'ad libitum'.

If Byron had rhymed 'philogyny' and 'misogyny', it would not be very funny, for one expects these two words to sound alike; they are formed alike from the Greek and make the end words of a natural antithesis. They are mere homoeoteleuton. 'Mahogany' makes a comic rhyme with 'philogyny' because of the wide disparity in meaning between the words. Mahogany, the Spanish name of a reddish hardwood, is not a likely companion for the learned Greek abstraction, but once an ingenious affinity in meaning is established, the rhyme sounds a triple surprise of ratification. Then comes 'dog any', and difference of meaning in rhyme has proceeded to the point of disintegration and mad abandon. What convinces us that 'dog any' belongs in this stanza is not so much its inevitable or appropriate meaning as the fact that it does rhyme.

'Rhyme,' says Henry Lanz, 'is one of those irrational satellites that revolve around reason. It is concerned not with the meaning of verse but only with its form, which is emotional. It lies within the plane of the alogical cross-section of verse.' It is within the scope of my argument to grant the alogical character of rhyme, or rather to insist on it, but at the same time to insist that the alogical character by itself has little, if any, aesthetic value. The music of spoken words in itself is meagre, so meagre in comparison to the music of song or instrument as to be hardly worth discussion. It has become a platitude of criticism to point out that verses composed of meaningless words afford no pleasure of any kind and can scarcely be called rhythmical – let them even be rhymed. The mere return to the vowel tonic (the chord or tone cluster characteristic of a vowel) is likely to produce the emotions of boredom. The art of words is an intellectual art, and the emotions of poetry are simultaneous with conceptions and largely induced through the medium of conceptions. In literary art only the wedding of the alogical with the logical gives the former an aesthetic value. The words of a rhyme, with their curious harmony of sound and distinction of sense, are an amalgam of the sensory and the logical, or an arrest and precipitation of the logical in sensory form; they are the icon in which the idea is caught. Rhyme and other verse elements save the physical quality of words – intellectualized and made transparent by daily prose usage. But without the intellectual element there is nothing to save and no reason why the physical element of words need be asserted. 'Many a man,' says Dr Lanz at the close of his book, 'was cruelly put to death for a "daring rhyme"'. And he regards it as a triumph of modern science that, instead of marvelling at the mystery of this force, we can "disect it as a corpse"'. These notions seem set up to provoke the retort that men are cruelly put to death not for melodies but for ideas, and that it is only when reduced to a purely 'physical basis' that rhyme becomes a 'corpse'.

When Adam dalf and Eve span,
Who was then a gentilman?

If there is something daring in this rhyme of John Ball's, it is certainly
not in the return to the overtone of 1840 vibrations per second
characteristic of ă [æ], but in the ironic jostle by which plebeian 'span'
gives a lesson in human values to aristocratic 'gentilman'.

T. S. Eliot

from *What Is a Classic?*   1945

You will have anticipated the conclusion towards which I have been
drawing: that those qualities of the classic which I have so far
mentioned – maturity of mind, maturity of manners, maturity of
language and perfection of the common style – are most nearly to be
illustrated, in English literature, in the eighteenth century; and, in
poetry, most in the poetry of Pope. If that were all I had to say on the
matter, it would certainly not be new, and it would not be worth
saying. That would be merely proposing a choice between two errors
at which men have arrived before: one, that the eighteenth century
is the finest period of English literature; and the other, that the classical
idea should be wholly discredited. My own opinion is that we have
no classic age, and no classic poet, in English; that when we see why
this is so, we have not the slightest reason for regret; but that,
nevertheless, we must maintain the classic ideal before our eyes.
Because we must maintain it, and because the English genius of
language has had other things to do than to realize it, we cannot
afford either to reject or to overrate the age of Pope; we cannot see
English literature as a whole, or aim rightly in the future, without
a critical appreciation of the degree to which the classical qualities
are exemplified in the work of Pope: which means that unless we
are able to enjoy the work of Pope, we cannot arrive at a full understanding of English poetry.

It is fairly obvious that the realization of classical qualities by Pope
was obtained at a high price – to the exclusion of some greater
potentialities of English verse. Now, to some extent, the sacrifice of

some potentialities in order to realize others is a condition of artistic creation, as it is a condition of life in general. In life the man who refuses to sacrifice anything, to gain anything else, ends in mediocrity or failure; though, on the other hand, there is the specialist who has sacrificed too much for too little, or who has been born too completely the specialist to have had anything to sacrifice. But in the English eighteenth century, we have reason for feeling that too much was excluded.

(16–16)

George Sherburn

from 'Pope at Work', *Essays on the Eighteenth Century Presented to David Nichol Smith* 1945

When Pope told Spence in 1730 that there was 'no judging of a piece from the scattered parts'; he was being modest and was recognizing the confused state of his fragmentary manuscripts. Spence properly interpreted the remark: one should 'survey the whole':

'Tis not a lip, or eye, we beauty call,
But the joint force and full result of all.
(*Essay on Criticism*, 245–6)

Pedantry may be permitted to remark, however, after examining Pope's manuscripts, that he composed by fragmentary paragraphs fully as often as by individual couplets, and far more often than he did from any sort of structural 'outline' of the whole poem. As he told Spence, the greatest trouble was in 'settling and ranging' these parts aright. The poet's habit of working in verse paragraphs can be seen anywhere. In the Harvard manuscript of the *Essay on Man*, Epistle I, for example, lines 29–34 of the standard editions are placed after line 22; lines 61–8 come after line 28, and are followed by lines 35–42; after line 186 come 207–32, etc. A comparison of early printed texts of the fourth *Moral Essay* (*Of Taste*) with later texts will show that the habit of rearranging paragraphs continued even after the poem was published. Both in the Harvard manuscript of the *Essay on Man*, Epistle I (which was obviously regarded as a final fair copy when begun), and in the fourth *Moral Essay*, the parts shuffled involve nearly always more than a single couplet. There has been too much stress on Pope's artistry in couplets; he is, as a matter of fact, quite as notably an artist in verse paragraphs. His art in varying the mood and tone and pace of succeeding paragraphs gives a diversity that indemnifies for any supposed monotony resultant from the closed couplet.

One may well suspect that in later days the *Essay on Man* would have been more favourably regarded by critics if the poet had printed his verse paragraphs frankly as such – if, in the manner of Traherne's *Centuries of Meditation* or of Tennyson's *In Memoriam*, he had been content to leave his verse units as fragmentary reflections on philosophic ideas that are bound to have recurrent interest. Pope did, of course, indicate units by marginal Roman numerals; yet he wished finally to think of his work as 'a short, yet not imperfect, system, of ethics'.

Of this 'system' he fell short, and of all the stages of poetic composition that of 'settling the parts' into a coherent and effective order worried him most. The difficulty is especially acute in the early thirties, when he is at work on different poems simultaneously; but perhaps the difficulty is inherent in the attempt to write fairly long poems that are discursively reflective.

Coming to the last stage of composition to be considered, we can have no doubt that the poet did make his fragmentary reflections 'agreeably enough to be read with pleasure'. Of his *limae labor et mora* already much has been said, and perhaps it is all summed up in the general opinion that Pope seldom altered without improvement. Examples may be superfluous, but the manuscripts of the *Essay on Man* are so full of them that one cannot forbear quoting. The opening lines of Epistle II –

Know then thyself; presume not God to scan;
The proper study of mankind is man –

are so natural an example of the firm, lapidary style that one can hardly imagine the couplet is the result of much reshaping. But in the Morgan Library manuscript the Epistle begins with the comparatively feeble

           we ourselves
Learn ~~then Thyself~~, not God presume to scan
But
~~And~~ know, the Study of Mankind is *Man.*

And the Harvard manuscript has as lines 13–14 of the Epistle (after
12 lines of apostrophe to Bolingbroke):

Know
~~Learn~~ we ourselves, not God presume to scan,
The only Science Convincd
~~But know~~, the Study of Mankind is *Man.*

Obviously the real inspiration here came after some floundering. The
couplet is a superb example of Pope's process of perfecting his
utterance. One may note that there is nothing inherently 'decorative' about the process. Another type of perfecting is seen in the
famous passage in Epistle I concerning the Indian concept of Heaven.
In part the Morgan manuscript reads:

Yet Nature's flattery this Hope has given;
Behind his cloud-topt Hills he builds a Heaven,
Some happier World, wch woods on woods infold,
Where never christian pierced for thirst of Gold.
Some safer World, in depth of Woods embrac'd,
Some happier Island in the watry waste,
Where slaves once more their native land behold,
No Fiends torment, nor Christians thirst for Gold.
Where Gold n'er grows, & never Spaniards come,
Where Trees bear maize, & Rivers flow wth Rum,
Exil'd, or chain'd, he lets you understand
Death but returns him to his native Land;
Or firm as Martyrs, smiling yields the ghost,
Rich of a Life that is not to be lost.

In the Harvard manuscript Pope had improved the first of these lines
into its standard printed form, doubtless because of the unsatisfactory
implications of *flattery*, which later Mr Elwin was at pains to point out.
Other verses, of some merit, were omitted to secure a firmer line of
thought or at least greater brevity. The problem *proprie communia
dicere* was encountered by Pope at every point in his revisions.

Of the fourteen lines just quoted Pope had crossed through for deletion lines 3 and 4 and the last six; the printed texts give variants of the remaining six. The case may serve as occasion to remark that Pope's method of composition by accreting paragraphs is in part balanced by this art of blotting. The Morgan manuscript of the four epistles of the *Essay on Man* contains almost 250 lines that did not appear in versions printed by Pope. Dr Johnson concluded from the Homer manuscripts of Pope that the poet's method 'was to write his first thoughts in his first words, and gradually to amplify, decorate, rectify, and refine them'. This statement is largely, but not completely true. There exists, for example, an early manuscript form of what was to become the *Epistle to Dr Arbuthnot*; and the manuscript runs only to about a hundred lines – less than one fourth the final length of the poem. But Pope practised condensation as well, and omitted much that he set down on paper in his working manuscripts. Concerning the decorative quality of his later composition there may be argument. If added illustrative details be regarded in the manner of gargoyles, these accretions are decorative. But if one considers Pope's imaginative phrasing after *The Dunciad* of 1729 – and apart from Book IV of that poem (1743) – the effect is not decorative but functional. His labour to produce

Know then thyself, presume not God to scan

is a fair example. The diction is chiselled and 'rectified', but not ornate. Through all the stages of composition – the turning of prose hints into verse paragraphs, the ranging of these paragraphs, and the final *limae labor* – Pope's object is the rectification of expression. For him poetry is perfected utterance, and his working manuscripts, especially those from the early thirties, testify to his unwearied attempts to polish his paragraphs and make them 'agreeable enough to be read with pleasure'.

Cleanth Brooks

from 'The Case of Miss Arabella Fermor', *The Well-Wrought Urn*
1947

Is Belinda [in *The Rape of the Lock*] a goddess, or is she merely a
frivolous tease? Pope himself was, we may be sure, thoroughly aware
of the problem. His friend Swift penetrated the secrets of the lady's
dressing room with what results we know. Belinda's dressing table,
of course, is bathed in a very different atmosphere; yet it may be
significant that Pope is willing to allow us to observe his heroine at
her dressing table at all. The poet definitely means to give us scenes
from the greenroom, and views from the wings, as well as a presentation 'in character' on the lighted stage.

Pope, of course, did not write *The Rape of the Lock* because he was
obsessed with the problem of Belinda's divinity. He shows, indeed,
that he was interested in a great many things: in various kinds of
social satire, in a playful treatment of the epic manner, in deflating
some of the more vapid clichés that filled the love poetry of the period,
and in a dozen other things. But we are familiar with Pope's interest
in the mock-epic as we are not familiar with his interest in the problem
of woman as goddess; and moreover, the rather lurid conventional
picture of Pope as the 'wicked wasp of Twickenham' – the particular
variant of the either-or theory as applied to Pope – encourages us to
take the poem as a dainty but rather obvious satire. There is some
justification, therefore, for emphasizing aspects of the poem which
have received little attention in the past, and perhaps for neglecting
other aspects of the poems which critics have already treated in
luminous detail.

One further point should be made: if Pope in this account of the
poem turns out to be something of a symbolist poet, and perhaps even
something of what we call, in our clumsy phrase, a 'metaphysical
poet' as well, we need not be alarmed. It matters very little whether
or not we twist some of the categories which the literary historian
jealously (and perhaps properly) guards. It matters a great deal that
we understand Pope's poem in its full richness and complexity. It
would be an amusing irony (and one not wholly undeserved) if we
retorted upon Pope some of the brittleness and inelasticity which we
feel that Pope was inclined to impose upon the more fluid and illogical

poetry which preceded him. But the real victims of the manoeuvre, if it blinded us to his poem, would be ourselves.

Pope's own friends were sometimes guilty of oversimplifying and reducing his poem by trying to make it accord with a narrow and pedantic logic. For example, Bishop Warburton, Pope's friend and editor, finds an error in the famous passage in which Belinda and her maid are represented as priestesses invoking the goddess of beauty. Warburton feels forced to comment as follows: 'There is a small inaccuracy in these lines. He first makes his heroine the chief priestess, then the goddess herself.' The lines in question [1 123 ff.] run as follows.

First, robed in white, the nymph intent adores,
With head uncovered, the cosmetic powers.
A heavenly image in the glass appears,
To that she bends, to that her eyes she rears.

It is true that Pope goes on to imply that Belinda is the chief priestess (by calling her maid the 'inferior priestess'), and that, a few lines later, he has the maid deck the goddess (Belinda) 'with the glittering spoil'. But surely Warburton ought not to have missed the point: Belinda, in worshipping at the shrine of beauty, quite naturally worships herself. Whose else is the 'heavenly image' which appears in the mirror to which she raises her eyes? The violation of logic involved is intended and is thoroughly justified. Belinda *is* a goddess, but she puts on her divinity at her dressing table; and, such is the paradox of beauty-worship, she can be both the sincere devotee and the divinity herself. We shall certainly require more sensitive instruments than Bishop Warburton's logic if we are to become aware of some of the nicest effects in the poem.

But to continue with the dressing-table scene:

The fair each moment rises in her charms,
Repairs her smiles, awakens every grace,
And calls forth all the wonders of her face;
Sees by degrees a purer blush arise,
And keener lightnings quicken in her eyes.

It is the experience which the cosmetic advertisers take at a level of dead seriousness, and obviously Pope is amused to have it taken seriously. And yet, is there not more here than the obvious humour?

Belinda is, after all, an artist, and who should be more sympathetic with the problems of the conscious artist than Pope himself? In our own time, William Butler Yeats, a less finicky poet than Pope, could address a 'young beauty' as 'dear fellow artist'.

In particular, consider the 'purer blush'. Why purer? One must not laugh too easily at the purity of the blush which Belinda is engaged in painting upon her face. After all, may we not regard it as a blush 'recollected in tranquillity', and therefore a more ideal blush than the spontaneous actual blush which shame or hauteur on an actual occasion might bring? If we merely read 'purer' as ironic for its opposite, 'impurer' – that is, unspontaneous and therefore unmaidenly – we shall miss not only the more delightful aspects of the humour, but we shall miss also Pope's concern for the real problem. Which is, after all, the more maidenly blush? That will depend, obviously, upon what one considers the essential nature of maidens to be; and Belinda, we ought to be reminded, is not the less real nor the less feminine because she fails to resemble Whittier's robust heroine, Maude Muller.

One is tempted to insist upon these ambiguities and complexities of attitude, not with any idea of overturning the orthodox reading of Pope's irony, but rather to make sure that we do not conceive it to be more brittle and thin than it actually is. This fact, at least, should be plain: regardless of what we may make of the 'purer blush', it is true that Belinda's dressing table does glow with a special radiance and charm, and that Pope, though amused by the vanity which it represents, is at the same time thoroughly alive to a beauty which it actually possesses.

There is a further reason for feeling that we shall not err in taking the niceties of Pope's description quite seriously. One notices that even the metaphors by which Pope characterizes Belinda are not casual bits of decoration, used for a moment, and then forgotten. They run throughout the poem as if they were motifs. For instance, at her dressing table Belinda is not only a priestess of 'the sacred rites of pride', but she is also compared to a warrior arming for the fray. Later in the poem she is the warrior once more at the card table in her conquest of the two 'adventurous knights'; and again, at the end of the poem, she emerges as the heroic conqueror in the epic encounter of the beaux and belles.

To take another example, Belinda, early in the poem [I 12–13], is compared to the sun. Pope suggests that the sun recognizes in Belinda a rival, and fears her:

Sol through white curtains shot a timorous ray,
And oped those eyes that must eclipse the day.

But the sun's fear of Belinda has not been introduced merely in order to give the poet an opportunity to mock at the polite cliché. The sun comparison appears again at the beginning of Canto II:

Not with more glories in th' ethereal plain
The sun first rises o'er the purpled main,
Than issuing forth the rival of his beams
Launched on the bosom of the silver *Thames*.

Belinda is like the sun, not only because of her bright eyes, and not only because she dominates her special world ('But every eye was fixed on her alone'). She is like the sun in another regard:

Bright as the sun, her eyes the gazers strike,
And like the sun they shine on all alike.

Is this general munificence on the part of Belinda a fault or a virtue? Is she shallow and flirtatious, giving her favours freely to all; or does she distribute her largesse impartially like a great prince? Or is she simply the well-bred belle who knows that she cannot play favourites if she wishes to be popular? The sun comparison is able to carry all these meanings, and therefore goes past any momentary jest. Granting that it may be over-ingenious to argue that Belinda in Canto IV (the gloomy Cave of Spleen) represents the sun in eclipse, still the sun comparison does appear once more in the poem, and quite explicitly. As the poem closes, Pope addresses Belinda thus:

When those fair suns shall set, as set they must,
And all those tresses shall be laid in dust,
This lock the Muse shall consecrate to fame,
And midst the stars inscribe Belinda's name!

Here, one notices that the poet, if he is forced to concede that Belinda's eyes are only metaphysical suns after all, still promises that the ravished lock shall have a celestial eternity, adding, like the planet Venus, 'new glory to the shining sphere!' And here Pope, we may be sure, is not merely playful in his metaphor. Belinda's name has been inscribed in the only heaven in which a poet would care to inscribe it. If the sceptic still has any doubts about Pope's taking Belinda very seriously, there should be no difficulty in convincing him that Pope took his own work very seriously indeed.

We began by raising the question of Belinda's status as a goddess. It ought to be quite clear that Pope's attitude toward Belinda is not exhausted in laughing away her claims to divinity. The attitude is much more complicated than that. Belinda's charm is not viewed uncritically, but the charm is real: it can survive the poet's knowledge of how much art and artifice have gone into making up the charm. The attitude is not wholly unrelated to that of Mirabell toward Millamant in Congreve's *The Way of the World*. Mirabell knows that his mistress has her faults, but as he philosophically remarks: '. . . I like her with all her faults; nay, I like her for her faults. Her follies are so natural, or so artful, that they become her. . . . she once used me with that insolence, that in revenge I took her to pieces, sifted her, and separated her failings; I studied 'em, and got 'em by rote. . . . They are now grown as familiar to me as my own frailties; and in all probability, in a little time longer, I shall like 'em as well.' The relation of author to creation can be more philosophical still; and though Pope's attitude toward his heroine has a large element of amused patronage in it, I find no contempt. Rather, Pope finds Belinda charming, and expects us to feel her charm.

To pursue the matter of attitude further still, what, after all, is Pope's attitude toward the iridescent little myth of the sylphs which he has provided to symbolize the polite conventions which govern the conduct of maidens? We miss the whole point if we dismiss the sylphs as merely 'supernatural machinery'. In general, we may say that the myth represents a qualification of the poet's prevailingly naturalistic interpretation. More specifically, it represents his attempt to do justice to the intricacies of the feminine mind. For, in spite of Pope's amusement at the irrationality of that mind, Pope acknowledges its beauty and its power.

In making this acknowledgement, he is a good realist – a better realist, indeed, than he appears when he tries to parade the fashionable ideas of the Age of Reason as in his *Essay on Man*. He is good enough realist to know that although men in their 'learned pride' may say that it is Honour which protects the chastity of maids, actually it is nothing of the sort: the belles are not kept chaste by any mere abstraction. It is the sylphs, the sylphs with their interest in fashion notes and their knowledge of the feminine heart:

With varying vanities, from every part,
They shift the moving toyshop of their heart;
Where wigs with wigs, with sword-knots sword-
     knots strive,
Beaux banish beaux, and coaches coaches drive.
(I 99–102)

Yet the myth of the sylphs is no mere decoration to this essentially cynical generalization. The sylphs do represent the supernatural, though the supernatural reduced, of course, to its flimsiest proportions. The poet has been very careful here. Even Belinda is not made to take their existence too seriously. As for the poet, he very modestly excuses himself from rendering any judgement at all by ranging himself on the side of 'learned pride':

Some secret truths from learned pride concealed
To maids alone and children are revealed;
What though no credit doubting wits may give?
The fair and innocent shall still believe.

In the old wives' tale or the child's fairy story may lurk an item of truth, after all. Consider the passage (I 27 ff.) carefully.

'Fair' and 'innocent' balance 'maids' and 'children'. Yet they act further to colour the whole passage. Is 'fair' used merely as a synonym for 'maids' – e.g., as in 'the fair'? Or is it that beauty is easily flattered? The doctrine which Ariel urges Belinda to accept is certainly flattering:

Hear and believe! thy own importance know
. . . unnumbered spirits round thee fly.

Is 'innocent' to be taken to mean 'guiltless', or does it mean 'naïve', perhaps even 'credulous'? And how do 'fair' and 'innocent' influence each other? Do the fair believe in the sylphs because they are still children? (Ariel, one remembers, begins by saying: 'If e'er one vision touched thy *infant* thought . . .'.) Pope is here exploiting that whole complex of associations which surrounded 'innocence' and connect it on the one hand with more than worldly wisdom and, on the other, with simple gullibility.

Pope, as we know, was clearly unjust in suggesting that Addison's advice against adding the machinery of the sylphs was prompted by any desire to prevent the improvement of the poem. Addison's caution was 'safe' and natural under the circumstances. But we can better understand how important the machinery was to become in the final version of the poem. For it is Pope's treatment of the sylphs which allows him to develop, with the most delicate modulation, his whole attitude toward Belinda and the special world which she graces. It is precisely the poet's handling of the supernatural – the level at which he is willing to entertain it – the amused qualifications which he demands of it – that makes it possible for him to state his attitude with full complexity.

The sylphs are, as Ariel himself suggests, 'honour', though honour rendered concrete and as it actually functions, not honour as a dry abstract. The sylphs' concern for good taste allows little range for critical perspective or a sense of proportion. To Ariel it will really be a dire disaster whether it is her honour or her new brocade that Belinda stains. To stain her honour will certainly constitute a breach of good taste – whatever else it may be – and that for Ariel is enough. Indeed, it is enough for the rather artificial world of manners with which Pope is concerned.

The myth of the sylphs is, thus, of the utmost utility to Pope: it allows him to show his awareness of the absurdities of a point of view which, nevertheless, is charming, delightful, and filled with a real poetry. Most important of all, the myth allows him to suggest that the charm, in part at least, springs from the very absurdity. The two elements can hardly be separated in Belinda; in her guardian, Ariel, they cannot be separated at all.

In this connection, it is well to raise specifically the question of Pope's attitude toward the 'rape' itself. We certainly underestimate the poem if we rest complacently in the view that Pope is merely laughing at a tempest in a teapot. There is such laughter, to be sure, and late in the poem Pope expresses his own judgement of the situation, employing Clarissa as his mouthpiece. But the tempest, ridiculous though it is when seen in perspective, is a real enough tempest and

related to very real issues. Indeed, Pope is able to reduce the incident
to its true importance precisely because he recognizes clearly its
hidden significance. And nowhere is Pope more careful to take into
account all the many sides of the situation than just here in the loss
of the lock itself.

For one thing, Pope is entirely too clear-sighted to allow that the
charming Belinda is merely the innocent victim of a rude assault.
Why has she cherished the lock at all? In part at least, 'to the
destruction of mankind', though mankind, of course, in keeping with
the convention, wishes so to be destroyed. Pope suggests that the
Baron may even be the victim rather than the aggressor – it is a moot
question whether he has seized the lock or been ensnared by it. Pope
does this very skilfully, but with great emphasis:

Love in these labyrinths his slaves detains,
And mighty hearts are held in slender chains.
With hairy springes we the birds betray,
Slight lines of hair surprise the finny prey;
Fair tresses man's imperial race ensnare,
And beauty draws us with a single hair.
(II 23–8)

Indeed, at the end of the poem, the poet addresses his heroine not as
victim but as a 'murderer';

For, after all the murders of your eye,
When, after millions slain, yourself shall die.

After all, does not Belinda want the Baron (and young men in
general) to covet the lock? She certainly does not want to retain
possession of the lock forever. The poet naturally sympathizes with
Belinda's pique at the way in which the Baron obtains the lock. He
must, in the war of the sexes, coax her into letting him have it. Force
is clearly unfair, though blandishment is fair. If she is an able warrior,
she will consent to the young man's taking the lock, though the lock
still attached to her head – and on the proper terms, honourable
marriage. If she is a weak opponent, she will yield the lock, and
herself, without any stipulation of terms, and will thus become a
ruined maid indeed. Pope has absolutely no illusions about what
the game is, and is certainly not to be shocked by any naturalistic

interpretation of the elaborate and courtly conventions under which Belinda fulfils her natural function of finding a mate.

On the other hand, this is not at all to say that Pope is anxious to do away with the courtly conventions as a pious fraud. He is not the romantic anarchist who would abolish all conventions because they are artificial The conventions not only have a regularizing function: they have their own charm. Like the rules of the card game in which Belinda triumphs, they may at points be arbitrary; but they make the game possible, and with it, the poetry and pageantry involved in it, in which Pope very clearly delights.

The card game itself, of course, is another symbol of the war of the sexes. Belinda must defeat the men; she must avoid that débâcle in which

The Knave of Diamonds tries his wily arts,
And wins (oh shameful chance!) the Queen of Hearts.

She must certainly avoid at every cost becoming a ruined maid. In the game as played, there is a moment in which she is 'Just in the jaws of ruin, and *Codille*', and gets a thrill of delicious excitement at being in so precarious a position.

If the reader objects that the last comment suggests a too obviously sexual interpretation of the card game, one must hasten to point out that a pervasive sexual symbolism informs, not only the description of the card game, but almost everything else in the poem, though here, again, our tradition of either-or may cause us to miss what Pope is doing. We are not forced to take the poem as either sly bawdy *or* as delightful fantasy. But if we are to see what Pope actually makes of his problem, we shall have to be alive to the sexual implications which are in the poem.

They are perfectly evident – even in the title itself; and the poem begins with an address to the Muse in which the sexual implications are underscored:

Say what strange motive, Goddess! could compel
A well-bred lord t'assault a gentle belle?
Oh say what stranger cause, yet unexplored,
Could make a gentle belle reject a lord?

True, we can take *assault* and *reject* in their more general meaning, not in their specific Latin senses, but the specific meanings are there just beneath the surface. Indeed, it is hard to believe, on the evidence of the poem as a whole that Pope would have been in the least surprised by Sir James Frazer's later commentaries on the ubiquity of hair as a fertility symbol. In the same way, one finds it hard to believe, after some of the material in the 'Cave of Spleen' section ('And maids turned bottles call aloud for corks'), that Pope would have been too much startled by the theories of Sigmund Freud.

The sexual implications become quite specific after the 'rape' has occurred. Thalestris, in inciting Belinda to take action against the Baron, cries:

Gods! shall the ravisher display your hair,
While the fops envy, and the ladies stare!

Even if we take *ravisher* in its most general sense, still the sexual symbolism lurks just behind Thalestris's words. Else why should honour be involved as it is? Why should the Baron desire the lock, and why should Belinda object so violently, not as to an act of simple rudeness, but to losing 'honour' and becoming a 'degraded toast'? The sexual element is involved at least to the extent that Belinda feels that she cannot afford to suffer the Baron, without protest, to take such a 'liberty'.

But a deeper sexual importance is symbolized by the whole incident. Belinda's anguished exclamation –

Oh hadst thou, cruel! been content to seize
Hairs less in sight, or any hairs but these!

carries on, unconsciously, the sexual suggestion. The lines indicate, primarily, of course, Belinda's exasperation at the ruining of her coiffure. The principal ironic effect, therefore, is one of bathos: her angry concern for the prominence of the lock deflates a little her protests about honour. (Something of the bathos carries over to the sexual parallel: it is hinted, perhaps, that the worst thing about a real rape for the belle would be that it could not be concealed.) But though Belinda's vehemence gives rise to these ironies, the exclamation itself is dramatically appropriate; and Belinda would doubtless have blushed to have her emphasis on 'any' interpreted literally and rudely. In her anger, she is obviously unconscious of the *faux pas*. But the fops whose admiring and envious comments on the exposed trophy Thalestris can predict –'Already hear the horrid things they say' – would be thoroughly alive to the unconscious *double entendre*. Pope's friend, Matthew Prior, wrote a naughty poem in which the same *double entendre* occurs. Pope himself, we may be sure, was perfectly aware of it.

In commenting on Pope's attitude toward the rape, we have suggested by implication his attitude toward chastity. Chastity is one of Belinda's most becoming garments. It gives her her retinue of airy guardians. As a proper maiden, she will keep from staining it just as she will keep from staining her new brocade. Its very fragility is part of its charm, and Pope becomes something of a symbolist poet in suggesting this. Three times in the poem he refers to the breaking of a frail china jar, once in connection with the loss of chastity, twice in connection with the loss of 'honour' suffered by Belinda in the 'rape' of the lock:

Whether the nymph shall break Diana's law,
Or some frail china jar receive a flaw. . . .
(II 105–6)

Or when rich china vessels, fall'n from high,
In glittering dust and painted fragments lie!
(III 159–60)

Thrice from my trembling hand the patch-box fell;
The tottering china shook without a wind. . . .
(IV 62–3)

Pope does not say, but he suggests, that chastity is, like the fine porcelain, something brittle, precious, useless, and easily broken. In the same way, he has hinted that honour (for which the sylphs, in part, stand) is something pretty, airy, fluid, and not really believed in. The devoted sylph who interposes his 'body' between the lock and the closing shears is clipped in two, but honour suffers little damage:

Fate urged the shears, and cut the sylph in twain
(But airy substance soon unites again).
(III 150–51)

It would be easy here to turn Pope into a cynic; but to try to do this is to miss the point. Pope does not hold chastity to be of no account. He definitely expects Belinda to be chaste; but, as a good humanist, he evidently regards virginity as essentially a negative virtue, and its possession a temporary state. He is very far from associating it with any magic virtue as Milton does in his *Comus*. The only magic which he will allow it is a kind of charm – a *je-ne-sais-quoi* such as the sylphs possess.

Actually, we probably distort Pope's view by putting the question in terms which require an explicit judgement at all. Pope accepts in the poem the necessity for the belle to be chaste just as he accepts the necessity for her to be gracious and attractive. But in accepting this, he is thoroughly alive to the cant frequently talked about woman's honour, and most of all, he is ironically, though quietly, resolute in putting first things first. This, I take it, is the whole point of Clarissa's speech. When Clarissa says:

Since painted, or not painted, all shall fade,
And she who scorns a man must die a maid,

we need not assume with Leslie Stephen that Pope is expressing a smug masculine superiority, with the implication that, for a woman, spinsterhood is the worst of all possible ills. (There is actually no reason for supposing that Pope thought it so.) The real point is that, for Belinda, perpetual spinsterhood *is* the worst of all possible ills. In her own terms, it would be a disaster to retain her locks for ever – locks turned to grey, though still curled with a pathetic hopefulness, unclaimed and unpossessed by any man. Belinda does not want *that*; and it is thus a violation of good sense to lose sight of the fact that the cherished lock is finally only a means to an end – one weapon to be used by the warrior in the battle, and not the strongest at that.

Clarissa is, of course, promptly called a prude, and the battle begins at once in perfect disregard of the 'good sense' that she has spoken. Pope is too fine an artist to have it happen otherwise. Belinda *has* been sorely vexed – and she, moreover, remains charming, even as an Amazon. After all, what the poet has said earlier is sincerely meant:

If to her share some female errors fall,
Look on her face, and you'll forget 'em all.

(II 17–18)

Though Pope obviously agrees with Clarissa, he is neither surprised nor particularly displeased with his heroine for flying in the face of Clarissa's advice.

The battle of the sexes which ensues parodies at some points the combat in the great epic which Milton fashioned on the rape of the apple. But the absurdity of a battle in which the contestants cannot be killed is a flaw in Milton's great poem, whereas Pope turns it to beautiful account in his. In *Paradise Lost*, the great archangels single each other out for combat in the best Homeric style. But when Michael's sword cleaves the side of Lucifer, the most that Milton can do with the incident is to observe that Lucifer feels pain, for his premises force him to hurry on to admit that

> . . . th'ethereal substance closed
> Not long divisible.

Lucifer is soon back in the fight, completely hale and formidable as ever. We have already seen how delightfully Pope converts this cabbage into a rose in the incident in which the sylph, in a desperate defence of the lock, is clipped in two by the shears.

The absurdity of a war fought by invulnerable opponents gives an air of unreality to the whole of Milton's episode. There is a bickering over rules. Satan and his followers cheat by inventing gunpowder. The hosts under Michael retort by throwing the celestial hills at the enemy; and the Almighty, to put a stop to the shameful rumpus, has the Son throw the troublemakers out. But if the fight were really serious, a fight to the death, why does the heavenly host not throw the hills in the first place? Or why does not the Almighty cast out the rebels without waiting for the three days of inconclusive fighting to elapse? The prevailing atmosphere of a game – a game played by good little boys and by unmannerly little ruffians, a game presided over by the stern schoolmaster – haunts the whole episode. The advantage is wholly with Pope here. By frankly recognizing that the contest between his beaux and belles is a game, he makes for his basic intention.

The suspicion that Pope in this episode is glancing at Milton is corroborated somewhat by Pope's general use of his celestial machinery. The supernatural guardians in *The Rape of the Lock* are made much of, but their effectiveness is hardly commensurate with their zeal. The affinities of the poem on this point are again with *Paradise Lost*, not with the *Iliad*. In Milton's poem, the angels are carefully stationed to guard Adam and Eve in their earthly home, but their protection proves, in the event, to be singularly ineffectual. They cannot prevent Satan from finding his way to the earth; and though they soar over the Garden, their 'radiant files, |Dazzling the moon', they never strike a blow. Even when they discover Satan, and prepare to engage him in combat, God, at the last moment, prevents the fight. Indeed, for all their numbers and for all their dazzling splendour, they succeed in determining events not at all. They can merely, in the case of Raphael, give the human pair advice and warning. Milton, though he loved to call their resonant names, and evidently tried to provide them with a realistic function, was apparently so fearful lest he divert attention from Adam's own freely made decision that he succeeds in giving them nothing to do.

If this limitation constitutes another ironical defect, perhaps, in Milton's great epic, it fits Pope's purposes beautifully. For, as we have seen, Pope's supernatural machinery is as airy as gossamer, and the fact that Ariel can do no more than Raphael, advise and warn – for all his display of zeal – makes again for Pope's basic intention. The issues in Pope's poem are matters of taste, matters of 'good sense', and the sylphs do not violate the human limitations of this world which Pope has elected to describe and in terms of which judgements are to be made. Matters of morality – still less, the ultimate sanctions of morality – are never raised.

One more of the numerous parallels between *The Rape of the Lock* and *Paradise Lost* ought to be mentioned here, even though it may well be one of which Pope was unconscious. After the Fall has taken place, Michael is sent to prepare Adam for his expulsion from the happy garden. The damage has been done, the apple has been plucked and eaten, the human pair must prepare to go out into the 'real' world, the 'fallen' world of our ordinary human experience. Yet, Michael promises that Adam can create within his own breast 'A Paradise ... happier far'. Clarissa's advice to Belinda makes the same point. For better or worse, the lock has been lost. That fact must be accepted. In suggesting Belinda's best course under the circumstances, Clarissa raises [v 9 *et seq.*] quite explicitly Belinda's status as a divinity:

Say, why are beauties praised and honoured most . . .
Why angels called, and angel-like adored?

The divine element cannot reside in mere beauty alone, painted
cheeks, bright eyes, curled locks. All human beauty is tainted with
mortality: true 'angelhood' resides in a quality of mind, and therefore can survive the loss of mere mortal beauty – can survive the loss
of the lock, even the destruction of its beauty by the shears of time.
The general parallel between the two speeches is almost complete.
Belinda's true divinity, like Adam's happier paradise, is to be found
within her. Pope, like Milton, can thus rationalize the matter in terms
which allow him to dismiss the supernatural machinery and yet
maintain the presence of a qualified supernatural in the midst of a
stern and rational world in which no longer one may expect 'God or
angel guest| With man, as with his friend, familiar used| To sit
indulgent' – an altered world in which Belinda will expect no more
intimate communications from Ariel, and where she, like Adam and
Eve, must rely on an inner virtue for advice and protection.

Indeed, one is tempted to complete the parallel by suggesting that
Belinda is, at this point, like Adam, being prepared to leave her happy
garden world of innocence and maidenly delight for a harsher world,
the world of human society as it is and with the poetic illusions
removed.

To return to the battle between the beaux and belles: here Pope
beautifully unifies the various motifs of the poem. The real nature of
the conventions of polite society, the heroic pretensions of that
society as mirrored in the epic, the flattering clichés which society
conventionally employs – all come in for a genial ragging. Indeed,
the clichés of the ardent lover become the focal point of concentration. For the clichés, if they make the contention absurd and pompous,
do indicate, by coming alive on another level, the true, if unconscious,
nature of the struggle.

No common weapons in their hands are found,
Like gods they fight, nor dread a mortal wound.
(v 43–4)

'Like gods they fight' should mean, in the epic framework, 'with
superhuman energy and valour'. And 'nor dread a mortal wound'

logically completes 'Like gods they fight' – until a yet sterner logic asserts itself and deflates the epic pomp. A fight in which the opponents cannot be killed is only a sham fight. Yet, this second meaning is very rich after all, and draws 'Like gods they fight' into its own orbit of meanings: there may be an extra zest in the fighting because it *is* an elaborate game. One can make godlike gestures because one has the invulnerability of a god. The contest is godlike, after all, because it is raised above the dust and turmoil of real issues. Like an elaborate dance, it symbolizes real issues but can find room for a grace and poetry which in a more earnest struggle are lost.

I have said earlier that Pope, by recognizing the real issues involved, is able to render his mock-epic battle meaningful. For the beaux of Hampton Court, though in truth they do not need to dread a mortal wound, can, and are prepared to, die. We must remember that 'to die' had at this period, as one of its submeanings, to experience the consummation of the sexual act. Pope's invulnerable beaux rush bravely forward to achieve such a death; for the war of the sexes, when fought seriously and to the death, ends in such an act.

The elegant battleground resounds with the cries of those who die 'in metaphor, and ... in song'. In some cases, little more is implied than a teasing of the popular clichés about bearing a 'living death', or being burnt alive in Cupid's flames. But few will question the sexual implications of 'die' in the passage in which Belinda overcomes the Baron:

Nor feared the chief th' unequal fight to try,
Who sought no more than on his foe to die. ....
'Boast not my fall,' he cried, 'insulting foe!
Thou by some other shall be laid as low. ....'
(v 77 *et seq.*)

The point is not that Pope is here leering at bawdy meanings. In the full context of the poem, they are not bawdy at all – or, perhaps we put the matter more accurately if we say that Pope's *total* attitude, as reflected in the poem, is able to absorb and digest into itself the incidental bawdy of which Pope's friends, and obviously Pope himself, were conscious. The crucial point is that Pope's interpretation of Belinda's divinity does not need to flinch from bawdy interpretations. The further meanings suggested by the naughty *double entendres* are not merely snickering jibes which contradict the surface meaning; rather, those further meanings constitute the qualifying background against which Belinda's divinity is asserted. Pope's testimony to Belinda's charm is not glib; it is not thin and one-sided. It is qualified by, though not destroyed by, a recognition of all the factors involved – even of those factors which seem superficially to negate it. The touch is light, to be sure; but the poem is not flimsy, not mere froth. The tone is ironical, but the irony is not that of a narrow and acerb satire; rather it is an irony which accords with a wise recognition of the total situation. The 'form' of the poem is, therefore, much more than the precise regard for a set of rules and conventions mechanically apprehended. It is, finally, the delicate balance and reconciliation of a host of partial interpretations and attitudes.

It was observed earlier that Pope is able to reduce the 'rape' to its true insignificance because he recognizes, as his characters do not, its real significance. Pope knows that the rape has in it more of compliment than of insult, though he naturally hardly expects Belinda to interpret it thus. He does not question her indignation, but he does suggest that it is, perhaps, a more complex response than Belinda realizes. Pope knows too how artificial the social conventions really are and he is thoroughly cognizant of the economic and biological necessities which underlie them – which the conventions sometimes seem to mask and sometimes to adorn. He is therefore not forced to choose between regarding them as either a hypocritical disguise or a poetic and graceful adornment. Knowing their true nature, he can view this outrage of the conventions with a wise and amused toler-ance – and can set it in its proper perspective.

Here the functional aspect of Pope's choice of the epic framework becomes plain. The detachment, the amused patronage, the note of aloof and impartial judgement – all demand that the incident be viewed with a large measure of aesthetic distance. Whatever incidental fun Pope may have had with the epic conventions, his choice of the mock-epic fits beautifully his general problem of scaling down the rape to its proper insignificance. The scene is reduced and the characters become small and manageable figures whose actions can always be plotted against a larger background.

How large that background is has not always been noticed.

Belinda's world is plainly a charming, artificial world; but Pope is not afraid to let in a glimpse of the real world which lies all about it:

Meanwhile declining from the noon of day,
The sun obliquely shoots his burning ray;
The hungry judges soon the sentence sign,
And wretches hang that jurymen may dine;
The merchant from th'exchange returns in peace,
And the long labours of the toilette cease –
Belinda now. . . .

(III 19–25)

It is a world in which business goes on and criminals are hanged for all that Belinda is preparing to sit down to ombre. This momentary glimpse of the world of serious affairs, of the world of business and law, of the world of casualness and cruelty, is not introduced merely to shrivel the high concerns of polite society into ironical insignificance, though its effect, of course, is to mock at the seriousness with which the world of fashion takes its affairs. Nor is the ironical clash which is introduced by the passage uncalculated and unintentional: it is not that Pope himself is unconsciously callous – without sympathy for the 'wretches'. The truth is that Pope's own perspective is so scaled, his totality of view so honest, that he can afford to embellish his little drama as lovingly as he likes without for a moment losing sight of its final triviality. A lesser poet would either have feared to introduce an echo of the 'real' world lest the effect prove to be too discordant, or would have insisted on the discord and moralized, too heavily and bitterly, the contrast between the gay and the serious. Pope's tact is perfect. The passage is an instance of the complexity of tone which the poem possesses.

W. K. Wimsatt

'Rhetoric and Poems: Alexander Pope', *English Institute Essays* 1948 (reprinted in *The Verbal Icon*, 1954)

When we seek to conrfont two such elusive entities as a theory of poems and poems themselves and to determine relations between these two, I think there is much to be said for placing them first, tentatively, in their most generic and non-committal relation. There is much to be said for the conjunctional form of title commonly given to the academic paper: X *and* Y, Shakespeare *and* Hall's Chronicle, Theory *and* Poems. I for one find it convenient to distinguish five main types of relation between theory and poems, all five of which are frequently to be observed in critical and historical studies, though often more or less confused.

1. There is for one thing the kind of relation between theory and poems with which we are concerned when our interest is chiefly in the theory itself, that is, when we try to describe and assess a given theory as objectively as we can with reference to whatever general norms for poems and hence for theory we possess. Is the classical theory of imitation in any sense a good or fruitful theory of poems? Or the classical theory of ornament and system of rhetoric? Or do these deserve to be completely demolished, as in the Crocean history of Aesthetic? Is Matthew Arnold's view of the high serious-ness and critical function of poems the right view? Or, does it, as Tate and others have argued, deliver poems into the hands of science and morals? My purpose at the moment is not to main-tain the importance of such questions, but merely to note their occurrence.

2. It may at times be difficult to distinguish between such a general evaluative interest in theory and what I consider a second kind of interest, that with which we approach a theorist, especially a tech-nical or rhetorical theorist and his cousins of the trivium, the gram-marian and logician, for the purpose of borrowing tools which we shall put to the partly unpredictable uses of our own analysis: *fable*, or *character*, or *metaphor* from Aristotle, *antithesis* or *parallel* from the rhetoricians, *sentences*, for that matter, and *nouns* and *verbs* from the grammarians. To do this may imply that we think a theorist a good theorist of poems, and yet I believe it may come short of that, in so far as concepts themselves may come short of integrated or achieved theory, and also in so far as this borrowing extends readily, and perhaps most profitably, to the less literary philosophers, the gram-marian and logician.

To look in the historical direction, I should say that when we take up the more generic concepts of rhetoric, grammar, and logic,

we ought to be on our guard against imputing to them special connections with the poems of any specific period – as would happen if
one were to note the Aristotelian 'categories' in Renaissance logic and
read in them an influence on the imagery of Drayton or Donne.
Richards in his *Philosophy of Rhetoric* has found the concept of the
morpheme as defined by Bloomfield a useful one for explaining
certain powers of words. But it would be somewhat wide of the
mark to learn that Auden had read either Richards or Bloomfield and
from that go on to discover such elements as morphemes in Auden's
poems. The idea of the circulation of the blood was expounded by
Harvey in 1616, but we do not conceive that it was about that time
that blood began to circulate in the human body.

3. A third relation between theory and poems is that which obtains
when a given theory does have a specific, historical relation to a poem,
but has this in virtue of the special fact that it appears in the poem as
part of the poem's meaning or content. One will recall numerous
instances in the history of English poetry; Chaucer's burlesque of
Geoffrey of Vinsauf in the mock-heroic of the cock and the fox,
Stephen Hawes's celebration of 'golden' words in his *Pastime of Pleasure*,
the Horatian arts of poetry (especially that of Pope), Mark Akenside's
Pleasures of the Imagination, Wordsworth's *Prelude*, and Shelley's *Ode
to the West Wind* (where the sparks from the unextinguished priestly
hearth mingle with the sparks of 'inextinguishable thought' which
appear twice in his prose *Defence of Poetry*). This relation between
theory and poems is that which for the most part obtains in historical
studies of the neutrally observational type – but often with some
implication that the relation established is of a more formal, or
actually theoretical, sort.

4. A fourth relation between theory and poems which I believe
it worth while to distinguish is again a specific historical relation, that
which obtains when in a given era a theory helps to determine poems
not as subject-matter but as an influence or cause why they are written
in a certain way. Perhaps the most important thing to note about this
relation is that (like number 3) it does not require that the theory as
theory be an adequate account of the poems. The classic theory concerning imitation of models, for instance, had a close bearing on the
Augustan vogue of translations, paraphrases, and 'imitations'. Yet
a theory of models is never really a literary theory, only a practical

rule of inspiration. And the classic theory in particular seemed almost unconscious of the paramount factor of parody, or allusiveness, which worked in the most lively Augustan instances. Again, the massive theory of epic which prevailed in that day might be taken as a partial cause of Blackmore's *Prince Arthur* or, in jocular reversal, *The Rape of the Lock*, or *The Dunciad*. But there are no successfully serious epics with which the theory can be compared. During the same period, the doctrine *Ut pictura poesis* may have joined with empirical views of imagination to determine the subject-matter of some poems; it may have been responsible for certain instances of the pictorial fallacy or opaqueness in word painting; but, as Lessing was partly to show, the analogy between words and marble or paint is of limited service for analysing the positive qualities of verbal art.

5. A fifth relation between theory and poems, that which will be the final of our argument, is that which obtains when in any historical era we can discern a specific affinity between theory as such and poems; that is, when what the theory says seems to be a specially appropriate description of what the poems are. Such a relation may of course coincide with the causal relation which we have just considered. There may be instances of a close causal connection between theory and poems and at the same time a high degree of validity for the theory as theory. A successful poet may be shown to have read a certain theory with profit, or he may even, though this I believe is rare, succeed in uttering a theory which explains his own poems. But these are matters for another sort of inquiry. It is only by keeping clear of such intentionalistic complications that we can focus upon the literary and critical issue: that is, the degree of resemblance between the theory and the poems or the adequacy of the theory to describe the poems.

To show a real correspondence between the theory of an era and the poems of the era would be, I take it, one of the most proper concerns of the student of criticism in its historical aspect, and to show that the theory gave an adequate account of the poems would be his masterpiece. Such an achievement, we ought at the same time to note, would be a special challenge to the student of either theory or poems who was interested in universal definitions or norms. Poems in different eras, it is assumed, will be to some extent different. But theory deals with universals. It is more disconcerting to find the theory of successive ages different than to find the poems different. No matter how well we, with our historical desires, succeed in localizing the theory or assimilating it to the poems of its own age, we can still see that the theory itself aims at the universal. If the poems and the theory vary in step with each other, then I suppose a great appearance of support is offered to historical relativism – unless indeed one's dialectic rises to reconciling certain valid special theories of poetry, say the Metaphysical theory of wit and the Romantic theory of imagination, in a more inclusive harmony. Or unless one is brave enough to decide in a given case that both poems and theory are bad – as Yvor Winters has not scrupled to say the poems of Poe are bad because they perfectly illustrate Poe's theory, a deliquescent version of Romantic imagination.

Not every theory found in a given age is equally relevant to describing the poems of that age. There are not only bad theories which have no special bearing on any kind of poems, but another and more important kind, those of such general significance (if not complete truth) that they transcend a special application to the poems of their age. Such, for example, I should call the neo-classic doctrine that poetry reveals the generic or universal. Despite the game of ombre and the all too specific and solid Dunces, the doctrine of the universal is if correctly interpreted a valid doctrine, and furthermore it is itself universal, that is, neither more nor less true of good neo-classic poems than of good poems in any other mode. Or the related doctrine that 'Style is the dress of thought' – true poetry is 'nature to advantage dressed'. This would appear to be the Augustan version of a paradox which literary criticism has so far by no means solved. Today we speak of art signs as iconic or as calling attention to their own excellence, or we speak of poetry as intensely realized meaning, or as dramatized meaning, or perhaps as structure of meaning. Poetic meaning still seems to contain other meanings and to make use of them, but seems to be tested in the end by the same norms. The doctrine that style is the dress of thought is as much our concern as it was Pope's, and, whatever its degree of truth, it applies no more specially to Augustan poems than to any other kind.

In somewhat the same way I believe we should have to discuss the whole classical theory of imitation and the antitheses deriving from the theory and flourishing in Pope's time between art and nature,

between invention and imitation of models, between wit and judgement, between genius and the rules. Or perhaps some of these
theoretical formulas do show a special relation to the poems of the
age, though one which will make acceptable sense to us only after a
certain adjustment. One such example seems to me of importance
here as a partial frame of reference for the more specific rhetorical
ideas which I wish to discuss. I have in mind the Augustan concept
of 'correctness', which, distinguished from greatness or 'genius',
sometimes took the form of an ideal, as in the well-known advice
of Walsh to Pope: that there had been *great* English poets, but no
great poet who was *correct*; but sometimes also was conceived as a fault
or limitation, as in Addison's *Spectators* nos. 160 and 291, where the
untrammelled productions of ancient Genius are preferred to the
scrupulous nicety or correctness of the moderns. As Sir Joshua
Reynolds was later to phrase it: 'So far, indeed, is the presence of
genius from implying an absence of faults, that they are considered
by many as its inseparable companions.' The paradox was still vital
in the next century, when Ruskin preferred the *imperfections*, that is,
the irregularities, of Gothic architecture to the *perfection*, that is the
regularity, of geometric ornaments in Greek architecture. This bizarre
critical tradition seems to arise from the capacity of the term *correctness*
to be taken not only (1) as a general term of value (certainly what is
'correct' is right and good), but (2) as a more specially descriptive
term, meaning something like symmetry and something like restraint
and precision. It is in the latter sense of course that we shall have to
take it if we apply it to Augustan poems – if we wish to say that Pope
followed the advice of Walsh and became a *correct* poet. The other
sense will hardly go with the liberal and usually accepted view that
Shakespeare's verse and rhetoric fit what Shakespeare is saying, just as
Pope's fit what Pope is saying. In the final sense of poetic value, each
kind of good poetry is correct.

It is under the head of correctness in its limited sense that the most
precise resemblances between neo-classic theory and neo-classic poems
seem to be available – I mean in the rhetoric of the closed couplet.
Perhaps it is not too much to say that the resemblance between theory
and poems which obtains here is one of the most precise in this history
of literature and criticism – that the hexameter couplets of Boileau

and Racine and the pentameters of Dryden and Pope represent the maximum fulfilment of a classic technical theory. Yet the relation between theory and poems which obtains even here is not, as we shall see, strictly a synchronous one.

The year 1935 gave us two highly competent studies, one by Professor Williamson, concerning the history of English couplet theory from Puttenham in 1589 to Edward Bysshe in 1702; and one by Miss Wallerstein, concerning the practice of English couplet writers, from the poems of Grimald in Tottel's *Miscellany* to Denham's lines on the Thames in 1655. Professors Williamson and Wallerstein, writing from these different directions, theory and poems, produced notably harmonious accounts of couplet rhetoric: the sententious closure, the balanced lines and half-lines, the antithesis and inversion, the strict metric and accordingly slight but telling variations, the constantly close and tensile union of what are called musical with logical and rhetorical effects. The dates embraced in the works of these two writers may, however, invite the reflection that so far as the couplets of Alexander Pope (at the English neo-classic zenith) conform to a theory of rhetoric, it is to a theory which had reached its full development a generation or two earlier. For a good account in English of the figures of speech and thought to be found in Pope's verse one will perhaps go even as far back as Puttenham's *Art of English Poesy*. In Puttenham one will find too the main metrical rules and even the important emphasis on the caesura. Edward Bysshe's *Art of English Poetry*, which may plausibly be taken as representative of what had happened to English poetics by the time Pope was a youth, says nothing at all of the figures, though it carries the metrics to a far greater degree of rigidity than Puttenham and includes the now famous dictionary of rhymes. The classical figures of speech and thought, joined with poetics during the Middle Ages, had by Bysshe's time been reseparated from poetics and confined again in the treatises on prose rhetoric – such as that of Thomas Blount, *The Academy of Eloquence* (1654), or that of John Smith, *The Mystery of Rhetoric Unveiled* (1657). Puttenham's *Art* of 1589, though it is only one of many English accounts of rhetorical figures up to Pope's day, remains the most lively and informative and the most precisely focused upon poems.

Pope himself in chapters 10 and 11 of *Peri Bathous* wrote a comic treatment of 'Tropes and Figures' (including 'The Antithesis, or See-Saw'), and he once observed to Spence that the 'stiffness of style' in Wycherley's plays was 'occasioned by his always studying for antithesis'. But neither in his *Essay on Criticism*, nor in his remarks to Spence, nor in his letters, even the elaborate letter on versification to Walsh, has Pope anything substantial to say about the system of artful figures which later critics have considered characteristic of his couplets. Pope talks of the metrical 'niceties', of suiting the sound to the sense, of caesura, of expletives, and of hiatus, or of avoiding extravagance in diction. The rhetorical sinews of the kind of verse in which he was the champion – the essential patterns where Waller's strength and Denham's sweetness joined, where Dryden had achieved the long resounding march and energy divine – these perhaps had been learned so well by Pope as a boy that he could forget them. 'It was our family priest,' he told Spence, 'who taught me the figures, accidence, and first part of grammar.' In later life perhaps the figures were assumed by Pope under the general head of 'correctness'. At any rate he seems to have been able to take them for granted.

Among the hundred odd figures, 'auricular', 'sensible', and 'sententious', presented by Puttenham, there are certain ones, a rather large number if all subdivisions of the main types are counted, which would seem to be fundamental to the logic of the formally ordered verbal style. Thus, '*Parison*, or the figure of even (clauses)', '*Omoioteleton*, or the figure of like-loose (like endings)', and '*Anaphora*, or the figure of report' (that is, repetition of a word at the beginning of successive clauses) are the figures in Puttenham which refer to formal parallels and which under one set of terms or another are a constant part of the rhetorical tradition from Puttenham back to Aristotle. Contrast or antithesis is the natural accompaniment of parallel. This appears in Puttenham as '*Antitheton*, or the quarreller, otherwise called the overthwart or recounter'. Wherever there is a parallel there is a distinction, and wherever a distinction, the possibility of a paradox, an antithesis, or at least a modulation. Thus, to illustrate now from the verse of Pope:

Who sees with equal eye, as God of all,
A hero perish, or a sparrow fall.
(*Essay on Man*, I 87–8)

Favours to none, to all she smiles extends;
Oft she rejects but never once offends.
(*The Rape of the Lock*, II 11–12)

Survey the whole, nor seek slight faults to find
Where nature moves, and rapture warms the mind.
(*Essay on Criticism*, 235–6)

This brings us, still quite naturally, to a third group of figures, those distinguished by Puttenham as '*Zeugma*, or the single supply' and '*Sillepsis*, or the double supply'. Zeugma is further distinguished by Puttenham into *Prozeugma* (or the Ringleader), *Mezozeugma* (or the Middlemarcher), and *Hypozeugma* (or the Rerewarder), accordingly as the zeugma, or yoking word, occurs at the beginning, the middle, or the end of a total construction. He treats zeugma among the figures 'merely *auricular* in that they reach no further than the ear', and among figures 'that work by defect', that, is, by the absence of 'some little portion of speech'. He does not say anything about the relation of zeugma to parallel. But we might observe that zeugma or ellipsis is almost the inevitable effect of a tightened and precise economy of parallel. If A, B, C and X, B, Z are presented, then A, B, C and X, Z is an easy result; or if A, B and X, B, then A, B and X – in the more usual case, the parallel of two elements. Thus, in Pope's verse:

Who could not win the mistress wooed the maid. (Prozeugma)
(*Essay on Criticism*, 105)

And now a bubble *burst*, and now a world. (Mezozeugma)
(*Essay on Man*, I 90)

Where nature moves, and rapture warms the *mind*. (Hypozeugma)
(*Essay on Criticism*, 236).

And, to note a special and significant kind of zeugma that occurs in Pope's verse, such examples as these:

Or lose her heart or necklace at a ball.
(*The Rape of the Lock*, II, 109)

Or stain her honour, or her new brocade.
(II, 107)

This is metaphor. I mention it here not simply to list the figure of metaphor among Pope's accomplishments. Puttenham also duly lists '*Metaphora*, or the figure of transport'. But here it seems to me curious, and worth noting, though it is not noted by Puttenham, that a series of several logical steps, distinction, parallel, then simplification or cancelling a common element, has led us to metaphor, something that has often, and notably by some in Pope's day, been considered the very essence of the irrational or merely imaginative in poetry. Let us carry our series to its conclusion, returning to Puttenham for help. Consider the figure of '*Sillepsis*, or the double supply', which occurs according to Puttenham when a verb is used either with a double grammatical congruity, or in a double sense. The latter may be thus illustrated from Pope's verse.

Here thou, great Anna! whom three realms obey,
Dost sometimes counsel take, and sometimes tea.
(III 7–8)

With earnest eyes, and round unthinking face,
He first the snuff-box opened, then the case.
(IV 125–6)

Worse and worse. We have now descended from logical parallel and ellipsis, through metaphor, into pun. In short, by starting with what might have been thought the most logical and prosaic aspects of Pope's verse (both *Antitheton* and *Parison* were mentioned by Puttenham as figures specially related to prose), and by moving through a few shades of meaning we have arrived at the very things which the modern critic Empson noticed first in looking for the shiftiness or ambiguity of this kind of verse. We may note too, as we pass, that the distinction between the two figures last described, the metaphoric zeugma and the punning syllepsis, is not always easy. Take the couplet preceding that about counsel and tea:

Here Britain's statesmen oft the fall foredoom
Of foreign tyrants and of nymphs at home.

It depends on how technically and specifically we are accustomed to think of a 'fall' from virtue, whether we take 'the fall of tyrants and of nymphs' as metaphor or pun.

But now I should like to backtrack into an area of rhetoric different from antitheses and parallels, though joining them or branching off from them, in Puttenham's *Art*, under the figure *Anaphora*, the word or phrase repeated at the beginning of successive clauses. Puttenham supplies a large battery of figures in this area: 'counterturns', 're-doubles', 'echo sounds', 'swift repeats', 'rebounds', and 'counter-changes', among which the pick is '*Traductio*, or the tranlacer'. This, says Puttenham, 'is when ye turn and tranlace a word into many sundry shapes as the tailor doth his garment, and after that sort do play with him in your ditty.' The principle of these figures is that a word or root is repeated in various syntactic positions, and sometimes in various forms, with a consequent shifting, version, turning, or translacing of the sense. These are the figures which Dryden in 1693 calls 'turns, both on the words and on the thought', and which, despite a report by Dryden to the contrary, are nowhere better illustrated than in Milton's *Paradise Lost*. The turn is one of the main sinews of the sense variously drawn out from line to line. 'So Man ... Shall ... die, And dying rise, and rising with him raise His Brethern, ransomed with his own dear life.' Toward the end of the seventeenth century this kind of wordplay had fallen into comparative disfavor. We need not be surprised that in Pope's verse it is less heavily underscored.

Yet graceful ease and sweetness void of pride
Might hide her faults, if belles had faults to hide.
(II 15–16)

Jilts ruled the state, and statesmen farces writ;
Nay wits had pensions, and young lords had wit.
(*Essay on Criticism*, 538–9)

These are lighter turns than Milton's – and at the same time wittier turns. By a different route we have arrived at somewhat the same terminus as when we pursued the forms of logical parallel, that is, at something like illogical pun – a difference being that whereas before we found the single word of two meanings, we find now two or more words of similar sound and one or another kind of play between their meanings.

In the couplet rhetoric which we have been examining, the abstract logic of parallel and antithesis is complicated and offset, then, by the turn and by the metaphoric zeugma and the punning syllepsis. It is complicated also by one other element of alogical counterpattern – the most important by far and, I believe, the apex of all the rhetorical phenomena which we have been considering – that is, rhyme. 'Symphony' or 'cadence', says Puttenham, meaning rhyme, is 'all the sweetness and cunning in our vulgar poesy'. And here we have too, as it happens, a theoretical statement by the master of practice. Pope told Spence:

I have nothing to say for rhyme but that I doubt whether a
poem can support itself without it in our language, unless it
be stiffened with such strange words as are likely to destroy
our language itself. The high style that is affected so much
in blank verse would not have been borne even in Milton
had not his subject turned so much on such strange,
out-of-the-world things as it does.

Rhyme, in this offhand statement, seems to be something like a stiffening or support of verse, rather than the commonly conceived music. Puttenham remarks that the Greeks and Latins 'used a manner of speech, by clauses of like termination, which they called *homoeoteleuton*', a thing somewhat like vernacular rhyme, yet different. The difference between *rhyme* and *homoeoteleuton* is, in fact, one of the most profound of rhetorical differences. For *homoeoteleuton*, the repetition of inflected endings (morphemes) to support logical parallels of statement, is that which added to parallel and antithesis makes the rhetoric of pointed prose. But rhyme, the use of alogical or accidental sound resemblances between different morphemes, is that which added to parallel and antithesis makes the rhetoric of the pointed couplet. As the turn was the characteristic stiffener of classical Latin verse and of its English counterpart the blank verse of Milton, so rhyme was the characteristic stiffener of vernacular verse and especially of the couplet.

Whatever nature has in worth denied
She gives in large recruits of needful pride.
(*Essay on Criticism*, 205-6)

The music of the rhyme is mental; it consists in an odd, almost magic, relation of phonetic likeness which encourages us to perceive and believe in a meaning otherwise asserted by the words of the couplet. The non-parallel or chiastic chime (worth[1]-denied,[2] gives[2']-Pride[1']) is the phonetic expression of the unhappy receptivity of the mental void. The principle is well illustrated in a few of Pope's proper-name rhymes, where we may note an affinity for a certain old-fashioned and childish form of riddle to be found in the pages of *The Farmer's Almanac.* Why is A like B? Because the name of A or of something connected with A means B or something connected with B. Why is a dog dressed warmer in summer than in winter? Because in winter he wears a fur coat, and in summer he wears a fur coat and pants. Why is a certain poet a dangerous influence upon married women? Because his name sounds like something.

Poor Cornus sees his frantic wife elope,
And curses wit, and poetry, and Pope.
(*Epistle to Dr Arbuthnot*, 24-5)

Why is a certain scholar a graceless figure? Because his name shows it.

Yet ne'er one sprig of laurel graced these ribalds,
From slashing Bentley down to pidling Tibbalds.
(163-4)

Here the words *sprig* and *pidling* play a part too in proving what it means to have a name like that. *Paronomasia,* '*Prosonomasia,* or the Nicknamer', is Puttenham's name for this figure. 'As *Tiberius* the Emperor, because he was a great drinker of wine, they called him by way of derision to his own name, *Caldius Biberius Nero,* instead of *Claudius Tiberius Nero.*' But Puttenham, I admit, does not connect this figure with the 'symphony' or 'tunable consent' called rhyme.

Poetry, it would appear, is not an affair of pure ideas – where X or Y could by agreement be substituted by any given word – nor strictly speaking is it an affair of sound as such or verbal music. Poetry is both sense and sound, and not by parallel or addition, but by a kind of union – which may be heard in onomatopoeia and expressive rhythm and in various modes of suggestion, extension, and secret verbal functioning. Of these the pun and its cousin the rhyme are but the most extravagant instances. Poetry exploits the *facts* of language, that words *do* mean so and so and acquire a kind of prerogative to do this.

English critics of the Renaissance, among them Milton and latterly even Dryden, were inclined to be hard on rhyme, calling it a jingling bondage, rude, beggarly, and Gothic. (Even Puttenham remarks that rhyme was brought into Greek and Latin by 'barbarous soldiers out of the camp'.) The Earl of Roscommon in polished couplets recited the bardic and monkish history of rhyme and hailed the glorious day when the British Muse should put on the rhymeless majesty of Rome and Athens. Critics of Pope's day – Dennis, Felton, and Gildon – took the same cue and called rhyme 'soft', 'effeminate', 'emasculating'. At the same time, as we have seen, the basic figures of parallel and antithesis originated as prose figures and by their nature tended to abstraction, order, and regular lines. Other factors too in the latter half of the seventeenth century – the scientific mistrust of inventive imagination, the plain style of scientists and pulpit orators, a refined and moderate way of talking adopted by society – are sometimes supposed to have helped in making the Augustan couplet poems the nearest things to prose poems in our language. Dryden and Pope, we remember Arnold said, are 'classics of our prose'. This of course we do not fully believe any more. Yet I suggest that we are confronted by an extremely curious and challenging situation in the heroic couplet of Pope: where a verse basically ordered by the rational rules of parallel and antithesis and showing at least a certain characteristic restraint of imagination, as contrasted say with metaphysical verse, at the same time is found to rely so heavily for 'support' or 'stiffening' – to use again the terms of Pope – on so barbarous and Gothic a device as rhyme.

In tracing the parallel between Puttenham and Pope we have observed perhaps the maximum degree of resemblance that obtains between the poems of Pope and any contemporary or nearly contemporary set of poetic rules. At the same time we have scarcely been able to refrain at each step from noting the incompleteness of Puttenham when compared to the fullness of the poetic actuality, even at the level specifically cited from Puttenham, the rhetorical. How far, we may now return and ask, does Puttenham or does any other rhetorician take us either in stating the main principles of couplet rhetoric or in exploring them? The answer, I believe, is: Not far.

Puttenham can list and to some extent describe our figures of speech for us. He does little to show their interrelation or total significance. We can improve on Puttenham by going back to antiquity, where in the third book of Aristotle's *Rhetoric* we find a chapter (11) saying that the smartest expressions consist in a concurrence of antithesis, parallel, metaphor, and 'metaphor of a special kind' – by the last of which it would appear that Aristotle means 'homonym'. All this may seem to relegate the rhetorical theory of Pope's age or that of earlier ages to the status described under the second heading at the start of this paper: rhetorical, grammatical, or logical theory upon which we draw merely for tools that we shall turn to the uses of our own analysis. Perhaps this is what happens. I do not know the remedy – unless in the interests of Puttenham and his fellows, we are to cut our criticism off from all that subsequent linguistics and rhetoric and our own insight may tell us.

'Rules,' said Sir William Temple and was paraphrased by Sir Thomas Pope Blount in his *De Re Poetica* of 1694, 'at best are capable only to prevent the making of bad verses, but never able to make men good poets.' This might have been interpreted in Pope's day and by Pope himself according to the well-known doctrine of the *je-ne-sais-quoi*, the 'grace beyond the reach of art', the Longinian concession to genius and the element of the unpredictable in art. It ought to be interpreted by us in the further sense that the rules of a given age never contain even all that can be subsequently formulated about the poems of the age and hence are never able to prescribe our interpretation or limit our understanding of the poems. Poems, if not always prior to theory – in the case of the couplet they seem not to be – are certainly always more concrete than theory.

What I have just said is the logical climax and completion of my argument. What I shall say now, briefly, may be taken as a kind of tailpiece. In the part of this essay where I made a brief survey of rhetorical theory in Pope's age and the preceding, I suppressed one curious facet of that history, for the purpose of introducing it at this point. It is a noteworthy fact that some of the most penetrating technical remarks made by critics during the age of Pope were made by those who disapproved of the devices they were describing. One will no doubt recall Addison's *Spectator* no. 62, where he mentions doggerel rhymes and puns as instances of that 'mixed wit' which consists 'partly in the resemblance of ideas, and partly in the resemblance of words'. Addison also promises to tell us something, on another day, about the 'wit' of antithesis. Far more spectacular are some of the analyses made by Pope's pre-Romantic enemy John Dennis. 'Rhyme,' says Dennis in a Miltonic demonstration prefixed to one of his own blank verse poems, 'is the same thing in relation to harmony that a pun is in relation to wit. . . . Rhyme may not so absurdly be said to be the pun of harmony.' And so far as puns proper and ambiguity are concerned, Empson was not the first to detect their presence in the poetry of Pope.

Nay wits had pensions, and young lords had wit.

'Here,' says Dennis, 'in the compass of one poor line are two devilish bobs for the Court. But 'tis no easy matter to tell which way the latter squinting reflection looks.' Cleanth Brooks has noticed the indecent pun upon the word 'die' in the fifth canto of The Rape of the Lock. It is not to be supposed that this had been overlooked by Dennis. 'That is to say,' observes Dennis, '*He wished for nothing more than to fight with her, because he desired nothing more than to lie with her.* Now what sensible meaning can this have?' Puns, says Dennis, are everywhere in The Rape of the Lock. 'Puns bear the same proportion to thought, that bubbles hold to bodies, and may justly be compared to those gaudy bladders which children make with soap.' Nor is it to be supposed that Dennis had overlooked the kind of pun by Puttenham in the figures of syllepsis and zeugma. 'A receipt for dry joking,' says Dennis. 'For by placing something important in the beginning of a period, and making something very trifling to follow it, he seems to take pains to bring *something* into a Conjunction Copulative with *nothing*, in order to beget *nothing*.' Perhaps it is needless to add that Dennis chooses for illustration of this formula the same examples which I have quoted in my own admiring analysis – those about staining her honor or her new brocade, and taking counsel and tea. At a certain level, Dennis saw very well what Pope was up to. Not an innuendo got past him. This, however, was not the kind of poetry which Dennis prescribed. These were not the rules he would write. We are confronted in our final exhibit with a relation between theory and poems which we have up to now scarcely canvassed. In this version of the critic's role there is a marked correlation not between poems and contemporary poetics but actually between poems and contemporary anti-poetics.

Maynard Mack

from 'Wit and Poetry and Pope: Some Observations on His Imagery', in James L. Clifford and Louis A. Landa (eds.), *Pope and his Contemporaries: Essays Presented to George Sherburn* 1949

We must notice that the closed couplet exercises on images a peculiarly muting subordinating influence. . . . This is Donne:

> Now
> The ladies come; as pirates, which do know
> That there came weak ships fraught with cochineal
> The men board them.

This is Pope:

> Painted for sight, and essenced for the smell,
> Like frigates fraught with spice and cochineal,
> Sail in the ladies. How each pirate eyes
> So weak a vessel, and so rich a prize!
> Top-gallant he, and she in all her trim,
> He boarding her, she striking sail to him.
> (*The Fourth Satire of Donne Versified*, 226–31)

Donne is not at his best in this case, and Pope has the advantage of maturing Donne's idea at length – about as much at length as he was ever inclined to go. Still, leaving all that aside, one can see, I think, that Pope's figure, in spite of its richer elaborations, is not the primary and exclusive focus of attention that Donne's is. Donne's. . . . is the sole occupant of the verse rhetoric which presents it; Pope's is jostled for *Lebensraum* by many other contenders. There is, first, the drama of the ladies' arrival, which the verse itself is at some pains to enact in the first two and a half lines. Then there is the confrontation of forces in line 3, and the double assessment of the booty in line 4, both again rhetorically enacted. Finally, in line 5 comes a brilliant chiastic *rapprochement* of male and female in their bedizenment, to be followed in line 6 by an extension and also a qualification of this *rapprochment* with respect to sex (both parties are interested in the amorous duel, but their functions differ), the former carried by the metrical parallel, the latter by the antithesis in the sense. All these effects grow out of the potentialities of couplet rhetoric, not out of the image; and though they may cooperate with imagery, as here, they have a life of their own which tends to mute it.

So far we have been discussing orthodox kinds of imagery in Pope's poetry, together with some of the modifications to which this imagery is subjected. It is time to turn now to some of his more reticent modes of imaging, which achieve metaphorical effect without using what it is customary to regard as metaphor. The first of these may be studied in his proper names.

Pope's names warrant an essay in themselves. With the possible exception of Milton, no poet has woven so many so happily into verse. And this is not simply because, as Pope said of himself,

Whoe'er offends, at some unlucky time,
Slides into verse, and hitches in a rhyme,
(*Imitations of Horace, Satires*, II i 77–8)

but because Pope saw, like Milton, the qualitative elements (including in Pope's case the humorous qualities) that could be extracted from proper names. For an effect of romance, sonority, and exoticism akin to Milton's, though much mitigated by the couplet, any passage of his translation of Homer's catalogue of ships will do:

The Paphlagonians Pylaemenes rules,
Where rich Henetia breeds her savage mules,
Where Erythinus' rising clifts are seen,
Thy groves of box, Cytorus! ever green;
And where Aegyalus and Cromna lie,
And lofty Sesamus invades the sky;
And where Parthenius, rolled through banks of flowers,
Reflects her bordering palaces and bowers.
(*Iliad*, II 1034–41)

For a combination of romance and humour, this passage:

First he relates how sinking to the chin,
Smit with his mien, the Mud-nymphs sucked him in:
How young Lutetia, softer than the down,
Nigrina black, and Merdamante brown,
Vied for his love in jetty bowers below,
As Hylas fair was ravished long ago.
(*The Dunciad*, II 331–6)

And for pure humour:

'Twas chattering, grinning, mouthing, jabbering all,
And noise and Norton, brangling and Breval,
Dennis and dissonance, and captious art,
And snip-snap short, and interruption smart,
And demonstration thin, and theses thick,
And major, minor, and conclusion quick.
(II 237–42)

It will be observed in all these passages that as the names slide into
verse they tend to take on a metaphorical colouring. Those in the first
and third passages are of real places and persons, but the poetry does
not require, any more than Milton's, that we identify them closely.
Instead they become vehicles of an aura of associations clinging to
epic warriors before Troy, or else of the vulgarity of a disputatious
literature, which swallows up writers as noise, brangling, dissonance
swallow up Norton, Breval, and Dennis. Pope is a master of this
metaphorical play with names. Sometimes the names he uses are
quasi-metaphorical to begin with, like those he has invented in the
Lutetia passage above. Or like those which allude – Adonis, Atossa,
Shylock, Balaam, Timon, Sporus. Or those which have an allegorical
cast – Uxorio, Worldly, Sir Morgan, Sir Visto, Patritio, Papillia,
Hippia. Or those which personify – Avarice, Profusion, Billingsgate,
Sophistry, Mathesis. Pope's habit with these classes of names is to
interlayer them among his real objects and real persons, so that there
results an additional and peculiarly suggestive kind of metaphorical
play between concrete and abstract: allegorical Sir Morgan astride
his cheese; allusive Adonis driving to St James's a whole herd of swine;
or personified morality, chicane, casuistry, and Dullness suddenly
brought into incongruous union with a judge named Page:

Morality, by her false guardians drawn,
Chicane in furs, and casuistry in lawn,
Gasps, as they straighten at each end the cord,
And dies, when Dullness gives her page the word.
(*The Dunciad*, IV 27–30)

Unquestionably, however, Pope's best metaphorical effects with
names were obtained from specific ones, as in the lines on Dennis and
Dissonance above. Did a certain duchess show an indiscriminate
appetite for men? How better image it than with a nice derangement
of proper names, opened with a particularly felicitous 'what':

What has not fired her bosom or her brain?
Caesar and Tall-boy, Charles, and Charlemagne.
(*Moral Essay II*, 77–8)

Did the vein of poetry in contemporary versifiers hardly weigh up
to a gramme? Then doubtless it was an age when

. . . nine such Poets made a Tate.
(*Epistle to Dr Arbuthnot*, 190)

Why was philosophy at Oxford so backward, so ponderous? Because
the Oxford logicians came riding whip and spur, through thin and
thick,

On German Crousaz and Dutch Burgersdyck.
(*The Dunciad*, IV 198)

Or, since the current drama was slavishly derivative, why not let the
patchwork image be projected partly with syntax and partly with
names – a roll-call of stately ones, a tumbling huddle of risible ones:

A past, vamped, future, old, revived, new piece,
'Twixt Plautus, Fletcher, Shakespeare, and Corneille,
Can make a Cibber, Tibbald, or Ozell.
(I 284–6)

A second restrained mode of imaging in Pope's poetry is the allusion.
Not simply the kind of descriptive allusion to persons, places, events,
and characters that all poets make continual use of, and of which I
shall say nothing here, but a kind that is specifically evaluative,

constructing its image by setting beside some present object or situation not so much another object or situation as another dimension, a different sphere – frequently for the purpose of diminishing what is present, but often, too, for the purpose of enlarging or elevating it. Familiar examples of the first use are the correspondence of Sporus to Satan in one of his more degrading disguises – at the ear of Eve, familiar toad' (*Epistle to Dr Arbuthnot*, 319); or (more humorously) of Cibber to Satan, on his exalted throne, at the opening of *The Dunciad*, II. A less familiar example is the witty correspondence suggested in *The Dunciad*, IV, between the dunces irresistibly drawn into the gravitational field of Dullness:

... by sure attraction led
And strong impulsive gravity of head –
(IV 75–6)

and the feeling Sin has in Milton's poem, after the Fall, of being pulled toward earth by 'sympathy, or some connatural force,'

Powerful at greatest distance to unite
With secret amity things of like kind. ...
Nor can I miss the way, so strongly drawn
By this new-felt attraction and instinct.
(x 244 ff.)

As for the second use, the *Essay on Man* begins with a particularly fine example in the 'garden tempting with forbidden fruit'; while *Windsor Forest* both begins and ends with one; the groves of Eden, which establish the central symbol of the poem – and the dove of Noah, also described as the dove of grace and peace, which throws around Pope's vision of England as she comes out of her continental wars all the seventeenth-century religious associations of covenant, happy rescue, and divine mission.

This evaluative kind of metaphor in Pope, whether diminishing or enlarging, is usually religious, and often very powerfully so. Here are some instances in the lighter hues (I limit myself to instances that I think have not been recorded by Pope's editors):

And Heaven is won by violence of song[1]

1 *Imitations of Horace, Epistles*, II, i, 240. cf. Matt., XI, 12.

And zeal for that great house which eats him up.[1]

Blest be the *great*! for those they take away[2]

And, instant, fancy feels the imputed sense.[3]

These colours are darker:

Each does but hate his neighbour as himself.[4]

What lady's face is not a whitewall?[5]

And this, though light in tone, carries a scathing indictment of the perversion of religious values in a money culture. Since it admirably illustrates the way allusion can construct a cogent metaphor without intruding on a casual surface and is, in fact, one of the most scarifying passages Pope ever wrote, I quote it in full:

On some, a *priest* succinct in amice white
Attends; *all flesh is nothing in his sight*!
Beeves, at his touch, at once to jelly *turn*,
And the huge boar is shrunk into an *urn*;
The board with specious *miracles* he loads,
Turns hares to larks, and pigeons into toads.
Another (for in all what one can shine?)
Explains the seve and verdeur of the *vine*.
What cannot copious *sacrifice atone*?
Thy treufles, Perigord! thy hams, Bayonne!
With French *libation* and Italian strain
Wash Bladen *white*, and *expiate* Hays's stain.
Knight lifts the head; for what are crowds undone
To *three essential* partridges *in one*?[6]
(*The Dunciad*, IV 549–62)

There are two other modes of imagery of which Pope is fond,

1 *Moral Essay III*, 208. cf. Psalms, LXIX, 9.
2 *Epistle to Dr Arbuthnot*, 255. cf. Job, I, 21.
3 *The Dunciad*, II, 200. cf. the theological sense of 'imputed'.
4 *Moral Essay III*, 110. cf. Matthew xxii 39.
5 *The Fourth Satire of Donne Versified*, 151. cf. Matthew xxiii 27. (The allusion is Pope's addition.)
6 The italics are mine.

modes that the concision of the closed couplet encourages and almost insists on, though no other writer of the couplet had perfected them to a like extent. These are pun and juxtaposition. Juxtaposition operates in Pope's poetry in several ways. One of them, as has lately been pointed out, is through zeugma, which the economy of this verse form often calls for and which can itself be modulated either into metaphor – 'Or stain her honour, or her new brocade', or into pun – 'And sometimes counsel take – and sometimes tea' (*The Rape of the Lock*, II 107, and III 8). (In either case, the effect is ultimately metaphorical, a correspondence being suggested between Belinda's attitudes to chastity and brocade, or between Queen Anne's, and her society's, to politics and tea.)

My own concern, however, is not with zeugma, but with the metaphorical effects that can arise from simple juxtaposition. For example, from a list of items *seriatim*, with one inharmonious term:

Puffs, powders, patches, Bibles, billets-doux.
(*The Rape of the Lock*, I 138)

Or from a simple parallel inside the line:

Dried butterflies, and tomes of casuistry.[1]
(V 122)

Or from a similar parallel inside the couplet:

Now lap-dogs give themselves the rousing shake,
And sleepless lovers, just at twelve, awake.
(I 15–16)

This is a very versatile device. In *The Rape of the Lock*, from which the above examples are taken, Pope uses it to mirror in his lines and couplets the disarray of values in the society he describes, the confounding of antithetical objects like lap-dogs and lovers, Bibles and billets-doux. On the other hand, in the *Essay on Man*, this same device, redirected by the context, can be made to mirror the 'equalizing' view of antithetical objects taken by the eye of God or by the god-like magnanimous man:

1 A particularly graceful comparison in its suggestion of a common animation, brilliance, delicacy of movement, and perishableness in the worlds of ethics and lepidoptera.

A hero perish, or a sparrow fall.
(I 88)

As toys and empires, for a god-like mind.
(IV 180)

It is also a very sensitive device. The potential metaphor that every juxtaposition tends to carry in suspension requires only the slightest jostling to precipitate it out. Sometimes a well-placed alliteration will do it:

The mind, in metaphysics at a loss,
May wander in a wilderness of moss.
(*The Dunciad*, IV 449–50)

Sometimes an inter-animation of words, as here between the 'smooth' eunuch and the 'eased' sea:

Where, eased of fleets, the Adriatic main
Wafts the smooth eunuch and enamoured swain.
(IV 309–10)

And sometimes a set of puns, as in this example, fusing the biologist with the object of his study:

The most recluse, discreetly opened, find
Congenial matter in the cockle-kind.
(IV 447–8)

Pun, of course, brings before us Pope's most prolific source of imagery in his comic and satiric poetry – which is to say, in the bulk of his work. His puns in other poems – *Windsor Forest*, *Eloisa*, the *Essay on Man*, the *Essay on Criticism* – are deeply buried and always reticent. But in the satires and *The Dunciad*, particularly the latter, he spends them openly and recklessly, with superb effect. They cease to be in these poems ordinary puns, like those we find in Metaphysical poetry, where, because of the conceit, pun has a lesser job to do; they become instead Metaphysical conceits themselves, yoking together violently, as Mr Leavis has noticed, the most heterogeneous ideas. Moreover, when they are used together with ordinary images, the real metaphorical power is likely to be lodged in them. Thus the following figures are not especially bold themselves, but the puns inside them open out like peacocks' tails:

Ye tinsel insects! whom a court maintains,
That counts your beauties only by your *stains*.[1]
(*Epilogue to the Satires*, Dialogue II 220–21)

On others interest her gay livery flings,
Interest that waves on *parti-coloured* wings.
(*The Dunciad*, IV 537–8)

At length corruption, like a general flood
(So long by watchful ministers withstood)
Shall deluge all; and avarice, creeping on,
Spread like a *low-born* mist, and blot the sun.
Moral Essay III, 137–40)

Here, then, are four classes of metaphorical effect in Pope's poetry, all of them obtained outside the normal channels of overt simile and metaphor. One of them, juxtaposition (its collateral descendant, zeugma, would make a second), stems from the structure of the closed couplet itself. Two more, allusion and pun, are encouraged to a large extent by its fixed and narrow room. And none of them, it is important to notice, calls attention to itself as metaphorical. Between them, nevertheless, without violating at all the prose conventions of the Augustan mode, they do a good deal of the work that we today associate with the extended metaphor and conceit.

The devices of complication touched on in the preceding sections pertain primarily to local texture: the line and couplet. I want to add to these, in conclusion, three patterns that are more pervasive; that help supply the kind of unity in Pope's poems which he is popularly not supposed to have. Actually, there is a wide variety of such patterns. There are the characteristics of the dramatic speaker of every poem, who shifts his style, manner, and quality of feeling considerably from poem to poem, as anyone will see who will compare carefully the *Essay on Criticism* with the *Essay on Man*, or the *Epistle to Dr Arbuthnot* with that to Augustus. There is the character of the interlocutor in the poems that have dialogue, by no means a man of

1 Italics in these quotations are mine.

straw. There is the implicit theme, usually announced in a word or phrase toward the outset of the poem, and while seldom developed in recurrent imagery, as in Shakespeare, almost always developed in recurrent references and situations. There is also, often, a kind of pattern of words that reticulates through a poem, enmeshing a larger and larger field of associations – for instance, words meaning light in the *Essay on Criticism*, or the word 'head' (and, of course, all terms for darkness) in *The Dunciad*. And there are a great many more such unifying agents.

The three that I shall examine briefly here are irony, the portrait, and mock-heroic. Pope's irony, fully analysed, would require a book. The point about it that is most relevant to our present topic is that it is a mode of complication closely resembling metaphor. At its most refined, in fact, as in Swift's *Modest Proposal* or Pope's praise of George II in the *Epistle to Augustus*, it asks us to lay together not two, but three different perspectives on reality. First, the surface, and second, the intended meanings, these two corresponding roughly to vehicle and tenor in a metaphor; and then, third – to use again the Pope and Swift examples – the kind of propositions that English projectors were *usually* making about Ireland, or the poets about George II. Pervasive irony of this type – of which there is a good deal in Pope – tends to resist the presence of bold imagery, for two reasons. In the first place, because it consists already in a mutual translation, to and fro, between one kind of complex whole with all its particularities clinging to it (what is said), and a different complex whole with all its revised particularities (what is meant); a translation that profuse or striking imagery only clutters and impedes. And in the second place, because the success of the medium depends on adopting the attitudes, motives, and so far as possible even the terms of a very conventional point of view. If one is going to write an ironic love song 'in the modern taste', one almost has to refer to 'Cupid's purple pinions'; or if a panegyric on George II, to the usual terms for kingly prowess:

Your country, chief, in arms abroad defend.
(*Imitations of Horace, Epistles*, II i 3)

To find a more striking phrase would destroy the subtlety of the ironic comment (i.e. its resemblance to what a Cibber might have said); and would, of course, too, destroy the mutual translation between the arms of battle and those of Madame Walmoden.

To all this, in the *Epistle to Augustus*, is added the further layer of metaphor that results from Pope's imitation of what Horace had written about *his* Caesar. Nor is this latter confined alone to the poems which are imitations. The Roman background, it has been well observed, is a kind of universal Augustan metaphor or 'myth'. It lies behind Pope's work, and much of Swift's and Fielding's, like a charged magnetic field, a reservoir of attitudes whose energy can be released into their own creations at a touch. Not through the Horatian or Virgilian or Ovidian tags; these are only its minor aspect; but through the imposed standard of a mighty and civilized tradition in arts, morals, government. At the same time, conveniently, it is a standard that can be used two ways: for a paradigm of the great and good now lost in the corruptions of the present, as in the comparison of George II with Augustus Caesar; or for the head-waters of a stream down which still flow the stable and continuing classic values:

You show us Rome was glorious, not profuse.
(*Moral Essay IV*, 23)

The world's just wonder, and even thine, O Rome!
(*Essay on Criticism*, 248)

Who would not weep, if Atticus were he?
(*Epistle to Dr Arbuthnot*, 214)

This last example brings us to Pope's portraits. These, again, have the complicating characteristics of metaphors, without drawing attention to themselves as such. They are often erroneously called 'illustrations', as if their content were exhausted in being identified with some abstraction implied or stated by the poem. But what abstractions will exhaust the characters of Atticus, Sporus, Atossa, Balaam, and a score of others? To instance from one of the simplest portraits, so that it may be quoted entire, here is Narcissa:

'Odious! in woollen! 'twould a saint provoke!'
(Were the last words that poor Narcissa spoke);
'No, let a charming chintz, and Brussels lace
Wrap my cold limbs, and shade my lifeless face:

One would not, sure, look frightful when one's dead:
And – Betty – give this cheek a little red.'
(*Moral Essay I*, 242–7)

This, to the extent that it illustrates anything, illustrates the poem's
prose argument that our ruling passion continues to our last breath.
But as a metaphor it explores, not without considerable profundity,
through the character of one type of woman, the character of the
human predicament itself. Here we have, as her name implies, the
foolish self-lover; but also – in a wider, more inevitable, and un-
censorable sense – the self-lover who inhabits each of us by virtue of
our mortal situation, the very principle of identity refusing to be
erased. Here, too, we have the foolish concern for appearances, vastly
magnified by the incongruity of its occasion; but also the fundamental
human clutching at the familiar and the known. And embracing it all
is the central paradox of human feelings about death and life. Cold
limbs don't need wrapping (the conjunction of terms itself suggests
that death can be apprehended but not comprehended), nor dead
faces shading; and yet, as our own death rituals show, somehow they
do. The levels of feeling and experience startled into activity in this
short passage can hardly be more than pointed at in the clumsiness of
paraphrase. The irony of words like 'saint', the ambiguities of
'charming' and 'shade', the tremendous compression in 'frightful', of
'the anguish of the marrow, The ague of the skeleton', accumulate as
one contemplates them.

All of Pope's portraits have at least the complexity of this one, and
all are equally metaphorical in effect. If they do not call attention to
themselves as metaphors, it is probably because in them the vehicle
has largely absorbed the tenor; for metaphors in general seem to take
on prominence according as both the tenor and the vehicle (viz.
lovers as well as compasses) are insisted on at once. In any case, they
behave like metaphors in Pope's poems, usually assuming, in addition
to their functions locally, an important unifying role. Sometimes they
define the entire structure of a poem, as in *Moral Essay II* where they
develop the easy-going aphorism of the opening – 'Most women
have no characters at all' – into a mature interpretation of what
personality is. Sometimes they supply the central symbols, as with
Timon in *Moral Essay IV*, 'Vice' in Dialogue II of the *Epilogue to the*

Satires, or the Man of Ross and Balaam in *Moral Essay III*. Likewise in *Arbuthnot*, Atticus and Sporus appear at just the crucial phases in the argument and knit up, as it were, the two essential ganglia in the sinews of the drama that the poem acts out between the poet and his adversaries. They give us, successively, the poet analytical and judicial, who can recognize the virtues of his opponents ('Blest with each talent and each art to please'), whose deliberation is such that he can even mirror it in his language – its subjunctives, its antitheses, the way it hangs the portrait over an individual without identifying it with him – the tentative, insinuating, never-wholly-committed hollow man who is Atticus; and then the poet roused and righteous, no longer judicial but executive, touching with Ithuriel's spear the invader in the garden, spitting from his mouth (with a concentration of sibilants and labials) the withered apple-seed. Both portraits are essential to the drama that unifies the poem.

The great pervasive metaphor of Augustan literature, however, including Pope's poetry, is the metaphor of tone: the mock-heroic. It is very closely allied, of course, to the classical or Roman myth touched on earlier and is, like that, a reservoir of strength. By its means, without the use of overt imagery at all, opposite and discordant qualities may be locked together in 'a balance or reconcilement of sameness with difference, of the general with the concrete, the idea with the image, the individual with the representative, the sense of novelty and freshness with old and familiar objects,' – the mock-heroic seems made on purpose to fit this definition of Coleridge's of the power of imagination. For a literature of decorums like the Augustan, it was a metaphor with every sort of value. It could be used in the large, as in *Joseph Andrews*, *Tom Jones*, *The Beggar's Opera*, *The Rape of the Lock*, *The Dunciad*, or in the small – the passage, the line. It could be set in motion by a passing allusion, not necessarily to the classics:

Calm temperance, whose blessings those partake
Who hunger, and who thirst, for scribbling sake;
(*The Dunciad*, I 49–50)

by a word:

Glad chains, warm furs, broad banners, and broad faces;
(I 88)

even by a cadence:

And the fresh vomit run for ever green.
(ii 156)

Moreover, it was a way of getting the local, the ephemeral, the pressure of life as it was lived, into poetry, and yet distancing it in amber:

That live-long wig, which Gorgon's self might own,
Eternal buckle takes in Parian stone.
(*Moral Essay III*, 295–6)

It was also a way of qualifying an attitude, of genuinely 'heroicizing' a Man of Ross, a Parson Adams, a school-mistress, yet undercutting them with a more inclusive attitude:

Rise, *honest* Muse! and sing the Man of Ross.[1]
(250)

Above all – and this, I think, was its supreme advantage for Pope – it was a metaphor that could be made to look two ways. If the heroic genre and the heroic episodes lurking behind *The Rape of the Lock* diminish many of the values of this society, they also partially throw their weight behind some others. Clarissa's speech (v 9 ff.) is an excellent case in point. Her words represent a sad shrinkage from the epic views of Glaucus which reverberate behind them, views involving real heroism and (to adapt Mr Eliot's phrase) the awful daring of a real surrender. Still, the effect of the contrast is not wholly minimizing. Clarissa's vision of life, worldly as it is when seen against the heroic standard, surpasses the others in the poem and points, even if obliquely, to the tragic conflict between the human lot and the human will that is common to life at every level.

This flexibility of the mock-heroic metaphor is seen in its greatest perfection in *The Dunciad*. There are, indeed, three thicknesses of metaphor in this poem: an overall metaphor, in which the poem as a whole serves as vehicle for a tenor which is the decline of literary and human values generally; a network of local metaphor, in which this poem is especially prolific; and in between, the specifically mock-heroic metaphor which springs from holding the tone and often the

1 The italics are mine.

circumstances of heroic poetry against the triviality of the dunces and their activities. But what is striking about this metaphor in *The Dunciad*, and indicative of its flexibility, is that it is applied quite differently from the way it is applied in *The Rape of the Lock*. There, the epic mode as vehicle either depresses the values of the actors, as with Belinda, or somewhat supports them, as with Clarissa. Here, the contrary, one of the two lines of development (the comic) grows from allowing the actors to depress and degrade the heroic mode, its dignity and beauty. Again and again Pope builds up in the poem effects of striking epic richness, only to let them be broken down, disfigured, stained – as the word 'vomit' stains the lovely movement and suggestion of the epic line quoted above. Thus the diving and other games in Book II disfigure the idea of noble emulation and suggest the befoulment of heroic values through the befoulment of the words and activities in which these values are recorded. Thus the fop's Grand Tour in IV mutilates a classical and Renaissance ideal (cf. also Virgil's Aeneas, to whose destined wanderings toward Rome the fop's are likened) of wisdom ripened by commerce with men and cities. Indeed the lines of the whole passage (IV 284 ff.) are balanced between the ideal and the fop's perversions of it:

A dauntless infant! never scared with God.

Europe he saw, and Europe saw him too.

Judicious drank, and greatly daring dined;

or between related ideals and what has happened to them:

To happy convents, bosomed deep in vines,
Where slumber abbots, purple as their wines.

or between epic resonances, the epic names, and the sorry facts:

To where the Seine, obsequious as she runs,
Pours at great Bourbon's feet her silken sons.

This is one line of development in *The Dunciad*. The other is its converse: the epic vehicle is gradually made throughout the poem to enlarge and give a status of serious menace to all this ludicrous activity. Here the epic circumstance of a presiding goddess proved invaluable. Partly ludicrous herself, she could also become the locus of inexhaustible negation behind the movements of her trivial puppets; her force could be associated humorously, but also seriously, with the powerful names of Chaos, Night, Anti-Christ, and with perversions of favourite order symbols like the sun, monarchy, and gravitation. Here, too, the epic backgrounds as supplied by Milton could be drawn in. Mr C. S. Lewis has remarked of *Paradise Lost* that 'only those will fully understand it who see that it might have been a comic poem'. *The Dunciad* is one realization of that might-have-been. Over and above the flow of Miltonic echoes and allusions, or the structural resemblances like Cibber's (or Theobald's) Pisgah-vision based on Adam's, or the clusered names of dunces like those of Milton's devils, thick as the leaves that strew bad books in Grub Street – *The Dunciad* is a version of Milton's theme in being the story of an uncreating Lōgos. As the poem progresses, our sense of this increases through the calling in of more and more powerful associations by the epic vehicle. The activities of the dunces and of Dullness are more and more equated with religious anti-values, culminating in the passage on the Eucharist quoted earlier. The metaphor of the coronation of the king-dunce moves always closer to and then flows into the metaphor of the Day of the Lord, the descent of the anti-Messiah, the uncreating Word. Meantime, symbols which have formerly been ludicrous – insects, for instance, or sleep – are given by this expansion in the epic vehicle a more sombre cast. The dunces thicken and become less individual, more anonymous, expressive of blind inertia – bees in swarm, or locusts blackening the land. Sleep becomes tied up with its baser physical manifestations, with drunkenness, with deception, with ignorance, with neglect of obligation, and finally with death. This is the sleep which *is* death, we realize, a *Narrendämmerung*, the twilight of the moral will. And yet, because of the ambivalence of the mock-heroic metaphor, Pope can keep to the end the tension between all these creatures as comic and ridiculous, and their destructive potentiality in being so. Certainly two of the finest puns in any poetry are those with which he continues to exploit this tension at the very end of the poem, when Dullness finally *yawns* and Nature *nods*.

The purpose of this essay has been to supply a few, a very few, of the materials that are requisite for giving the phrase 'poetry of statement' specific content. I have tried to suggest that Pope is poetic, but not in the way that the Metaphysicals are poetic, even where he is most like them; that if the prominent metaphor is the distinctive item in their practice, this has been replaced in Pope's poetry partly by devices of greater compression, like allusion and pun, partly by devices that are more distributive, like irony and mock-heroic, and of course by a multitude of other elements – the net effect of all these being to submerge the multiplicities of poetic language just beneath the single-ness of prose. Twenty-five years ago it would have been equally important to say that Pope is not poetic as the Romantics are poetic, for in this century there has always been a tendency to subsume him as far as possible under the reigning orthodoxy. It is true that in certain areas Pope's poetry faintly resembles that of the Romantics; in certain others, that of the line of wit. But the task of criticism for the future, when we are likely to be paying more and more attention to Pope as our own poetry moves in the direction suggested by Mr Auden, and by Mr Eliot in his *Quartets*, is not with Pope as a pre-Romantic or a post-Metaphysical, but as an Augustan poet whose peculiar accomplishment, however we may choose to rate it on the ultimate scale of values, was the successful fusion of some of the most antithetical features of verse and prose.

F. W. Bateson

from his Introduction to *Epistles to Several Persons (Moral Essays)*, the Twickenham edition of Pope, vol. 3, part 2, edited by John Butt   1951

Epistles to Several Persons is a better title than *Moral Essays*, not only because it was the title of Pope's own choice, but because it describes more accurately the nature of these four poems. To a reader of the early eighteenth century the word 'essay' had a more formidable connotation than it has today. The combinations of 'moral' and 'essays', instead of suggesting, as it might to us, Addison's Saturday numbers of *The Spectator*, would then have been more likely to suggest some such dismal treatise as James Lowde's *Moral Essays wherein some of Mr Locke's and Monsr Malebranche's opinions are briefly examined* (1699). The effect of Warburton's title for these poems therefore was to put all the emphasis on the didactic elements in the poems. Here, it proclaimed, is another *Essay on Man*. It called attention, in other words, to all that is weakest and most pretentious in the four Epistles and ignored altogether the social satire and worldly wisdom in which their real strength lies.

If there is a certain convenience in the term *Moral Essays* as differentiating the Epistles that are associated with the *Essay on Man* from Pope's other letters in verse, such as those to Addison, Harley, Craggs and Jervas, this is more than counterbalanced by the reminder that the word 'Epistle' conveys that Pope is using in these poems one of the accepted neo-classic forms. As a vehicle for political compliment, literary criticism, and social correction the Horatian epistle had long been a favourite of the Augustan poets, and Dryden, in 'To My Honoured Kinsman, John Dryden', and Congreve, in 'Of Improving the Present Time' (which had been addressed to the same Lord Cobham as Pope's epistle), had already shown that ethics could also be treated 'in the Horatian way' in excellent English verse.

In the *Spectator* no. 618, Ambrose Philips provides a long list of 'The qualifications requisite for writing Epistles, after the model given us by Horace': 'a good fund of strong masculine sense'; 'a thorough knowledge of mankind'; 'an insight into the business and the prevailing humours of the age'; a 'mind well seasoned with the finest precepts of morality'; and a mastery of 'refined raillery, and a lively turn of wit, with an easy and concise manner of expression'. Philips adds that the illustrations and similes should be drawn from 'common life', and that 'strokes of satire and criticism, as well as panegyrics', are particularly desirable, provided that 'a vulgar diction' and 'too negligent' a versification are avoided. It will be seen that Pope's Epistles adhere closely to Philips's ideal recommendation, which is indeed only an elaboration of the prescription in Horace's tenth *Satire* that Pope used as an epigraph to the 'death-bed' edition [of these four poems]. *To Burlington* was criticized on its publication as insufficiently 'correct' in its versification. Sir Thomas Hanmer, for example, was informed by Dr Delany, Swift's friend, on 23 December 1731 (only ten days after the poem had come out) that 'There is a general outcry against that part of the poem which is thought an abuse of ye Duke of Chandos – other parts are quarrelled with as obscure and unharmonious; and I am told there is an advertisement that promises a publication of Mr Pope's Epistle versified . . .'[1] Except for an occasional tiring of the ears with open vowels it is difficult to find more than a line or two in *To Burlington* that could possibly be considered 'unharmonious'. But Aaron Hill refers to the same criticism of the poem in a letter to Pope himself of 17 December (only four days after publication):

We have poets, whom heaven visits with a taste, as well as planters and builders. What other inducement could provoke some of them, to mistake your epistolary relaxation of numbers, for an involuntary defect in your versification?

As Hill hints, a great deal more was in fact involved than the precise degree of metrical negligence appropriate to a Horatian epistle. The Dunces were moving in to the counter-attack, and Pope was forced under this new pressure to reconsider the moral basis of epistolary satire. . . .

Pope's answer, when anybody impugned his motives, was to appeal to 'virtue'. Applying to himself the character that Horace had attributed to Lucilius, he proclaimed himself (in capital letters)

TO VIRTUE ONLY and HER FRIENDS, A FRIEND.
(*Imitations of Horace, Satires*, II i 121)

Pope's modern friends have found such passages, which are by no means rare in his writings, embarrassing and distressing. But for Pope 'virtue' did not mean quite what it means to us. The most specific reference, though it does not quite amount to a definition, is in one of the later *Imitations of Horace* (*Epistles*, i i 77–80):

Here, Wisdom calls: 'Seek virtue first! be bold!
As gold to silver, virtue is to gold.'
There, London's voice: 'Get money, money still!
And then let virtue follow, if she will.'

1 *The Correspondence of Sir Thomas Hanmer*, ed. Sir H. E. Bunbury (1838), p. 217. The charge of obscurity was also brought against *To Bathurst* by Lady Anne Irwin, in a letter to her father, Lord Carlisle, 18 January 1733/4: 'there are good thoughts wrapped up in obscurity, but that is so much the fashion that to be plain and intelligible is a meanness in writing the moderns are resolved not to be guilty on . . .'.

Here Pope seems to be saying that the opposite of the pursuit of virtue is the pursuit of money. And therefore presumably, if London symbolizes money, virtue must be symbolized by the country. (God made the country, in fact, and man made the town.) Virtue, on this interpretation, is a class-concept, the system of values of the 'landed interest', the 'Country Party'. Vice is therefore the social philosophy of the urban capitalists, the rising middle classes who, with their champions in Parliament and at Court, where already a potential threat to the supremacy of the squirearchy.[1]

It is significant at any rate that Burlington, Bathurst, and Cobham were all prominent members of the landed aristocracy. They were at the opposite social and economic pole, that is, from such contemporary notabilities as Sir Gilbert Heathcote, who was one of the founders of the Bank of England, Sir John Blount, the projector of the South Sea Company, Peter Walter, the moneylender, and the rest of the financiers and crooks who are satirized in *To Bathurst*. Politically Burlington was neutral (he is the exemplar of 'Sense' rather than 'Virtue'), but Bathurst was a prominent Tory and Cobham, who had voted against Walpole's Excise Bill in 1733, became from then one of the most influential of the Opposition Whigs. And their country seats at Chiswick, Cirencester, and Stowe were, of course, object lessons in the new gardening, at once picturesque and utilitarian,

Whose ample lawns are not ashamed to feed
The milky heifer and deserving steed.
(*Moral Essay IV*, 185-6)

Pope's 'virtue' was closely related therefore to Bolingbroke's 'patriotism'. (In Epistle I Cobham's last, and therefore most edifying, words are foretold to be 'Oh, save my country, Heaven!') It was a quality that had little or nothing to do with the respectability of one's private life. Bathurst, the 'philosopher and rake', is held up as an example of the golden mean,

1 This is not the place for a detailed exposition of the Augustan *Weltanschauung,* but some understanding of the social basis of Pope's poetry is essential if the modern reader is not to be unfair to him. Of course, it is not suggested that Pope himself would have accepted a class definition of 'virtue', such as that given above, which is an attempt to get behind what he *thought* he meant to the basic implications of his satire.

There, English bounty yet a while may stand,
And honour linger ere it leaves the land.
(*Moral Essay III*, 247–8)

'Virtue', in fact, is primarily a social quality, the positive element of
which the negative is 'vice', and Pope's satires are exercises in
'contrast' (a pictorial term to which he often reverts) between the
two elements. On the one hand, they applaud the exemplars of
'virtue', the living representatives of what is to Pope the ideal social
order. On the other hand, they attack and ridicule 'vice', or the
deviation from this social order. Each of the two aspects presented its
own literary problem. The positive problem Pope solved, or thought
he had solved, by piling up rhetorical compliments. And at any rate
the recipients of the compliments seemed to have liked them. This is
what Cobham, for example, had to say when he had read the
Epistle addressed to him:

Though I have not modesty enough not to be pleased with
your extraordinary compliment I have wit enough to know
how little I deserve it. You know all mankind are putting
themselves upon the world for more then they are worth
and their friends are daily helping the deceits, but I am afraid
I shall not pass for an absolute patriot. However I have the
honour of having received a public testimony of your
esteem and friendship and am as proud of it as I could be
of any advantage which could happen to me.

But the positive social elements are not important in satire, except
by implication. The literary problem presented by the negative
elements was the crucial one. How was Pope to be the fearless social
critic without seeming to be a libeller?

It is important to recognize that the basis of Pope's satire is *fact*.
It was by stooping to Truth, i.e. the kind of evidence that would be
accepted in a court of law, that he was able to moralize his song.
Unlike his friend Young, whose five satires called *The Universal
Passion* (1725/6) Pope had certainly read and admired, he was not
content with what Charles Lamb, speaking of Restoration comedy,
was to call 'a speculative scene of things, which has no reference
whatever to the world that is'. His satire, in contradistinction to that

of Wycherley and Congreve, is rooted in topical and contemporary life, and his progress as a satirist can best be measured by the degree of social actuality that each poem achieved. In *To Burlington*, for example, though the illustrative details are real, the satiric butts are personified abstractions, almost all without any living originals. The 'subject' of the poem, according to the letter that Pope prefixed to the third edition, was the 'pride' of his 'betters'; in other words, the extravagant ostentation of the Augustan aristocracy that a modern sociologist has called 'the ritual of conspicuous waste'. 'Lord Timon' is obviously intended to personify this 'pride'. His villa is 'proud' (line 101), his chapel exhibits 'the pride of prayer' (line 142), his 'civil pride' (line 166) is sickening, though eventually 'all his pride has planned' (line 175) will pass away.[1] On the other hand, some of the details that Pope introduces to illustrate 'Timon's' pride can be traced to the actual grounds and mansions of contemporary noblemen. Blenheim Palace, for example, certainly contributed some items. It is not impossible either that, though 'Timon' is not the Duke of Chandos, Cannons, the Duke's 'place' at Edgware, may have provided one or two suggestions, e.g. the 'statues thick as trees' (line 120). Chandos himself admitted to a friend, 'I am not so ignorant of my own weakness, as not to be sensible of its [Timon's character's] justness in some particulars.' Pope points out some of the topical allusions in the poem in his notes. To line 75, for example,

Or cut wide views through mountains to the plain,

Pope added the following note in 1735:

This was done in Hertfordshire, by a wealthy citizen, at the expense of above £5,000, by which means (merely to overlook a dead plain) he let in the north wind upon his house and parterre, which were before adorned and defended by beautiful woods.[2]

1 'Pride' is a key-word in Pope. He uses it twice as often as Milton, surprisingly enough. The word occurs twenty-four times in the *Essay on Man* alone.
2 Pope's purpose in such notes has, I think, been misunderstood. They were not primarily for the benefit of the provincial reader who needed an explanation of the allusions. Their essential function is to supply the *evidence* on which Pope's satiric charges are based.

Here Pope is clearly alluding to Moor Park, Rickmansworth, where the two vistas that Benjamin Styles, a successful South Sea speculator, cut through the hill can still be seen.

The presence of so much contemporary topical detail no doubt explains why the first readers of *To Burlington* jumped to the conclusion that 'Timon' and the six other offenders against taste who are pilloried in the poem must be caricatures of real people. A catch-penny production called *A Miscellany on Taste* (1732) even provided a 'Clavis' in which all the fictitious names are equated with contemporary notabilities. Not only is 'Timon' the 'Duke of C—', but 'Villario' is 'Lord C—le—n' (i.e. Castlemaine), 'Bubo' is 'Lord C—d—n' (i.e. Cadogan), and 'Sir Shylock' is even identified with 'Sir R— W—' (i.e. Walpole). It was all very annoying to Pope, not only because of the social hot water in which he found himself, but also because it meant that his satiric gun had misfired. What he had intended to be read as general 'satire', illustrated by ideal types,[1] had been taken as topical and personal 'libel'.

In *To Bathurst* he succeeded in avoiding the mistake he had made in *To Burlington*. In the letter inserted in the third edition of *To Burlington* he had promised that his next poem would 'make use of real names and not of fictitious ones', and he gave three reasons for this change of tactics, (1) 'to avoid misconstruction', (2) 'to lessen offence', and (3) 'not to multiply ill-natured applications'. The first and third of these reasons were valid ones on the literary as well as the social plane. For an Augustan poet the first essential was to be intelligible. But the second was really a betrayal of the satirist's function ; satire only succeeds by being *offensive* to its victims. It is true that it might have been extremely dangerous at this stage for Pope to have attacked one of his 'betters', a Member of the House of Lords, for example, under his own name. In the end, therefore, he compromised. Of the thirty-one satiric butts introduced into *To Bathurst* sixteen appear under their own names and fifteen under fictitious names. Real names are used for all the middle-class victims such as Ward, Waters, Bond, etc., as well as for the Dukes of Buckingham and Wharton, who were both safely dead, and also for such

1 Pope's own description of his method in *To Burlington* was 'telling truths, and drawing exemplary pictures of men and manners' (letter to Tonson, senior, 7 June 1732, Sherburn, III 291).

disreputable aristocratic adventurers as Sir William Colepepper, Joseph Gage, and Lady Mary Herbert who were safe game, though still alive. The fictitions names fall into three categories, (i) parallel Latin or pseudo-Latin names of the Horatian type, (ii) pseudonyms sounding something like the victims' real names, and (iii) miscellaneous names, scriptural, national, etc. The first and second of these categories seem to include the 'living examples, which enforce best' that Pope told Caryll he intended to restrict the poem to. Most of the victims can be identified with some certainty because the real names, or at any rate one or more letters of the real names, often appear in the early drafts of the poem. They were almost all contemporary aristocrats, like the Herveys, the Wortley Montagus, General Cadogan, and Lord Selkirk.[1] The only ideal figure in these categories seems to be 'Harpax' (line 93).[2] The third category only includes two names, 'Sir Morgan' (line 49) which Pope assured Caryll 'is a fictitious name', and 'Balaam' (lines 339 ff.), who may conceivably be Thomas Pitt but is more likely to be nobody in particular.

Although less consistently, Pope adheres on the whole to 'living examples' in *To Cobham*. The fidelity to fact is underlined in a note to line 251, which was added in 1735: 'The rest of these instances are strictly true, though the persons are not named.' And the central 'example' – the character that plays the role in this poem that 'Timon' played in *To Burlington* – is supplied by a contemporary, the Duke of Wharton, who appears in the final text under his own name.[3] But there are a number of figures that seem to be mere

1 The exceptions are 'Cato' (line 68), who is certainly Sir Christopher Musgrave, who had died in 1704, and 'Cotta' (lines 179 ff.), who must be Sir John Cutler, who was neither contemporary nor an aristocrat. Cutler comes in under his own name in lines 315–34, and his appearance as 'Cotta' may be due to the fact that the point of the passage is the contrast between Cutler and his son-in-law the Earl of Radnor (whose successor was a neighbour of Pope's at Twickenham). Pope may have felt that if the son-in-law did not appear under his own name, the father-in-law should not either.

2 The ideality of 'Harpax' seems to be guaranteed by *Imitations of Horace, Satires*, II i 42–4:
A hundred smart in Timon and in Balaam:
The fewer still you name, you wound the more;
Bond is but one, but Harpax is a score.

3 In the earlier editions he had been called 'Clodio' – a name that had been applied to his father, the first Marquis, by William Shippen in *Faction Displayed* (1704).

general types, e.g. the 'gay free-thinker' (lines 162–5), 'Catius' (lines 136–9), and the politician (lines 130–5), and others, which seem to derive from real people, are apparently in process of generalization. Thus Godolphin is called 'Patritio' (line 140), though he had been dead over twenty years and the reference is more complimentary than satirical, and James Johnston, who is 'J**n' in the first edition, ends up as 'Scoto'.

Pope was, in fact, on the horns of a dilemma. If he used fictitious names for real people, how could he be sure that the reader identified them correctly?[1] If he used fictitious names for mere ideal types, how could he secure himself from the 'ill-natured applications' that the Dunces would be sure to propagate? The solution that he ultimately adopted in the later *Imitations of Horace* was to use real names for real people all the time, however influential and aristocratic they might be. For factual satire this was the course that logic demanded. Short of this, however, there were ways and means by which the reader could be helped to interpret a fictitious name correctly. One has already been noticed in discussing *To Bathurst*. Such names as Worldly (=Wortley Montagu), Shylock (=Lord Selkirk), and Bubo (=Bubb Doddington) told their own story. Another device, first used in the second volume of the *Works* (April

---

1 The copies of the Epistles that have been annotated in MS. by eighteenth-century readers show how difficult even the best informed of them, e.g. Horace Walpole, Wilkes, and William Cole, found it to make the correct identifications. Pope's intimate friend the second Earl of Oxford, recognized that 'G—' stood for Gage, 'Maria' for Mary Herbert, and 'Bl—t' for Sir John Blount in the first edition of *To Bathurst*, but failed apparently to identify any of the fictitious names. (His copy is now in the Bodleian.)

On the appearance of Faulkner's Dublin reprint of *To Bathurst* early in 1733 Swift reported to Pope 'we have no objection but the obscurity of several passages by our ignorance in facts and persons, which makes us lose abundance of the satire. Had the printer given me notice, I would have honestly printed the names at length, where I happened to know them; and writ explanatory notes . . .'. In Faulkner's reprint of *To Cobham* a year or so later somebody (presumably Swift) has done exactly that; e.g. on 'Clodio' (line 180), 'It is supposed the author means the late Duke of Wharton.' But the expansion of 'J**n' (line 158) to 'Jaunssen' – with a note on this South Sea millionaire – illustrates the hazards of such identifications. By 'J**n' Pope had really meant his Twickenham neighbour James Johnston, and on learning the mistake Faulkner had to insert in the unsold copies a cancel leaf, which is without the note and just reads 'J—n' in the text.

1735), was to retain the same fictitious name for a real person in a number of poems. Lady Mary Wortley Montagu was called 'Sappho' so often by Pope – he had inherited the name from Peterborough – that he could soon count on the reader making the correct identification. A similar case is that of 'Bubo'. A more interesting device is exemplified by 'Atossa' and 'Philomedé' in To a Lady. Here the names, though Horatian in appearance, are much more specific than the run of Latin or pseudo–Latin names. There was only one Atossa in literary history, the Atossa of Herodotus, whose main claim to fame was that she was the daughter of Cyrus and the sister of Cambyses. And there was only one woman in England that the name could fit, viz. the Duchess of Buckinghamshire, who was enormously proud of being James II's illegitimate child and so half-sister to the Old Pretender. 'Philomedé' is an equally unusual name, though a 'Lover of the Mede' (if that is the sense intended) may mean more than one thing and could apply to many grandes dames of the period.

Finally, if the worst came to the worst, it was always possible to tell the reader which fictitious names concealed a living original and which did not. This is what Pope does more than once in To a Lady. To the first edition he prefixed an 'Advertisement' in which he declared 'upon his honour, that no one character is drawn from the life'. This was true, or almost true,[1] of the first edition, which did not include the characters of 'Atossa', 'Philomedé' and 'Cloe'. And the 'death-bed edition', which adds these characters, gives the reader a fairly broad hint in the note to line 199 that there had been a good reason why they had not been included in the earlier editions.

Pope's satirical progress in the Epistles, from 'Timon' to 'Wharton', had been considerable. He had learnt, as he told Arbuthnot, that 'general satire in times of general vice has no force', and that ''tis only by hunting one or two from the herd that any examples can be made.' Henceforth he was to avoid 'harmless Characters that no one hit'. And, even more salutary, he had learnt the importance of fact. There is an interesting admission in a letter Pope wrote to the elder Tonson

---

1 Pope's friend Lord Oxford thought 'Arcadia's Countess' (line 7) was the Countess of Pembroke. If she was, Pope might have excused himself by claiming that she had not been 'drawn from the life', as Pope had not known the Countess in question personally.

on 7 June 1732 to thank him for the biographical details he had collected about the Man of Ross:

You know, few of these particulars can be made to shine in verse, but I have selected the most affecting, and have added two or three which I learned from other hands. A small exaggeration you must allow me as a poet; yet I was determined the ground work at least should be truth.

He had allowed himself too much exaggeration in *To Bathurst*. *To a Lady* is a much better poem, not only because it is gayer, but because it is more honest and more accurate. When he claimed, in the 'Advertisement' to the *Epistle to Arbuthnot*, that that poem included 'not a circumstance but what is true', he was pointing to what is its, and Pope's, real greatness. Veracity did not come easily to the *mens curva in corpore curvo*. In the *Epistles to Several Persons* we can trace the process of self-discipline, moral as well as technical, by which he eventually taught his Muse to stoop to Truth.

W. K. Wimsatt

from 'The Augustan Mode in English Poetry', *ELH*, *A Journal of English Literary History*, vol. 20   1953 (reprinted in *Hateful Contraries*, 1965)

Near the end of the *Essay on Man* Pope himself makes what seems to me a lamentable recantation of a classical doctrine received in childhood.

> I turned the tuneful art
> From sounds to things, from fancy to the heart;
> From wit's false mirror held up nature's light.
> (IV 391–3)

The pity is that he was more or less telling the truth. If, for example, the unearned optimism of the 'ruling passion' which runs through Epistle II of the *Essay on Man* falls a bit short of being Pope's most impressive poetry, as I at least am inclined to think it does, one way

to suggest the character of the shortcoming is to say that the lines
would have trouble passing the salon test.

See some strange comfort every state attend,
And pride bestowed on all, a common friend.
(II 271–2)

This may be somewhat tedious, somewhat too comforting. A more
tart expression, one that took proper advantage of human vanity and
was safe from being found a partisan with it, would no doubt have
been inappropriate in the context. Yet in a different context Pope
had once before shown the witty side of the same platitude.

Whatever nature has in worth denied
She gives in large recruits of needful Pride.
(*Essay on Crtiticism*, 205–6)

Lord Chesterfield's advice to his son about cultivating poetic diction
and his advice about cultivating the precise, unpretentious speech of
a gentleman are equally in earnest, but these utterances do not occur
in the same letter. They represent a split in the Augustan ideal of
eloquence – between a social side and a purely literary side – an
opposition which the greatest of the Augustan poets was able to
harmonize no more completely than the greatest of the salon conver-
sationalists. . . .

My view is that the English Augustans were, at their best and at their
most characteristic, laughing poets of a heightened unreality. The
world which the Augustan wit found most amusing and into which
he had his deepest visions was an inverted, chaotic reality, the unreality
of the 'uncreating word', – the 'true no-meaning' which 'puzzles
more than wit'. The peculiar feat of the Augustan poet was the art
of teasing unreality with the redeeming force of wit – of casting upon
a welter of unreal materials a light of order and a perspective vision.
    That is the truth despite all the intimations to the contrary which
Augustan poets themselves may have uttered, all the rules which
later scholars may have identified, to the effect that Augustanism is
the direct incorporation of ideal reality, of reason and light – 'one
clear, unchanged, and universal light'. That passage on Nature in
Pope's *Essay*, like the rules for every poetic emergency urbanely

recited by Horace, is perhaps best taken as a part of the author's mask. Augustan poets (along with the critic Dennis) could talk about the rules, they could in various ways introduce the rules as material into their poetical Arts of Poetry; but Augustan poets could not formally demonstrate the rules without being chilly. The *Essay on Criticism* furnishes positive examples only of how to accommodate the sound to the sense. The best these poets could do for the rules – and it was uncommonly good – was to give burlesque examples of how the rules are violated. This explains why the liveliest Augustan prose criticism (it is not found in the Longinian terms of a Preface to Homer or of notes to Homer) sounds so much like the actual performance of Augustan poetry.

Thus, there was a rule derived from Aristotle and Horace that a literary character portrayal should be consistent and plausible – it should observe its 'decorum'.

> ... si forte reponis Achillem,
> impiger, iracundus, inexorabilis, acer.
> (*Ad Pisones*, 120–21)

But this rule is not very exciting. It does not invite extra-illustration. Or at least the Augustans were not really so much interdested in illustrating it as a Scaliger or a Vida might have been. The only way to make such a rule interesting is to subvert it. Chapter V of Pope's Scriblerian *Peri Bathous* prescribes how a modern poet of the 'profound' might do this.

In the very manners he will affect the marvellous; he will draw Achilles with the patience of Job; a prince talking like a jack-pudding; a maid of honour selling bargains; a footman speaking like a philosopher; and a fine gentleman like a scholar.

With the important difference in consciousness that made wit, this kind of garbled character was what the Augustan poet himself would execute in his poems.

> Rufa, whose eye quick-glancing o'er the park,
> Attracts each light gay meteor of a spark,
> Agrees as ill with Rufa studying Locke,
> As Sappho's diamonds with her dirty smock. ...

Now deep in Taylor and the Book of Martyrs,
Now drinking citron with his grace and Chartres.
Now conscience chills her, and now passion burns;
And atheism and religion take their turns.
(*Moral Essay II*, 21–4, 63–6)

Now high, now low, now master up, now miss,
And he himself one vile antithesis.
(*Epistle to Dr Arbuthnot*, 324–5)

The principle of unreality comes out in Pope's *Peri Bathous* even
more starkly when he talks about outdoor nature. And here let me
cite a curious parallel to a modern philosopher's view of the whole
meaning of our modern Western art. In his *Dehumanization of Art*
Ortega y Gasset remarks:

It would be interesting to find out whether in the new
artistic inspiration, where they fulfil a substantive and not
merely a decorative function, images have not acquired a
curious derogatory quality and, instead of ennobling and
enhancing, belittle and disparage poor reality. I remember
reading a book of modern poetry in which a flash of
lightning was compared to a carpenter's rule and the leafless
trees of winter to brooms sweeping the sky. The weapon of
poetry turns against natural things and wounds or murders
them,

Beside that place the following passage of *Peri Bathous*.

He [the poet of the profound] ought therefore to render
himself master of this happy and *anti-natural* way of thinking
to such a degree as to be able, on the appearance of any object,
to furnish his imagination with ideas infinitely *below* it. And
his eyes should be like unto the wrong end of a perspective
glass, by which all the objects of nature are lessened. For
example, when a true genius looks upon the sky, he
immediately catches the idea of a piece of blue lutestring or
a child's mantle. . . . If he looks upon a tempest, he shall
have an image of a tumbled bed.
(chapter v)

Ortega y Gasset begins his essay by professing a neutral descriptive purpose. Yet his description is so sympathetic as to sound much like an apology. Say what you will, he argues in effect, these *are* the modern values in art. See what you can make of them. Pope, on the other hand, is putting a finger on deviations from the norm of classical sanity. 'Nobody can write that way without being ridiculous.' The similarity of the two critiques, however, is striking, as is the general correspondence of *Peri Bathous* to the lavish subversions which characterize Pope's own poetry.

In cold December fragrant chaplets blow,
And heavy harvests nod beneath the snow.
(*The Dunciad*, I 77–8)

The forests dance, the rivers upward rise.
Whales sport in woods, and dolphins in the skies.[1]
(*The Dunciad*, III 245–6)

In all this there appears, I believe, more than a slight affinity between Augustan burlesque and the kind of unreality which during the period of Ortega's survey flourished in various forms of 'expression' and 'surrealism'. The parallel between *Peri Bathous* and the conceptions of Ortega reaches its most exquisite in Ortega's introduction of the term 'infrarealism.' The English translation of the sentence by which this term is defined could scarcely sound more like a borrowing from Pope's ironic treatise. 'Instead of soaring to poetical heights, art may dive beneath the level marked by the natural perspective.'

1 cf. Horace, *Ad Pisones*, 29: 'Delphinum silvis adpingit, fluctibus aprum' (the negative rule) with Horace, *Odes*, I ii 9–12:

Piscium et summa genus haesit ulmo
Nota quae sedes fuerat columbis,
Et superjecto pavidae natarunt
Aequorae dammae.

Donald Davie

from *Articulate Energy: An Enquiry into the Syntax of English Poetry*
1955

We are accustomed to think, quite rightly too, that trisyllabic metre
is more rapid than the iambic:

The Assyrian came down like the wolf on the fold,
And his cohorts were gleaming in purple and gold.

We certainly get the impression, which may even be true to fact,
that in reading these lines (even silently) we have read twenty-four
syllables in the time we take, in iambic verse, for sixteen. Hence we
call it rapid. But now consider Pope:

The thriving plants, ignoble broomsticks made,
Now sweep those alleys they were born to shade.
(*Moral Essay IV*, 97–8)

Here too, in this iambic verse, we get an impression of rapidity, but
of a quite different sort. This is rapid because it expresses so much in
so short a time. The rapidity of Byron is a rapid movement of lips
and tongue; Pope's rapidity is a rapid movement of the mind. Pope's
rapidity we perceive by empathy; Byron's we do not. . . .

The couplet, in fact, at least as used by Dryden and by Pope, is
capable of rendering only one sort of movement through the mind;
it is committed by its very nature to a syntax of antithesis and razor-
sharp distinctions. That may be one reason why all the Romantic
poets, except Byron, eschewed it. . . .

In Valéry's formula, it is not necessary that the structure of expressions
should be *the only* source of interest in the poem, only that this should
be more interesting than anything else. And even Valéry's formula
is too narrow. For there is no reason why this sort of syntax, any more
than any of the other sorts, should be more than one source of pleasure
among many others. It is *poetic* syntax in that it gives poetic pleasure,
and it differs from other kinds of syntax only in this – that the pleasure
it gives has nothing to do with mimesis. On these terms, any amount

of older poetry can be seen to employ syntax-like-mathematics and indeed this category becomes more crowded than any of the others. In particular, the Augustan age sends up one candidate after another:

Within the couplet the poet worked out as many contrasts and parallels as he could, providing the maximum number of internal geometrical relationships. Denham's lines on the Thames had fascinated later poets with the possibilities of this kind of configuration. They were frequently imitated – too frequently for Swift's pleasure. Their kind of verbal manipulation was improved on, until in Pope a couplet will often suggest a difficult figure in Euclid, its vowels and consonants, its sense-oppositions and sense-attractions, fitted together like arcs and lines.

'A fop their passion, but their prize a sot;
Alive, ridiculous, and dead, forgot!'[1]

The Euclidean reference here is exact. This is a syntax like mathematics, as is Mallarmé's. I have given examples from Pope to illustrate another category of poetic syntax which I have called 'objective', and and I think there is some danger that the high shine of artifice over the surface of the best Augustan verse will lead readers to think of their syntax as 'like mathematics' when in fact it has a more mimetic function, clinging closely to the experience behind it. Still, it cannot be denied that it is in the eighteenth century that we find most of this Euclidean syntax.

Yeats may seem to speak of the same thing, though he compares it with mechanics rather than mathematics, when he writes to H. J. C. Grierson in 1912:

The over childish or over pretty or feminine element in some good Wordsworth and in much poetry up to our date comes from the lack of natural momentum in the syntax. This momentum underlies almost every Elizabethan and Jacobean lyric and is far more important than simplicity of vocabulary. If Wordsworth had found it he could have any amount of elaborate English. Byron, unlike the

1 *Times Literary Supplement*, 4 January 1936.

Elizabethans though he always tries for it, constantly allows
it to die out in some mind-created construction, but is I
think the one great English poet – though one can hardly
call him great except in purpose and manhood – who sought
it constantly.

But here there is the difficulty of what Yeats means by 'natural'.
He opposes it to 'mind-created', which is obviously much the fitter
word for the constructions of Denham and Pope. . . .

H. M. McLuhan selects two lines by Pope to illustrate how the
couplet can contrive a main plot and a sub-plot:

The hungry judges soon the sentence sign,
And wretches hang that jurymen may dine.
(*The Rape of the Lock*, III 21–2)

Here there is proximity in sense in so far as (the rhyme suggests) the
signing of a death-warrant and eating one's dinner are actions equally
momentous to the coarsened and dehumanized mind. But here the
rhyme only clinches an effect prepared by the syntax; if the sub-plot
is a parallel to the main plot, obviously the climax of the one is
likely to resemble the climax of the other. And this is only a particularly obvious example. Professor W. K. Wimsatt, in a sustained and
admirable analysis of Pope's rhyming, shows that such an exercise
becomes inevitably an analysis of syntax – 'In fact, words have no
character as rhymes, until they become points in a syntactic succession.'[1]
In other words, articulation by rhyme depends upon syntax as much
as articulation by images.

Hugh Kenner

from 'In the Wake of the Anarch', *Gnomon*   1958

Pope was aware, with more than Yeatsian lucidity, that in his lifetime
millennial traditions were suddenly fading. The Universal Darkness

1 W. K. Wimsatt, 'One Relation of Rhyme to Reason', in *The Verbal Icon*,
University of Kentucky Press, 1954, p. 156 [see pp. 345–55 above].

into which he gazed with such prophetic horror was no mere sensational reflex of a provincial inability to grasp the mutability of cultures. Misled by a look of gradualness, however, we suppose that he was misled. When Mr Eliot reminded us that the eighteenth century was 'like any other age', an age of transition, he was speaking of its poetic sensibility, which 'alters from generation to generation, whether we will or no', impelled by the accumulation of events, retarded by the tenacity of human habit, not a seismograph to register intellectual cataclysms but a turbid fluid medium of awareness holding in suspension their settling dust. The gradual downward sloping of the arts into the Romantic century misleads us into supposing that Pope's age modulated into Shenstone's just as Dryden's modulated into Pope's; but to approach history through poetry anthologies, with an ear for the morphology of sensibility, is to apprehend not events but their protracted reverberations. Scholarly ears, attuned to this mull of sound, readily suppose that when Pope spoke of Art after Art going out he was 'exaggerating magnificently' (as his Twickenham editor puts it) the death of an age which he refused to believe was like all ages mortal: a first trombonist standing up in the pit to announce the extinction of music because the phrases allotted for the passage of which he bore the burden were drawing to a close.

Yet it is easy to show that he was not exaggerating: the proof is that Pope himself became in fifty years all but unintelligible. His editors could not read him; his commentators cannot read him. Though our dictionaries contain all his words and our handbooks all his allusions, his poems have grown as inaccessible as (to exaggerate magnificently) those of the Etruscans. We are situated, since the Romantic explosion, on another planet; in the finale to The Dunciad we intuit a desperate vatic urgency and applaud a pomp of sound, but suppose that the same thing is being said over and over. On the contrary: a most precise analysis goes forward, according to premises desperately in need of recovery.

She comes! She comes! the sable throne behold
Of night primeval and of chaos old!
Before her, fancy's gilded clouds decay,
And all its varying rainbows die away.
Wit shoots in vain its momentary fires. . . .

The light that is being negated is no mere blurry metaphor for intelligence, but an illumination whose modes of operation are conceived with speculative exactness. Fancy stands in relation to it as sunset colours and rainbows to the sun – the clouds and raindrops not objects made visible but pretexts for a tenuous virtuosity of the luminescent principle itself, to be anticipated (Coleridge, Shelley) just after the full light has vanished. Wit in its absence is condemned to be self-luminous and transient, a fugitive display (Byron, Peacock) –

The meteor drops, in a flash expires.

The sun of learning has set before, but in a previous Dark Age the stars held their places; an Erigena put Greek tags in his verses, a stray monk took bearings from Virgil. But this time the primal light itself is being withdrawn from all things luminous:

As one by one, at dread Medea's strain,
The sickening stars fade off th' ethereal plain,
As Argus' eyes, by Hermes' wand oppressed,
Closed one by one to everlasting rest,
Thus at her felt approach, and secret might,
Art after art goes out, and all is night. . . .

The arts are stars as civilization's steering marks, flowers as its products and ornaments, eyes as its guardians; now the flowers fade, the eyes close, the very stars are occulted. Hermes, the undoing of the many-eyed Argus, was the god of luck and wealth, the patron of merchants and of thieves – in Pope's usage, emblem of the opacities of commerce. The booksellers and the money-spinners of the City are among the efficient causes of *The Dunciad*'s action.

The 'Universal Darkness' that buries all is therefore a negation of a universal light concerning whose functioning Pope was willing to be more specific than elocutionists suppose. We hear about it, in fact, as early as the *Essay on Criticism*, published when he was too young (twenty-three) to have done any more than intuit a set of regnant intellectual conventions.

Unerring nature, still divinely bright,
One clear, unchanged, and universal light,

Life, force, and beauty must to all impart,
At once the source, and end, and test of art. . . .
(70–73)

This Light comes, by a long tradition, out of St John's gospel; it
shone in the darkness and the darkness did not comprehend it, it was
in the beginning with God, and it was the Word, the Logos which
the Romans, lacking a single term, denominated as *ratio et oratio*.

In some fair body thus th' informing soul
With spirits feeds, with vigour fills the whole,
Each motion guides, and every nerve sustains;
Itself unseen, but in th' effects remains.
(76–9)

These passages, to be sure, are flaccid gestures toward the conventional
– but a lost convention. The identity of the Universal Light and the
Universal Reason was a commonplace of a thousand sermons; St
Augustine's doctrine of human knowledge, never abandoned from
the fourth century to the Cambridge Platonists, turns on this identity.
The Holy Spirit, furthermore, stood to the world in the same
relation as the human soul to the body; hence a tissue of analogies
whereby the polysemous 'Nature', divine, human, and created, could
be 'at once the source, and end, and test' of a human activity which
paralleled that of the Divine Artificer. All this, by Pope's time, had
come to be believed 'in memory only, reconsidered passion'; and
Pope for his part reports no visions of the light, though he talks about
it with a born paraphraser's suavity. He has nothing comparable to
Dante's

Chè la mia vista, venendo sincera,
e più e più intrava per lo raggio
dell' altra luce che da se e vera,

or even Mr Pound's

that the body of light come forth
            from the body of fire. . . .

He handled the ideas that were in circulation, and rubbed them
smoother; he was content enough in Locke's ambience, and allowed
Bolingbroke credit as a philosopher, and wrote about

strong connexions, nice dependencies,
Gradations just.
(*Essay on Man*, I 30–31)

What rouses him to visionary intensity isn't metaphysical radiance
but the processional triumph of obfuscation:

She comes! She comes! . . .

The Dunciad, as Mr Aubrey Williams shows in his well-mannered,
vastly informative study,[1] plays its energies on a process of thickening
and fattening, perceived with hallucinatory particularity: literature
inertly copied from other literature, drama no longer aspiring to
conceive with austre passion an action like a moving arrow, plunging
instead into stupefying sensation, the stage manager rather than the
dramatist 'immortal';[2] the prestige of learning become an inducement for pedagogy to ally itself with advertisement and scholarship
to agitate itself like a tireless worm:

Let standard-authors, thus, like trophies born,
Appear more glorious as more hacked and torn,
And you, my critics! in the chequered shade,
Admire new light through holes yourselves have made.
Leave not a foot of verse, a foot of stone,
A page, a grave, that they can call their own.
(IV 123–8)

It is a terrible, compelling apocalypse, and when its detractors complain of spleen its champions have found nothing better to do than
concede exaggeration, albeit magnificent.

One would never guess from Mr Williams's genteel manner that

1 *Pope's Dunciad, A Study of Its Meaning*, 1955.
2 'Immortal Rich! how calm he sits at ease
'Mid snows of paper, and fierce hail of pease;
And proud his mistress' orders to perform
Rides in the whirlwind, and directs the storm.'
(IV 261–4)
As for the spectator, he goggles like a tourist in Radio City:
'Joy fills his soul, joy innocent of thought;
"What power," he cries, "what power these wonders wrought?"'
(IV 249–50)

he had walked into the professional Popeans' Natchez-Augustan manor with the components of a time bomb under his raincoat. Possibly he doesn't guess it either. In his first two chapters he appears to be setting up the equipment for a lantern lecture, complete with map. The impatient reader may well start on the last four chapters, which are informative enough to discontent the lecturer's tone; and then reflect that the large perspectives of learning there afforded may well be more systematically accessible to Mr Williams's generation than they were to Pope's. As one may sail along coasts without a map, or any idea of what a map would look like, so a reader living in Pope's age would have encountered the capes and headlands of the poem with a readiness of habitual response which the historian, mistaking tradition for doctrine, can extrapolate into a statement of principle the Augustan might not have recognized. The way to profit by Mr Williams's exposition is to transpose it into the specific assumptions behind Pope's local devices.

The chief technical device in *The Dunciad* is to mime perversity by systematically perverting what we are meant to recognize as the normative images of orderly encomium. Bentley's great paean to the scholars affords a condensed instance:

Like buoys, that never sink into the flood –

his learning a mark to steer by, he and his fellows fixed points amid tempests and opinions; it seems a neatly predictable image, until the dénouement –

On learning's surface we but lie and nod.
(IV 241-2)

In the passage about standard-authors, the first couplet perverts into Yahooesque jubilation the regimental pride and orderly decorum of armies, the second into simian self-congratulation a tranquil pietism about the fullness of age. We are meant to recall how Waller had written,

The soul's dark cottage, battered and decayed,
Lets in new light through chinks that time has made;

but the plenitude of senescent wisdom gives way to its parody, the annotator's idiotic delight that new beams penetrate a text (which before his arrival on the scene had been merely an impediment to the light) every time his forefinger punches a hole in it.

Pope's way of moving mock earths requires his taking a stand on such minimal and cliché-ridden orderliness as can still be evoked; he postulates the intelligibility of created things, the normality of their symbolic functions, the rationality of poetic images. We hear much about the aptness of his literary parody; but the literary order upon the prestige of which Pope depends for so many effects isn't to his mind venerable because it happens to exist, but radiant because sanctioned by those very analogies between divine and human intelligence which permit and render fructive the ready resemblances between wise men and seamarks, light and intelligence, the playwright and God; which enable the writer to see in ordonnance an image of order, to co-operate with his material rather than fight it, and make with ease intelligible statements about the intelligible – which in short reveal a world interesting enough to write about.

When no one believed such things any longer, no one could read in depth what had been so written. The mind coming close slips over Pope's mirrorlike surface, and drawing back sees reflected there its own banalities. 'Not a classic of our poetry,' said Arnold, 'a classic of our prose.' Pope opened his Fourth Book with a prophetic apostrophe to the powers of oblivion:

Ye powers! whose mysteries restored I sing,
To whom time bears me on his rapid wing,
Suspend a while your force inertly strong,
Then take at once the poet and the song.

It was so: a criticism which assumed that the writer situated before an opaque world expressed only himself transformed Pope into a spiteful little hunchback.

J. S. Cunningham

from *Pope: The Rape of the Lock*   1961

'A poem on a slight subject requires the greatest care to make it considerable enough to be read.' When Pope made this remark to his friend Joseph Spence, he had (it seems) *The Dunciad* chiefly in mind; and recent criticism of that poem has dwelt on the meticulous and often furtive care with which Pope, while apparently preoccupied with the ephemera, the sweepings and nonentities of Grub Street and Fleet Ditch, attempts to persuade us of their paradoxical importance as symptoms of a widespread, perhaps irretrievable decline in civilized standards. The duncos act out their grossly comic *charade* on a stage which reverberates with mutilated hints, distorted echoes, of very 'considerable' things – classical epic, the Scriptures, Milton. As embodiments of the reductive will, defacers of the ideals these echoes call to mind, the dunces attain in the poem an unenviable significance far beyond their mere status in Pope's London. Conversely, as the posturing mimics of nobler figures, they are dwarfed by their own pretensions. This double activity of inflation and deflation, through which the dunces are at once below consideration *and* a serious menace, Pope achieves in so far as he contrives to expose the trivial by insinuation, allusion and parody – in so far as he 'implies and projects the possible other case, the case rich and edifying where the actuality is pretentious and vain' (Henry James, *The Lesson of the Master*).

Marshall McLuhan

from *The Gutenberg Galaxy*   1962

Pope's Dunciad indicts the printed book as the agent of a primitivistic and Romantic revival. Sheer visual quantity evokes the magical resonance of the tribal horde. The box office looms as a return to the echo chamber of bardic incantation.

In 1683–4 there appeared in London by Joseph Moxon, *Mechanic Exercises on the Whole Art of Printing*. The editors point out (p. vii) that 'it put in writing a knowledge that was wholly traditional', and that Moxon's book 'was by forty years the earliest manual of printing in any language'. Like Gibbon in his retrospect of Rome, Moxon seems to have been animated by a sense of print as having reached a terminus. A similar sentiment inspires *The Tale of a Tub* and *The Battle of the Books* by Dean Swift. But it is to *The Dunciad* that we must turn for the epic of the printed word and its benefits to mankind. For here is the explicit study of plunging of the human mind into the sludge of an unconscious engendered by the book. It has been obscured to posterity, in keeping with the prophecy at the end of Book IV, just why literature should be charged with stupefying mankind, and mesmerically ushering the polite world back into primitivism, the Africa within, and above all, the unconscious. The simple key to this operation is that which we have had in hand throughout this book – the increasing separation of the visual faculty from the interplay with the other senses leads to the rejection from consciousness of most of our experience, and the consequent hypertrophy of the unconscious. This ever-enlarging domain Pope calls the world 'of chaos and old night'. It is the tribal, non-literate world celebrated by Mircea Eliade in *The Sacred and the Profane*.

Martinus Scriblerus in his notes to *The Dunciad* reflects on how much more difficult it is to write an epic about the numerous scribblers and industrious hacks of the press than about a Charlemagne, a Brute, or a Godfrey. He then mentions the need for a satirist 'to dissuade the dull and punish the wicked', and looks at the general situation that has brought on the crisis:

We shall next declare the occasion and the cause which moved our poet to this particular work. He lived in those days when (after providence had permitted the invention of printing as a scourge for the sins of the learned) paper also became so cheap, and printers so numerous, that a deluge of authors covered the land: whereby not only the peace of the honest unwriting subject was daily molested, but unmerciful demands were made of his applause, yea, of his money, by such as would neither earn the one or deserve the other. At the same time, the liberty of the press was so unlimited that it grew dangerous to refuse them either: for they would forthwith publish slanders unpunished, the authors being anonymous; nay the immediate publishers thereof lay skulking under the wings of an Act of Parliament, assuredly intended for better purposes.

Next he turns . . . from the general economic causes to the private moral motivation of authors inspired by 'dullness and poverty; the one born with them, the other contracted by neglect of their proper talents. . . .' In a word, the attack is on applied knowledge as it manifests itself in 'industry' and 'plodding'. For authors inspired by self-opinion and the craving for self-expression are driven into 'setting up this sad and sorry merchandise'.

By means of the agglomerate action of many such victims of applied knowledge – that is, self-opinionated authors endowed with industry and plodding – there is now the restoration of the reign of chaos and old night and the 'removal of the imperial seat of Dullness their daughter from the city to the polite world'. As the book market expands, the division between intellect and commerce ends. The book trade takes over the functions of wit and spirit and government.

That is the meaning of the opening lines of the first editions of the poem:

Books and the man I sing, the first who brings
The Smithfield muses to the ears of kings.

It seemed quite unnatural to the 'polite world' of the time that decision-making and kingly rule should be accessible to popular authors. We no longer consider it odd or revolting to be ruled by people for whom the book of the month might appear quite respectable fare. Smithfield, where Bartholomew Fair was kept, was still a place for book-peddling. But in later editions Pope changed the opening:

The mighty mother, and her son who brings
The Smithfield muses to the ear of kings. . . .

He has encountered the public, the collective unconscious, and dubbed it 'the mighty mother', in accordance with the occultism of his time. It is Joyce's 'Lead kindly Fowl' (foule, owl, crowd), which we have seen earlier.

As the book market enlarged and the gathering and reporting of news improved, the nature of authorship and public underwent the great changes that we accept as normal today. The book had retained from manuscript times some of its private and conversational character, as Leibniz indicated in his evaluation. But the book was beginning to be merged in the newspaper, as the work of Addison and Steele reminds us. Improved printing technology carried this process all the way by the end of the eighteenth century and the arrival of the steam press.

Yet Dudek in *Literature and the Press* (p. 46) considers that even after steampower had been applied to printing:

English newspapers in the first quarter of the century,
however, were by no means designed to appeal to the whole
population. By modern standards they would be considered
too dull to interest more than a small minority of serious
readers. . . . Early-nineteenth-century newspapers were run
largely for the genteel. Their style was stiff and formal,
ranging between Addisonian gracefulness and Johnsonian
elevation. The contents consisted of small advertisements, of
local affairs and national politics, especially of commercial
news and long transcriptions of parlimentary reports. . . . the
best current literature was noticed in the newspapers. . . . 'In
those days', Charles Lamb recalled, 'every morning paper,
as an essential retainer to its establishment, kept an author,
who was bound to furnish daily a quantum of witty
paragraphs. . . .' And since the divorce between the language
of journalism (journalese) and the literary use of language
had not yet been brought about, we find in the eighteenth
and early nineteenth century that some of the principal men
of letters contributed to the newspapers or made a living by
writing.

But Pope peopled his *Dunciad* with these very figures, for his perceptions and criticisms were not personal or based on a private point of view. Rather he was concerned with a total change. It is significant that this change is not specified until the fourth book of *The Dunciad*, which came out in 1742. It is after introducing the famous classics master, Dr Busby of Westminster School, that we hear the ancient and especially Ciceronian theme concerning the excellence of man (IV 147–50):

The pale boy-senator yet tingling stands,
And holds his breeches close with both his hands.
Then thus: 'Since man from beast by words is known,
Words are man's province, words we teach alone.'

Earlier we had noted the meaning of this theme for Cicero who regarded eloquence as an inclusive wisdom, harmonizing our faculties, unifying all knowledge. Pope is here quite explicit in citing the destruction of this unity as deriving from word specialism and denudation. The theme of the denudation of consciousness we have followed continuously throughout the Renaissance. It is also the theme of Pope's *Dunciad*. The boy-senator continues:

When reason doubtful, like the Samian letter,
Points him two ways, the narrower is the better.
Placed at the door of learning, youth to guide,
We never suffer it to stand too wide.
To ask, to guess, to know, as they commence,
As fancy opens the quick springs of sense,
We ply the memory, we load the brain,
Bind rebel wit, and double chain on chain,
Confine the thought, to exercise the breath;
And keep them in the pale of words till death.
Whate'er the talents, or howe'er designed,
We hang one jingling padlock on the mind.
A poet the first day, he dips his quill;
And what the last? a very poet still.
Pity! the charm works only in our wall,
Lost, lost too soon in yonder house or hall.

Pope has not received his due as a serious analyst of the intellectual *malaise* of Europe. He continues Shakespeare's argument in *Lear* and Donne's in the *Anatomy of the World*:

'Tis all in pieces, all coherence gone,
All just supply and all relation.

It is the division of sense and the separation of words from their functions that Pope decries exactly as does Shakespeare in *King Lear*. Art and science had been separated as visual quantification and homogenization penetrated to every domain and the mechanization of language and literature proceeded:

Beneath her foot-stool science groans in chains,
And wit dreads exile, penalties and pains.
There foamed rebellious logic.) gagged and bound,
There, stripped, rhetoric langushed on the ground. . . .
(*The Dunciad*, IV 21–4)

*The new collective unconscious Pope saw as the
accumulating backwash of private self-expression.*

Pope had a very simple scheme for his first three books. Book I deals with authors, their egotism and desire for self-expression and eternal fame. Book II turns to the booksellers who provide the conduits to swell the tides of public confession. Book III concerns the collective unconscious, the growing backwash from the tidal wave of self-expression. It is Pope's simple theme that the fogs of Dullness and new tribalism are fed by the printing press. Wit, the quick interplay among our senses and faculties, is thus steadily anaesthetized by the encroaching unconscious. Anybody who tried to get Pope's meaning by considering the content of the writers he presents would miss the needed clues. Pope is offering a formal causality, not an efficient causality, as an explanation of the metamorphosis from within. The entire matter is thus to be found in a single couplet (I, 89–90):

Now night descending, the proud scene was o'er
But lived in Settle's numbers one day more.

Print, with its uniformity, repeatability, and limitless extent, does give reincarnate life and fame to anything at all. The kind of limp life so conferred by dull heads upon dull themes formalistically penetrates all existence. Since readers are as vain as authors, they crave to view their own conglomerate visage and, therefore, demand the dullest wits to exert themselves in ever greater degree as the collective audience increases. The 'human interest' newspaper is the ultimate mode of this collective dynamic:

Now mayors and shrieves all hushed and satiate lay,
Yet eat, in dreams, the custard of the day;
While pensive poets painful vigils keep,
Sleepless themselves to give their readers sleep.
(191-4)

Of course, Pope does not mean that the readers will be bored by the products of sleepless poets or news-writers. Quite the contrary. They will be thrilled, as by seeing their own image in the press. The readers' sleep is of the spirit. In their wits they are not pained but impaired.

Pope is telling the English world what Cervantes had told the Spanish world and Rabelais the French world concerning print. It is a delirium. It is a transforming and metamorphosing drug that has the power of imposing its assumptions upon every level of consciousness. But for us in the 1960s, print has much of the quaint receding character of the movie and the railway train. In recognizing its hidden powers at this late date we can learn to stress the positive virtues of print but we can gain insight into the much more potent and recent forms of radio and television also.

In his analysis of books, authors, and markets, Pope, like Harold Innis in *The Bias of Communication*, assumes that the entire operation of print in our lives is not only unconscious but that for this very reason it immeasurably enlarges the domain of the unconscious. Pope placed an owl at the beginning of *The Dunciad*, and Innis entitled the opening chapter of *The Bias of Communication*, 'Minerva's Owl'; 'Minerva's Owl begins its flight only in the gathering dusk. . . .'

Aubrey Williams has a fine treatment[1] of the second *Dunciad* of 1729 in which he quotes Pope's own words to Swift:

The Dunciad is going to be printed in all pomp. . . . It will
be attended with *Proeme, Prolegomena, Testimonia Scriptorum,
Index Authorum*, and Notes *Variorum*. As to the latter, I desire
you to read over the text, and make a few in any way you
like best, whether dry raillery, upon the style and way of
commenting of trivial critics; or humorous, upon the authors
in the poem; or historical, of persons, places, times; or
explanatory; or collecting the parallel passages of the ancients.

1 *Pope's Dunciad* (1955), p. 60.

Instead, that is, of a mere individual book attack on Dullness, Pope has provided a collective newspaper format and much 'human interest' for the poem. He can thus render the plodding industry of Baconian applied knowledge and group toil with a dramatic quality that renders, yet irradiates, the very Dullness he decries. Williams points out (p. 60) that the reason why 'the new material attached to the poem has never been adequately defined is due, I think, to the assumptions most critics and editors have made: that the notes are to be taken at the level of history, and that their main purpose is to continue the personal satire in a prose commentary.'

The last book of The Dunciad *proclaims the metamorphic power of mechanically applied knowledge as a stupendous parody of the Eucharist.*

The entire fourth book of *The Dunciad* has to do with the theme of *The Gutenberg Galaxy*, the translation or reduction of diverse modes into a single mode of homogenized things. Right off (lines 44–5), this theme is rendered in terms of the new Italian opera,

When lo! a harlot form soft sliding by,
With mincing step, small voice, and languid eye;

In the new chromatics, Pope finds (lines 57–60) the all-reducing and homogenizing power that the book exercises on the human spirit:

One trill shall harmonize joy, grief, and rage,
Wake the dull church, and lull the ranting stage;
To the same notes thy sons shall hum, or snore,
And all thy yawning daughters cry, *encore*.

Reduction and metamorphosis by homogenization and fragmentation are the persistent themes of the fourth book (lines 453–6):

O! would the sons of men once think their eyes
And reason giv'n them but to study *flies*!
See nature in some partial narrow shape,
And let the author of the whole escape:

But these were the means by which, as Yeats tells us:

Locke sank into a swoon;
The Garden died;
God took the spinning jenny
Out of his side.

The popular mesmerism achieved by uniformity and repeatability, taught men the miracles of the division of labour and the creation of world markets. It is these miracles that Pope anticipates in *The Dunciad*, for their transforming power had long affected the mind. The mind [is] now afflicted with the desire and power to climb by sheer sequential additive toil:

Why all your toils? Your sons have learned to sing.
How quick ambition hastes to ridicule!
The sire is made a peer, the son a fool.

Then follows a decisive passage of explicit comment (lines 549–57) on the Gutenberg miracles of applied knowledge and human transformation:

On some, a priest succinct in amice white
Attends; all flesh is nothing in his sight!
Beeves, at his touch, at once to jelly turn,
And the huge boar is shrunk into an urn:
The board with specious miracles he loads,
Turns hares to larks, and pigeons into toads.
Another (for in all what one can shine?)
Explains the *seve* and *verdeur* of the vine.
What cannot copious sacrifice atone?

Pope deliberately makes the miracles of applied knowledge a parody of the Eucharist. It is the same transforming and reducing power of applied knowledge which has confounded and confused all the arts and sciences, for, says Pope, the new *translatio studii* or transmission of studies and disciplines by the printed book has not been so much a transmission as a complete transformation of the disciplines and of the human mind as well. Studies have been translated exactly as was Bottom the Weaver.

How closely Pope's progress of Dullness over the earth conforms to the concept of *translatio studii* can be seen easily if

lines 65–112 of *Dunciad*, III, are compared to this statement
of the historic theme by an English humanist of the fourteenth
century, Richard de Bury: 'Admirable Minerva seems to
bend her course to all the nations of the earth, and reacheth
from end to end mightily, that she may reveal herself to all
mankind. We see that she has already visited the Indians, the
Babylonians, the Egyptians and Greeks, the Arabs and the
Romans. Now she has passed by Paris, and now has happily
come to Britain, the most noble of islands, nay, rather a
microcosm in itself, that she may show herself a debtor both
to the Greeks and to the Barbarians.'
(Aubrey Williams, *Pope's 'Dunciad'*, p. 47)

And Pope in making Dullness the goddess of the unconscious is
contrasting her with Minerva, goddess of alert intellect and wit. It is
not Minerva but her obverse complement, the owl, that the printed
book has conferred on Western man. 'However ill-fitting their
heroic garb,' Williams remarks (p. 59), 'one at last finds the dunces
invested with uncivilizing powers of epic proportions.'

Supported by the Gutenberg technology, the power of the dunces
to shape and befog the human intellect is unlimited. Pope's efforts to
clarify this basic point have been in vain. His intense concern with the
pattern of action in his armed horde of nobodies has been mistaken for
personal spite. Pope was entirely concerned with the *formalistic pattern*
and penetrative and configuring power of the new technology. His
readers have been befogged by 'content' obsession and the practical
benefits of applied knowledge. He says in a note to Book III, 337:

Do not, gentle reader, rest too secure in thy contempt of the
instruments for such a revolution in learning, or despise such
weak agents as have been described in our poem, but
remember what the Dutch stories somewhere relate, that a
great part of their provinces was once overflowed by a small
opening made in one of their dykes by a single water-rat.

But the new mechanical instrument and its mesmerized and homogenized servants, the dunces, are irresistible:

In vain, in vain – the all-composing hour
Resistless falls; the Muse obeys the power.

She comes! She comes! the sable throne behold
Of night primeval and of chaos old!
Before her, fancy's gilded clouds decay,
And all its varying rainbows die away.
Wit shoots in vain its momentary fires,
The meteor drops, and in a flash expires.
As one by one, at dread Medea's strain,
The sickening stars fade off th' ethereal plain;
As Argus' eyes, by Hermes' wand oppressed,
Closed one by one to everlasting rest,
Thus at her felt approach, and secret might,
Art after art goes out, and all is night.
See skulking truth to her old cavern fled,
Mountains of casuistry heaped o'er her head!
Philosophy, that leaned on heaven before,
Shrinks to her second cause, and is no more.
Physic of metaphysic begs defence,
And metaphysic calls for aid on sense!
See mystery to mathematics fly!
In vain! They gaze, turn giddy, rave, and die.
Religion, blushing, veils her sacred fires,
And unawares morality expires.
Nor public flame nor private dares to shine;
Nor human spark is left, nor glimpse divine!
Lo! thy dread empire, Chaos! is restored;
Light dies before thy uncreating word.
Thy hand, great anarch! lets the curtain fall;
And universal darkness buries all.

This is the night from which Joyce invites the Finnegans to Wake.

Winifred Nowottny

from *The Language Poets Use*   1962

[Leigh Hunt] sums up his case against Pope's versification with the words, 'this kind of sing-song'.[1] The sing-song effect (if this is

1 For fuller quotation of Hunt's attack, and discussion of it, see Geoffrey Tillotson, *Pope and Human Nature*, Oxford University Press, 1958, pp. 182–8.

indeed a proper description of the effect of having a marked pause after the fourth syllable of the line in each successive line) is confined to the group of lines beginning with 'On her white breast . . .' and ending at '. . . you'll forget 'em all' (*The Rape of the Lock*, II 7–18); the six lines which in Hunt's quotation precede these, do not in fact show the same feature, and after '. . . you'll forget 'em all' the placing of the pause is again varied. It is, certainly, striking to find a solid block of lines displaying no variation in the placing of the caesura; more striking that these lines constitute one unit (the description of Belinda's person and demeanour), before and after which there is no comparable monotony of caesura: more striking still that this unit displays 'an additional monotony', the inversion in four contiguous lines of the first foot of the line. It would almost seem that the poet had gone out of his way to be repetitious in his versification, and it is possible to see in the nature of his subject-matter a good reason why he should have done so, for the sense itself invites us to infer that beneath the outward animation of Belinda's looks there lies a level imperviousness, the even-handed indifference of the enthroned beauty to her rout of admirers; the critic may then conclude that the monotonies of this passage (in diction so animated) are contrived, and are intended to be a metrical equivalent to Belinda's indifference. If this seems a speculation too generous to Pope, we must at least admit that he himself devises as the climax of this ironically animated passage a line which explicitly says that, glorious as Belinda is, her condescension is perhaps as meaningless as it is universal:

[Bright as the sun her eyes the gazers strike,]
And like the sun they shine on all alike

–a line whose diction seems to aim at an ultimate in banality. Not content with the explicit 'all alike', Pope selects a banal simile ('Sun' for favour) and has the sun do the the least original thing possible (it does not beam, blaze, or glow – it merely shines), and to complete the obviousness the last word of the line ('alike') chimes with the second (like') and its dullness is emphasized by the force of the word with which it rhymes ('strike'). Would it not be ungenerous to Pope to suppose that he could, without conscious contrivance, arrive at a diction of such bland nullity?

Pope's intentions may be irrecoverable and, as some would hold, irrelevant in considering the actual merits of the passage, but the attempt to take a bearing on his treatment of metrics by reference to his treatment of diction and rhyme, and to relate the metrics, the diction and the rhyme to the explicit sense of the passage, may serve to make the point that the sense borne by a passage is closely related to the technicalities of the medium and also to make the further point that any attempt to relate the thing done to the manner of doing it rapidly involves the critic in a desperate scamper to keep pace in prose words with the articulateness of the poet's manifold techniques. Poetry's means of imitating the thing it talks of go far beyond what Pope called 'style of sound' (complex though that, in his hands, was) and they include the poetic management of linguistic necessities not peculiar to poems, as rhyme and metre are. . . .

. . . In many cases there will prove to be a fruitful interplay between syntactical relations and other formal systems – as for instance the rhyme-scheme. This is so in Pope's well-known lines (*Pastorals*, II 73–6):

Where'er you walk, cool gales shall fan the glade,
Trees, where you sit, shall crowd into a shade,
Where'er you tread, the blushing flowers shall rise,
And all things flourish where you turn your eyes.

Here the management of the rhymes cannot be fully appreciated unless one relates them to the flow and ebb of expectations set up by skilful management of syntax. The first of these lines balances almost the pause after 'walk'; before the pause comes the human action, after it the effect on Nature. The second line repeats this strong pause but introduces a syntactical variation: 'Trees' (which corresponds syntactically to 'cool glades') is put first in the line and is further emphasized by an irregular strong stresss; 'where you sit', which follows, makes us expect that this second line will in some way repeat the pattern of the first. So we expect to be told what the trees will do, and because we are made to wait for the verb, this expectation becomes a felt desire for the completion of the pattern – a desire which is then not only satisfied but amply satisfied when the pattern expands ('shall crowd into') and then returns to rest when 'a shade' brings this line into correspondence with 'the glade' in the line before. The opening of the third reaffirms the formula of the opening of the first, with the words 'Where'er you tread', and one interprets this as a recapitulation of theme that must lead to a further variation. When that variation does come ('the blushing flowers'), it provides at the same time a dilation of that element of the pattern which had contrasted in the previous line (where 'Trees' had replaced 'cool glades'). This third line does not, like the second, return to rest, for it ends with 'shall rise'; here there is no counterpart to 'the glade', 'a shade'. The fourth line is a complex and surprising resolution of this crisis in the pattern. First it sums into a satisfactory climax the sequence 'gales'–'Trees'–'flowers' with the phrase 'And all things'. The following verb, however, still leaves unsatisfied our wish for a counterpart to 'glade' and 'shade'. Delayed thus, the urge to fulfilment is stronger, and to it is added the pressure of expectation of a counterpart to 'Where[-e'er] you walk/sit/tread'. Suddenly both demands are fulfilled simultaneously: the latter in 'where you turn your eyes', the former in the fact that *this* phrase now provides the transitive verb and the object, so that 'you turn your eyes' is a return to the syntactical pattern of the second half of the first line ('cool gales shall fan the glade'; subject–verb–object) and at the same time it brings the quatrain to an end by neatly reversing the initial disposition of the two major parts of the overall pattern:

Where'er you walk,   cool gales shall fan the glade,

· · · · · · ╳ · · · · · ·

And all things flourish   where you turn your eyes.

It is only with respect to these manipulations of expectancy that one can estimate the art shown in the rhymes. The rhyme 'glade'/'shade' is unsurprising[1] (it rhymes noun with noun, the nouns naming comparable things) and this is suitable for this point in the pattern (for here the second line returns to rest); in contrast, the rhyme 'rise'/'eyes' more surprisingly rhymes a verb with a noun, and the verb occupies a position on the crest of a wave of expectancy whereas the noun occupies such a position in the pattern that it resolves all the remaining expectations of the poem in a simultaneous fulfilment. Moreover it

1 For discussion of Pope's interest in telling rhymes (seen in his concern to rhyme different parts of speech, and words from different semantic spheres) see W. K. Wimsatt, *The Verbal Icon* (Lexington, Kentucky, 1954) and pp. 345–55 above.

is only with respect to all this activity with patterns of rhyme and syntax that one can estimate the fitness of the diction for its purposes. Such a diction, worn smooth with use, has no anfractuosities to distract us from the witty evolution of the patterns I have discussed; its unruffled surface is almost a necessary condition of our being set at ease to follow the patterns moving beneath it with such agile assurance.

Donald Davie

from *The Language of Science and the Language of Literature,*
1700–1740   1963

The particular range of puns which Empson isolates accounts for a great deal of the wittiest writing in the anti-mechanist tradition. Take the word 'profundity'. By relying implicitly on the truthfulness of etymology, we get an irrefragable chain of logic: 'Profound' is 'deep'; to go deep is to sink; lead sinks fastest; therefore the most profound thinkers are the most leaden. This is the logic behind that elaborate spoof of the Scriblerus Club, *The Art of Sinking in Poetry, or a Treatise of the Bathos*. 'Bathos' represents an extension of the same logic from Latin etymology into Greek, and comes up with the surprising conclusion that the most profound writers are the most bathetic. Conversely, 'elevation'. 'Elevation' is 'rising high'; what rises high is levity; nothing rises so high as balloons, which are bags of wind; therefore the most elevated writers are the biggest windbags or those who display most levity. Once admit that there is no gulf fixed between the material and the immaterial worlds (which was the admission that Locke demanded), and the reasoning is impregnable.

   It is doubtless no accident that a moving spirit behind *The Memoirs of Martinus Scriblerus* was Dr John Arbuthnot, the Queen's physician, whom we have met already as the author of an *Essay on Aliments*. The baffling ambiguity in the terminology of contemporary medicine, an ambiguity which we illustrated from that work, would not be lost on a man like Arbuthnot, who combined the physician and the man of letters. Out of the Scriblerus Club, where Pope and Swift were Arbuthnot's associates, and out of 'The Memoirs of Martinus

Scriblerus', came both *Gulliver's Travels* and *The Dunciad*. And so it is no surprise that the pun on 'profundity', for instance, is constantly in evidence in Pope's poem. His duncies, you recall, are led to profundity, that is, to the bottom of the Thames, by the leaden weight of their own stupidity:

Not so bold Arnall; with a weight of skull,
Furious he dives, precipitately dull.
Whirlpools and storms his circling arm invest,
With all the might of gravitation blest.
No crab more active in the dirty dance,
Downward to climb, and backward to advance.
He brings up half the bottom on his head,
And loudly claims the journals and the lead.

This is from Book II [315–22]; there is the same pun in Book IV [75–80], when the duncies are attracted to their mother-goddess, Dullness, by 'strong impulsive gravity of head':

None needs a guide, by sure attraction led,
And strong impulsive gravity of head;
None want a place, for all their centre found,
Hung to the goddess, and cohered around.
Not closer, orb in orb, conglobed are seen
The buzzing bees about their dusky queen.

'Gravity' is a particularly good example. Traditionally used to designate the spiritual quality of certain temperaments and personalities, it is forced back, when Newton with learned propriety adopts it to designate a principle of physics, upon its root meaning in Latin. 'Gravity' becomes 'weight'. And so, once again, a grave thinker becomes a leaden-footed thinker. His weightiness is all in his lack of buoyancy – one sees how the joke could be extended indefinitely. This is a much better pun than the one in Shakespeare about how, when someone is dead, he'll be a 'grave' man. For Shakespeare's pun is a matter of merely accidental likeness of sound, whereas Pope's feels back along the lines of etymological development to a genuine likeness of meanings. It is used to comic effect, yet the comedy has an edge to it. For it is refusing to take seriously a view of the relationship of the material to the supposedly immaterial, which was being taken very seriously indeed by many of Pope's contemporaries. It is therefore an extremely serious joke. And incidentally, in an age when physics was trying to explain all phenomena without exception by reference to the laws of motion, 'impulsive', the word that goes with 'gravity', partakes of the same crucial ambiguity. (28–31)

J. B. Broadbent

'The Rape of the Lock', from *Poetic Love* 1964

The Rape of the Lock (1712, expanded 1714) is the last poetic analysis of love in the courtly tradition. It is a satire on the very diminution that it practises as a satirical device. The heroic, glamorous, morally solemn events of romantic epic are shown to have dwindled, through the seventeenth century, to the febrile behaviour of a society whose rule is vanity. The mythology of Renaissance Christianity has become gnomes and sylphs attendant on a girl's toilet, as though Herrick were writing *Paradise Lost*. Spenser's portentous pageants become the Cave of Spleen. Battle is a game of ombre, rape the snipping of a hair. All this makes it irritating, and sometimes disheartening reading; but the poem is excellent because Pope is conscious that the relation is close between the satire and its object. Pope knew all the characters and was distantly related to some; the central incident occurred (but the Baron married someone else between the publication of the two versions). The subtle moral ironies are expressed in the idiom of the society they satirize, so there is no escape. But the satire is not disqualified by its own criticism because Pope exploits the social idiom, and his own poetic diction, very subtly, to simultaneously delineate and judge reality. And the satire is not superficial, merely of manners: being so verbal, it exposes an insidious corruption of fundamental concepts and sentiments.

For example, Sir Plume is a ludicrous figure:

Sir Plume, of amber snuff-box justly vain,
And the nice conduct of a clouded cane,
With earnest eyes, and round unthinking face,

He first the snuff-box opened, then the case,
And thus broke out – 'My lord! why, what the devil!
Zounds! damn the lock! 'fore God, you must be civil!
Plague on't! 'tis past a jest! – nay, prithee, pox!
Give her the hair!' – he spoke, and rapped his box.
(IV 123–30)

But his chaotic blah exposes an infection that is endemic to the
poem's society: the devil, damnation, God and civility are mixed
in moral disorder like Belinda's 'Puffs, powders, patches, Bibles,
billets-doux'; and pox infects her hair by association.

    The Baron's love is mock-heroic:

For this, ere Phoebus rose, he had implored
Propitious Heaven, and every power adored,
But chiefly love – to love an altar built
Of twelve vast French romances, neatly gilt.
There lay three garters, half a pair of gloves,
And all the trophies of his former loves;
With tender billets-doux he lights the pyre,
And breathes three amorous sighs to raise the fire.
(II 35–42)

But real epic mocks back. The Baron's love is a surrogate adventure,
a bookish and fetichistic vanity. The game, the garter, gloves and hair,
are his concern, not the girl herself.

    Belinda has no love; her attachment is to herself:

And now, unveiled, the toilet stands displayed,
Each silver vase in mystic order laid.
First, robed in white, the nymph intent adores,
With head uncovered, the cosmetic powers.
A heavenly image in the glass appears,
To that she bends, to that her eyes she rears;
Th' inferior priestess, at her altar's side,
Trembling begins the sacred rites of pride.
(I 121–8)

The satire of this passage works to and fro in literary history, at so
elevated a level that Belinda becomes the archetype of vanity. The

earliest analogue is Narcissus admiring himself in the pool, the latest,
Eliot's sterile neurotic in *A Game of Chess*:

The Chair she sat in, like a burnished throne,
Glowed on the marble, where the glass
Held up by standards wrought with fruited vines
From which a golden Cupidon peeped out
(Another hid his head beneath his wing)
Doubled the flame of sevenbranched candelabra
Reflecting light upon the table as
The glitter of her jewels rose to meet it.
(*Waste Land*, II)

This relates Belinda to the sexy sterility of the Bower of Bliss, with
its imitation fecundity ('wrought with fruited vines'); and back to
the idolatry (the candelabra belong to the Temple) of material goods
– her jewels – in Pope's description of 'the sacred rites'. It also makes
of her a shrivelled Cleopatra, bereft of gorgeous barge and breezes.
She is shamed – the hiding Cupidon. The other Cupidon, gold
mimicry of love, repeats a device of Pope's in his description of
Timon's villa, where

Two Cupids squirt before; a lake behind
Improves the keenness of the northern wind.
(*Moral Essays IV*, 111–12)

– the god of love can only piss, shivering by an artificial lake which
attracts not the fecundating zephyrs but the freezing blasts. But Pope's
Belinda is judged as well as analysed: between her and Narcissus is
Eve, who saw first her own reflection in a lake of Paradise:

It started back, but pleased I soon returned,
Pleased it returned as soon with answering looks
Of sympathy and love, there I had fixed
Mine eyes till now, and pined with vain desire,
Had not a voice thus warned me, What thou seest,
What there thou seest, fair creature, is thy self . . .
(*Paradise Lost* IV 463–8)

So Belinda's pride is that which caused the Fall.

Belinda encloses love in her personal vanity; and the vanity turns out to be not even sentimental, but commercial. The sylphs look after her and her kind:

> What guards the purity of melting maids,
> In courtly balls and midnight masquerades,
> Safe from the treacherous friend, the daring spark,
> The glance by day, the whisper in the dark?
> When kind occasion prompt their warm desires,
> When music softens, and when dancing fires?
> 'Tis but their sylph, the wise celestials know,
> Though honour is the word with men below.
> (i 71–8)

The verse just contains, and judges, the lubricity its words suggest – the accurate mixture of fiery and liquid response to incessant stimuli. What we call honour turns out to be a sylph – that is, either a non-existent fancy, or a celestial lady's maid: in either case, vanity, whether intellectual or physical. The sylphs of vanity attend especially to Belinda, in case

> the nymph shall break Diana's law,
> Or some frail china jar receive a flaw;
> Or stain her honour, or her new brocade,
> Forget her prayers or miss a masquerade.
> (ii 105–8)

The famous lines, in which zeugma operates as simile (to Belinda, prayers = masquerade), are more complex than they look. To break chastity (Diana's law) is equivalent, in Belinda's mind, to cracking a china jar. The point is made delicately, but it takes up a coarse idiom – to crack a jar meant to deflower; a frail was (still is, I believe, in parts of the USA) a prostitute. Gay explains the passage fully:

> When I some antique jar behold,
> Or white or blue or specked with gold,
> Vessels so pure and so refined
> Appear the type of womankind.
> *To a Lady, on her passion for old china*)

So far, compliment. But:

Are they not valued for their beauty,
Too fair, too fine, for household duty? . . .
How white, how polished, is their skin,
And valued most when only seen!

So Belinda is merely an ornament. But a valuable one:

She who before was highest prized,
Is for a crack or flaw despised.
I grant they're frail, yet they're so rare
The treasure cannot cost too dear!

In short, Belinda's chastity has only ornamental value; and, as an ornament, it has a price. Pope takes it even further. Belinda equates her honour with her new dress – another ornament, but one that she puts on (and would take off) to increase her apparent value. There is no distinction, in Belinda's mind, between china ornament, dress, hymen and viginity itself.

Yet the whole poem turns on Belinda's outraged modesty at having had a lock of her hair cut off. It now appears that her rage is at having lost value in the market. Her modesty is in any case dubious. In the Cave of Spleen, Affectation goes to bed, pretending to be sick, so as to show her bosom to admirers:

On the rich quilt sinks with becoming woe,
Wrapped in a gown, for sickness (and for show).
(IV 35–6)

This is funny; but the further implication is that this vanity actually infects love; and that the kind of love it leads to infects with real disease, the pox:

The fair ones feel such maladies as these
When each new nightdress gives a new disease.
(IV 37–8)

The final criticism of Belinda is that she is frigid. She is angry at the rape because it insults her and, she fears, lowers her market value, though she pretends her concern is honour. Beyond that, she recognizes it as a symbolically sexual assault, and would have preferred a real one because it would have devalued her less:

Oh hadst thou, cruel! been content to seize
Hairs less in sight, or any hairs but these!
(IV 175–6)

This is the final criticism of her 'honour'; but it criticizes her frigidity as well: for all her airs and outrage and sexual vanity, she is no more interested in real sex than in symbolic rape.

Pope made this criticism of other women too:

'Yet Chloe, sure, was formed without a spot.'
Nature in her then erred not, but forgot.
'With every pleasing, every prudent part,
Say, what can Chloe want?' She wants a heart.
She speaks, behaves and acts just as she ought,
But never, never reached one generous thought;
Virtue she finds too painful an endeavour,
Content to dwell in decencies for ever;
So very reasonable, so unmoved,
As never yet to love, or to be loved.
She, while her lover pants upon her breast,
Can mark the figures on an Indian chest;
And, when she see her friend in deep despair,
Observes how much a chintz exceeds mohair.
(*Moral Essay II*, 157–70)

That complaisance, prudence, decency and reasonableness are not enough is a sign of how inaccurate it is to view the Augustan period as merely rational; while Pope's silent positives – a heart, generosity, active virtue, passion, sympathy – reveal the characteristics of 'pre-Romanticism' so early (1731) that we might as well call them 'post-Renaissance Humanist'. Pope insists on humanity by showing his loveless women as things:

Flaunts and goes down, an unregarded thing.
(*Moral Essay II*, 252)

A vain, unquiet, glittering, wretched thing.
(*Epistle to Miss Blount with Voiture*, 54)

The images suggest bright mechanical toys – these women have turned into the material goods they desire.

Pope's villainesses cannot tell the difference between breast and chest, despair and mohair. To an early seventeenth-century writer, or a nineteenth-century one, this could be sinful; to Pope, though, it is only a solecism, a social mistake, an unrewarding failure of prudence. What makes the Augustans seem 'rational' is not their ethic but the secular utilitarianism which motivated it. Until about 1640 some kind of passionate love, whether stirring the earth or all fire and air, Platonic or heavenly, could be admired in literature for its own sake: it was heroic, magnanimous; even its baser forms could quickly sublimate, as in Cleopatra; for all virtue lay in love. In the 1790s Blake restored individual and intense love to that status. But for the 150 intervening years the word is rather *benevolence* than love. This is, fundamentally, why the literature of that period is still not popular, not itself loved.
(266–71)

Allan Rodway

from 'By Algebra to Augustanism', in Roger Fowler (ed.), *Essays on Style and Language* 1966

No one doubts that Pope is a master of antithesis. Indeed, it is popularly supposed that his work consists of little else. What is less appreciated – owing to his clarity – is the amazing complexity of its meshing with linguistic devices of all kinds from the sublime or the beautiful to the deliberately ridiculous. Much, then, is debarred from examination here (even if we had the space) for this essay is concerned primarily not with those uses of language which are likely to be found in any good poetry, but only with this one, syntactical, use which is as special to Augustanism as the emotional glow from a friction of verbal connotation is to Romanticism. The following fairly simple couplet from the *Essay on the Characters of Women* (263–4), however, may serve as a preliminary to other less antithetical usages. This exceptional woman

Charms by accepting, by submitting sways,
Yet has her humour most when she obeys.

The second line is slightly paradoxical in its internal relationships,
considerably so in its relationship to the first line. This latter relationship plays against the former, since the slight element of paradox in
the idea of liking to obey would be entirely cancelled by the realization that *this* obedience is in fact a mode of rule (sway) were it not for
the syntactical pull of the antithetical syntax which insists on an
opposition logic could not sustain. The result, an aesthetic *frisson*
comparable to that of a melodic discord. Something similar takes
place in the first line alone. Grammatically, we have a straightforward
mirror-antithesis (main verb. participle/participle. main verb). 'Accepting' is certainly much the same thing as 'submitting', and the structure
insists that the relationship of 'charms' to the one is the same as that
of 'sways' to the other and therefore that they are equivalent to each
other. But neither of these things is true. To sway by submitting is
paradoxical, but to charm by accepting is what one might expect;
and one might well sway without charming and charm without
swaying; they are by no means equivalent. Of course, 'charm' *can*
mean 'influence' as well as 'please', and this secondary meaning is
inevitably made present by the structure though it is contrary to the
context. In terms of meaning, then, the antithesis is (a & —b): b :: b:
—b. The effect of this discord, however, is in the main not aesthetic
but psychological; it makes the rather underhand business of wheedling
seem charming.

But more interesting than this sort of thing is the extraordinary
extent to which Pope, the high priest of 'correctness', is prepared
to sacrifice grammar for effect. At least as much credit must be given
to this device as to the often-noted tension between colloquial language
and formal structure, when we try to account for the pressure and
intensity of his poetry – pressure and intensity quite different in kind
from that of Romantic work. It can be shown that psychological
attention is not distributed evenly. As one might expect it fastens
most firmly on the comparatively infrequent words that bear the
burden of meaning and least firmly on the very frequent, but merely
structural words ('the', 'was', 'were', 'have', 'to' and the like). This
principle obviously provides the driving power behind the famous

passage immediately preceding that from which the last couplet came:

See how the world its veterans rewards!
A youth of frolics, an old age of cards;
Fair to no purpose, artful to no end,
Young without lovers, old without a friend;
A fop their passion, but their prize a sot;
Alive, ridiculous, and dead, forgot!

The terrible bite of that last line, in which every word (save *and*) hammers a nail into the coffin, comes from the omission of 'they were' and 'they are' quite as much as from the antithesis. The words left out are as much part of the poem as those put in. It is probable, too, that the feeling of climax comes not so much from the progression of the sense as from the fact that this line is syntactically more concentrated than the others (which leave our 'see' (line 2), 'they are' (3 and 4), 'was' and 'is' (5) and keep in a number of structural words).

Such grammatical economy is not exceptional but habitual in Pope, and so is much other deliberate grammatical mistaking. Mr Eliot has been much commended for a couple of daring instances of fused grammar in *The Waste Land* and Joyce for many instances in *Ulysses*. One is tempted to assert that the only reason Pope has not is that he works with an appearance of incomparable ease. The whole structure seems well cut and stylish and the stitches don't show. His is the art that conceals art. In the 'Atticus' passage of the *Epistle to Dr Arbuthnot*, for instance, we have an extraordinary sentence of eighteen lines in which the main clause 'Who but must laugh' comes at the end as a long-awaited climax, everything before it being a sequence of dependent clauses. These build up expectation, for we don't know what they depend on, since their ten completed verbs ('Bear', 'View', etc.) and five incomplete ('Willing', 'afraid', etc., which need a 'be') are all hung economically from one unrepeated auxiliary, 'Should' (which therefore fuses three operations: should exist, act so, be such – and, to begin with, also suggests the question 'Should such a man ... [be allowed to] ...?'):

Should such a man, too fond to rule alone,
Bear, like the Turk, no brother near the throne;

View him with scornful, yet with jealous eyes,
And hate for arts that caused himself to rise;
Damn with faint praise, assent with civil leer,
And, without sneering, teach the rest to sneer;
Willing to wound, and yet afraid to strike,
Just hint a fault, and hesitate dislike;
Alike reserved to blame, or to commend,
A timorous foe, and a suspicious friend;
Dreading ev'n fools; by flatterers besieged,
And so obliging that he ne'er obliged;
Like Cato, give his little Senate laws,
And sit attentive to his own applause;
While wits and Templars every sentence raise,
And wonder with a foolish face of praise.
Who but must laugh, if such a man there be?
Who would not weep, if Atticus were he?
(197–214)

In an interesting essay on 'One Relation of Rhyme to Reason'[1]
W. K. Wimsatt, Jr, demonstrated the contribution rhyme may make
to sense or aesthetic pleasure, or both, by setting a difference in parts of
speech, or in function of the same parts of speech, against parallel
structures of line or sense-units. Thus, of the four lines – parallel in
structure – from 'Dreading ev'n fools . . .' to '. . . his own applause',
he writes:

Here the same parts of speech are rhymed, but one verb is
passive, one active; one noun is plural, one singular. The
functions are different, in each case what he does being set
against what he receives.

Most of the remainder of the Atticus passage, of course, is characterized by the rhyming of different parts of speech. Such 'irregularity'
is certainly an important part of the total effect, but is hardly so
essential to it as the larger grammatical irregularity. The one gives
Pope's rapier its dazzling movement, but the other is the source of
the killing muscular thrust.

A similar slight sacrifice of grammatical correctness for syntactical

1 See pp. 345–55 above.

strength is to be seen in the following passage (and many others), where 'shall' must be carried on through all four lines but 'in vain' only as far as the second:

In vain thy reason finer webs shall draw,
Entangle justice in her net of law,
And right, too rigid, harden into wrong;
Still for the strong too weak, the weak too strong.
(*Essay on Man*, III 191–4)

It is noteworthy that *weak* and *strong* are each used both as nouns and adjectives, so that the antithesis of sound is counterpointed by a different antithesis of sense, and this in turn is complicated by the tonal alikeness (pejorative) in the adjectival uses of words opposite in sense. This could be elaborated symbolically, as Crabbe's couplet was. But no doubt enough has been done on these lines, and there is a risk of giving the impression that there is nothing more to Augustan poetry than syntactical ingenuity lending muscular vitality to a body of common sense – an impression obviously falsifiable (in this case by noting the suppressed metaphors behind *webs* and *reason, justice* and *net*, the ambiguity of *rigid* and *harden*, the use of alliteration, and so on).

The present approach has simply been intended to indicate the possibility of a special way into Augustanism at a point where modern criticism has faltered – a way which takes advantage of one general difference between Augustan and Romantic or symbolist works. Where they are typically concerned with states, and thus with evocative imagery, it is more concerned with relations, and therefore relies to a greater extent on patterns of syntax.

It proceeds systematically where they proceed by leaps, sparking gaps of sense, yet it proceeds no less excitingly if our attention is not misguided. Their syntax is subordinated to emotive effects or metaphysical persuasion, and if it draws attention to itself it is probably failing in those effects. Augustan syntax can afford to be so patterned as even to play a pure aesthetic of composition against other emotive effects. But it commonly subserves a general desire for reasonable, or apparently reasonable persuasion. So it comes to provide a rather unexpected sort of 'animation' over and above that of metre and matter. At times, indeed – when the syntactical form is closely linked with the matter of argument – it provides what can only be described as an aesthetic of intellection – not the pleasure of thinking itself, but a pleasure deriving from the same area of mind: something akin to what the mathematician presumably means when he refers to the 'beauty' of an equation.

The New Critics eliminated the word 'aesthetic' from the vocabulary of modern criticism – perhaps rightly, for it had come to be used in a vague, sloppy way. But if stylists can bring it back refurbished, as above, that alone would justify the present attempt, for however important a work may be in other respects, if it is not aesthetic if it is not art.

(62–7)

Maynard Mack

from his Introduction to the Twickenham edition of Pope's *Iliad* and *Odyssey* 1967

Pope's Homer: Its Relations to his Life and Work

Pope's love affair with Homer began, as we have seen, in childhood and endured throughout his life. From Homer, he told Broome in 1715, and Spence much later, he first caught 'the itch of poetry', reading the *Iliad* as a boy of eight in 'that great edition with pictures' which contained the English of John Ogilby.[1] He was fifty-four when he mentioned this to Spence, yet 'he still spoke of the pleasure it then gave him, with a sort of rapture, only in reflecting on it.'[2]

We may be teased in passing by the implications of Spence's sentence. Does it contain a glimpse of an only son, protected and too much tended by elderly parents eager to shelter him from rough sports and youthful mayhem, finding escape from domesticity, and no doubt from an incessant round of devotional duties, on the ringing plains of Troy; where the violences, however terrifying, left no scars, and the heroisms, though ideal, could be possessed by anyone who

1 Pope to Broome, 16 June [1715], *Correspondence*, I 297; *Spence's Anecdotes* pp. 276–9, no. 29. Spence assigns the conversation to 1742–3.
2 Spence, p. 276, no. 30.

would perform the necessary act of imagination? Possibly. But possibly not. All that is certain is that Spence's word 'rapture', and the state of mind it describes, recur with a significant frequency in such records as we have of Pope's response to the Greek poet. The view of Homer's 'distinguishing Excellencies' which he communicated to Ralph Bridges in 1708 makes rapture already a key term: 'that rapture and fire, which carries you away with him, with that wonderful force, that no man who has a true poetical spirit is master of himself, while he reads him'.[1] Seven years later in the *Iliad* Preface, it remains a key term, linked now to the poetical imagination itself – the 'Invention' in which Homer is held to have excelled all others: 'It is to the strength of this amazing Invention we are to attribute that unequalled fire and rapture, which is so forcible in *Homer*, that no man of a true poetical spirit is master of himself while he reads him.'

The rhetoric of these tributes is Longinian, stemming from an idea of elevated style as the source of 'transport'; but the experience they describe was clearly Pope's own. Bathurst, at whose house Pope often stayed while engaged on his *Iliad* translation, told Hugh Blair that when they gathered for breakfast 'Mr Pope used frequently to repeat, with great rapture, the Greek lines which he had been translating.'[2] Spence, after taking down the poet's observation that he was always 'particularly struck' with the passage where Homer makes Priam's grief for dead Hector brim over into anger against his living sons, and could never read it 'without weeping for the distress of that unfortunate old prince', adds this note: 'He read it then; and was interrupted by his tears.'[3]

Rapture in an allied sense asserts its presence frequently in the correspondence of 1714–20, while the *Iliad* version was in progress:

. . . what can you expect from a man who has not talked these five days? who is withdrawing his thoughts as far as he can, from all the present world, its customs and its manners, to be fully possessed and absorbed in the past? When people talk of going to Church, I think of sacrifices and libations; when I see the parson, I address him as *Chryses* priest of *Apollo*; and instead of the Lord's Prayer, I begin

1 5 April, *Correspondence*, I 44.
2 Boswell, *Life of Johnson*, Hill and Powell (ed.) III 403.
3 Spence, p. 260 no. 529.

– God of the silver bow, etc.[1]

Adieu! I am going to forget you. This minute you took up all my mind, the next I shall think of nothing but the terms of Agamemnon, and the recovery of Briseis.[2]

We know, too, that such withdrawals could be profound. Pope does not specify in a letter of 1712 the occasion of his reverie, but it is clear from his description that it belongs among the phenomena of imagination with which the testimony of many poets has made us familiar:

Like a witch, whose carcase lies motionless on the floor, while she keeps her airy sabbaths, and enjoys a thousand imaginary entertainments abroad, in this world, and in others, I seem to sleep in the midst of the hurry, even as you would swear a top stands still, when 'tis in the whirl of its giddy motion. 'Tis no figure, but a serious truth I tell you when I say that my days and nights are so much alike, so equally insensible of any moving power but fancy, that I have sometimes spoke of things in our family as truths and real accidents, which I only dreamt of; and again when some things that actually happened came into my head, have though (till I enquired) that I had only dreamt of them.[3]

Pope's descriptions of the experience are always whimsical, but they point to an intensity of occupation and possession – an 'agony of trance', as Yeats might have put it – which, sustained for days or weeks at a time through the period of a dozen years when Homer (and, in a different sense, his translator) was undergoing translation, cannot be supposed to have vanished, when the job was finished, leaving no trace. At the very least, one would expect to find the process had brought about some degree of interpenetration of Pope's world by Homer's, at all levels, in a way difficult, perhaps impossible, to assess or describe, but nevertheless important for the life of his imagination and his career as poet.

1 To Jervas, 28 July 1714, *Correspondence*, I 240. See also to Jervas, 16 August 1714; to Gay, 4 May 1714; to Ford, 19 May [1714]: *Correspondence*, I, 243, 223, 223–4.
2 To Robert Digby, 2 June 1717, *Correspondence*, I 408.
3 To John Caryll, Jr, 5 December, *Correspondence*, I 163.

Much in the relation of Homer to Pope's imagination necessarily remains conjectural, but this does not make it less interesting or less important. The famous grotto at Twickenham will serve as a first example. Did this have any sort of imaginative affiliation with the grotto in *Odyssey* v (59–74; Pope, 72–96), where Odysseus is entertained by Calypso? That grotto, as pictured by Pope's friend William Kent in the headpiece to Book v, shows some interesting resemblances of structure to the 'perspective view' of the Twickenham grotto published by John Searle in his *Plan of Mr Pope's Garden* (1745). Its contents and surroundings, as detailed by Pope in the translation, rouse recollections of the poet's own garden; the 'groves', the shade of 'nodding cypress', the 'path that winded to the cave', all composed in a 'various sylvan scene', as at Twickenham; while, inside the cavern, 'fountains from the clefts distill', as 'lingering drops from mineral roofs' distilled in the grotto by the Thames. Is it reasonable to suppose that Kent recalled Pope's grotto in sketching Calypso's? Can Pope have recalled Calypso's in planning, or imagining, his own?

The Naiads' grotto in Book XIII of the *Odyssey* is similarly suggestive (96–112; Pope 116–35). Here Odysseus was first restored to his homeland after his ten years' journeying, approximately the length of years that Pope had journeyed in Homer when he completed the first version of his Twickenham grotto in 1725.

Long hast thou, friend! been absent from thy soil,
Like patient Ithacus at siege of Troy –

Gay had hailed him in these words on the completion of the *Iliad* in 1720.[1] Was the edge of this analogy still visible to the poet when he completed the rest of Homer in 1726, contemplating in his grotto and small villa the visible emblems of a homecoming more royal than King Odysseus had, though also treasure-laden?

Cheer up, my friend, thy dangers now are o'er;
Methinks – nay, sure the rising coasts appear;
Hark how the guns salute from either shore,
As thy trim vessel cuts the Thames so fair.
Shouts answering shouts from Kent and Essex roar,
And bells break loud thro' every gust of air.

1 *Mr Pope's Welcome from Greece*, 1–2.

Bonfires do blaze, and bones and cleavers ring,
As at the coming of some mighty king.
(*Mr Pope's Welcome from Greece*, 17–24)

In the Naiads' grotto Pope placed urns and bowls of 'living stone',
a material not found in Homer which he seems to have borrowed
from the *vivoque sedilia saxo* of Virgil's grotto of the Nymphs, where
Aneas found shelter after his long voyaging from Troy to Carthage
(1 167). Since he also borrowed from Virgil's grotto the phrase 'sylvan
scene' (*silvis scaena coruscis*) to describe the surroundings of Calypso's
grotto,[1] it becomes apparent that his imagination apprehended all
three of these grottos as if in a *montage*. How far did his own exercises
in 'grottofying' enter into this characteristic act of generalizing
through allusion? What was the relation in his consciousness between
his own 'shadowy cave', as he calls it in the *Verses on a Grotto by the
River Thames at Twickenham*, and Homer's ἄντρον ἠεροειδές (*Odyssey*,
XIII 103), of which 'shadowy cave' is a literal translation? Or between
his own 'Nymph of the Grot', imagined in verse even if never
realized in stone, and the Nymphs of Virgil and Homer, who served,
like her, as tutelary deities of a sacred precinct?

An interesting specimen of the way in which Pope and Homer
interpenetrate may be found in the figure of Axylus, toward the
beginning of *Iliad* VI:

... Axylus, hospitable, rich and good:
In fair Arisba's walls (his native place)
He held his seat; a friend to human race.
Fast by the road, his ever-open door
Obliged the wealthy, and relieved the poor.
To stern Tydides now he falls a prey,
No friend to guard him in the dreadful day!
Breathless the good man fell, and by his side
His faithful servant, old Calesius died.

This is not quite Homer's Axylus. Pope has retouched Homer's fleet-
ing sketch of a bountiful man whose bounties did not save him with

1 v 80. Milton had of course also borrowed it for the 'verdurous wall' of his
garden: *Paradise Lost*, IV 140.

colourings from other times and climes. There are traces here of Stoic ethic, out of which will subsequently be fashioned the 'good man' of the *Essay on Man*, IV, whose benevolence grows to 'take every creature in, of every kind':

Friend, parent, neighbour, first it will embrace,
His country next, and next all human race.
(367–8)

There are stronger traces of New Testament instruction about the poor, and certainly also, as Reuben Brower has suggested, of a new social consciousness about the poor as a class: the passage could serve, he notes, as an epitaph for Ralph Allen.[1] It could also serve, and evidently did in Pope's case, as one of those exemplary images which linger in every man's mind of his own ideal identity. 'This beautiful character', Pope says in his note on the passage,

has not been able to escape the misunderstanding of some of the commentators, who thought Homer designed it as a reproof of an undistinguished generosity. It is evidently a panegyrick on that virtue, and not improbably on the memory of some excellent, but unfortunate man in that country, whom the poet honours with the noble title of *A Friend to Mankind*. It is indeed a severe reproof of the ingratitude of men, and a kind of satire on [the] human race, while he represents this lover of his species miserably perishing without assistance from any of those numbers he had obliged. This death is very moving, and the circumstance of a faithful servant's dying by his side, well imagined, and natural to such a character. His manner of keeping house near a frequented highway, and relieving all travellers, is agreeable to that ancient hospitality which we now only read of. There is abundance of this spirit everywhere in the Odysseis. The Patriarchs in the Old Testament sit at their gates to see those who pass by, and entreat them to enter into their houses . . .

1 *Alexander Pope: The Poetry of Allusion* (1959), p. 113. cf. for the same type of modernization, *Odyssey*, XV 398–9.

Later, when Pope himself keeps a 'house near a frequented highway', he likes to see himself as in some measure sharing in the preservation of these ancient hospitalities. 'My house', he tells Bethel, 'is like the house of a Patriarch of old, standing by the highway side and receiving all travellers.'[1] Readers of the Satires and Epistles will recognize in this genial feeling one of the chief attributes of the idealized figure who speaks in them:

> But ancient friends (tho' poor, or out of play)
> That touch my bell, I cannot turn away ...
> My lands are sold, my father's house is gone;
> I'll hire another's, is not that my own,
> And yours, my friends, through whose free-opening gate
> None comes too early, none departs too late.
> (For I, who hold sage Homer's rule the best,
> Welcome the coming, speed the going guest.)
> (*Imitations of Horace*, Satire II ii 139–40, 155–60)

It belongs also to the idealized friends of the idealized figure – Oxford, Bathurst, and the rest, in whose charitable practices:

> English bounty yet awhile may stand,
> And honour linger ere it leaves the land.
> (*Epistle to Bathurst*, 247–8)

And it is made on a number of occasions the satirist's chief measure of the shift which has taken place away from the seventeenth-century's still feudal ideal of 'housekeeping':

> Where are those troops of poor, that thronged of yore
> The good old landlord's hospitable door?
> (*The Second Satire of Dr John Donne*, Versify'd, 113–14)

toward a social theory more Benthamite and Mandevillian, which Pope finds tolerable only in so far as it can be subsumed under a Providential scheme of checks and balances:

> Ask we what makes one keep and one bestow?
> That power who bids the ocean ebb and flow,
> Bids seed-time, harvest, equal course maintain. ...

1 To Hugh Bethel, 9 August 1726, *Correspondence*, II 386.

Who sees pale Mammon pine amidst his store
Sees but a backward steward for the poor;
This year a reservoir, to keep and spare,
The next a fountain spouting through his heir.[1]
(*Epistle of Bathurst*, 165-6, 173-6)

The spendthrift Timon is thus as deficient in true bounty, though the sums he lavishes on 'taste' prove to have social utility:

Yet hence the poor are clothed, the hungry fed;
Health to himself, and to his infants bread
The labourer bears. What his hard heart denies,
His charitable vanity supplies.
(*Epistle to Burlington*, 169-72)

as the miser Cotta, who, unlike Axylus, neither obliges the wealthy nor relieves the poor:

To cram the rich was prodigal expense,
And who would take the poor from providence? . . .
Benighted wanderers, the forest o'er
Curse the saved candle, and unopening door.
(*Epistle to Bathurst*, 187-8, 195-6)

The standard against which Pope habitually judges such ways of life in the Horatian poems is a conflation deriving partly from the Bible, partly from the tradition of seventeenth-century English housekeeping at its best, partly from Rome – as Professor Brower remarks, 'the country house and the villa and the kind of life they harboured had very real affinities'[2] – and last, but not necessarily least, from Homer. Beside Cotta's 'unopening door' stands the tacit censure not only of Pope's 'free-opening gate' at Twickenham and the 'hospitable' door of the 'good old' seventeenth-century landlords, but 'sage Homer's rule', and – most moving perhaps of all that rule's exemplifications in the two great guest-honouring epics which Pope translated – the house of Axylus. In Axylus's 'ever-open Door' (a

1 *Epistle to Bathurst*, 165-6, 173-6. The reservoir and fountain were images familiar from ethical sermons, as Earl Wasserman has pointed out in *Pope's Epistle to Bathurst* (1960), p. 17.
2 *Alexander Pope: The Poetry of Allusion* (1959), p. 113.

detail added by Pope to the original) the poet has imaged his sense of πάντας γὰρ φιλέεσκεν ὁδῷ ἔπι οἰκία ναίων (*Iliad*, VI 15) – which the last nine words of his sentence in the letter to Bethel very nearly literally translate.

An instance which clearly shows Pope's imagination of his life and role at Twickenham drawing nourishment from Homer may be found in his imitation of Horace's first satire of the second book. Here the imitator develops Horace's insinuating reference to Lucilius, and to the great men with whom Lucilius had remained on easy terms throughout his attacks on corruption, into a ringing ethical manifesto and applies it to himself. Horace says simply:

What! when Lucilius first dared to compose poems after this kind, and to strip off the skin with which each strutted all bedecked before the eyes of men, though foul within, was Laelius offended at his wit, or he who took his well-earned name from conquered Carthage? Or were they hurt because Metellus was smitten, and Lupus buried under a shower of lampooning verses? Yet he laid hold upon the leaders of the people, and upon the people in their tribes, kindly in fact only to Virtue and her friends. Nay, when virtuous Scipio and the wise and gentle Laelius withdrew into privacy from the throng and theatre of life, they would turn to folly, and flinging off restraint would indulge with him in sport while their dish of herbs was on the boil.
(62–74)

Pope says:

What! armed for virtue when I point the pen,
Brand the bold front of shameless guilty men;
Dash the proud gamester in his gilded car;
Bare the mean heart that lurks beneath a star;
Can there be wanting, to defend her cause,
Light of the church, or guardians of the laws?
Could pensioned Boileau lash in honest strain
Flatterers and bigots even in Louis' reign?

Could Laureate Dryden pimp and Friar engage,
Yet neither Charles nor James be in a rage,
And I not strip the gilding off a knave,
Un-placed, un-pensioned, no man's heir, or slave?
I will, or perish in the generous cause.
Hear this, and tremble! you who 'scape the laws.
Yes, while I live, no rich or noble knave
Shall walk the world, in credit, to his grave:
To VIRTUE ONLY and HER FRIENDS A FRIEND.
The world beside may murmur, or commend.
Know, all the distant din that world can keep
Rolls o'er my grotto, and but soothes my sleep.
There my retreat the best companions grace,
Chiefs out of war, and statesmen out of place.
There St John mingles with my friendly bowl
The feast of reason and the flow of soul;
And he, whose lightning pierced the Iberian lines,
Now forms my quincunx, and now ranks my vines,
Or tames the genius of the stubborn plain,
Almost as quickly as he conquered Spain.
(105–32)

Readers familiar with Pope's style in the Homer translations will hear
almost at once in the tone of the first part of this passage, and in
some portions of its vocabulary ('point the pen', 'Brand the bold
front', 'shameless guilty men', 'gilded car', 'lights', 'guardians',
'strip', 'generous cause', etc.) reverberations of challenge and defiance
from the Augustan *Iliad*, more than matching the epic implications
of Horace's *et qui Duxit ab oppressa meritum Carthagine nomen* (65–6).
They will also hear in the second half of the paragraph the marked
change of tone. The ambience now is not that of the *Iliad*, but that of
the 'great eating poem', as Fielding calls the *Odyssey*, with its
innumerable ritual feasts crowned by the 'friendly bowl', and its
recurrent celebration of poets and the respect that great men pay them:

Phemius, whose voice divine could sweetest sing
High strain, responsive to the vocal string.
(I 155; Pope, 199–200)

> Demodocus, the bard of fame,
> Taught by the Gods to please, when high he sings
> The vocal lay responsive to the strings.
> (VIII 44–5; Pope, 40–42)

> Lives there a man beneath the spacious skies,
> Who sacred honours to the bard denies?
> The Muse the bard inspires, exalts his mind;
> The Muse indulgent loves the harmonious kind.
> (VIII 479–84; Pope 523–6)

> But chief to poets such respect belongs,
> By rival nations courted for their songs;
> These states invite, and mighty kings admire,
> Wide as the sun displays his vital fire.
> (XVII 382–6; Pope 466–9)

> A deed like this thy future fame would wrong,
> For dear to Gods and men is sacred song.
> Self-taught I sing; by heaven, and heaven alone
> The genuine seeds of poesy are sown;
> And (what the Gods bestow) the lofty lay,
> To Gods alone, and god-like worth, we pay.
> (XXII 345–8; Pope 381–6)

This is a note struck often in the poems of the 1730s. It varies from simple assertion of the poet's place in a good society:

> There, my retreat the best companions grace.
> (*Imitations of Horace*, Satire II i 125)

> The courtly Talbot, Somers, Sheffield read,
> Even mitred Rochester would nod the head,
> And St John's self (great Dryden's friends before)
> With open arms received one poet more.
> (*Epistle to Dr Arbuthnot*, 139–42)

> Thus Somers once and Halifax were mine.
> (*Epilogue to the Satires*, Dialogue II 77)

to proud acknowledgement of the responsibilities that go with this privileged position:

Not proud, nor servile, be one poet's praise
That, if he pleased, he pleased by manly ways;
That Flattery, even to kings, he held a shame.
(*Epistle to Dr Arbuthnot*, 338–40)

The rights a court attacked, a poet saved.
(*Imitations of Horace*, Epistles II i 224)

Ye tinsel insects! whom a court maintains,
That counts your beauties only by your stains,
Spin all your cobwebs o'er the eye of day!
The Muse's wing shall brush you all away.
(*Epilogue to the Satires*, Dialogue II 220–23)

Conspicuous scene! another yet is nigh
(More silent far) where kings and poets lie.
(*Imitations of Horace*, Epistles I, vi 50–51)[1]

It is typical of the marked tonal difference between Pope's Horatian poems and their originals that he should so often juxtapose poet and king, poet and court, as he does in the passages above.[2] He would have seconded heartily the remark of Schiller's Charles VII, which incorporates, perhaps for the last time in modern history, that ideal view of the relations of culture and power of which the *Odyssey* is an early and massive expression: 'The minstrel should be at the king's side.'[3] This situation being quite unimaginable for a poet in the time of George II, Pope is constrained to present an alternative – his own court, composed of all those whom the king's court lack wit to value:

But does the court a worthy man remove?
That instant, I declare, he has my love.
I shun his zenith, court his mild decline;
Thus Somers once, and Halifax were mine.

[1] Horace refers only to Numa and Ancus, both kings; Pope inserts poets among the kings – not simply, I think, because of the allusion to Westminster Abbey.

[2] cf. also his *Part of the Ninth Ode of the Fourth Book of Horace*. The four stanzas of Horace's thirteen that Pope translates are precisely those that celebrate the immortalizing power of poets.

[3] *Jungfrau von Orleans*, 484–5: 'Drum soll der Sänger mit dem König gehen, Sie beide wohnen auf der Menschheit Höhen!'

Oft in the clear, still mirror of retreat,
I studied Shrewsbury, the wise and great.
(*Epilogue to the Satires*, Dialogue II 74–9)

In the passage with which we began, the names are different, but
the implication of a good society existing in 'Retreat', and standing
opposed to the Court and the Court's ways, is also there. Pope
receives in his grotto 'the best companions', not the 'Companions'
of the Bath and Garter whom George and Walpole receive. One is a
'statesman', one a 'chief'; together with their poet they sum up a
world. The military member of the partnership is a figure of epic
powers straight out of the *Iliad*,[1] who wields lightning and tames
lesser deities, like a Jove, yet is, nevertheless, in the manner of all the
Homeric heroes, not above sharing in the humblest chores of life.[2]
The other figure, the statesman, perhaps belongs rather to the *Odyssey*.
Is not his original (somewhere deep in the recesses of the poet's
imagination) Bolingbroke-Odysseus – 'the much enduring man', the
knower of men and cities, the exile long prevented from return, the
philosopher and man of eloquence, in whose 'feast of reason and flow
of soul' the poet hears a reminiscence of moments peculiarly and
graciously Odyssean?

To feastful mirth be this white hour assigned
And sweet discourse, the banquet of the mind.
(Pope's *Odyssey*, IV 329–30)

Whether this particular analogy is justified or not, there is a
quality in this passage as a whole, and in others in the poems of the
1730s, which appears to owe less to Horace than to a vocabulary
of attitudes (as well as words) learned during many years of seeking
to anglicize and Augustanize Homer. One cannot avoid wondering
whether these particular lines owe something of the peculiar felicity
which readers have always recognized in them to a joyous sense of
triumph and fulfilment – the fulfilment of a boy's dream, who had

1 See also *Aenid*, VI 842.
2 'There is a Pleasure in taking a view of that Simplicity in Opposition to the
Luxury of succeeding Ages ...' (Pope's Preface to the *Iliad*). '... Nay, a skill
in such works as Agriculture was a Glory even to a King: *Homer* here places it
upon a level with military science, and the knowledge of the cultivation of
the ground is equall'd to glory in war' (*Odyssey*, XVIII 412n).

read the *Iliad* in 'that great edition with pictures' and felt stir in him premonitions of a kind of greatness that could in very deed be made one's own by an act of imagination.

So far our path has lain through a shadowy country of the mind where it is impossible to be sure whether the tracks one thinks one sees are the poet's footprints or one's own. We come a little further into the light when we turn from Pope's mind to his poetic practices, though here too it is perplexing to know where the nicer boundaries of the subject begin and end. This is notably the case if we examine the more general and pervasive features of his poetry. In the striking animation of his best writing, for example, is there possibly a residue deposited by his long effort dating from boyhood to duplicate the animation he admired in Homer? ('What he writes', says the *Iliad* Preface, 'is of the most animated nature imaginable; every thing moves, every thing lives, and is put in action. If a council be call'd, or a battle fought, you are not coldly informed of what was said or done as from a third person; the reader is hurryed out of himself by the force of the poet's imagination, and turns in one place to a hearer, in another to a spectator.') One is inclined to answer this question: Yes. Yet the qualities of style one is tempted to select to support the answer prove on scrutiny to be no closer (often less close) to Homer than to Virgil, Horace, Ovid, Statius, and to Milton, Waller, Cowley, Dryden, etc. None of them make Pope's poetry very much resemble Homer's, even in the translations.

We do better to stay with identifiable obligations. One of these unquestionably lies in the area of vocabulary. Pope's years of mining in the common vein of epic diction gave him a second language. Its heaviest incidence occurs not unexpectedly in the *Rape of the Lock* and the *Dunciad*, where fates 'impend', warnings are given 'thrice', 'care' is the word for every responsibility, carriages become 'chariots' or 'cars', breasts 'swell', rivers 'roll tribute' or 'disembogue', Vandals and other beings *en masse* are 'embodied', papers 'fly diverse', smoke 'involves' the poles, minds 'revolve' their plans, blankets (like walls and tapestries) are 'storied', cards and corpses 'strow' the plain or green in 'heaps on heaps' or 'whole battalions', dead are either 'more than mortal', or else, compared to some other dead, 'not half so', most buildings are 'domes', sounds 'reecho' whenever they do not 'resound', and wanderers travel a 'watery way' or 'watery plain' under an 'aetherial' one. This list could be extended from *The Rape of the Lock* and *The Dunciad* almost indefinitely.

The vocabulary is by no means confined, however, to these two poems. If the playwright in the *Epistle to Augustus* 'pants for glory' (line 300), if Cobham's love of country persists 'to the latest breath' (*Epistle to Cobham*, 262), if Walpole has been seen by Pope 'uncumbered with the venal tribe' (*Epilogue to the Satires*, Dialogue I 31), if Caesar scorns the poet's 'lays' (*Imitations of Horace*, Satire II i 35), if John Cutler's 'reverend temples' are 'crowned' with a few grey hairs (*Epistle to Bathurst*, 327), if happiness is sought in 'iron harvests of the field' (*Essay on Man*, IV 12), if the grape gives 'juice nectareous' (*Essay on Man*, I 136) and the bubble Joy 'laughs' in Folly's cup (*Essay on Man*, IV 12), the reason is to be sought partly in Pope's years of translating Homer. Obviously, some necessary qualifications must be made. Part of this vocabulary comes to Pope from the Latin epics directly. Still more comes to him from English translators of these and of Homer, not forgetting Dryden, whose *Aeneid* was a paramount inspiration. Much comes from Milton. But the experience that forged these several levies into a language whose use was second nature must have been primarily the effort of translation itself. And though much that this effort produced cannot, we now think, be found in Homer's Greek, it populated the translator's mind with locutions whose epic resonances could thereafter be sounded at will – or involuntarily. Pope does not always sound them with equal skill. Here and there, as with 'bleed' for the manner of Socrates's death in the *Essay on Man*, IV 235, they contribute tone at the expense of meaning and have a 'glossiness' which Romantic criticism will deplore. But for the most part, they facilitate those ironic zeugmas and antithetic worlds of feeling for which Pope's poetry is famous:

Our Generals now, retired to their estates,
Hang their old trophies o'er their garden gates,
In life's cool evening satiate of applause,
Nor fond of bleeding even in Brunswick's cause.
(*Imitations of Horace*, Epistle I i 7–10)

'Bleedings' in *this* passage – announced by the epic 'satiate'; alliterated to a proper name insinuating loss of English blood for interests not

English; and punning on a medical and possibly financial sense – could hardly be improved. These effects, especially as found in the poems of the 1730s, are well known and need no special illustration here.

Close to epic vocabulary among the acquisitions to which translating Homer contributed comes the world of Homeric character and event, considered as a treasury of allusion. Homer, Pope says in the *Iliad* Preface, 'opened a new and boundless walk for his imagination . . . in the invention of Fable'. To an extent, his translator did likewise for himself by immersing so deeply in that fable that thereafter it kept thrusting forward for his use in his original poetry an almost inexhaustible supply of analogues. Furthermore, the English rendering, once it was achieved, or even while it was in progress, facilitated allusion not simply to Homer's fable, but to the English dress it wore or was about to wear. In the years before and during translation of the *Iliad*, the relationships of the original text to its 'versions' assume an almost comical complexity. The *Rape of the Lock* echoes passages in Homer which presumably Pope had not yet translated but whose Englishing, when he does translate them, is patently influenced by the English he had given them in the *Rape of the Lock*. Formulas and phrases evidently found first for *Windsor Forest* (though their ultimate origin was in some instances Homer's Greek):

(a) To plains with well-breathed beagles we repair.
(121)

(b) Oft, as in airy rings they skim the heath.
(131)

(c) They fall, and leave their little lives in air.
(134)

(d) Not half so swift the trembling doves can fly,
When the fierce eagle cleaves the liquid sky.
(185–6)

(e) And now his shadow reached her as she run
(His shadow lengthened by the setting sun),
And now his shorter breath with sultry air
Pants on her neck, and fans her parting hair.
(193–6)

(f) High in the midst, upon his urn reclined.
(349)

(g) That Thames's glory to the stars shall raise.
(356)

(h) Though foaming Hermus swells with tides of gold[1] –
(358)

were reworked for a variety of contexts in the *Iliad* translation:

(aa) The well-breathed beagle drives the flying fawn.
(XXII 244; cf. XV 697).

(bb) In airy circles wings his painful way.
(XII 238)

(cc) The wounded bird . . .
A moment hung, and spread her pinions there,
Then sudden dropped, and left her life in air.
(XXIII 1037, 1039–40)

(dd) Not half so swift the sailing falcon flies,
That drives a turtle through the liquid skies.
(XV 260–7)

(ee) Full on his neck he feels the sultry breeze,
And hovering o'er, their stretching shadows sees.
(XXIII 459–60)

(ff) High in the midst the great Achilles stands.
(XVI 204)

(gg) Achilles' glory to the stars to raise.
(XV 82)

(hh) And plenteous Hermus swells with tides of gold.
(XX 452)

The intertraffic between the *Iliad* translation and the *Elegy to the Memory of an Unfortunate Lady* was particularly intricate. The description of the stabbing of Rhesus by Diomed in *Iliad* X (published 1717):

1 This is a sampling, not an exhaustive list.

Just then a deathful dream Minerva sent;
A warlike form appeared before his tent,
Whose visionary steel his bosom tore.
(578–80)

either owes something to, or is owed something by, the apparition
in the *Elegy* (also published 1717):

Tis she! – but why that bleeding bosom gored,
Why dimly gleams the visionary sword?
(3–4)

The exultation of Odysseus over the dead body of Socus, son of
Hippasus, in *Iliad* XI (1717):

Ah wretch! no father shall thy corpse compose,
Thy dying eyes no tender mother close –
(569–70)

seems to stand in a similar tangled relationship to what in the *Elegy* is
pure elegiac lament:

By foreign hands thy dying eyes were closed,
By foreign hands thy decent limbs composed.
(51–2)

The direction of indebtedness is perhaps clearer in the case of the
vengeance envisioned in the *Elegy* for the persecutor of the unfortunate
lady. 'If eternal justice rules the ball', his whole tribe is to be brought
low, while bystanders, watching the 'long funerals', comment:

Lo these were they, whose souls the Furies steeled
And cursed with hearts unknowing how to yield.
(35, 41–2)

The comment echoes Ajax's reproach to Achilles in Book IX (1717),
as the Greek embassy to his tent comes to an unavailing close:

The Gods that unrelenting breast have steeled,
And cursed thee with a mind that cannot yield.
(754–5)

Yet in turn it possibly modifies the reproach that Achilles in *Iliad* XVI (published 1718) says his Myrmidons have been in the habit of applying to him because of his stubborn wrath: 'O nursed with gall, unknowing how to yield!' (244). And it may, because it combines reproach with a prophecy of retribution, have modified Hector's dying words to Achilles in *Iliad* XXII, influencing the shift from Gods to Furies, and from mind to heart:

The Furies that relentless breast have steeled,
And cursed thee with a heart that cannot yield.
Yet think, a day will come, when Fate's decree
And angry Gods shall wreak this wrong on thee.
(447–50)

In the later poems there is of course no longer a question of intertraffic. Homer in Greek and Homer in English now make up together the rich treasury of allusion which Pope's editors and critics from Warburton to the present have been engaged in recovering. The dragging of 'Old England's Genius' at the wheels of Vice's 'Triumphal Car', in the first dialogue of the *Epiloge to the Satires* (151–4), crosses a Spenserian pageant (and Petrachan *Trionfo*) with memories of Hector's fate and intimations of the doom of England mirrored in the doom of Troy. A line (396) in the final apostrophe to George II in the *Epistle to Augustus* – 'What seas you traversed! and what fields you fought!' echoes slyly for the initiated an accent earlier granted on a more heroic occasion:

Not so Achilles . . .
Restless he rolled around his weary bed,
And all his soul on his Patroclus fed: . . .
What toils they shared, what martial works they wrought,
What seas they measured, and what fields they fought
(XXIV 5, 9–10, 13–14)

In the *Epistle to Augustus*, the line precedes a couplet pointedly referring to the king's 'repose':

Oh! could I mount on the Maeonian wing,
Your arms, your actions, your repose to sing!
(395–5)

in such a way as suggests allusion to Cibber's birthday ode of 1731:

From whose high veins this greater day arose,
A second George, to fix our world's repose.
(*An Ode for His Majesty's Birthday . . . October 30, 1731*, 30–31)

It is followed by a couplet:

How, when you nodded, o'er the land and deep,
Peace stole her wing, and wrapped the world in sleep
(*Epistle to Augustus*, 400–401)

that Pope will echo in the 1742 *Dunciad* – possibly to make the hinted identification of Geoge with Dullness in the *Epistle to Augustus* unmistakable for those in the secret:

While the Great Mother bids Britannia sleep,
And pours her spirit o'er the land and deep.

In any case, the Homeric echo in line 390 gives special relevance to the invocation in line 394 (which is not in Horace) of the 'Maeonian' wing.

Sometimes the background of Pope's Homeric allusions is more obscure than this and brings us perhaps closer to the mind of the poet than to his poetic meaning. Thus his contemptuous dismissal of French *petits-maîtres* in *Dunciad* IV:

To where the Seine, obsequious as she runs,
Pours at great Bourbon's feet her silken sons
(297–8)

probably has its origin in Juvenal's allusion to the Orontes pouring a freight of Greek parasites into Tiber (Satires III 62–5); but there evidently hovers in the form of the couplet a memory of his own Catalogue of Ships:

Or where by Phoestus silver Jardan runs,
Crete's hundred cities pour forth all her sons.
(*Iliad*, II 789–90)

Likewise the poetic justice accorded to Atossa – who, 'childless with all her children, wants an heir' – and to her great wealth:

To heirs unknown descends the unguarded store
(*Epistle to a Lady*, 148–9)

may have had for subconscious archetype the fate of Homer's
Phoenops (a 'covetous old Man' says the note on the passage, v 202)
whose two sons fall victim to Diomed in *Iliad* v:

Vast was his wealth, and these the only heirs
Of all his labours, and a life of cares;
Cold death o'ertakes them in their blooming years,
And leaves the father unavailing tears.
To strangers now descends his heapy store,
The race forgotten, and the name no more.
(198–203)

Since this was a fate that Pope at one time anticipated for the Duke
of Marlborough, and insists on in the character of him written but
never included in the *Essay on Man* (247–8), it is possible that the
Phoenops of the English Homer owes something to its creator's
politics; at the very least he has been 'moralized' as compared with
Homer's figure of simple pathos.

  Pope's later poetry is full of problematical echoes of this kind. If we
ask whether, in the *Essay on Man*, the 'hound sagacious on the tainted
green' recollects a formula evolved for *Iliad* xxII:

Sure of the vapour in the tainted dews,
The certain hound his various maze pursues

our answer is at best, 'Possibly'; and the possibility has no significance
except as evidence of the degree to which the Homer translations
affected everything Pope touched thereafter. On the other hand, if
we inquire whether something is owed by the famous epigram
written for the collar of one of Bounce's whelps when given by the
poet to the Prince of Wales:

I am His Highness' dog at Kew;
Pray tell me Sir, whose dog are you?

to the last two lines of Ulysses' comment on seeing his dog Argus:

What noble beast in this abandon'd state
Lies here all helpless at Ulysses' gate?

His bulk and beauty speak no vulgar praise;
If, as he seems, he was, in better days,
Some care his age deserves. Or was he prized
For worthless beauty – therefore now despised?
Such dogs, and men, there are, meer things of state,
And always cherished by their friends, the great . . .
(*Odyssey*, XVII 368–75)

our conclusion cannot be much more affirmative, but the resemblance
is far more interesting; the two passages illuminate each other and
refresh our consciousness that the man who translated Homer is very
much the same man who will say of himself in the first Horatian
imitation (and dare to say it partly because of his success with Homer):
'Un-placed, un-pensioned, no man's heir, or slave' (Satire II i 116). . . .

We come at length to the epic posture. The single hero, or small
saving-remnant, defending a narrow place against overwhelming
odds – this, according to W. P. Ker, is the essential situation of epic,
and the *Iliad* is of course its supreme embodiment. It is also one of
the possible situations of satire, since satire has always potential within
itself the call to defend the storehouses of communal virtue. Perhaps
it is not accidental that the only English satirist who assumes this
posture often, and so boldly that it becomes almost his trademark:

Yes, while I live, no rich or noble knave
Shall walk the world, in credit, to his grave.
(*Imitations of Horace*, Satire II i 119–20)

Yet may this verse (if such a verse remain)
Show there was one who held it in disdain.
(*Epilogue to the Satire*, Dialogue I 171–2)

Yes, I am proud; I must be proud to see
Men not afraid of God, afraid of me . . .
(Dialogue II 208–9)

should be the poet who spent nearly two decades of his life in intermittent translating of Homer. One connection, at any rate, seems
plausible. The language of the epic posture is characteristically grand-
iose, and Pope's effort to render this language in the translation, as

was noted on an earlier page, is often strained. Yet this was precisely
the feature of Homer and of Pope's translating idiom which had only
to be slightly rearranged to give us in the satires those splendid scenes
in which a single leaf of currency wafts an army, Phryne buys the
whole auction, 'slaughtered hecatombs' and 'floods of wine' are
required to 'fill' the 'capacious squire' and 'deep Divine', etc.
Particular lexical reminiscences are perhaps not so revealing as the
general tendency of the satiric poems, which is often exaggerative
in just this epic way. Without Pope's work on Homer, one feels,
Timon's Villa, Cotta's 'lone Chartreux', Selkirk's 'Nepenthe of a
Court', the back-handed praise of George Augustus, and many
another of Pope's outsized creations could not have been what they
are. . . . .

Yvor Winters

from *Forms of Discovery*, chapter 2   1967

In Dryden and his followers there is not much left of the older
English traditions: the models are mainly Latin, and to some extent
Greek and French, but in a general way the poets of this line have
styles which correspond to the older ornate and plain styles. We might
say, at least figuratively, that the heroic style corresponds to the old
ornate style and the directly didactic or satiric to the plain. I use the
adverb *directly* with the explicit intention of excluding the mock-
heroic, which is something else. We can see the heroic style in a fairly
distinguished form in Dryden's Virgil, and it is not without minor
virtues in Pope's Homer. We can see it, or something very like it, in
the 'great odes', more or less Pindaric in intention, which obsessed so
many poets from Dryden until late in the nineteenth century.
Alexander's Feast, by Dryden, will serve as an example. It is, I suppose,
the most coldly misbegotten monster in the history of English verse,
yet Dryden considered it his greatest work. The best single poem by
Dryden is certainly *MacFlecknoe*, and the best by Pope *The Rape of the
Lock*. Yet these are mock-heroic poems; their principal virtues arise
from the fact that they exploit the ridiculous aspects of the style that
both poets held in the highest esteem. This is a sad commentary on

the main preoccupations of the period; and parody is a dangerous style, because it depends upon clichés for its effectiveness, and clichés are still clichés even when used in the interest of wit. Even poems as remarkable as these two are essentially a kind of light verse. Churchill employs the mock-heroic method, but in most poems occasionally, and in his last work with great discretion. He never employs the heroic.

The directly satiric and didactic are not invariably combined with each other, but we find them together in the most memorable poems. I will take *Absalom and Achitophel* and the *Epistle to Dr Arbuthnot* as examples. Most readers – myself among them – remember these poems fragmentarily: the portraits of Zimri, Achitophel and Atticus, and a handful of Pope's epigrams stay in the mind, but the poems do not. The reason for this is simple: neither poem has any really unifying principle. Dryden employs a dull narrative, which elaborately and clumsily parallels the biblical narrative, and he does this in order to praise a monarch who was a corrupt fool. One cannot take the whole poem seriously, but one can find interest in the brilliant details. Pope's poem is more honest, and for that reason more obviously fragmentary: nothing holds it together except Pope's exasperation with people who have exasperated him. They were doubtless exasperating, but so are most people; so is life. The form of each poem is an excuse for satirical portraits and epigrams, rather than a unifying principle.
(125–6)

Peter Dixon

from 'Alexander Pope of Twickenham', *The World of Pope's Satires* 1968

On more than one occasion Swift expressed regret over the topicality of Pope's satire. He pointed out that the day-to-day affairs of London, however sensational, would quickly be forgotten; even at the time of writing, a witty allusion to some metropolitan rogue or fool might well be simply mystifying to a reader twenty miles from the capital. In another way Pope's eagerness to name contemporary names could defeat the avowed purpose of his saitre. Instead of extinguishing the dunces of the age he might succeed only in conferring on them the immortality of great art. 'Take care the bad poets do not outwit you,' Swift warned him, 'as they have served the good ones in every age, whom they have provoked to transmit their names to posterity. Maevius is as well known as Virgil, and Gildon will be as well known as you if his name gets into your verses.'[1] Swift's fears were prophetic. One reason for the eclipsing of Pope's reputation in the nineteenth century was that he was felt to have been ignobly enmeshed in the mundane and the trivial. Francis Jeffrey reproved the writers of the early eighteenth century because 'they never pass beyond "the visible diurnal sphere", or deal in anything that can either lift us above our vulgar nature, or ennoble its reality'.[2] And, to take Swift's second point, Pope has certainly endowed the dunces with a dubious kind of immortality. The details of obscure lives and works have been patiently exhumed by editors and commentators in order to elucidate the names preserved in the amber of *The Dunciad*, the *Epistles* [*Moral Essays*], and the *Imitations of Horace*.

If the reader of Pope cannot avoid learning something of the career of Charles Gildon, that is partly because Pope himself, as his own first editor, supplied plentiful (and not unprejudiced) information about the names and events to which his poems allude. The immediate ethical occasion of the *Epistle to Lord Bathurst*, for example, is provided by the misdemeanours of Peter Walter and Francis Chartres, of directors of the South Sea Company and the fraudulent governors of the Charitable Corporation; Pope's copious annotations on the lives and works of these malefactors serve both to justify his satirical attacks and to anchor in reality the absurd obsessions of the avaricious and the prodigal. The truth about men's behaviour may be quite as bizarre as satirical fiction paints it. Yet the *Epistle to Lord Bathurst* also exists to honour the Man of Ross, whose philanthropy, transcending the local and temporary, assumes in Pope's lines a Christ-like significance:

---

1 Letter to Pope, 26 November 1725, *Correspondence*, Vol. II, p. 343. (Maevius, one of a group of poetasters who attacked Horace and Virgil, is ridiculed in Virgil's third *Eclogue*.) For Swift's other reservations about Pope's topicality see *Correspondence*, Vol. II, p. 504, and Vol. III, p. 343.

2 Review of Sir Walter Scott's edition of Swift, *Edinburgh Review*, Vol. XXVII (1816), p. 3.

Behold the marketplace with poor o'erspread!
The Man of Ross divides the weekly bread.
Behold yon alms-house, neat, but void of state,
Where age and want sit smiling at the gate.
Him portioned maids, apprenticed orphans blest,
The young who labour, and the old who rest.
(263–8)

This portrait goes some way towards meeting Jeffrey's objection, for the charity of the Man of Ross ennobles our real human nature. Yet it does so only because Pope reminds us of reality by describing charitable acts which belong to the recent past, to a recognizable world of 'portions' and apprenticeships. The exemplary force of such good works depends upon our acknowledging that they are both divinely sanctioned and humanly practicable. Lest we try to shrug off their implications for our own conduct, and deny their practicability, Pope's own footnote insists upon the historical identity of this anonymous patriarch, and upon the actuality of his deeds: 'The person here celebrated, who with a small estate actually performed all these good works, and whose true name was almost lost . . . was called Mr John Kyrle. He died in the year 1724, aged ninety, and lies interred in the chancel of the church of Ross in Herefordshire.'

In the poems of the early 1730s Pope speaks both for and against his age. The 'visible diurnal sphere' at once provokes him to satire and provides him with patterns of those very qualities, aesthetic, social, and moral, which the objects of his satire signally lack. If he condemns Cloe and Timon and Peter Walter, he writes with an opposite but equal warmth on behalf of Martha Blount, Lord Burlington, and John Kyrle. Hence the note of authority in his poetry, its characteristic air of confidence; true standrads and values are demonstrably being upheld by a select circle which includes the poet and his friends. Hence, too, the infrequency with which Pope makes any sustained use of what Henry James called 'operative irony', the irony which 'implies and projects the possible other case, the case rich and edifying where the actuality is pretentious and vain'.[1] The ironic Epistle to Augustus is unique among Pope's works precisely because the man it addresses is unique. Comparisons with an inadequate monarch have to be fetched

1 Preface to The Lesson of the Master.

from afar, and the 'possible other case' is here implied and projected by means of Horace's unironical Epistle to Augustus, the poem which Pope has so brilliantly inverted. Rome's Augustus Caesar, a man of culture, a patron of the arts, confronts the stolid indifference and meagre materialism of England's George Augustus.
(1–3)

Appendix : Notes

A. Pope's interpretation of 'correctness' was primarily metrical.
    The two letters reprinted here derive their special interest from
    their relationship to *An Essay on Criticism* lines 337–83, which
    follows them. The letter to Walsh, the squire-cum-poet-cum-
    man about town whom Dryden had called the best critic of the
    nation, may be a later concoction, though a surviving draft of
    parts of the *Pastorals* shows Pope consulting Walsh on similar
    details of technique. But the resemblance to the letter to
    Cromwell is suspicious. Walsh had died in 1708 and Pope may
    have wished to give the impression that he was more intimate
    with him than he had in fact been. The Cromwell letter
    survives; he had given it to his blue-stocking mistress Elizabeth
    Thomas who sold it (and other letters from Pope) to the
    unscrupulous publisher Curll.
    An Essay on Criticism, though published in mid-May 1711, did
    not receive its first review until mid-December – but the
    reviewer was Addison (though this fact was not revealed until
    December 1712) and the periodical in which it appeared was
    the *Spectator*, incomparably the most influential literary journal
    of the period. Pope was already a friend of Steele, but he did not
    know Addison personally at the time. And though the review
    led to their meeting the preliminary generalizations about 'envy
    and detraction' – presumably inspired by the attack on Dennis –
    must have irritated Pope, even if the general tone of the review
    is complimentary.

B. The *Guardian*, number 40, is one of Pope's cleverest perform-
    ances, combining mock-eulogy of Ambrose Philips's pastorals
    with mock-depreciation of his own. The simplicity that is
    continuously applauded in Philips's silliest lines may be part of
    the general attack on Addison, at its height in 1713, or it may
    refer directly to Philips's preface to *The Distressed Mother*, a
    version of Racine's *Andromaque*, in which simplicity is repeatedly
    asserted to be the supreme literary virtue. 'Namby-Pamby',

as he was nicknamed, did not enjoy Pope's ridicule and is even said to have hung a birch rod in Button's Coffee House for purposes of physical retaliation in case Pope ever ventured inside. Johnson's considered critical verdict was that the essay is 'a composition of artifice, criticism and literature to which nothing equal will easily be found'. It follows a series of papers on pastoral poetry in *The Guardian* by Thomas Tickell, Addison's candidate for the translation of the *Iliad*, in which Philips's pastorals were frequently quoted or referred to, whereas Pope's were ignored.

C.   In addition to his 'public' poems Pope wrote a number of 'private' pieces, often of a blasphemous or obscene character, that were intended only for the circle of his intimates. Pope must however have allowed his friends to take copies and eventually an unscrupulous bookseller such as Curll would get hold of them and publish them, though of course always without Pope's authorization. But Pope had no difficulty in extricating himself from such situations as the advertisement on p. 56 demonstrates. By 1734 when *Sober Advice from Horace to the Young Gentlemen about Town* was published, he only found it necessary to change his usual publisher and add on the title-page *Imitated in the Manner of Mr Pope*. The advice contained in this amusing modernization of Horace's Satire I ii was in fact far from sober – or even respectable.

D.   In addition to the *Anecdotes*, specimens of which appear under the appropriate dates above, Spence wrote when a young Fellow of New College, Oxford, these appreciative but not uncritical Platonic dialogues upon Pope's *Odyssey*. The dialogues, indeed, were directly responsible for the acquaintance with Pope of which the *Anecdotes* were the fruit. Spence's *Essay* consists in its final form of five dialogues, three on Books One–Fourteen (published in 1726) and the last two on Books Fifteen–Twenty-four (published in the complete collection of the dialogues in 1728). The invitation to visit Pope at Twickenham came in 1726 soon after the appearance of the first instalment of dialogues. Pope made a number of minor suggestions, which were generally adopted by Spence, in the manuscript of the last two dialogues, but Spence does not show himself aware in either instalment (including the careful revision of the first three dialogues in 1728) of Broome's and Fenton's share in the translation. Many of the passages that his Antiphaus objects to, even in the first edition of the *Essay* (which has been followed in this selection), were not – except in so far as he may have revised them – the work of Pope but of his collaborators. Thus in the extracts given Fenton (who only translated two of the first fourteen Books) is criticized for eleven passages, whereas Pope, who translated eight of the first fourteen, receives only nine censures. Broome, who undertook four of the fourteen Books, receives eight criticisms, but his work had been much more thoroughly revised by Pope than Fenton's. The preference for Pope as a translator revealed by these statistics, together with the sensible extenuations often preferred by Philypsus (a name presumably meaning 'lover of the sublime', with Antiphaus meaning 'objector to stylistic glare') may explain Pope's unusual cordiality to Spence.

E. Much the most interesting comments by Pope himself on his own poems are to be found in the records of his conversation known as *Spence's Anecdotes*. Joseph Spence's *Essay on Pope's 'Odyssey'* (from which an extract appears on pp. 59–71 above) had secured him an invitation to Twickenham in 1726, and on subsequent visits from 1728 to Pope's death Spence recorded in some detail and with apparent accuracy various conversations that he had had both with Pope and with other literary figures of the period. Pope, however, was his hero and he had intended to write his life – a project that he abandoned only on learning that Warburton, Pope's official editor, was also proposing to be his biographer. The *Anecdotes* were first published in 1820 in two separate editions by S. W. Singer and Edmond Malone, of which Singer's is much the fuller. The definitive edition is by James M. Osborn (2 vols. 1966).

F. *A Master Key to Poetry*, which remained unpublished until 1949, is a by-product of the 'Epistle to Burlington' (now better known as *Moral Essay IV*), and of the hot water that Pope found himself in because of its resemblances, almost certainly unintended, between his Lord Timon and the Duke of Chandos. The episode is more effectively dealt with in the first *Imitation of Horace* (Satire II i), which was written a year or so later. The malicious gossip in aristocratic circles that had been accumulating against Pope for many years was hydra-headed and it is difficult to identify all of the individuals he had intended to satirize.

G.   *A Pipe of Tobacco* (1736) describes its 'low' subject in the characteristic styles of six contemporary poets. They are pastiches rather than parodies, 'and Mr Pope himself used to speak of those likenesses as very just and very well taken' (Spence's *Anecdotes*). Jane Austen must have agreed. In *Mansfield Park* Mary Crawford asks Mrs Grant, 'Do you remember Hawkins Browne's "Address to Tobacco" in imitation of Pope?' (vol. 1, ch. 17).

H.   When Pope changed the hero of *The Dunciad* from the scholarly Lewis Theobald, who had exposed the inadequacies of the Pope edition of Shakespeare (1725), to the actor-dramatist Colley Cibber, he invited the retaliation of an expert in ludicrous controversy. Cibber's anecdote of their brief encounter in a brothel twenty-five years earlier – when he found Pope 'in the act' and extricated the puny poet bodily 'before he had exhausted his tender frame' – was exactly the kind of satiric thrust that Pope could not answer.

I.   Johnson has occasional references to Pope in *The Rambler* (1750–52), but his earliest serious critique of Pope was the detailed commentary on Pope's epitaphs – extracts pp. 95–101 above – that he contributed to *The Universal Visitor* (1756), a short-lived and undistinguished journal from which they were exhumed to provide the final section of the *Life*. The original function of the *Life* was to introduce Pope's poems in an ambitious reprint of the principal English poets (beginning with Cowley) in which the London publishers co-operated, 1779–81, with Johnson providing a biography and critical estimate prefixed to each poet's works. But Johnson's *Lives of the English Poets* detached themselves from this merely introductory capacity as early as 1781 and have survived in their own right as one of the masterpieces of English literary criticism. The *Life* of Pope, the last to be written, is the longest of the series and is perhaps Johnson's critical masterpiece. An excellent account of Johnson's haphazard methods of composition will be found in 'The Making of *The Life of Pope*' by Frederick W. Hilles in *New Light on Dr Johnson* (1959).

J. This passage from Pope's *Iliad* – which seemed especially offensive to Southey, Wordsworth and Coleridge (see pp. 185, 187 and 189) – is typical of the 'picturesque' manner. Charles Jervas, a professional painter who gave Pope lessons in painting at this time, added suggestions on the proofs which Pope incorporated. Norman Callan (*Review of English Studies*, April 1953, p. 111) points out that the whole passage is full of painter's terms and bears an obvious relation to Rembrandt's *The Night Watch*.

K. The Rev. W. L. Bowles – a minor poet whose *Fourteen Sonnets* (1789) had a considerable influence on Coleridge (see *Biographia Literaria*, ch. 1) – revived the critical views of Joseph Warton in his ten-volume edition of Pope's *Works*, published in 1806. These afterwards involved him in a long controversy with Thomas Campbell, Byron, and others concerning Pope's moral character as well as his rank as a poet. The seven years' war of pamphlets and articles began in 1819 and dragged on until 1826. The earlier stages of the controversy are illustrated here in Bowles's 'Concluding Observations' (p. 170), Campbell's *Specimens* (p. 199), Bowles's *Invariable Principles* (p. 201), Isaac D'Israeli's article in the *Quarterly Review* (p. 202), Byron's *Letter*, etc. (p. 203) and Hazlitt's 'Pope, Lord Byron, and Mr Bowles' (p. 209).

L. Wordsworth's essay 'Upon Epitaphs' was to have been published in three instalments in Coleridge's periodical the *Friend* (1809–10). However, the *Friend* ceased publication shortly after the first part appeared, and the second and third parts (from which the passage in the text is taken) were only published in Wordsworth's *Prose Works*, ed. A. B. Grosart (1876).

M.   Various explanations have been offered for Byron's intense admiration of Pope. Goethe thought that he ignored Shakespeare because he sensed his own inferiority, but praised Pope because he had no cause to fear him (*Conversations with Eckermann*, 24 February 1825); and Sainte-Beuve later endorsed this opinion ('Qu'est-ce qu'un classique?', 1850). On the other hand, James Russell Lowell suggested that the sincerity of Byron's admiration of Pope had been 'too hastily doubted', even if his polemics were 'written rather more against Wordsworth than for Pope' ('Pope', 1871). Byron himself says in his *Letter to* [*John Murray*]: 'As a child I first read Pope's Homer with a rapture which no subsequent work could ever afford'.

N.   Ruskin tells us that as a child he had Scott's novels and Pope's *Iliad* 'for constant reading . . . on weekdays' (*Praeterita*, ch. 1). In his earlier pronouncements on Pope, he vacillated between admiration and disgust – as, for example, in a letter to his father (23 November 1851): 'Pope is very wonderful – but turns sour on the stomach.' However, his admiration increased as he grew older, and in 1873 he contemplated a work that would 'rescue Pope from the hands of his present scavenger biographer' (i.e. Whitwell Elwin) (*Fors Clavigera*, Letter 32, note).

O.   Ruskin refers in *Fors Clavigera* (Letter 40) to 'an unhappy wretch of a clergyman I read of in the papers – spending his life industriously in showing the meanness of Alexander Pope – and how Alexander Pope cringed and lied'. This was the Rev. Whitwell Elwin, editor of the *Quarterly Review* from 1853 to 1860, who produced five volumes (1871–72) of the great Victorian edition of Pope, which had been conceived by John Wilson Croker in 1831 and was finally completed by W. J. Courthope in five further volumes (1881–89). Mark Pattison described Elwin's commentary as 'a running fire of depreciation kept up at the foot of the page', and Gladstone is said to have remarked: 'It seems as though Elwin has edited Pope in order to show that he is not worth editing.'

Select Bibliography

The Works of Mr Alexander Pope, with his Last Corrections, Additions and Improvements. Together with the Commentaries and Notes of Mr Warburton, 9 vols., 1751. The official edition. Includes new notes and revisions by Pope. Some of the textual changes seem to be due to the officious Warburton.

The Works, 10 vols., 1871–89. Edition begun by W. Elwin who was superseded by W. J. Courthope because of his lack of sympathy with Pope. Still standard for Pope's acknowledged prose other than the letters.

The Prose Works, edited by Norman Ault, vol. 1 (all published), Blackwell, 1935. Includes some anonymous matter, scurrilous or obscene, that may not be by Pope, though most of the identifications are plausible.

The Twickenham Edition of the Poems, 11 vols. Methuen, 1939–67. General editor John Butt, whose one-volume edition (1963) conflates and abbreviates the first seven volumes. Maynard Mack has acted as general editor of the Homer translations (4 vols., Yale University Press, 1967), which include Pope's notes but do not annotate them.

The Correspondence, 5 vols., Oxford University Press, 1956. Fully annotated by George Sherburn.

Facsimiles of Pope's own manuscripts: *Windsor Forest* (edited by R. M. Schmitz, St Louis, 1952); *Epistle to Bathurst* (edited by Earl R. Wasserman, Johns Hopkins Press, 1960); *Essay on Man* (Roxburghe Club, 1962); *Essay on Criticism* (edited by R. M. Schmitz, St Louis, 1962).

Acknowledgements

For permission to use copyright material acknowledgement is made to the following:

For the extracts from *Seven Types of Ambiguity* by William Empson to New Directions Publishing Corporation and Chatto & Windus Ltd; for the extract from *ABC of Reading* by Ezra Pound to New Directions Publishing Corporation and Faber & Faber Ltd; for the article 'Alexander Pope' to *The Times Literary Supplement*; for the extract from *Revaluation* by F. R. Leavis to Chatto & Windus Ltd; for the extract from *The Great Chain of Being* by Arthur O. Lovejoy to Harvard University Press; for the essay 'Alexander Pope' from *Anne to Victoria: Essays by Various Hands* to Curtis Brown Ltd; for the extract from the *New Statesman and Nation* by Cyril Connolly to the *New Statesman*; for the article 'One Relation of Rhyme to Reason' by W. K. Wimsatt reprinted in *The Verbal Icon* to the *Modern Language Quarterly*; for the extract from 'What is a Classic?' from *On Poetry and Poets* by T. S. Eliot to Faber & Faber Ltd; for the extract 'Pope at Work' by George Sherburn from *Essays on the Eighteenth Century Presented to David Nichol Smith* to The Clarendon Press; for the extract 'The Case of Miss Arabella Fermor' from *The Well-Wrought Urn* by Cleanth Brooks to Harcourt Brace Jovanovich Inc. and Dennis Dobson; for the essay 'Rhetoric and Poems: Alexander Pope' by W. K. Wimsatt to Columbia University Press; for the extract 'Wit and Poetry and Pope' by Maynard Mack from *Essays Presented to George Sherburn* to The Clarendon Press; for the extract from *Epistles to Several Persons* by F. W. Bateson to Yale University Press and Methuen & Co. Ltd; from the extract from 'The Augustan Mode in English Poetry' by W. K. Wimsatt reprinted in *Hateful Contraries* to the Johns Hopkins Press; for the extract from *Articulate Energy* by Donald Davie to Routledge & Kegan Paul Ltd; for the extract from 'In the Wake of the Anarch' by Hugh Kenner to Astor-Honor Inc.; for the extract from *The Rape of the Lock* by J. S. Cunningham to Edward Arnold Ltd; for the extract from *The Gutenberg Galaxy* by Marshall McLuhan to Routledge & Kegan Paul Ltd and The University of Toronto Press; for the extract from *The Language Poets Use* by Winifred Nowottny to the Athlone Press; for the extract from *The Language of Science and the Language of Literature* by Donald Davie to Sheed & Ward Ltd; for the essay 'The Rape of the Lock' from *Poetic Love* by J. B. Broadbent to Chatto & Windus Ltd; for the extract 'By Algebra to Augustanism' by Allan Rodway from *Essays on Style and Language* to Routledge & Kegan Paul Ltd and Humanities Press Inc.; for the extract from the Introduction to the Twickenham edition of Pope's *Iliad* and *Odyssey* by Maynard Mack to Yale University Press and Methuen & Co. Ltd; for the extract from *Forms of Discovery* by Yvor Winters to the Swallow Press Inc.; for the extract from *The World of Pope's Satires* by Peter Dixon to Methuen & Co. Ltd.

Index

Extracts included in this anthology are indicated by bold page references

Achitophel (in Dryden's *Absalom and Achitophel*) 214, 260

Addison, Joseph (1672–1719) 23, 28, 37, 86, 104, 127, 166, 212, 213, 217, 232, 234, 392

    portrait of him in *Epistle to Dr Arbuthnot* 197, 243, 272 ⟡ **Atticus**
    review of *Essay on Criticism* in the *Spectator* **44–7**

Akenside, Mark (1721–70) Poet and physician, author of *The Pleasures of the Imagination* 192

Alexandrine (12-syllable line) 40, 42, 43

Alsop, Anthony (d. 1726) Scholar and wit 87

Amhurst, Nicholas (1697–1742) Political pamphleteer, edited Bolingbroke's *Craftsman* 35

Anne, Queen 212, 229, 258, 260

Antitheses 65, 384

Apollo God of music and poetry 190, 264

Arbuthnot, John (1667–1735) Doctor and wit; collaborated with Pope 23, 24, **447–8**

Ariosto, Ludovico (1474–1533) Italian poet, author of the romantic epic *Orlando Furioso* 187

Aristides Athenian general and statesman, known as 'The Just', ostracized in 482 B C **204–5**

Aristotle (384–322 B C) 45, 384

Arnold, Matthew (1822–88) 35, 165–6, 168, **240–42, 249–53**, 272–4, 293

Atossa (in *Moral Essay II*) 260 ⟡ **Marlborough, Sarah, Duchess of**

Atterbury, Francis (1662–1732) Bishop of Rochester; exiled as Jacobite 58

Atticus Portrait of Addison in *Epistle to Dr Arbuthnot* 239, 260, 269 ⟡ **Addison**

Auden, W. H. 328–43

Augustan verse forms 335–8

Ault, Norman Editor of Pope's prose 493

Austen, Jane (1775–1817) Reference in *Mansfield Park*, 490

B., T. Contributor to Aaron Hill's *Prompter* (1735) **83–4**

Bagehot, Walter (1826–77) Writer on economics, politics and literature **234–6**

Bashi Bazouk, Bashi Bazouks were Turkish irregular soldiers notorious for their lawlessness and brutality, but Bagehot uses the term to mean bizarre in character or composition 235

Bateson, F. W. 405–19

Bathurst, Allen, Earl (1684–1775) One of Pope's closest aristocratic friends 158–60

Bible, (Authorized Version, 1611) 169, 223

Binfield (Berkshire) Pope family residence from *c.* 1700 23

Blacklock, Thomas (1721–91) Blind poet 75

Blackmore, Sir Richard (1653–1729) Successful doctor; his epics the butt of the coffee-house wits **56,** 170, 380

Blair, Hugh (1718–1800) Professor of Rhetoric at Edinburgh **150–52**

Blake, William (1757–1827) Notebook, containing poems, epigrams and the draft of his 'Public Address', ed. G. Keynes (1935) **174**

Blasphemy (in Pope's 'Universal Prayer') 56

Blount, Martha (1690–1763) Catholic friend, apparently became Pope's mistress 24, 195

Blount, Thomas (1618–79) Author of *The Academy of Eloquence* 383

Boileau-Despréaux, Nicolas (1636–1711) French poet, satirist, and critic, author of *L'Art poétique* 101, 170, 171, 184, 190, 382

Bolingbroke, Henry St John, Viscount (1678–1751) Tory politician, became Pope's 'guide, philosopher and friend' on return from exile as Jacobite 23, 30, 158–60, 197, 229, 249, 256, 412

Boswell, James (1740–95) **155–161,** 265

Bouhours, Dominique (1628–1702) Jesuit literary critic 108

Bowles, William Lisle (1762–1850) Sonneteer and critic 166–7, **169–73,** 199–210, **201,** 491

Break, Break, Break (Tennyson's) 271–2

Broadbent, J. B. 449–55

Brooke, Henry (?1703–83) Poet and novelist 86

Brooks, Cleanth 360–77

Broome, William (1689–1745) Minor poet; translated twelve books of Pope's *Odyssey* 65, 70, 71, 93, 104, 174

Browne, Isaac Hawkins (1705–60) His *A Pipe of Tobacco* includes pastiche of Pope's style **85,** 490

Brunel, Sir Marc Isambard (1769–1849) French-born civil engineer 218

Buckingham, George Villiers, 2nd Duke of (1628–87) 214

Buckingham, John Sheffield, Duke of (1648–1721) Author of *Essay on Poetry*; his *Works* edited posthumously by Pope 47, 104

Buffon, Georges Louis Lederc, Comte de (1707–99) French naturalist and author of *Discours sur le style* 262

Bufo, (in *Epistle to Dr Arbuthnot*) 260

Buonaparte, Napoleon (1769–1821) 233

Burns, Robert (1759–96) 206, 259

Butler, Samuel (1612–80) Author of *Hudibras* 64, 104

Butt, John General editor of Twickenham Pope 285, 493

Button's Coffee-House (in Covent Garden) Frequented by Addison and his protégés 33

Byron, George Gordon, Baron Byron (1788–1824) Eulogized Pope in public and private letters in *Letters and Journals*, ed. R. E. Prothero (1898–1901) 163, 167, **201–2, 203–8,** 209–10, 259, 265, 491–2

Bysshe, Edward (*fl.* 1712) Compiler of *Art of English Poetry* 383

Cadogan, William Cadogan, Earl of (1675–1726) 267

Caesura (Pope's preferences) 39–40, 42

Callan, Norman 491

Campbell, Thomas (1777–1844) Poet, anthologist, critic; author of *The Pleasures of Hope*, 167, **199–200,** 201, 209, 491

Caryll, John (?1666–1736) Catholic friend of the Popes; responsible for *The Rape of the Lock* 127

Cawthorne, James (1719–61) Poet 174

Chandos, James Brydges, Duke of (1673–1744) Identified with Pope's 'Timon' (*Moral Essay IV*) 410

Chapman, George (?1559–1634) Poet, dramatist and translator of Homer 250

Charles II (1630–85) 191, 218, 219, 260

Chartres (Charteris), Francis (1675–1732) Rake portrayed in *Moral Essay III* 197

Chatterton, Thomas (1752–70) 212

Chaucer, Geoffrey (?1343–1400) 25, 187, 192, 246, 265, 278, 345–50

Chesterfield, Philip Dormer Stanhope, Earl of (1694–1773) Statesman, patron of literature and letter-writer **92, 94, 120,** 420

Chiabrera, Gabriello (1552–1637) Italian poet 175

Chiasmus (favourite figure of speech with Pope) 351–2

Christ 204

Churchill, Charles (1731–64) Poet and satirist 174

Cibber, Colley (1671–1757) Whig dramatist, actor-manager 24, 87–8, 89, 213, 231, 232, 272, 490

Clare, John (1793–1864) Poet, author of *The Shepherd's Calendar*; Journal in *The Prose of John Clare*, ed. J. A. and Anne Tibble (1951) 211

Clarendon, Edward Hyde, Earl of (1609–74) Statesman, author of *History of the Rebellion and Civil Wars in England* 255

'Classic', Pope recognized as in his life-time 355

Claudian (*fl.* 393–404) Latin poet 214

Cobbett, William (1762–1835) Radical; author of *Rural Rides* 205

Cobham, Richard Temple, Viscount (?1669–1749) Aristocratic friend of Pope; creator of Stowe (Buckinghamshire) 413

Coleridge, Samuel Taylor (1772–1834) 163, 164, 165, 167, **188–90,** 213, 249, 281, 491

   Ancient Mariner 280

   lectures and marginalia in *Coleridge's Miscellaneous Criticism,* ed. T. M. Raysor (1936) **179, 198, 214**

   Table Talk, ed. H. N. Coleridge (1835) **214**

   Notebook 17 quoted in *Inquiring Spirit: A New Presentation of Coleridge,* ed. K. Coburn (1951) **215**

Collins, William (1721–59) 211

Common sense (the Augustan criterion *par excellence*) 35–6

Congreve, William (1670–1729) Dramatist; *Iliad* translation dedicated to him 35, 83, 256, 261, 410

Connolly, Cyril 343–5

Continental school 179 ◊ **French school**

Cooper, Samuel (1609–72) Miniaturist; Pope's maternal uncle 25

'Correctness' (the neo-classic ideal, to be reached by following the 'rules') 89, 108, 382–4

Couplet, heroic 335–7

   Closed couplet 347–8, 424–6

Courthope, W. J. (1842–1917) literary critic and historian; editor of Pope 492

Cowley, Abraham (1618–67) 90, 104

Cowper, William (1731–1800) **121–2,** 164–5, 167, 172, 201, 215, 234, 258, 261

   his translation of Homer compared with Pope's 169, 240

Crabbe, George (1754–1832) 201

Croker, John Wilson (1780–1857) politician and editor of Pope 492

Cromwell, Henry (*fl.* 1710) Early man-about-town friend of Pope 41

Crousaz, Jean Pierre de (1663–1748) Swiss theologian, exposed deism of *Essay on Man* 23, 249

Cunningham, J. S. 433

Curll, Edmund (1675–1747) Unscrupulous publisher; used by Pope for surreptitious edition of his letters 23, 232

Cynthia Goddess of the moon 194

Dante Alighieri (1265–1321) 202, 229

Davie, Donald 424–6, 447–9

Defoe, Daniel (?1661–1731) 59

Denham, Sir John (1615–69) 25, 29, 43, 104
  Cooper's Hill 107
Dennis, John (1657–1734) Literary critic in almost continuous warfare
with Pope 30–31, 45, 169, 232, 392
  Remarks upon Translation of Homer **57–8**
  Remarks upon 'Rape of the Lock' **73–4**
  Reflections upon 'Essay on Criticism' 47, **49–55**
De Quincey, Thomas (1785–1859) 167, **216–17, 220–28, 230, 234**
Dilke, Charles Wentworth (1789–1864) Antiquary and critic 167
D'Israeli, Isaac (1766–1848) Literary historian; father of Benjamin
Disraeli 167, **179–80**, 202–3, 491
Dixon, Peter 483–6
Doeg (in Dryden's *Absalom and Achitophel*) 260
Donne, John (?1571–1631) 82, 101, 104, 130, 214, 393
Dorset, Charles Sackville, Earl of (1638–1706) Restoration poet and
courtier 106
Dryden, John (1631–1700) 39, 40, 42, 43–4, 64, 89–90, 101, 104, 164,
168, 171, 172, 173, 174, 180, 186, 187, 191, 192, 201, 215, 219, 221–2,
242, 247, 249–53, 265, 410
  compared with Pope 118, 135–7, 154–5, 197–8, 214, 220, 230,
  260–63, 269–71, 272, 281
  Absalom and Achitophel 201
  Aeneis 65, 91
  Fables 81
  Palamon and Arcite 201
  Religio Laici 260
Dyce, Alexander (1798–1869) Scholar and editor of Elizabethan
dramatists 211–12
Dyer, John (1699–1758) Poet, author of *Grongar Hill* 174, 211

Edinburgh Review 164, 178–9
Eliot, George (1819–80) **239**
Eliot, T. S. (1888–1965) 26, **272**, 318–21, **355–6**
Elizabeth I (1533–1603) 212
Elwin, Whitwell (1816–1900) Editor of Pope's poems **247, 248, 249,**
492
Emerson, Ralph Waldo (1803–82) 253
Empson, William 283–4, **297–306**
Encyclopaedia Britannica 216–17
Epanaphora Synonymous with anaphora, a rhetorical figure in which
the same word or phrase is repeated at the beginning of several
successive sentences or clauses 267

Epicede Anglicized form of the Latin *epicedium*, a poem in honour of a dead person 267

Epicurean system Philosophy of Epicurus (341–270 B C), expounded by Lucretius in *De Rerum Natura* 204

Excursion Wordsworth's long philosophical poem 201, 213

'Expletives' (to be avoided) 40, 41, 43

Fairfax, Edward (d. 1635) Poet and translator of Tasso's *Gerusalemme Liberata* 104, 263

Fanny, Lord Pope's nickname for Lord Hervey 169 ◊ **Hervey**

Fenton, Elijah (1683–1730) Minor poet, translated four books of Pope's *Odyssey*, 63, 65, 70, 71, 104, 204

Fielding, Henry (1707–54) **79, 94–5,** 469

Figures of speech used by Pope 384–8

Fitzgerald, Edward (1809–83) Translator of the *Rubáiyát of Omar Khayyám*; letter of Thackeray quoted in Alfred M. Terhune, *The Life of Edward Fitzgerald* (1947) **213**

Ford, John (1586–1639) Dramatist 164, 178

Freind, Robert (1667–1751) Headmaster of Westminster School 87

French school Term applied to the 'school' of Dryden and Pope, whose poetic theory and practice were influenced by French neo-classical critics, particularly Boileau; sometimes distinguished from an 'Italian school' represented by Spenser and Milton 163, 164, 171, 186, 187, 188, 191, 219, 221–2

Frere, John Hookham (1769–1846) Writer of humorous verse **153**

Frontinus (A D 30–104) Roman author of *Strategemata*, a manual of military strategy 180

Frye, Northrop 35

Fuseli, Henry (1741–1825) Swiss-born painter, friend of Blake **174**

Garth, Sir Samuel (1661–1719) Physician and poet, author of *The Dispensary* 104, 262, 263, 268

Gay, John (1685–1732) 23, 99–101, 104, 186, 231, 256, 452–3, 463–4

Genre criticism 285–6

George II (1683–1760) 254

Gibbon, Edward (1737–94) 164

Gifford, William (1756–1826) Poet, translator of Juvenal, and first editor of the *Quarterly Review* 201

Gilfillan, George (1813–78) Scottish literary critic **238**

Giotto (1266–1336) 260

Gladstone, W. E. (1809–98) 492

Goethe, Johanne Wolfgang von (1749–1832) 235, 491

Goldsmith, Oliver (1730–74) **118–19, 119–20, 120–21,** 229
Góngora y Argote, Luis de (1561–1627) Spanish poet, exemplar of
the affected style known as Gongorism 215
Gradus Short for *Gradus ad Parnassum* (steps to Parnassus), Dictionary
of prosody, poetical epithets and phrases, formerly used in English
schools as an aid to Latin versification 189, 243, 263–8
Graves, Robert (b. 1895) 286–7
Gray, Thomas (1716–71) **92,** 107, 164, 192, 252

Hamilton, Sir William (1788–1856) Scottish philosopher 254
Haydon, Benjamin Robert (1786–1846) Historical painter 191
Hazlitt, William (1778–1830) 164, **173,** **192–8, 209–10,** 491
Headley, Henry (1765–88) Poet and critic **153–4**
Hearne, Thomas (1678–1735) Medievalist **74**
Henriade Epic poem by Voltaire 244
Herbert, Edward, Lord Herbert of Cherbury (1583–1648)
Philosopher and poet 88
Herodotus (*c.* 480–*c.* 425 BC) 235
Herschel, Sir William (1739–1822) Astronomer 185
Hervey (Harvey), John, Baron Hervey (1696–1743) **34, 81,** 170
◊ **Fanny, Lord**
portrait of him in *Epistle to Dr Arbuthnot* 166, 243 ◊ **Sporus**
Hiatus (prosodic) 40, 41, 43
Hill, Aaron (1685–1750) Minor poet and dramatist 36, 411
Hilles, Frederick W. 491
Hind and the Panther, The (Dryden's) 260
Hobbes, Thomas (1588–1679) 185–6, 333
Homer, 165–6, 169, 181, 184–5, 187, 193, 200, 240–42, 250, 268, 460–82
◊ *Iliad* and *Odyssey*
echoes of in Pope's own poems 466–82
Hoole, John (1727–1803) Translator of Tasso's *Jerusalem Delivered* and
Ariosto's *Orlando Furioso* 218, 268
Hopkins, Gerard Manley (1844–89) Letter to Baillie in *Further
Letters of Gerard Manley Hopkins* (1938) **245**
Hopkins ◊ **Sternhold**
Horace (Quintus Horatius Flaccus) (65–8 BC) 46, 80, 171, 189, 192,
231
compared with Pope 218, 270
Pope's *Imitations* 82, 343–5, 472–3
Housman, A. E. (1859–1936) **281–2**
Hughes, John (1677–1720) Poet, author of the successful tragedy *The
Siege of Damascus* 204

Hume, David (1711–76) 164

Hunt, James Henry Leigh (1784–1859) 163, 166, **180–3, 187–8, 191–2, 214, 219–20, 228**

Huxley, Aldous (1894–1963) Novelist and essayist **306–7**

Hyperbole (in Pope's Homer) **92**

Irwin, Lady Anne (*fl.* 1734) Complained of Pope's obscurity 411

Italian school, 171, 221 ◊ French school

Jacob (in Genesis) 190

Jeffrey, Francis, Lord Jeffrey (1773–1850) Scottish critic and lawyer; one of the founders and first editor of the *Edinburgh Review* 164, **178–9,** 484

Jervas, Charles (?1675–1739) Professional painter who gave Pope lessons 28

Johnson, Samuel (1709–84) 160–61, 163, 164, 171, 172, 175, 177, 181, 183, 187, 244, 266, 267, 282
   on *Dunciad* **143–4**
   on *Elegy (on) Unfortunate Lady* **125–6, 137–8**
   on *Eloisa to Abelard* **142–3**
   on *Epitaphs* **95–101**
   on *Essay on Criticism* **92–3, 138–40**
   on *Essay on Man* **128, 144–6**
   on *Imitations of Horace* 147
   on *Letters* **134**
   on *Moral Essays* **146**
   on *Rape of the Lock* **140–42**
   comments on Pope recorded by Boswell **155–61**
   comparison with Dryden **135–7**
   Pope's life and habits **160–61**
   Pope's versification **93–4, 147–8**

Jonson, Ben (1572–1637) 218, 282

Juvenal (AD ?60–?130) Roman satiric poet 171, 224–5

Keats, John (1795–1821) 190, 191, 277, **308–9**
   letter to Haydon in *The Letters of John Keats*, ed. H. E. Rollins (1958) 191

Kenner, Hugh **426–32**

King, William (1650–1729) Archbishop and philosopher 158

Knowles, John (1781–1841) Biographer of Henry Fuseli **174**

Knox, Vicesimus (1752–1821) Essayist **150**

La Bruyère, Jean de (1645–96) French moralist, author of *Charactères* on the model of Theophrastus 101, 243

Lake Poets, Lake School Terms applied to Wordsworth, Coleridge and Southey, who resided in the Lake District; Charles Lamb, though a Londoner, was sometimes included in the 'Lake School' 164, 173

Lamb, Charles (1775–1834) 173

Langton, Bennet (1737–1801) Friend of Dr Johnson 265

Lansdowne, George Granville, Baron (1667–1735) Politician, poet and dramatist 104

Lausus (in Virgil's *Aeneid*) 246

Lanz, Henry 354–5

Leavis, F. R. 315–25

Leibniz, Gottfried Wilhelm von (1646–1716) German philosopher and mathematician 249, 254

Lintot, Bernard (1675–1736) Publisher 23

Locke, John (1632–1704) 64, 90

London Magazine (1748) Anonymous article **92–3**

Longinus Supposed author of the Greek treatise *On the Sublime* 46, 267, 461

Lowell, James Russell (1819–91) American poet, essayist and diplomat **247–8**, 492

Louis XIV (1638–1715) 229

Lucretius (Titus Lucretius Caro), (94–55 BC) Roman poet and philosopher, author of *De Rerum Natura* 204, 253, 265, 269

Macaulay, Thomas Babington, Baron Macaulay (1800–1859) 166, 167, **212–13**, **217–18**, 257
   note on Pope's *Imitations of Horace* in *Marginal Notes by Lord Macaulay*, ed. G. O. Trevelyan (1907) **218**

MacFlecknoe (Dryden's) 198, 269

Machiavelli, Niccolò (1469–1527) 180

Mack, Maynard 20, 284–5, **393–409**, **460–82**

McLuhan, H. Marshall 433–43

Mahomet 206

Malherbe, François de (1555–1628) French apostle of 'correctness' 41

Mandeville, Bernard (?1670–1733) Sceptical philosopher 88, 466–7

Marino, Giambattista (1569–1625) Neapolitan poet, exemplar of the affected style known as Marinism 215

Marlborough, Sarah, Duchess of (1660–1744) Supposed original of Atossa in *Moral Essay II* 243

Marvell, Andrew (1621–78) 218

Mary, Lady ⟡ **Montague, Lady Mary Wortley**

Massinger, Philip (1583–1640) 198, 260

Maximin (in Dryden's heroic play *Tyrannic Love*) 213

Mephistopheles 225
Michelangelo (1475–1564) 244
Milton, John (1608–74) 86, 103, 152, 174, 180, 187, 192, 194, 200, 202, 205, 206, 216, 221, 223, 229, 250, 265, 272, 372–4, 387, 397, 451
   Paradise Lost 186
Miscellany on Taste (1732) Provoked by *Moral Essay IV* 415
'Mock-heroic' (analysis of term) 405–8
Monosyllabic lines (Pope's dislike of) 40, 41, 43
Montagu, Lady Mary Wortley (1689–1762) Aristocrat with whom Pope flirted before attacking her outrageously 23, 34, **83**, 133, 169, 271
'Moonlight scene' in Pope's Iliad 161–2, 165, 181, 185, 187, 189–90, 213, 241–2, 491
More, Henry (1614–87) Cambridge Platonist and poet 185
Murray, John Byron's publisher 203–8, 492

Names of satiric characters 415–18
Nelson, Horatio, Viscount Nelson (1758–1805) 233
Newdigate prize Prize for English verse at Oxford University 217
Newman, Francis William (1805–97) Translator of Homer 240
Newman, John Henry (1801–90) **211**
Nisus (in Virgil's *Aeneid*) 246
Nowottny, Winifred 443–7

Og (in Dryden's *Absalom and Achitophel*) 260
Oldham, John (1653–83) Poet and satirist 64, 104, 218
Onomatopoeia (Pope's interest in) 39, 42, 43, 93–4, 139–40
Ovid (Ovidius Naso) (43 BC–AD 17) 90, 189, 197
Oxford, Edward Harley, 2nd Earl of (1689–1741) Close friend of Pope's complimented in *Moral Essay III* 82

Parnell, Thomas (1679–1718) Poet and member of the Scriblerus Club 104, 212
Pascal, Blaise (1623–62) 243
Pattison, Mark (1813–84) Rector of Lincoln College, Oxford; edited Pope's *Essay on Man* (1869) and *Satires and Epistles* (1872) **248–9, 253–5,** 492
Peacock, Thomas Love (1785–1866) 164
Pegasus Winged horse of Greek mythology, the favourite of the Muses 190
Persian Tales (Arabian Nights) 81
Personal satire 30–32, 80, 83
Philips, Ambrose (?1675–1749) Rival pastoralist, protégé of Addison; ridiculed by Pope in the *Guardian* 33, 49, **72–3,** 169

Pindar (*c.* 522–442 BC) 167
Pitt, Christopher (1699–1748) Translator of *Aeneid* 104
Plato (?427–348 BC) 206
Poetic diction (Augustan) 339–42
Plutarch's Lives 191
Pope, Alexander (1688–1744) *Dunciad* 143–4, 156, 157, 174, 197, 198, 217, 231, 232–3, 246, 249, 254, 255–6, 261, 265, 267, 269, 270, 271, 278, 279, 280–81, 288–9, 302, 313, 321, 323–4, 407–8, 427–32, 433–43
  eclogues ⟡ **Pastorals**
  Elegy to the Memory of an Unfortunate Lady 109, 125–6, 137–8, 180, 262, 266–7, 281, 282, 297, 476–8
  Eloisa to Abelard 109–10, 142–3, 152, 170, 171, 174, 180, 181, 200, 201, 223–4, 262, 267–8, 291–2
  Epilogue to the Satires 257, 286–7
  Epistle to Dr Arbuthnot (Prologue to the Satires) 28, 146, 204, 207, 211, 257, 272, 273, 301–2, 322, 323, 349–50
  Epistle to Robert Earl of Oxford 200
  Epistles 173, 179, 193, 197, 248, 254 ⟡ *Moral Essays*
  Epitaphs 95–101, 175–8, 211
  Essay on Criticism 47, 49–55, 108, 122–5, 196, 212, 216, 220, 247, 254, 257, 265
  Essay on Man 111–15, 128–9, 144–6, 173, 188, 197, 201, 208, 211, 224, 226–8, 243, 246, 248–9, 254, 256, 260, 261, 277, 292, 321, 326–7, 356–9
  Homer (Pope's translation of) 165–6, 169, 173, 184–5, 188, 189–90, 191, 215, 222, 228, 240–2, 245, 268, 460–82, 492 ⟡ *Iliad*, (Pope's translation of)
  Iliad (Pope's translation of) 57–8, 128, 143, 161–2, 165, 181–2, 185, 187, 188, 189–90, 196–7, 213, 240–2, 244, 262, 281, 460–82, 491, 492 ⟡ **Homer**
  Imitations of Horace 117–18, 130, 147, 205, 218, 248, 249, 251, 257, 265, 270, 292, 343–5, 485–6
  Messiah 169, 264–5
  Moral Essays 103, 115–16, 129–30, 146, 183, 189, 200, 223, 224–6, 254, 268–9, 274, 303–6, 306–7, 322–3, 403–5, 405–19, 484–5 ⟡ *Epistles* (Pope's)
  Ode for Music on St Cecilia's Day 201, 258
  Ode on Solitude 212, 219
  Odyssey (Pope's translation of) 59–71, 460–82 ⟡ **Homer**
  Pastorals 104–6, 135, 186, 211, 218, 237, 239, 254
  Prologue to Mr Addison's Tragedy of Cato 200
  Prologue to the Satires ⟡ *Epistle to Dr Arbuthnot*

Rape of the Lock 71–2, 126–8, 138–42, 166–7, 170, 171–2, 174, 180, 182–3, 188, 191, 195–6, 201, 202, 219, 231, 247–8, 254, 255–6, 260, 261, 263, 265–6, 269, 270, 278, 279–80, 281, 284, 297–300, 311, 314, 317, 360–77, 449–55, 482

Satires 173, 179, 189, 193, 197, 224–5, 239, 248, 254, 268–9, 270 ⊳

Imitations of Horace

Sober Advice from Horace 80–81

Temple of Fame 28

'Universal Prayer' 157

Windsor Forest 28, 106–8, 181, 186, 264–5, 475

Prose works:

Discourse on Pastoral Poetry **25**

Guardian no. 40, **49–55**

Iliad preface 25

Letters 134

Notes to his own poems and translations 26

Odyssey postscript 25

Preface to *Works* (1717) 25

Modern Key to Popery **76–8**

Newspaper advertisements **56, 80,** 488

Peri Bathous 86, 383–4, 422–3

Shakespeare edition 23

Themes, technique, influences:

Antitheses 65, 384, 455–60

Closed couplet 424–6

Comparison with Dryden 289–93, 319–20

Correctness, neo-classic rules 89, 108, 382–4, 421

Deism 24

'Epistle' defined 410

Hiatus 40, 41, 43

Influence of Bolingbroke, 30, 132, 158–60

Influence of Milton 372–4, 387, 397

Influence of Swift 29–30

Personal satire 30–32, 80, 83, 413–19

Portraits in verse 403–4

'Pride' 414, 420

Puns 324–5, 366–70, 375, 386, 392, 401, 447–9

Repetitions 291

Revisions 288, 338–9, 356–9

Rhyme in Pope 288, 345–55

Verbal juxtapositions 399–400

Versification 443–7

508   Index

Pope, Alexander – *continued*
''Virtue' 411
Virtuosity in invention of proper names 394–6
Vocabulary 473–8
Personal and biographical:
Family and social background 23, 24, 328–43, 411–13
Garden, grotto and villa 20, 23, 464, 466
Lessons in painting 26, 28
Portraits of Pope 20
Scriblerus Club 447–8
Spence's Anecdotes 489
Comments on his own poems:
Dunciad 27, 75, 81, 87, 91
Essay on Criticism 42–4
Essay on Man 30, 88–9
Iliad 57–8, 75, 81, 91, 93
Imitations of Horace 85
Messiah 67, 91
Odyssey 75, 86–7, 91
Pastorals 26–7, 28, 91
Rape of the Lock 27, 71–2, 81
General critical comments by Pope 71, 74, 75, 82, 84, 90, 91
'Correctness' 89, 108
'Delicacy' 87
Personal satire 30, 79
'Picturesque' 25
'Soft' and 'Sweet' verses 28, 75
Versification 39–41, 41–2, 42–4, 89
'Pope controversy' 167, 199–210, 491
Popple, William (1701–64) Journalist, frequent contributor to
Aaron Hill's *Prompter* 36
Pound, Ezra (b. 1885) **307–8**
Pre-romantic poetry 35
Prior, Matthew (1664–1721) 104, 231, 232
Prompter, The (1734) Theatrical periodical hostile to Pope **83–4**
Puns (in Pope) 324–5, 386, 401, 447–9
sexual puns 366–70, 375, 392

Quarterly Review 165, **184–6**, 189, **202–3**, 491, 492
Quintilian (*c.* 37–*c.* 100) *Institutio Oratoria* cited by Pope 103

Rasselas Johnson's philosophical tale 241
Rees's Cyclopaedia *The Cyclopaedia, or Universal Dictionary of Arts,*

Sciences and Literature, ed. Abraham Rees (1743–1825) 185
Religious allusions 397–8
Revision (Pope's habitual) 27, 135–6, 356–9
Reynolds, Sir Joshua (1723–92) 189
Rhyme (in Pope) 40, 41, 43, 345–55
Ribera, José (Lo Spagnoletto) Painter 26
Richardson, Jonathan (1665–1745) Portrait painter 231
Richardson, Samuel (1689–1761) 200
Rochester, John Wilmot, Earl of, (1648–80) 64, 106, 218
Rodway, Allan 455–60
Rogers, Samuel (1763–1855) Poet and banker; author of *The Pleasures of Memory* 201
Rosa, Salvator (1615–73) Painter 26
Roscommon, Wentworth Dillon, Earl of (?1633–85) Author of *Essay on Translated Verse* 47
Rousseau, Jean-Jacques (1712–78) 164
Rubens, Peter Paul (1577–1640) 245
Ruskins, John (1819–1900) **236–7, 239,** 245–6, 492
   Letter to his father printed in his *Works*, ed. E. T. Cook and A. Wedderburn (1903–12) **230–31**

Sainte-Beuve, Charles Augustin (1804–69) French critic; *Causeries du lundi* translated by E. J. Trechmann **229,** 491–2
Saintsbury, George (1845–1933) Literary critic and historian 166, **262–9,** 277
Sandys, George (1578–1644) Translator of Ovid 104
Sawney (1728) 72
Scott, Sir Walter (1771–1832) 173, **183–4,** 213, 492
Seasons, The Descriptive poem in four parts (1726–30) by James Thomson 186
Seatonian prize Prize for sacred poetry at Cambridge University 217
Settle, Elkanah (1648–1724) Poet and dramatist, satirized by Dryden and Pope 261
Scriblerus Club 447–8
'Sensibility' (literary sentimentality) 36
Shaftesbury, Anthony Ashley Cooper, 1st Earl of (1621–83) 214
Shaftesbury, Anthony Ashley Cooper, 3rd Earl of (1671–1713) Philosopher 88
Sexual puns (in Pope) 366–70, 375, 392
Shakespeare, William (1564–1616) 103, 163, 174, 187, 192, 193, 194, 205, 206, 213, 216, 221, 223, 229, 246, 248, 260, 267, 491
Shelley, Percy Bysshe (1792–1822) 163, 234–5, 265

Shenstone, William (1714–63) Pre-romantic poet **120**, 156–7

Sherburn, George 27, 356–9

   Early Career of Alexander Pope 284

   Correspondence of Alexander Pope 284

Sheridan, Richard Brinsley (1751–1816) 261

Shiels, Robert (d. 1753) Compiler of biographical dictionary, Johnson's assistant on *Dictionary* 293

Shrewsbury, Charles Talbot, Duke of (1660–1718) 83

'Simplicity' (slogan of Addison group) 33, 487

Sitwell, Edith (1887–1964) **276–81**

Skelton, John (?1460–1529) Poet and courtier 186

Smith, Adam (1723–90) Rhetorician and political economist **119**

Smith, John (*fl.* 1657) Author of *The Mystery of Rhetoric Unveiled* 383

Socrates (?469–399 B C) 204, 206

Somerville, William (1675–1742) Country gentleman and minor poet 106

Southey, Robert (1774–1843) 165, **169**, 184–6, **215**, 491

Spence, Joseph (1699–1768) Fellow of New College; Pope's would-be biographer 32, 71, 210

   Essay on Pope's Odyssey **59–71**

Spenser, Edmund (?1552–99) 90, 103, 180, 187, 192, 221, 223

Sporus Portrait of Hervey in *Epistle to Dr Arbuthnot* 166, 207, 239, 260 ⟡ Hervey

Sprat, Thomas (1635–1713) Poet and author of *The History of the Royal Society* 174

Squire, Sir John Collings (1884–1958) Poet, parodist and critic **271–2**

Statius (Publius Papinius) (*c.* 45–96 A D), Silver Age epic poet: translated in part by Pope 90

Steele, Sir Richard (1672–1729) 232

Stendhal (Marie Henri Beyle) (1783–1842) 243

Stephen, Sir Leslie (1832–1904) Philosopher, critic and biographer 167, **255–9**, 277

Sternhold, Thomas (d. 1549), and **Hopkins, John** (d. 1570) Authors of the old metrical version of the Psalms 183

Stockdale, Percival (1736–1811) Critic and biographer **121**

Strachey, Lytton (1880–1932) Biographer and critic, member of 'Bloomsbury Group' **272–4**

Sutherland, James 31–2

Swift, Jonathan (1667–1745) 23, 29–30, **79**, 85, 104, 183, 229, 232, 248, 256, 417

   compared with Pope 169, 238

Swinburne, Algernon Charles (1837–1909) **259–61**

Taine, Hippolyte Adolphe (1828–93) French philosopher, historian and critic; *Histoire de la Littérature anglaise* translated by H. Van Laun 242–5

Tate, Allen (b. 1899) American poet and critic **275–6**

Temple, Sir William (1628–99) 90, 208, 391

Tennyson, Alfred, Baron Tennyson (1809–92) **261–2**, 265
   Break, Break, Break

Tennyson, Hallam Son of Alfred **261–2**

Thackeray, William Makepeace (1811–63) 213, **231–4**

Theobald (Tibbald), Lewis (1688–1744) Criticized Pope's edition of Shakespeare in *Shakespeare Restored*; hero of first version of *The Dunciad* 23, 232

Theocritus (*c.* 310–250 BC) 104, 105

Thompson, Francis (1859–1907) Poet and critic, author of *The Hound of Heaven* **269–71**

Thomson, James (1700–1748) Poet, author of *The Seasons* 165, 186, 211

Tibbald ▷ **Theobald, Lewis**

Tickell, Thomas (1686–1740) Poet whose translation of the first book of the *Iliad* occasioned Pope's quarrel with Addison; author of papers on pastoral in the *Guardian* 30, 267

Tillotson, Geoffrey 308–15

Tillotson, John (1630–94) Archbishop and stylist 90

Timon (in *Moral Essay IV*) 214

Tonson, Jacob (?1656–1736) Successful publisher 23

Twickenham (site of Pope's villa from 1718) 23

Tytler, Alexander Fraser, Lord Woodhouselee (1747–1813) Scotch lawyer; his *Essay on the Principles of Translation* praises Pope **161–2**

Versification 28, 39–44, 75, 89, 147–8

Virgil (Vergilius Maro) (70–19 BC) 189, 242, 246, 250, 253
   Aeneid 82
   Eclogues 67, 91, 105, 106
   Georgics 109

Voltaire (François-Marie Arouet) (1694–1778) 164, 181, 247

Waller, Edmund (1606–87) Initiator with Denham of English Augustan poetry 43, 104, 263

Wallerstein, Ruth 383

Walsh, William (1663–1708) Minor poet and critic; Pope's earliest literary adviser 39, 89, 154–5

Warburton, William (1698–1779) Pope's friend and literary executor; controversial theologian, annotated first complete edition of Pope's poems 24, 91, 249, 493

Warton, Joseph (1722–1800) minor pre-Romantic 35, **86**, 163, 166, 206, 257, 491
   Essay on the Genius and Writings of Pope 37, **101–18**, 143, 149
   on *Elegy (on) Unfortunate Lady* **109**
   on *Eloisa to Abelard* **109–10**
   on *Essay on Criticism* **108**
   on *Essay on Man* **111–15**
   Four 'classes' of English poets **103–4**
   on *Pastorals* **104–6**
   on *Windsor Forest* **106–8**
   on *Moral Essay I* (in prose) **103**
Warton, Thomas (?1688–1745) minor poet 152
Warton, Thomas (1728–90) Poet and literary historian 35, **152**
Watts Isaac (1674–1748) Poet and hymn writer 282
Wellek, René 164
West, Richard (1716–42) Gray's and Horace Walpole's tubercular friend 34
Weston, Joseph (*fl.* 1788) **154–5**
Welsted, Leonard (1688–1747) Poet, involved in quarrel with Pope 232
Wharton, Philip, Duke of (1698–1731) Principal specimen of 'ruling passion' in *Moral Essay I* 243, 254, 416
Williamson, George 383
Wimsatt, W. K. Jr 20, **345–55**, **377–93**, **419–23**
Winchilsea, Anne Finch, Countess of (1661–1720) Poetess 186
Winters, Yvor 381, **482–3**
Woolf, Virginia (1882–1941) **274–5**
Wordsworth, William (1770–1850) 163, 164, 165, **169**, **186–7**, 188, 213, 242, 249, 252, 265, 491, 492
   Letters in *The Letters of William and Dorothy Wordsworth*, ed. E. de Selincourt (1935–9) **173**, **211–12**
   'Upon Epitaphs' **175–8**, 491
Wycherley, William (?1640–1716) Dramatist; early friend of Pope 35

Yalden Thomas (1670–1736) Poet 174
Young, Edward (1683–1765) Poet and satirist, author of *The Complaint*, or, *Night Thoughts on Life, Death and Immortality* 75, 101, 192, 237, 239, 268, 413

Zeugma, (one of Pope's favourite figures of speech) 284, 385
Zimri (in Dryden's *Absalom and Achitophel*) 214, 260